DATE DUE			
May 5 '75			

The Early Meisterlieder
of
Hans Sachs (1514-1518)

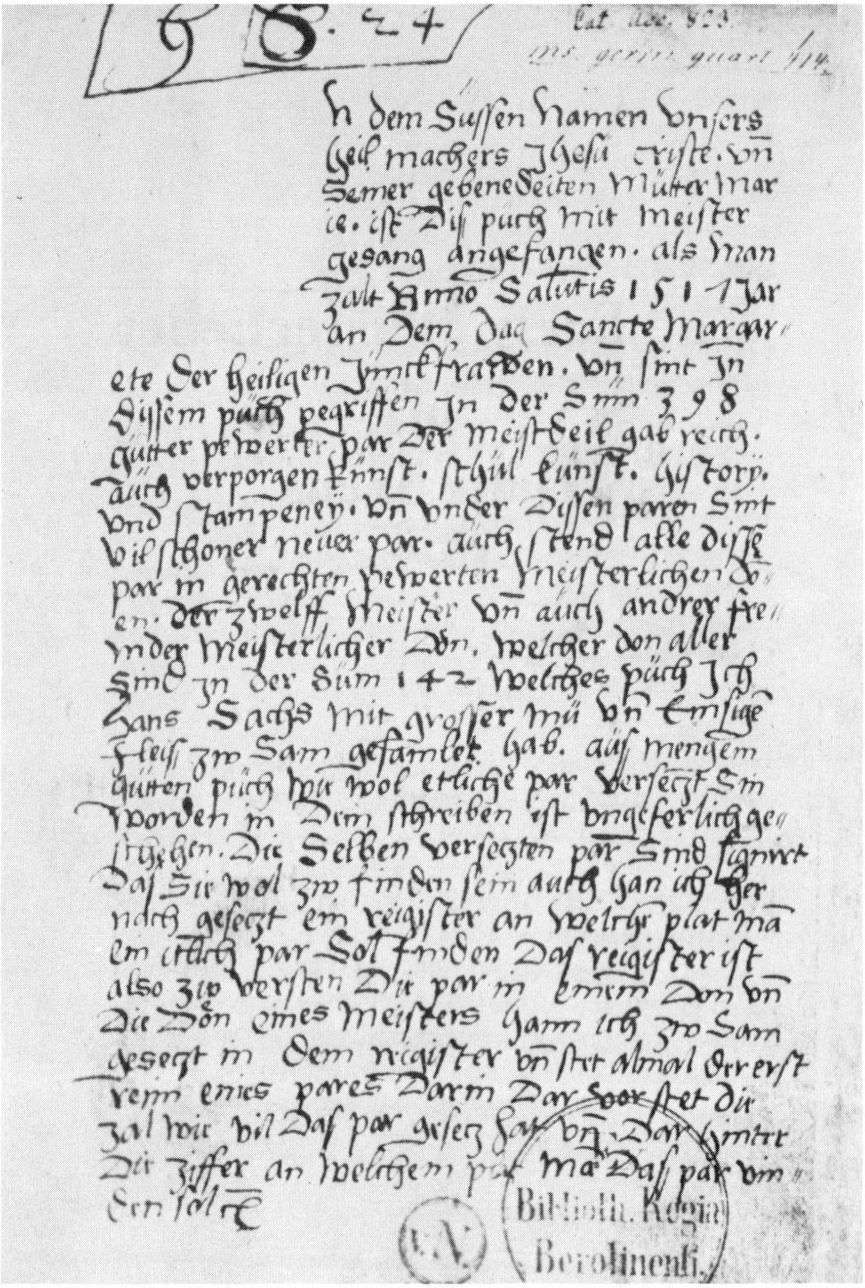

9 8.24

Cat. acc. 823.

Ms. germ. quart 414.

In dem Sussen namen unsers
heil machers Jhesu criste. vn
seiner gebenedeiten Mutter mar
ie. ist dis puch mit meister
gesang angefangen. als man
zalt Anno Salutis 1517 Jar
an dem dag Sancte Margar
ete der heiligen Junckfrawen. vn sint In
dissem puch pegriffen In der sum 398
gutter pewerter par der meist teil gab reich.
auch verporgen kunst. schul kunst. historj.
vnd stampeney. vn vnder dissen paren sint
vil schoner newer par. auch stend alle disse
par in gerechten pewerten meisterlichen do
en. der zwelff meister vn auch andrer fre
mder meisterlicher don. welcher don aller
sind in der sum 142 welches puch Ich
Hans Sachs mit grosser mu vn emsige
fleiss zu sam gesamlet hab. aus mengem
gutten puch wie wol etliche par versezt sin
worden in dem schreiben ist vngeferlich ge
schehen. die selben versezten par sind signiert
das sie wol zu finden sein auch han ich her
nach gesezt ein register an welcher plat ma
ein ytlich par sol finden das register ist
also zu versten die par in einem don vn
die don eines meisters hann ich zu sam
gesezt in dem register vn stet almal der erst
reim eines pares darin dar vor stet die
zal wie vil das par gesez hat vn dar hinter
die ziffer an welchem plat ma das par vin
den sol

The Preface to Berlin 414 *frontispiece*

The Early Meisterlieder
of
Hans Sachs

by

Frances H. Ellis

Indiana University Studies

Bloomington

83/.4

sale

93/09

april 1975

Published in Canada by Fitzhenry & Whiteside Limited, Don Mills, Ontario
Library of Congress catalog card number: 73-81163
ISBN: 0-253-31853-X
Manufactured in the United States of America

This book is published under the sponsorship of the Department of Germanic Languages, Indiana University.

Contents

The Early Meisterlieder
of
Hans Sachs

List of Illustrations

Preface

This Study offers a complete edition of the first forty Meisterlieder which Hans Sachs wrote (1514-1518), taken from the anthology into which he copied them, a manuscript now known simply as Berlin 414. While making an analysis of this manuscript in 1946 I discovered that the young poet had actually copied forty of his own poems into it and not thirty-nine as the scholars kept repeating. Twenty of these songs have never before been published; the other twenty, of which three were transcribed from manuscripts of a later date than that of Berlin 414, have appeared at different times and in diverse places. Here, therefore, all forty are made available as a unified whole in an exact transcription. Their themes are both religious and secular with more than half of the latter devoted to matters concerned with Meistergesang. This edition is intended for scholars interested in Hans Sachs and in his language before the Reformation; in the original patterns of his own first five melodies; in Meistergesang as the poet practiced it many years before the earliest extant copy of the rules (1540); and in Hans Sachs' detailed listing of items penalized, which is thus our earliest "Schulzettel" *in nuce*, and which is here published for the first time.

My most heartfelt thanks go to Professor Norbert Fuerst for his constructive criticism; to Professor Foster W. Blaisdell for several suggestions; to Professor Frank G. Banta for reading the linguistic summary with a critical eye; and to Mrs. Gail Matthews of the Inter-Library Loan Department of Indiana University for her friendly assistance in locating books and articles in other libraries. I am particularly indebted to the Research and Development Committee and to Chancellor Herman B Wells for his encouragement in dark hours.

Frances H. Ellis

Introduction

Hans Sachs is a familiar figure in the literature of the sixteenth century, the author of numerous Meisterlieder and *Spruchgedichte*, of rhymed fables and farces, of tragedies, comedies, and Shrovetide plays, and of a few prose dialogs. Familiar, too, is the broad outline of his life which he recorded in sundry of his Summaries.[1] There is, however, another Hans Sachs, the youthful one, who, while still a journeyman, wrote verse which is known only in part, but which already heralds his later fame. To become acquainted with the young Sachs it is necessary to go back to the first two decades of the sixteenth century, back before he achieved the grade of master artisan, back before the Reformation and his own change of faith, back also before he took upon himself the responsibilities of the head of a family and of a prosperous middle-class burgher, and before he won the high esteem of his fellow citizens. In going back it is also necessary to slough off the conceptions and judgments of the intervening centuries and to view life and thought, as these affected Hans Sachs, from the standpoint of the time in which he was young.

Like boys of any century who are growing out of their teens into manhood, he had problems, needed guidance, and had to make decisions. He was only seventeen when he started out in the spring of 1512 to gain the necessary skills in his trade under the tutelage of master shoemakers in one town after another. Aside from becoming proficient in his chosen work, there was the excitement of seeing new places, of observing the kaleidoscopic company encountered on the roads, of meeting all kinds of people, of acquiring a variety of experiences, and of being able to enjoy a hitherto unknown freedom. These journeyman years, in anticipation, probably denoted the great adventure, but in reality they also brought with them unforeseen hardships. In retrospect Hans Sachs describes what may well have befallen himself, when he says he was often weary to the point of exhaustion while trudging along with blistered feet. Sometimes he even got lost. How glad he was then to see a town in the distance, but how disappointed when at times he found no work there and, to keep on going, had to spend all of the money he had saved. Masters, too, differed in kind, and the hours of work were long.[2] This was life, and he was learning about it. God-fearing as he was, and mindful of his home training and of the good advice given him by his father, as well as of the code for conduct and work prescribed by his guild, he soon began to look askance at the usual pastimes indulged in by the journeymen.[3] He had been drawn to such pleasures the first year that he was away from home, he later remembered, had sampled them, but then had rejected them, even though his companions had derided him for so doing. His reason was that each brought with it some aftermath of grief.[4]

In Wels in 1513, he tells us in a poem, he came to the conclusion that he would have to find something useful and honorable to do besides his hard work, and so, to think the matter over, he took a long walk, something he did frequently. Aside from the literary tradition involved, this may very well have been the one means he had of getting away from the tumult and bustle all around him, of being

13

by himself in the country where he would have the quiet to listen to the thoughts within him. As he lay daydreaming beside a little spring, he relates, the nine Muses appeared to him and, after ascertaining what troubled him, offered their help with the words:

> ... O jüngling, dein dienst sey
> Das dich auff teutsch poeterey
> Ergebst durch-auß dein leben lang
> Nemblichen auf meistergesang.

Each Muse in turn endowed him with the attributes which would further his poetic creations and then, as a parting injunction, Clio proclaimed:

> ... all deine gedicht
> Zu Gottes ehr werden gericht
> Zu straff der laster, lob der tugendt
> Zu lehre der blüenden jugendt
> Zu ergetzung trawriger gmüt.

These words forecast the substance of all the poet was to write. As he bowed toward the Muses in deep gratitude, he says, they disappeared. Joyously he came back from his walk and straightway began to put the gifts he had just received from them into practice.[5] Although Hans Sachs did not narrate this imaginary happening until years later, it may already have been latent in his mind at that early time, for it fits in well with his inclination to turn aside from those entertainments which his fellow journeymen enjoyed, to a more intellectually satisfying way of spending the little spare time at his disposal. Furthermore, he liked to read, which no doubt also set him apart.[6]

Soon verse after verse flowed from his pen. From the years 1514 through 1518 the youthful poet produced forty-two Meisterlieder and composed five original melodies; in addition he wrote two Shrovetide plays and four *Spruchgedichte*.[7] The Meisterlieder already show a wide range of subject matter. Divided almost equally between the religious and the secular, each category in turn brings a variety of topics. Most of the observations, however, which Hans Sachs made during his journeyman years seem to have been stored away in his mind for the future, at which time he drew upon them at will to picture life and people as he had found them, but for these early Meisterlieder it is just as if, to a great extent, he had tuned out the world in which he moved. Surprisingly, on the other hand, he does reveal bits of information regarding himself, especially in several of the songs on Meistergesang. Indirectly, too, he gives glimpses of his suffering anent an unhappy love affair, and tells us about a day in the life of a journeyman shoemaker. Fleetingly a verse may also touch upon a wish or an ideal. And in the Meisterlied on brotherly love we gain an insight into the fact that he was well aware of conditions around him.[8] Two of the songs on Meistergesang are a distinct contribution to its early history.[9]

Hans Sachs copied all but two of the Meisterlieder which he wrote during these years, along with those he had collected from other Meistersinger, into his first manuscript-book, Berlin 414.[10] He began the copying on July 13, 1517 (he would have been twenty-four years old on November 5 of that year), in Nuremberg, and may have finished it by the end of the year 1518, because none of his songs carry a later date. Twenty of his forty poems have never before been published; twenty have been published in their entirety in books printed in the nineteenth and in the early part of the twentieth century, some of which are not always easily accessible. Three of the published songs, however, were not transcribed from Berlin 414, but from manuscripts in Dresden. Moreover, only the eight poems which Wackernagel published follow Berlin 414 closely, and even those differ slightly *passim*.[11] Other editors, for comparison, have sometimes drawn upon additional manuscripts into which the Meisterlieder were later copied, have often normalized the spelling, supplied punctuation, umlauts, and capitalization, and have frequently changed the dialectal and Middle High German forms into New High German ones.[12] Therefore, in order to give a true picture of the poetry and language of the youthful Hans Sachs, I have faithfully transcribed all forty Meisterlieder from Berlin 414 with the exception of two minor matters: I have resolved all abbreviations, and, since the poet's use of capital letters is capricious, I have kept only those which he sometimes uses for names and those with which he begins the three divisions of a strophe. I have made no emendations, nor have I changed rhyme schemes or tried to impose the Puschmann rules of 1571 upon Meisterlieder written more than fifty years prior to that time. Wherever corrections made at a later date overlie the original wording, I have kept the original, if at all discernible, and have so stated. At the same time, where either a word necessary for the syllable count, or a whole verse essential to the structure of the strophe, has been omitted, but has been inserted by some later hand, I have included it in italics and have called attention to it in the Notes. There also I have commented on linguistic matters, literary allusions, source material, and other details including errors of one kind or another which Hans Sachs may have made due to oversight, and have noted and rectified misstatements and inaccuracies in articles bearing on these Meisterlieder.

Hans Sachs entered his Meisterlieder into Berlin 414 in prose form, but indicated the end of a verse by means of a slanting line which I have chosen to call a virgule. He set off the three parts of the strophe by beginning each part on a new line and by affixing a special mark at its close, a mark to which I have given the name partite sign. At the end of a line he divides a word without regard to syllabification; even monosyllables are divided. He frequently runs words together; on the other hand, he sometimes leaves a prefix unattached. He uses no punctuation. In addition to emendations which appear to have been made at a later time, the poet himself made a number of corrections at the time that he was copying the poems into his manuscript-book. Where he has written part of a verse out of order, he indicates the proper sequence of words by means of superscribed numbers. Sometimes omissions appear in the right-hand margin. With very few exceptions the strophes are numbered. Occasionally space has been left for a large initial letter of the first word in a song. Fading is apparent on a few folios, and a finer quill seems to have been used on folios 464^V-465^r. Here and there an ink blot mars a folio.

Hans Sachs availed himself of the following abbreviations: a long mark over the *n* to indicate the *d* of *vnd*; a long mark over the vowel in a word to indicate an *m* or an *n*; a diagonal line through the top part of the beginning of the initial letter *v* to indicate the prefix *ver*; a *g* with its tail a short, straight, downward line to indicate the suffix *us*; a kind of half circle extending upward from a *d* to indicate the ending *er*; a short line through the tail of an initial *p* to indicate *per* or *pro*; and a kind of 3 to indicate the Latin ending *ue* (as in *atque*, for instance). I have not called attention to any of these, nor to the unregulated use of capital letters which sometimes are even used to make a correction within a word.

Hans Sachs did not enter his Meisterlieder on consecutive folios; instead there are twenty-eight on foll. 1^r-41^r; one on foll. 84^V-85^V; one on 88^r-88^V; two on foll. 437^V-438^V; and eight on foll. 460^r-469^r. Thus changes in calligraphy, which were taking place gradually, become all the more apparent in the last eight poems, all of which were written in 1518. Sporadically as early as folio 13^r an occasional letter, more particularly the *d, j,* and *s,* begins to look like a capital, and on folio 14^r a final *r* now and then is similar to a *z*. Beginning with folio 460^r the *u* is written, with very few exceptions, with a hook over it (*ŭ*), and the *g* is noticeably altered. There are also changes in the writing of the letters *d* and *e*. On folio 463^V a long *s* has a line paralleling it midway down (once this even appears on folio 24^r), and from then on such a line is to be found here and there both medially and in final position. The *h, p,* and *l* likewise show changes. In the poem on folio 468^r the *d* has taken on an entirely different character, and the virgule, which usually slants forward, is now and then made to slant backwards, or to stand in vertical position. The reproductions of folios 1^r and 463^V in Appendix A serve to illustrate Hans Sachs' handwriting at the beginning and towards the end of the manuscript.

A few of the rhyme schemes which Hans Sachs uses differ from their final form and here and there point to the fact that the rules set down later were not yet in force. A discussion of each of Hans Sachs' five *Töne*, together with the change of name in two of them, will be found under the Heading of the first Meisterlied which is set to that particular *Ton*. The photostat copies of the five melodies which the poet composed 1513 through 1518 and entered into the second volume of his Meisterlieder, Mg. 2, will be found in Appendix B. The rhyme schemes for all of the *Töne* to which he set his forty Meisterlieder are in Appendix C. A Linguistic Summary preceding the Notes is basic for an understanding of the poet's language in these poems.

In presenting the Meisterlieder I have divided them into five chapters, each of which is supplied with background information on the subject matter of the poems in the chapter and/or details on that portion of Hans Sachs' life closely connected with that specific group of songs. Within each chapter the Meisterlieder, with few exceptions, are arranged in chronological order. Their original sequence in Berlin 414, a sequence which follows no special order, is always indicated by a number at the top right of the first page introducing a new song. The folio pagination for the whole poem is at the left. Folio numbers have also been placed in the right-hand margin at the side of the verse which begins on that folio. The Meisterlieder vary in length from three to thirteen strophes: twenty-five have three strophes, five have five, seven have seven, and only three are thirteen strophes long. The number of verses to a song ranges from thirty-six to two hundred and eight; twenty-one of the poems have under a hundred. The total count of verses is four thousand two hundred and sixty. Hans Sachs closes his Meisterlieder in a variety of ways. In sixteen he offers a brief prayer (in one of these he presents his song to the Virgin, and in another to St. Catherine before the prayer); he gives praise and honor to the Virgin in one, praises her and pays court to her in another, and in one he just presents his new song to her; in five poems he gives spiritual advice; seven songs end with suggestions, and three of these make use of proverbs to support the counsel; two poems express wishes; one extends an invitation to the Masters, and at the close of one Hans Sachs presents his Meisterlied to them; the remaining five simply end with a statement of fact.

The poet's great talent for spinning out his verses and the amount of reading he did, all the while working long and hard to perfect himself in his trade, are astounding. After a close study of these early Meisterlieder one realizes how extremely deft he was in saying what he wanted to within the confines of an often complicated poetic pattern. But one can also see from some of the songs on Meistergesang that Wagner's words (in his opera *Die Meistersinger*) fittingly apply to Hans Sachs just after he returned home from his journeyman years: "Denn wer als Meister ward geboren / Der hat unter Meistern den schlimmsten Stand."[13]

Chapter I / Meisterlieder of a General Religious Nature

Background

The years during which Hans Sachs conceived and wrote his Meisterlieder dealing with religion were the very threshold of the Reformation. For the Meistersinger, as well as for almost everyone else at that time, religion was an integral part of life. As boys they had all been drilled in chanting or singing Latin hymns and in an understanding of the rites of the Church for the purpose of taking a small part therein.[1] In addition, year in and year out, they heard the liturgy of the Mass and the sermons based on the Bible and on the works of the Church Fathers, whereby, indirectly, an assured amount of doctrine was impressed upon their minds.[2] Unwittingly they may sometimes have wondered about the divine mysteries. Certain it is that very early the Meistersinger became so interested in various theological questions that they made them the subject matter of their songs. It is amazing to see how some of these men without any higher education spell out their explications.[3] Advantageously they now and then use learned methods for clarifying a statement by asking and answering a question, by raising and refuting an objection, by drawing upon a parallel illustration, and by translating or paraphrasing an inserted Latin word or phrase.[4] Without doubt the Masters took pride in their borrowed learning and felt called to elucidate in their verses the great truths of Christianity, and to delineate a few of the finer distinctions.[5] In doing so they do not reveal a deep conception, but an attempt to understand the divine mysteries on their own level.[6] Deeply in earnest, and ever conscious of man's sinful nature, they admonished their fellow artisans to be contrite, not some time in the future, but in the immediate present, for as Hans Sachs reminded them: "spatte rew düt selten güt."[7] The Meistersinger recognized the vital importance of this inner repentance, yet at the same time they were cognizant of the inadequacy of man to fulfill God's commandments and so, over and above all, they advised their hearers to place their trust in His divine justice.[8] In the event, however, that a Christian feared the wrath of God too much, he could always turn to the Virgin Mary to intercede with Christ for him.[9] Furthermore, whenever explanation of a point in theology became too involved, or when reason mocked, there was one sure way of resolving the question, namely, in the words of Hans Sachs: "die ding in dem gelaüben sten."[10] Faith was indeed a bulwark, but it likewise set the limits beyond which man's thinking did not go.[11] Infrequently the Meistersinger touched upon current controversies concerning Church doctrine.[12] These poems with their theological import could of course be heard only in the *Singschulen*; nevertheless their subject matter would of necessity reach a wider audience indirectly through references to it or even discussions of it which may very well have occurred both in the homes of the Meistersinger and at their work. In this manner, therefore, they helped to ready a small patch of the ground in which the seeds of the Reformation could take root.[13]

Similarly to the sons of the more prosperous citizens of Nuremberg, Hans Sachs, too, attended a Latin school from his seventh to his fifteenth year.[14] The school day was six hours long. According to age and ability pupils were placed into three groups. After the elementary instruction in reading and writing, and learning two Latin words a day, they progressed to the middle section. Now only four hours were given over to lessons; the other two were devoted to duties pertaining to the Church. Various subjects were taught and much practice was given to learning Latin, so that by the time the pupils reached the upper division they could read the gospels in the Vulgate Bible. Furthermore, at this third level sundry medieval texts were used to impart instruction in grammar, exposition, and in the explanation of verse.[15] Hans Sachs specifically enumerates six of the Seven Liberal Arts, omitting only *geometria*, among the subjects which he studied.[16] During the second hour of the afternoon there was a lesson, "Die nicht allein nützlich, sunder auch lustig und lieblich sei," on a fable of Aesop for instance, or on something from Avianus or Terentius. Exceptional pupils, and this would of course include Hans Sachs, had an extra hour, "ein besonder Actus in arte humanitatis oder in leichten Episteln als Aeneae Sylvii. . ."[17] Religious instruction consisted of the daily recitation of the *Pater Noster*, the *Ave*, and the *Credo*, and on Feast Days one of the teachers read excerpts from the gospels.[18] From the very beginning, however, the pupils were drilled in group singing in order that, as soon as they advanced to the middle class, they could take part in the ceremonies of the daily worship: mass, choral-prayer, and processional songs.[19] Certain responses and antiphons were sung only by them.[20] Memorizing and singing these undoubtedly had a special appeal for Hans Sachs, as did the Latin hymns used in the liturgy and the festival hymns which accompanied the feasts of the ecclesiastical year. Besides these there were the sequences, ornaments "to the mass . . . created for each and every festival with a particular theme in mind," and in Nuremberg, as elsewhere, there were also the "extra-liturgical" processional hymns of praise.[21] Songs so varied may well have provided Hans Sachs with a more poetic insight into Biblical lore and have made him more familiar with the lives of those saints whose days were being celebrated. At the same time, however, overexposure to such participation in singing seems also to have induced boredom in the young boy, for in a farcical poem, written many years later, which describes the fourfold nature of a pupil, he has an old priest explain,

> Zŭmb andren so ist der schŭeler ein engel,
> Wen er zuechtig an mengel
> Got lobet in der kirchen mit gesang;
> Wen er in dem cor das hoch ambt hilft singen,
> Vesper, complet verpringen,
> Wie wol im oft darpey sein weil ist lang.[22]

But in memory this tedium induced by helping the priests two hours daily with the rituals of the Church seems also to have been forgotten, for the words "Darzu mit hertzlichen begerden / Begriff gesangeskunst subtil" show his love for music.[23] Thus his formal education, short and meager as it was, had sent him on his way with a desire to know more about a variety of things, had also perhaps given him a modicum of training in the art of versification and in the technique of musical composition, but above all it had provided him with intellectual substance for the rest of his life by opening up to him the world of books.[24]

His school days over, there began the learning of a trade, that of making shoes. But for a boy with a "sinnreich ingenium," as he puts it, the work of his hands, hard as it was for an apprentice, did not suffice; he wanted something to occupy his mind as well.[25] This need was supplied by Lienhart Nunnenbeck, the weaver and Meistersinger who taught him the rudiments of Meistergesang, selecting, no doubt, Meisterlieder religious in character to serve as models. Just as the boy had done in school, he most likely applied himself "mit hohem fleiß," and may have been pleased to find in this new form the content of some of the hymns he knew so well.[26] Two years, then the apprenticeship was over, and Hans Sachs started out on his long trek as a journeyman, an untried youth facing he knew not what.[27]

In all probability he was unafraid, for, as he informs us, he was "zogen auff gut sittn und tugendt / von mein eltern, auff zucht und ehr, / Dergleich hernach auch durch die lehr / Der praeceptori auff der schul," and ready to enter into each new experience with zest. On the pleasurable side was his contact with Meistersinger in various cities, for even many years later he recollected that he was "... behafft / Mit hertzenlicher lieb und gunst / Zu meistergsang der löbling kunst / ... Wo ich im land hört meistergsang / Da leret ich in schneller eil / Der bar und thön ein großen teil."[28] He learned about life as well during those years when he was growing into manhood. Zealously, too, he started to collect Meisterlieder, divided almost equally between the religious and the secular.[29]

In view of the fact that the very first Meisterlied which Hans Sachs asserts he wrote is of a general religious nature, I shall begin with poems in that category.[30] Both by training in matters religious and by the fact that he had already read or heard a number of Meisterlieder which treated doctrines of the Church, he follows tradition, yet, at the same time, with youthful zeal he imparts new spontaneity to his subject. His faith was strong; it was a faith which fortified him in his theological concepts and helped him in bearing a great disappointment in his young life. For the seven songs in this group he chose first of all to sing of the Trinity. Following this he considers the Holy Sacrament of the Eucharist, recounts the Atonement, and gives a kind of sermon on sin in which he depicts the sinner's doleful plight when in the hour of death he has to give an accounting of his life before God. Then, as if to dispel the gloom, he describes the twelve fruits of blessedness awaiting those in the hereafter who have served God, proceeds to reflect on the two natures of Christ, and ends with the clarion call of a dawn song.

In no less than three of his Summaries Hans Sachs tells us that he was twenty years old when, in Munich, he wrote his first Meisterlied. He affixes the exact date to a copy of it in the Dresden MS. M 190: "Dis par ist Hans Sachsen erst gedicht anno salutis 1414 den 1. Mai."[1] For his subject he chose the mystery of the origin of the Trinity and let the old familiar chant, *Gloria patri et filio et spiritui sancto, sicut erat in principio et nunc et semper in saecula saeculorum*, together with a paraphrase of it, serve as introduction.[2] This done, he states that the Son was begotten of the Father high in the Trinity, an enigma which no one on this earth has ever really explained, or for that matter has ever been worthy of understanding completely. To show the inadequacy of even the greatest minds in the Church to fathom such an inscrutable mystery, he refers to John and to his visions in the Apocalypse, to Athanasius, who was inspired by the Holy Spirit in many things that he wrote, and to St. Augustine and his encounter with the child on the seashore. Hans Sachs then contends that a matter such as this is rooted in faith, and he echoes Church doctrine when he adds that probing beyond the bounds of belief could lead to heresy. With a brief petition to God who rules eternally, a word which takes his hearers back to the *saecula saeculorum* of the first strophe, he skillfully brings his song to a close.

Goedeke published the Meisterlied under a title of his own invention, *Geheimnis der Gotheit*, and Arnold, who included it among his selections from Hans Sachs, took both text and title from Goedeke.[3]

    In des Marners langer don 3   10^r
    lieder Hans Sax gedicht

1   Gloria patrÿ lob vnd er
        got vatter in dem dron
        et fillio dem sün so her
        et spiritüi sancto fron
    5   lab er seÿ dem heilligen geist
        dreÿ nommen vnd ein got genent $\overline{fe}$

        Sicüt erat vnd ÿmer mer
        in principio schon
        der ÿe was et nüncet semper
   10   in secüla on abelon
        secülor vm aüch aller meist
        von welt zw welt / ewig vn ent $\overline{fe}$

        Got vatter seinen sün gepirt
        hoch in der drinidat
   15   Wie das geschicht kein lerer das beschriben hat   10^v

aüf disser erden kreis
kein mensch aüch des nie wirdig wür
der disse ding gancz grüntlich weis
disse gepürt verporgen ist
20 den siben künsten freÿ
geamatreÿ
rethorica philossoffeÿ
loica vnd astronomeÿ
gramatia mit müsica
25 mit irer süssen melodeÿ
da mit al meister sind gespeist
haben das klerlich nie erkent /ℇ

2 Johannes gottes adelar
der sach hoch in dem dron
dreÿ person vnd ein wessen clar
peÿ in ein maget also fron
5 vil heimlikeit wart in bekünt
als vns apocalipsis seit /ℇ

Er sach hoch in der himel kar
dreÿ vnder einer kron
gar hoch ob aller engel schar
10 ein licht in dreÿen flamen pron
noch west er nit den rechten grünt
der hohen gepürt der gotheit /ℇ

Seit Johannes den grünt nit weis
vnd kam doch also hach
15 vil weniger ein schlechter laÿ sol gründen nach
gepürt der drinidat
seit das sant Athanasius
von gothet solich gras genat
ein sprechen des heilligen geist
20 hat heimelich vnd stil
geschriben vil
von der driüaltikeit süptil
vnd ereichet doch nit das zil
des sünes ewiger gepürt
25 dar vm so ist ein kinder spil
was dichtet aller meister münt
von der hohen driüaltikeit /ℇ

3 Der lerer sant Aügüstinus
hat aüch gar schon vnd vein
von der gepürt altissimus

11ʳ

geschriben clar laüter vnd rein
5   vnd hat beweget manig frag
da er ging peÿ dem mere preit Ƒ℮

Da horet er ein stime süs
von einem kindelein
als wenig ich des wassers flüs
10   mag schopffen in das grubl klein
also wenig dürch gründen mag
dein hercz das wessen der gotheit Ƒ℮

Aügüstinus müst lassen ab
vnd ander lerer mer
15   zw gründen nach der hohen drinidat so her
ir weissen mercket das
die ding in dem gelaüben sten
keiner sol gründen vüre pas
welicher weitter gründen wolt
20   wan der gelaüb berÿrt
der wir verirt
wan es keinem nit zw gepÿrt
manig doctor zw keczer wirt
der gründen wil nach der gepürt
25   got vatters der ewig reigirt
der helff vns hie aüs aller clag
in freud ewiger selikeit Ƒ℮
1514 Ƒ℮

In this Meisterlied, written the same year as the preceding one, 1514, Hans Sachs takes up the mystery of the Eucharist. Since this is a difficult subject, he attempts to clarify the points he makes in each of the three strophes by means of homely examples. He declares that the efficacy of the Holy Sacrament is wondrous if received worthily, but eternal damnation for him who receives it unworthily, in the same way that the nectar of a flower becomes either honey or poison depending upon whether a bee or a spider withdraws it. The second strophe brings two points: one, the potency of the Lord's Supper never decreases no matter how many Christians far and wide share in it; and two, God comes to earth to be present in the numerous particles of the Eucharist while actually remaining on his heavenly throne. To illustrate he cites the sun and its rays for the first point and the many reflections of a man standing in a hall of a hundred mirrors for the second. In the third strophe he considers the doctrine of Transubstantiation in support of which he calls attention to God's transformation of Lot's wife, and also gives the very curious example of a snake's losing its venom through the power of a word. Hans Sachs' comment that it is discordant to say appearance and taste are lacking in the Eucharist may refer to something he had heard and is a rather surprising indication of lay criticism, but at the same time evidence that the tenets of the Church were being discussed by the laity. Devoutly, therefore, he urges his fellow Meistersinger not to be blinded by error, but to believe in the Holy Sacrament because with God all things are possible. Whereas he had begun his Meisterlied with a plea to the Virgin for help in writing it, he closes it with a direct prayer to the Lord Jesus Christ.

The Meisterlied has been published three times, by Wackernagel with the title *Von dem heiligen sacrament*, by Goedeke entitled *Geheimnis des sacraments*, and by Arnold who, however, took both text and title from Goedeke; in addition, Friedman quoted several verses from both Wackernagel and Goedeke.[1]

>
> **Marners langer don H S gedicht**   11ʳ
> **3 lieder**

1
      Maria himel keisserin
      dw hoch wirdige meit
      verleich mir wicz vernünfft vnd sin
      das ich bewer die heimlikeit
   5 von dem heiligen sacrament
      vnd von der himelischen speis /℮

      Die der künig aüs seraffin
      lies hie der cristenheit
      aüs rechter lib vnd warer mÿn
  10 e· er vür vns am creücze streit

da mit er vns helff aüs ellent
vnd schlos mit aüff das paradeis *ꝛc̄*

Die würckvng die ist wünderpar
des sacramentes fron
15 wer das enpfahet wirdiklichen also schon
dem kümet es zw steür
wer das vnwirdiklich enpfecht
dem wirt zw lon ewiges feür
des selben im gelichnüs nÿm
20 peÿ einer plümen her
die pin mit ger
nÿmet dar aüs ir speis mit ler
dar aüs wirt honig vnferffer
so aber ein spin neüsset dÿ
25 plümen dar aüs wirt gifft gefer
dar peÿ ist clerlich zw verstent
des prottes fricht zwaierleÿ weis *ꝛc̄*

2   Manigen nÿmet wünder ser
wie das fron sacrament
wirt in der cristen heit so fer
gewandlet an manigem ent
5 vnd hat doch hÿ vnd dort sein crafft
nÿndert kein abegang es hat *ꝛc̄*

Dürch die natür so nÿm ein ler
schaw wie der sün *her* sent
den seinen schein aüf erden her
10 vnd beleibet doch vndzwdrent
hat vmb vnd vmb sein aigenschafft
als er am firmamente gat *ꝛc̄*

Also kümet gott her aüf erd
in das sacrament fron
15 vnd beleibet wessenlich ein der himel dronn   12^r
noch ist zw mercken not
wÿ so vil partickel entpfa
hen mügen allein einen got
des selben ich geleichnüs gib
20 das ist zw mercken ring
merck ob da hing
hündert spigel ich eüch da sing
vnd das ein mensch dar vüre ging
ein ÿder spigel sünderlich
25 gancz des menschen gestalt enpfing

25

also vil partickel warhafft
enpfahen einen got verstat /ℭ

3 Mag sich verwandlen prot vnd wein
   in fleisch vnd plüt gar drot
   dürch wortes crafft der priester rein
   so er ob dem altare stot
5 wider wertig zw sprechen ist
   gesicht geschmack felt daran gar /ℭ

   Exempel geit die schrifft so vein
   wie das der ewig got
   ein weip verwandelet in stein
10 da der engel aüszfüret lot
   von Sodoma in kürczer frist
   saget vns genesis vürbar /ℭ

   War vmb wolt sich dan wandlen nicht
   prot wein in fleisch vnd plüt
15 dürch worttes krafft / die der priester da sprechen dut
   seit offt dürch worttes krafft
   ein schlang verlissen ist ir gifft
   die sie doch hat von aigenschafft
   dar vmb gelaüb warhafftiklich
20 an das fron sacrament
   dar von nit went
   schaw das dich kein irsal nit plent
   wan alle ding got müglich sent
   der verleÿch vns reÿ peicht vnd püs
25 dar nach ein güt seliges ent
   ich pitt dich herre Jesw crist
   hilff vns dort an der engel schar /ℭ 1514 /ℭ

This Meisterlied, written in 1517 three years after the preceding one, calls upon the Christian to meditate on the atonement. To induce him to do so, Hans Sachs poignantly depicts Christ, not as a distant figure, but as someone close and very human, someone to whom our heart goes out because of His hard lot. In the first strophe the poet surveys His life from the time of His entering into this world in poverty on through the years of His mission. The second stanza concentrates on the Passion and Crucifixion. Again by means of words and phrases from out of his everyday vocabulary, interspersed only occasionally with terminology from the Biblical account, Hans Sachs gives us a compassionate portrayal of Christ. The third strophe is theological in content. Three questions are asked. The answers to the first two are sound, according to Catholic theology, but the third offers only one of the total number of reasons which the Catholic Church advances for the magnitude of the suffering and death of Christ. At the close of the song the Christian is admonished to give thanks to God and to be ever mindful of His death. Of the seven Meisterlieder in this group this is the only one which neither opens nor closes with a petition or prayer.

In Six peckmessers korweis 3   27^V
lieder / Hans Saxen gedicht

1   Pe
         tracht dw ondechtiger krist
         in disser frist
         was cristus hat erlitten
    5   ee er vns hat erstritten
         in dissem jamerdal
         nim war
         wie er ein ging in disse welt
         in ar
   10   emüt drübsal vnd grosser kelt
         ellent nacket vnd dar zw plos /ℭ

         Ge
         wünden in die düchel klein
         in ein kriplein
   15   recht sam ein armes kinde
         vür essel vnd vur rinde
         geleit in odem stal
         dar noch
         merck wie er lies beschneiden sich
   20   vnd floch

27

künig Herodem ermigklich
in egipten in armüt gros ⁓

Darnach so merck
aüf al sein werck
25 wie er dürst hünger het
hicz frost erlet
vnd manig net
parvüs
cristus
30 ging frw vnd spet
er pet vastet vnd wachet
dar zw er auch nit lachet
vnd het gar wenig freüd
aüf erdt
35 macht er die krancken offt gesünt
vnd lerdt
den weg der warheit alle stünd
des drügen im die Jüden neid ⁓

2 Dar
nach betracht wie cristus wart
gefangen hart
gefüret hertikleichen
5 mit raüffen packenstreichen
mit scheltwort vnd schmach ret
verspeit
geworffen zogen her vnd hin
aüs neit
10 velschlich gezeiget vber in
darnach betracht wie mon in schlüg ⁓

Gar
hart mit geissel rütten mer
vnd aüch bÿ er
15 mit dornen wart gekrönet
verspottet vnd verhönet
vnd valsch vervrteilet
darnach
wie er sein schmehen ganck verpracht
20 müd schwach
mit stossen velen vnd vnmacht
do er sein selbes creücze drüg ⁓

Darnach wie man
in schmit daran

25 mit engstiklicher not
    mit schant vnd spot
    von plüt gancz rot
    er stündt
    hart wündt
30 pis in den dot
    vnd wie er aüch mit peine
    an sach die müter seine
    petracht aüch wie er starb
    schmelich
35 vnschüldiklich drostlos ellent
    nün sich
    an sein gepürt leben vnd ent
    wie hart er dir das hail erwarb *ꝛc̄*

3 Doch
    ist ein frag wÿ vns gemein
    cristus allein
    hat mügen huld erwerben
5 mit dem einigen sterben
    nün mercke seit vns al
    Adam
    der einig mensch zw vale pracht
    alsam
10 vns widervmb erlossen macht
    cristus ein person mensch vnd got *ꝛc̄*

    Noch
    ist ein frag ob die gotheit
    aüch etbas leit
15 in seiner marter schwere
    ob sie bedriebet were
    merck got ist an zw val
    gancz freÿ
    darvmb er vnleidenlich ist
20 doch peÿ
    wont sie der menschheit Jessw crist
    die starb mit dem herbesten dot *ꝛc̄*

    Ein frag ist wÿ
    der dot cristi
25 hab hie vür droffen gar
    alle döde clar
    der martrer schar
    nün her
    seit er

30   von natür war
an seinem laÿb der zartest
des was sein dot der hartest
o crist des im danck sag
bedenck
35   sein marter vnd dotlichen schmercz
vnd senck
sein strenges sterben in dein hercz
das seÿ dein spigel alle dag /xͤ 1517 /xͤ

With dismal words of woe Hans Sachs ushers in this Meisterlied, also composed in 1517, which is akin to a medieval sermon in rhyme. Its picturization of sin, despair, death, and hell reminds one of a story in the *Gesta Romanorum* in which a King is greatly sorrowful because hell is beneath his throne, the sword of divine justice above his head, the sword of death before him, and the sword of his sins, ready to accuse him before God, behind his back.[1] Hans Sachs may very well have read this tale, for the *Gesta Romanorum* appeared in a German translation in 1489.[2] Certainly there is nothing in his own life at this time which would have produced such turmoil within himself; hence a borrowing seems more to the point. Gone, he declares, is his joyful frame of mind for he sees death in the offing. No matter which way he turns there is desolation. Even when he lifts up his eyes he sees a heaven that is barred to him. The only brightness in all of this gloom is the portion addressed to the Virgin. Upon her he centers his hopes as he pleads with her to place her shield between him and her angry child. From out of his own unworthiness he then exhorts the sinner in general to heed his words, to repent, and to call fervently upon God for forgiveness. This shift to God Himself is brief, for almost immediately the poet returns to Mary, because, as the "Mead of Mercy," it is she who can gain favor for us. His closing words are addressed directly to her.

Wackernagel published this Meisterlied with its first two verses as title.[3]

In der vberhohen perck weis Hanss   40^v
Saxen vnd sein gedicht 3 lieder

1   Ach
          we mir armen sünder we
          wie ste
          ich so ÿn jemerlicher not
5   mit sch*m*erczen jch vmbfangen pin   39^r
          hin
          ist hercz müt vnd freud frecher sin
          ich sÿ vor mir den grimen dot
          dar zw die vngewissen zeit
10   die scheit
          mich von der welt
          geit meinen leib der erden /ȓ

          So
          ich schaw hinter mich geschwint
15   so fint
          ich hinder mir das streng gericht
          da alle parmung wirt verspert
          hert

```
      richt got den sünder mit dem schwert
20    da hilffet aüch kein fürpit nicht
      er stost in ein das ewig mort
      vnd dort
      in zw geselt
      dem deuffel ewigcleichen /c̄
25  O
      schaw ich zw der lincken hant merck eben
      da vint ich armer mein sündiges leben
      dar von ich got müs schwere rechnung geben
      van
30    hochfart geitikeite
      neite
      von zoren drünckenheite
      mit
      vnkeusch des geleichen
35    von posheit vnd von schande
      da
      mit ich det vnere
      mein
      en schepffer so here
40    schwere
      mere
      merck ich von mir nit vere
      wa
      ich armer mich kere
45    zw meiner rechten hande
      nit
      drostes mag mir werden
      wan
      dar peÿ ich kein wercke
50    mercke
      das mich in hoffnüng stercke
      kein
      güt dat volget mir nit nach /c̄

2     Heb
      ich dan aüf die aügen mein
      mit pein
      sich ich verspert der himel dar
5     da in doch ist ewige wün
      vün
      anplickvng der gotlichen sün
      von frolockvng der engel schar
```

dar zw ich aüch erschaffen pin
10 ist hin
des leid ich not
vor angst mŏcht ich verczagen /c̄

Och
schaw ich vnder mich gen dal
15 in qüal
so find ich offen sten die hel
dar in weis ich gros be vnd ach
rach
drübsal angst clag vnd vngemach
20 dar ein sol aüch mein arme sel
dar von mich got doch het gedrost
erlost
mit seinem dot
ist nün on mir verloren /c̄

25 Doch
sie ich ob mir gelenczen von veren
den hellen himelischen meres steren
zw dem so wil ich armer sünder keren
das
30 ist maria milde
pilde
secz deiner parmüng schilde
vir
deines kindes zoren
35 zw dir stet al mein hoffen
cle
himelischer gartte
heil
der petripten harte
40 zarte
arte
des dodes ich icz wartte
we
meiner hine fartte
45 dÿ hel die stet mir offen
dir
jünckfraw dw ich clagen
las
mir genad her flisse
50 sisse
das ich mein sunt hÿ pisse

weil
ich noch aüf der erden leb /℮

3   O
sünder peÿ mir dein gedenck
nit wenck
schaw wÿ dw stest in einem stant
5   von wegen cleiner freüden hie
die
doch alle ist zw gencklich ÿe
vnd gilt dir gar ein draürigs pfant
dw verleüsest das ewig heil
10   zw deil
wirt dir der val
in ewiklichen schmerczen /

Pas
merck sünder was ich dir sag
15   palt schlag
dein hercz gancz mit reüichem müt
von allen sünden dich behent
went
spar sie nit on dein lecztes ent   41^r
20   wan spatte rew düt selten güt
aüch ist die zeit gar vngewis
aüs dis
em jamerdal
misen wir alle sterben /℮
25   Las
dich dein sünt von ganczem herczen reÿe
mit inikeit zw got dem heren schreÿe
so wil er dir genediklich verzeihe
der
30   vir vns aüf ert kame
name
den dot an creüczes stame
wolt
dich zweiffel verderben
35   nÿm zw vir sprecherine
Mar
iam die jünckfrawe
gilff
schreÿ zw ir in drawe
40   pawe

schawe
sie ist der parmüng aüe
dar
zw der genad dawe
45   sie kan dir huld gewine
holt
hat sie dich von herczen
wer
sich von sünt düt kere
50   here
dw küngin der ere
hilff
vns zw dir so werd wir fro ꝑ̄ 1517 ꝑ̄

Written the same year as the preceding Meisterlied, 1517, this one contrasts sharply with it, for here Hans Sachs speaks of the blessedness which, in the heavenly Jerusalem, God bestows upon the Christian who has served Him with love and devotion. For his basis the poet uses the second verse in the last chapter of The Revelation, where St. John records that he saw "the tree of life which bare twelve manner of fruits," and proceeds to interpret these (which St. John does not do) to be the twelve spiritual joys awaiting the Blessed in Paradise. A few of these might very well have expressed some of Hans Sachs' inmost wishes for this life: health with never a pain, love without hindrances, joy without envy in another's honor, and peace without animosity. From the delineation of the joys it would seem that he envisioned the transfigured as leading a blessedly active life, and yet, at the end of the song he contradicts this by admonishing Christians to turn to God so that they will come to eternal rest, a traditional conception.

In der schlag weis linhart 84ᵛ
nünnenpecken Hans Saxen gedicht
5 lieder

1 Erhebe 85ʳ
dw cristenliche zünfft
in got das dein gemütte
gen im dich ieb
5 im werck der lieb
mit iniger andachte /ℇ

Pedrachte
wie dir got in zw künft
wil geben dürch sein gütte
10 die seligkeit
dar in zwelff freit
zw fellig die merck ebe /ℇ

Johannes clÿg
lich seit von dem
15 dürch heimlich sin
an dem lesten capitel
spricht ich sach in
Jerüsalem
das lebentig
20 holcz sten freÿ in dem mittel
das drüg
zwelff frische klug
dissen aüs züg

      al hie vernem
25   nach dem geistlichen titel /ꝛ̄

2   Die state
      ierüsalem pedeit
      das himelische reiche
      vnd die zwelff fricht
5   ich vnderricht
      zwelff zw fellig freid herste /ꝛ̄

      Die erste
      ist die ewige freit
      an draüren ewikleiche
10   der frolockvng
      kein irdisch züng
      gancz kein aüs sprechen hatte /ꝛ̄

      Die ander ist
      ewig gesünd
15   vnd an al we
      der seligen merck eben
      die drit verste
      in solcher wund
      an endes frist
20   sie ÿmer ebig leben
      der dot
      düt in kein not
      der ewig got
      hat in den fünd
25   in seinem reiche geben /ꝛ̄

3   Die virte
      ist ebig lÿb habvng
      an alle hindernüsse
      dar in lebent
5   ewig an ent
      die himelische zünffte /ꝛ̄

      Dÿ vünffte
      ist die er settigung
      ewig on al verdrüsse
10   wan in ewick
      al aügenplick
      freidt neüe freid gepirte /ꝛ̄

      Dy sechst ist gros
      wan sie al dort

15   von angesicht
zw angesicht got kennen
vnd zweiflen nicht
das wort lob wort
sie sechen plos
20   die sibent wil ich nennen
ist frit
der im wont mit
kein vnwil nit
ist an dem ort
25   den frid mag nimant drennen /c̄

4   Dy achte
ist ir freÿheit so gancz
al dinst ist in gar ferne
sÿ sind vn mie
5   got loben sie
an mü die gottes freünte /c̄

Die neünte
ir clarheit vnd gelancz
sie leuchten als dÿ sterne
10   ir leib aüch wirt
clarifizirt
peÿ in ist aüch kein nachte /c̄

Die zehent stat
in geselschafft
15   der zehenn stent
des himelÿschen here
wan sie al sent
mit günst pehafft
das ÿdes hat
20   freüd in des andren ere
kein neit
nÿmand nit dreit
gunstige freit
die geit in crafft
25   dort ewiklich imere /c̄

5   Des schallen
der engelischen stim
mit gar sussem hoffirenn
ist die eilfft freit
5   ir seligkeit
der aüser welten geste /c̄

Die leste
ist sicher heit vernÿm
das sie nit mer verliren
10 dÿ freide sis
vnd sein gewis
das sie nit mügen vallen x̄c̄

O weltlich zir
wie gar pehent
15 zw schmilczet gar
dein freüd ist pald verloffen
o cristen schar
zw got dich went
auf das dort dir
20 der himelpfort ste offen
das dw
aüch kumest zw
ewiger rw
das ist das ent
25 da hin wir alle hoffen x̄c̄ 1517 iar

By means of the word "surexit," which effectively begins this Meisterlied composed in 1518 on the two natures of Christ, Hans Sachs epitomizes a Christian event of the greatest importance in that, as he says, Christ lives forevermore and reigns eternally with the Father and the Holy Spirit. The young poet has a clear understanding of the dogma of the two natures of Christ, the one human and the other divine, united into one substantial whole throughout all eternity at the same time that they remain completely distinct, but he does not seem too sure of himself when he begins to speculate about this mystery. Consequently in each of the three strophes he finds it necessary to address himself to an unnamed master for help in answering his questions. It is only towards the very end that he briefly refers to a master by name, namely to St. Francis, then abruptly brings his song to a close with a short prayer to Jesus.

In six peckmessers kor weis   460^r
Hans Sachsen gedicht
3 lieder

1   Sǔ
        rexit cristǔs de morte
        vns vǔr pas me
        er lebet aǔch ӱmere
5   vnd in gotlicher ere
        dort ewiklich reigirt
        mӱt got
        vatter vnd dem heiligen geist
        aǔs not
10   cristus der war sǔn gottes heist
        die ander persan der dreӱheit /℮ /℮ /℮

        Zwǔ
        natǔr sint in cristo fron
        doch ein person
15   gotlich vnd aǔch menschliche
        ӱmer vnd ewikliche
        aldo kein schidvng wirt
        vnd was
        man von einer natǔre ret
20   merckt das
        man vǔn der andren aǔch verstet
        von welt zw welt in ewikeit /℮̄

        Aǔs dem ich mag
        hie ton ein frag

25   seit die menscheit cristi
vereint ist ẙe
der gotheit wẙ
on endt
erkendt
30   aŭch schidlich nie
nŭn ist die frag erkoren
ob cristus werdt geporen
von got dem vatter zart
ewick
35   in seiner gotlichen gepŭrt
vnd strick
aŭch meister dissen spehen gŭrt
pistŭ in hoher kŭnst gelart ℞

2   Pin
ich hie reden aigentlich
so antwordt ich
das die gepervng pŭre
5   an dreff gotlich natŭre
vnd nit die menscheit wert
seit got
vatter gotlich natŭr gepirt
aŭs not
10   menschlich natŭr geschiden wirt
meister pescheid mich disser frag ℞

        In
der gepervng solt verstan
wirt die persan
15   personlich nit geschiden
nẙm geleichnŭs herniden
da cristus starb aŭf ert
das mort
lit cristŭs nach der menscheit hie   460ᵛ
20   merck fort
gotlich natŭr was leidlich nie
doch wart kein schidvng da ich sag ℞

        Es spricht paŭlŭs
wie das cristus
25   geporen seẙ ein fart
sein mŭtter wart
maria zart
von der
nam er

30 menschliche art
nŭn seit die schrifft *hÿe* voren
gottes sun wert geporen
aŭs des vatters sŭbstancz
merck wo
35 got vatter geper die menscheit
also
wŭr sein sŭbstancz menschlich geseit
das mag cristlich reden nÿmancz /k͞c

3 Nŭn
ich hie weiter fragen mŭs
seit das cristŭs
ist nach der menscheit clare
5 ein creatŭr vŭr ware
dar aŭs mag sprechen ich
das in
geporen hab die war gotheit
den sin
10 der schopfvng man sitlich aŭs leit
ein geperŭng gotlicher kŭr /k͞c /k͞c

Vŭn
wegen der schopfŭng verste
so spricht man ee
15 Cristŭm geporen seÿe
von der gotheit dar peÿe
zv reden hie sitlich
sag dv
meister mag man dŭrch dÿ schopffvng
20 aŭch zw
legen die gotlich gepervng
allen geschopff der creatŭr /k͞c

Seÿ wer die wel
in himel hel
25 oder aŭf disser erdt
die frag peclerdt
franciscus wert
vnd spricht
gericht
30 an al geferdt
mag man das aŭch wol sprechen
der schopffvng nach zwrechen
nŭn pitten wir Jesŭm
das er

42

35   vns mach von allen sǔnden heÿl
      vnd ver
      leÿ vns ewigen erbe deil
      in dem ewigen keisser dǔm $\overline{Ke}$ ·1·5·18· $\overline{Ke}$

The last of these religious songs, written also in 1518, is a dawn song which has been pronounced one of the best religious *Tagelieder* we have.[1] As a model Hans Sachs chose the courtly dawn song of the Minnesinger. The opening verses are epic in character, but then the watchman speaks directly to the stranger-guest, bidding him flee, and warning him with regard to what will befall him and the high-born lady if the lord of the castle should come upon them. At the beginning of the second stanza the poet, by means of a question as to the identity of the bold knight, skillfully introduces the interpretation of the allegory, an interpretation which closely parallels the first strophe and emphasizes the danger of an abrupt end and its consequent punishment. In the third stanza Hans Sachs delineates this last motif in greater detail because he wants to impress upon man that, if death overtakes him while he is entrapped in sin, God's punishment will be immediate. The poet's closing plea to the Virgin to awaken him with her merciful voice, should he fall asleep in sin, is in keeping with the idea of the dawn song and rounds out its motifs.

Goedeke published the Meisterlied under the title *Vermahnung zur buß*; Wackernagel used the words of verse fourteen from the second strophe for his title, *Wach auf von sünden, es ist spat*; Kochs quoted some twenty verses taken from the first two stanzas, all according to Wackernagel; Schweitzer published the first two *Stollen* as he found them in Goedeke.[2]

In der hohen dag weis Hans   461ᵛ
Sachsen vnd sein gedicht
3 lieder

1   Es rŭft ein wachter faste
     des hohen dages glaste
     dringet von orient
     dÿ nacht gen occident sich lent
5   es nahet gen dem morgen /℘ /℘

     Dar vm dŭ frembdter gaste
     alhie nit lenger raste
     von deinem lib dich went
     vnd mach dich aŭs der pŭrg pehent
10   gar heimlich vnd verporgen /℘

     Mein her leit in dem sale
     in seines schlaffes qŭale
     der gen dem dag aŭf stet
     vnd so er hie pegreiffen det
15   dich vnd dye hoch geporen
     die er im hat erkoren

so er die fünd geschmecht
dürch sein vrteil vnd scharpffes recht
het ir den leib verloren
20 dem seinen schwinden zoren
ir nit entrinen mecht
wan er stürczet eüch peide schlecht
ab in das diffe dale
dan würdt eüer freüdt schmale
25 dar vmb weich aüs dem pett
pewar dich vnd dein lib vor not
dw stest in schweren sorgen /ꝛ̄ /ꝛ̄

462ʳ

2 Wer ist der küne helde
der sich hat zw geselde
dem zarten frewenlein
mensch merck das ist der leibe dein
5 ist aüf der pürg entschlaffen /ꝛ̄ /ꝛ̄

In sünden manigfelde
das freülein aüserwelde
pedeüt die sele rein
die got hat nach der pildnüs sein
10 gar adelich erschaffen /ꝛ̄ /ꝛ̄ /ꝛ̄

Der wachter an der zinen
ist die vernünfft mit sinen
wach auf so rüfft er drat
wach auf von sünden es ist spat
15 vergangen ist dein zeite
der dot ist dir nit weite
pedeüt das dages licht
got ist der her ich hie pericht
der in dem sal noch leite
20 seiner parmherczikeite
wart aüf güt zw versicht
dar vm zw rew peicht püs dich pflicht
dar dürch magstü entrinen
kümen frolich von hinen
25 ·e· dich erschleicht der dat
vnd volgest dü nit weisem rat
leib vnd sel wirt got straffen /ꝛ̄ /ꝛ̄

3 Merck so in sünden diche
der grime dot erschliche
zw hant er wachet got

mit der gerechtikeite drot
5 vŭnd er eŭch dan peflecket /e̅ /e̅

Das selb er an eŭch riche
stŭrczet eŭch schneliklich
in den ewigen dot
der fal ewig kein ende hot
10 kein reŭ eŭch dar nach klecket /e̅ /e̅

Sŭnder in dem gefilde
ist alle freŭd gancz wilde
der fal ist also diff
kein lebend hercz die pein pegriff
15 merckt der verdampten schare
gotlichen anplick klare
sehen sÿ nit ewick
wan sie dŭncket ein aŭgenplick
wol hŭndert daŭsendt jare
20 sŭnder nÿm der straff ware
vnd lös dem schlaff dich schick
vnd los dich aŭs der sŭnden strick
maria jŭnckfraŭ milde
dŭ senftmŭtiges pilde
25 so ich in sŭnd entschliff
mit der genaden stim mir riff
das ich wir aŭf gewecket /e̅ Am en /e̅ 1518 /e̅ /e̅

462ᵛ

Chapter II / Songs to the Virgin Mary

Background

To show how strong and deep the roots of tradition were which Hans Sachs inherited for his Meisterlieder in honor of the Virgin Mary, I find it necessary to sketch the history of Mariology.

The oldest literary accounts of the Virgin are the legends recorded in the apocryphal gospels of the New Testament, legends which became well known since they supplied the desired details so lacking in the canonical books of the Bible.[1] As a result the Church had to begin examining its own position with regard to the Virgin.[2] In defense of her against unbelievers the apologists, as early as the second century, applied metaphorical language from the Scriptures to her. During the next 200 years this practice increased to such an extent that we find most of the prefigurations of the Virgin, which were current throughout the Middle Ages and beyond, already present in the patristic writings.[3] Yet the development of doctrine and dogma with regard to her was still in the background, although allusions to her exalted position were plainly visible. The greatest single impetus given to Mariology was the pronouncement at the Council of Ephesus in 431 that the Virgin was *theotokos*, the God-bearer. Thereafter the propagation of her veneration in the West as well as in the East made tremendous progress through the establishment of church feasts honoring certain events in her life; through the continuous portrayal in art of various scenes in which she figured in both the canonical and the apocryphal gospels; through the renaming of churches after her; through the addition of Mary-miracles to the Saints legends prepared for meditation in the monasteries; and, most important of all, through the inclusion of her name in the liturgy of the Church.[4]

In the West the Virgin's place in the theology of the Church was espoused with great zeal in Latin homilies, exegeses, litanies, and in verse. But whatever the genre, the authors drew upon prefigurations for her to lend weight to an argument, to embellish an account, or simply to praise her.[5] Despite the fact that controversy about certain points of doctrine pertaining to the Virgin continued throughout the tenth century, in the eleventh Marian devotion reached a height which could scarcely ascend further.[6] Now it was necessary to maintain her pre-eminence by bringing her closer to the common people both as the mother of God and as a mother who had known joy and great grief. The observation of Saturday as her own special day was advocated and adopted.[7] Then, beginning with the twelfth century, the movement of various monastic orders to make Mary their particular patroness brought about the flowering of the Mary-cult.[8] Furthermore, knights from the time of the Crusades on remained steadfast in their devotion to her, and other laymen formed Mary-guilds and Mary-brotherhoods to honor and serve her.[9]

Yet nothing that was inaugurated to keep the remembrance of Mary ever fresh in the minds of the people even approximated the great influence engendered by the introduction of the angel Gabriel's simple salutation to her: *Ave, gratia plena: Dominus tecum: Benedicta tu in mulieribus.*[10] From time to time this greeting was expanded, first by inserting *Maria* after the *Ave*, whereby the name of the prayer was created, then by excerpting from Elizabeth's welcome to Mary the phrase: *benedictus fructus ventris tui*, to which, as a fitting close, the name *Jesus*, or *Jesus Christus*, was subsequently appended.[11] Later a second half came into existence with the petition: *Sancta Maria, ora pro nobis*; but the last seven words, *peccatoribus, nunc et in hora mortis nostrae*, were not included officially in the prayer until after the Reformation.[12] The first documentation admonishing the people to pray the *Ave*—the first part only—along with the *Credo* and the *Pater Noster*, is to be found in the twelfth century. By the end of the thirteenth these three, but particularly the *Ave* and the *Pater Noster*, constituted the core of all oral prayers for the laity.[13] Nevertheless the people needed constant reminders to pray the *Ave* often. Legends proclaiming the efficacy of repeated *Aves* were resorted to and grew in number until by the beginning of the fourteenth century there was a sizable collection centering on Mary.[14] In tale after tale she comes to the aid of those who through their many *Aves* show their love for her. But the device which had the greatest appeal in popularizing the *Ave* was the rosary.[15] The pattern for the saying of the prayers was not uniform, and, if we may judge from a pamphlet which appeared in Nuremberg as late as 1503, instructions seem to have been needed for rosary devotions. However, toward the end of the fifteenth century it was thought to be sufficient for the common man to recite fifty *Aves* with a *Pater Noster* inserted between every ten.[16]

Imbued as men were with love for the Virgin Mary, not a few seemed to feel a need to express their devoutness in a form aside from formal prayers, and so they turned to poetry, both to epic and, more abundantly, to lyric. Once begun it came forth in a constant outpouring from the second half of the twelfth century on into the fifteenth. But no matter whether the poems possess great literary quality or are only passingly fair, whether they are anonymous or named, the predominant note in all is praise for the Virgin conveyed for the most part through traditional and newly invented metaphors.[17] Considering the lyric poetry only, one finds it quite natural that the *Ave* itself should have served in various ways as the basis for poetic greetings to the Virgin. Numerous poems also deal with her life, death, and assumption, with her virtues, her joys, and her sorrows, and a goodly number paraphrase Latin hymns dedicated to her.[18] Again and again she is requested to plead with her Son for mercy, a reflection of the doctrine that the Virgin acts as mediatrix between man and Christ.[19] From out of this conviction the popular belief that even the greatest sinner could find pardon through the Virgin's intercession gained ground. Often there is also a plea at the close of a poem that she stand by the author in the hour of death, a petition which, over a period of time, may have been conducive in bringing about the second part of the *Ave*.[20]

Thus religion with its liturgy, hymns, and sermons, together with poetry and the arts, revealed a deep reverence for the Virgin Mary. All portrayed her in the various aspects of her life, but the part allotted to her in the Passion story as the sorrowing mother inspired perhaps the finest works of all.[21] Consequently a close relationship to Mary, which manifested itself in these forms within and without the Church, permeated the lives of both rich and poor up to and beyond the Reformation. In Nuremberg we find the *Liebfrauenkirche* (1349); the *Marienbruderschaft Kapelle* (1355); Mary-statues and other works of art, often presented in her honor, in the large churches of the city; rosaries depicted in both paintings and wood carvings either as a motif or as the framework for a picture, usually that of the Virgin.[22]

Hans Sachs must have been just as familiar with the tangible proofs of Marian devotion in Nuremberg as he was with the hymns and poems dedicated to the Virgin, with legends about her, and with numerous Meisterlieder which sang her praises.[23] It is not surprising, therefore, that he too paid homage to her with songs of his own fashioning. Eleven such are included in Berlin 414. Instead of arranging these in chronological order, I have chosen rather to present them relative to their subject matter: the Virgin as the *mater dolorosa*, the Annunciation, the Nativity (to which he devoted three songs), and the three Conceptions of Mary. He also paraphrased two well-known Latin hymns, one of them twice, and wrote two songs to glorify her, which are made up almost entirely of metaphors and epithets. Included in the descriptive language are common prefigurations, a few of which occur more than once. However, in one instance only, and that by means of the word "figvrirt," supported a little further on by the word "bedÿdt," does Hans Sachs call attention to the fact that an event in the Old Testament foreshadows Mary.[24] As a rule he employs prefigurations merely as metaphors. The substance of the poet's Mary-songs is in the vast stream of tradition, but he often varies that which has been handed down to him and frequently highlights the old with new figurative phraseology and with realistic details drawn from life as he saw it about him.

For the theme of the first of the eleven Meisterlieder which Hans Sachs wrote in honor of the Virgin Mary from 1514-1518, he took that of the sorrowing mother. Whether he was familiar with the *Stabat mater*, a Latin rhymed prayer which had already been translated into German during the fourteenth century, or whether he had heard the *Stabat iuxta iesu crucem*, which is related to it and which was being sung in Germany as a sequence in the Votive-Mass *de compassione beatae Mariae*, cannot be ascertained, but does not seem too remote a conjecture.[1] It is possible also that he may have seen one of the *Marienklagen*-plays which were performed on Good Friday and in which the chief actors were Christ, Mary, and John. No matter what aroused his first interest, the final incentive which prompted his own composition may very well have been a Meisterlied by Folz, which he copied into Berlin 414, for aside from certain items which were common property, a few verses are quite similar in wording, sometimes in their entirety, sometimes in part, sometimes merely as an allusion to, or as a reflection of a thought.[2] Nevertheless, the two Meisterlieder differ materially from each other because Hans Sachs displays a greater power of realistic description and is able to depict Mary's love for her child in a more natural manner. He does not forget that the grief of the Virgin is the central theme and that we are seeing the crucified Christ through her eyes. And what she sees overwhelms her because the figure on the cross is her own dearly beloved child, a fact which the poet stresses over and over again. Yet this very relationship brings added sorrow to Jesus in that He understands her compassion for Him, and so, even in the midst of His own anguish, He speaks to her with a gentle voice as He gives her into the keeping of John. It is not until Christ has been removed from the cross and laid beside her that she voices her poignant complaint, all the while calling Him her child, her son. Only at the end of the lament, as if suddenly remembering who this child of hers really is, does she address Him as her dear Lord Jesus Christ. And as He is carried away to be laid in the tomb, she follows, disconsolate.

Even though we find the traditional details, both apocryphal and Biblical, in the poem, Hans Sachs brings them closer to us by motivating his statements. To mention only a few: Mary could scarcely recognize her dear child because there was so much blood streaming over His face from the crown of thorns; His human strength was ebbing away because He had received so many blows and was so wounded; it is Mary's motherly desire which prompts her to wish that she might hang beside Him; and it is the taunting of the Jews which increases her suffering even more. Incidentally and skillfully the young poet weaves in the doctrine of atonement when he has John try to console Mary by reminding her that Christ had to die thus shamefully in order to save mankind and that on the third day He would joyously arise. Unlike the poet of the *Stabat mater*, who took up three-fifths of his poem with a plea to Mary, Hans Sachs devotes only the last eight verses to a prayer in which he requests her to free him from sin and, along with John, to stand by him in the hour of death and to intercede for him with God.

The Meisterlied was published in the doctoral dissertation of Sister Mary Juliana Schroeder.[3]

In des Marners langer don 7
lieder die gülde clag vnser liben
frawen H S gedicht

1   O cristenn mensch fleissig betracht
      das weinen vnd die clag
      so von Maria wart verpracht
      an dem heilligen kar freitag
5   da ir kint an dem creücze hing
      was schwerlich in den dot verwündt /c̄

      Vnd het solich grosse amacht
      nach aller lerer sag
      der dot mit seinem leben facht
10   wan der her da manigen schlag
      empfangen het das im entging
      sein menschlich krafft mÿt pleichem mündt /c̄

      Sein libe müter stan vor im
      sach an die grossen pein
15   die da ir liebes kint het in der marter sein
      aüs müterlicher gir
      dacht sie o herczenlibes kint
      ich wolt aüch das ich hing peÿ dir
      aüf hüb sie da ir angesicht
20   vnd sach in draürig an
      ein dürne kran
      het er aüf seinem haübet stan
      das plüet vber sein antlicz ran
      das sie in kaüm erkennen mocht
25   dar ab sie solich leid gewan
      das grosser schmerczen vmefing
      ir reines hercz die selben stündt /c̄

2   Sie sach hangen ellentikleich
      ir herczenlibes kin
      on alle schüld gar lesterleich
      bedrüebet waren al sein sin
5   sein leiden was so manigfalt
      sein leib was nacket vnde plos /c̄

      Der edel künig aller reich
      in aremüt erschin

sein angesicht wart worden pleich
10 sein menschlich krafft was gar da hin
sein leib würd gancz dotlich gestalt
dar vber das rot plüet ab flos /c̄

Gar jemerlich verspeiet wart
sein zartes angesicht
15 die jüden hetten mitt im kein mitleiden nicht
sachen doch wol die not
wie im mit krefften wonet peÿ
der grimiklich vnd grimer dot
wan er was schwach müd vnde kranck
20 mit armen aüs gepreit
on pitterkeit
aldo ein scharpffes schwert verschneÿt   8ᵛ
Maria hercz vor grossem leit
als ir doch vor manigem jar
25 Her Simeon het weis geseit
ein schwert dein hercz noch mit gebalt
dürch dringen wirt vor jamer gros /c̄

3   Das da genczlich erfüllet war
wie sant Anshelmus spricht
zw schmacheit im der jüden schar
zwen schacher hetten aüf gericht
5 dar zwischen mit schweigendenn münd
hing cristus als ein lemelein /c̄

Vnd weinet an dem creücze clar
als vns die schrifft vergicht
wan er verlassen was so gar
10 kein hilffe het von nÿmant nicht
was doch pis in den dot verwünd
on alle schüld led er dÿ pein /c̄

Aüch het der her besünder leit
da er sach an den schmercz
15 dar mit vmbgeben wart das müeterliche hercz
die im kein hilff mocht dün
vnd doch geren gestorben wer
vir iren ein gepornen sün
den sie an sünd erczogen het
20 al hie aüf disser ert
der hing versert
vor den falschen jüden vnwert
vnd het sein reines plüet verrert

52

die driben aus im iren spot
25 dar ab der müter laid sich mert
vnd da ellentiklichen stünd
vnd wartet aüf das ende sein /c̄

4 On allen drost so gar ellent
sein mütter er an sach
ir mit leiden er wol erkent
mit senffter stim er zw ir sprach
5 beib schaw das ist der süne dein
Johan nÿm deiner mütter war /c̄

Als ob er sprech mein lecztes ent
das ist mir also nach
dar vmb Johannes in dein hent
10 mein libe mütter dw enpfach
ich mag ir nÿmer vor gesein
ich müs mich von ir scheiden zwar /c̄

Wan es doch alles ist verpracht
aüf dissem erterich
15 o lieber sün wiltw dan hÿ verlassen mich
nim mich aüch mit dir hin
wan ich dÿ betrieptest mütter
aüf disser ganczen erden pin
Johannes gab ir seinen drost
20 sprach meit genaden vol
weistw doch wol
das er hie schmelich sterben sol
da mit losset er vnferhol
menschlich geschlecht aüs dodes val
25 misten sünst ewig kümer dol
am dritten dag aüs aller pein
wirt er der sten mit freüden clar /c̄

5 O mensch gedenck der grossen not
da die mütter an sach
wie irem kint der grime dot
sein minikliches hercz zw prach
5 er schreÿ vatter mit laütter stim
mein geist befilch ich in dein hent /c̄

Zw hant ein plinder jüde drot
in ein die seiten stach
dar aüs flos wasser plüt so rot
10 gar miltiklich ein schoner pach

wie wol im vor der dot mit grim
sein zartte aügen het verbent /℮

Da peÿ die mütter mercket wie
ir kint verschiden was
15 dar von ein scharpffes schwert ir hercz vnd sel dürch mas
vnd sach in on mit fleis
wie er mit armen aüs gespan
en hing da in cleglicher weis
aüf die prüst er geneiget het
20 das dote haübet sein
solt da nit pein
haben die werde müter rein
seit die sün ver lor iren schein
vnd aüch dürch grosses mitleiden
25 zerspilten sich die hertten stein
vnd in dem tempel aüch vernim
der vmehang sich gar zw drent /℮

6   Dar nach mon zw der vesper zeit
in ab dem creücze nam
zw seiner mutter mon in leit
aüf die erd peÿ des creüczes stam
5 die manigen zeher vergos
vnd sach in permiklichen an /℮

Vnd küsset ÿm mit pitterkeit
sein antlicz wünesam
vnd aüch manige wünden weit
10 da von ir grosser schmerczen kam
vor leit ir hent zw sam da schloss
die himelische küngin fran /℮

Sie sprach wie gros gewessen sint
der schmercz mein libes kint
15 wie jemerlich dein hent vnd fües dürch graben sint
vnd aüch dein antlicz clar
zerstossen vnd zerschlagen ist
vnd aüch dein seit dürch stochen gar
wie pistw hÿ an allen drost
20 verschiden so schmelich
kein drost han ich
mer hÿ auf dissem erterich
seit dw hast gar verlassen mich
ich wolt das ich verschiden wer
25 mein herczenlibes kint vür dich

so het ein ent mein ellent gros
das ich aüf disser erden han /c̄

7   Versigen ist in disser frist
     aller weisheit ein prün
     o wie gar nün versigen ist
     dein münd mein herczen lieber sün
5   wie hastw hÿ dein reines plüt
     vergossen so mit grosser not /c̄

     Mein lieber Herre Jesw crist   10ʳ
     seit dw in reicher wün
     ein künig aller engel pist
10   wie pistw dan so ellent nün
     wie leistw hÿ in aremüt
     vnd pist so pitterlichen dot /c̄

     Man nom alda van ir do hin
     ir libes kint Jesus
15   Joseph von Aramathia Nicodemus
     drügen in zw dem grab
     die ellent mütter volget nach
     grosser schmerczen sie vmegab
     desselbigen ich dich ermon
20   küngin der jeracheÿ
     o matter deÿ
     mach mich von allen sünden freÿ
     wan meines lebes nÿmer seÿ
     so küm zw meinem leczten ent
25   dw vnd Johannes stet mir peÿ
     vnd halt mein sel in eüer hüt
     pit für sie den ewigen got /c̄ 1514 /c̄

No. 9, foll. 36ʳ-37ʳ   Orig. 24

Hans Sachs enframes the first of his three Meisterlieder on the Nativity, written in 1514, 1515, and 1517 respectively, in traditional theology: in the first strophe David pleads with God to send His Son to earth so that the prophets and he himself may be released from limbo, where they have all been languishing for so many centuries, and in the very last *Abgesang* the concept of salvation is rounded out by a brief reference to Christ's suffering on the cross. To add conviction to the fact that God heard David and that the incarnation came about in a supernatural way through a Virgin, the poet cites prophecies and prefigurations in the Old Testament. Then with a brief reminder to his audience to praise and honor this wondrous birth because of its great import, Hans Sachs is ready for the story proper, which, however, he restricts to four events: the decree of Caesar Augustus, the coming of Mary and Joseph to Bethlehem, Mary's giving birth to God and man in one person, and the arrival of the Three Kings bearing gifts. For the most part the short account follows the New Testament, but there is one strophe, the fourth, which sets the song apart; in it the poet describes with homely realism the joy of the young mother in her infant Son and lets her love for Him find expression in her endearments and in the little things which she does for His comfort. Hans Sachs then closes with a few words of prayer to Mary that she not forsake us, but protect us and stand by us on the Day of Judgment.

Wackernagel published the Meisterlied under the title "Von der Geburt Christi."[1]

In dem güldin don Hans Saxen vnd   36ʳ
sein gedicht 5 lieder

1   Da zweÿ vnd fünfczig hündert iar
           zwar
           gar
           vergangen was
5   in gottes has
           manch proffet sas
           diff in varhelle qüal /ꝛ

           Der edel weis künig Daüit   36ᵛ
           mit
10   pitt
           erlicher stim
           rüffet in grim
           her vns vernim
           sendt vns dein sün zw dal /ꝛ

15   Er hor vns küng sabaotht
           sent vns das himelische prot

so wirt geent al vnser not
drot
hot
20 got
den sun becleit
mit der menscheit
peÿ einer meit
in irem keuschen sal /꞊

2   Meitlichen rein on alle mon
fron
von
gotlicher kür
5   clar laütter pür
vber natür
die meit ir kint entpfing /꞊

Der früm proffet Isaias
das
10   bas
in septimo
capitülo
spricht er also
ein maget schwanger ging /꞊

15   Irer entpfencknüs vnzw stört
nün hört esechielis wört
peschlossen ist vnd pleibt die port
fort
hort
20   dort
Moisem grün
der püsch vnd prün
kein meil gewün
kein pletlein nie so ring /꞊

3   Ir christen sprechet lob vnd er
der
her
lichen gepürt
5   dar dürch vns würt
gros leit enpfürt
schlos aüf der himel pon /꞊

Der früm keisser aügüstus lies
his

10   gwis
      aüs gen vnd melt
      in aller welt
      man pringen selt
      ein czins pfenig gar schon *ke̅*

15   Do das gepot aüs gangen war
      Maria vnd Joseph kam dar
      zw petlahem die meit gepar
      gar
      clar
20   zwar
      in kalter zeit
      mit grosser freit
      die clar gotheit
      vnd mensch in einr person *ke̅*

4   Sie sach in also liplich an
      schan
      fran
      mit ganczer gerd
5   den fürsten werd
      himel vnd erd
      da in menschlicher art *ke̅*

      Vnd in gar freüntlichen aüf zückt
      schmückt
10   drückt
      in an ir prüst
      nach herczen lust
      vnd liplichen küst
      in on sein mündlein zart *ke̅*

15   Vnd wicklet in ein düchel clein
      das adeliche kintelein
      vnd neigt in ein das criplein rein
      ein
      schein
20   vein
      der gotheit clar
      vmbgab sie gar
      der engel schar
      süngen schon zw der fart *ke̅*

5   Zw hant ein lichter steren schein
      fein
      rein

in orient
5 da wart erkent
das het benent
die schrifft balaam schon /c̄

Gar schnel dreÿ edel küng vür bar
zwar
10 dar
zügen in gir
mit reicher zir
golt weÿraüch mir
prachten dem kindlein fron /c̄

15 Das vns pracht aüs des flüches neit
dar vür es an dem creücze leit
dar vmb sein lob singt vnde seit
weit
preit
20 meit
verlas vns nicht
halt vns in pflicht
am iüngsten gricht
dw vns dreulich peÿ stan /c̄ 1514 /c̄

The second song of the Nativity, composed at Christmas time, 1515, one year after the first one and shorter than it by two strophes, is a New Year's gift to the Virgin.[1] After greeting her both as "star of the sea" and as "morning star" Hans Sachs requests that she grant him inspiration in singing her praise. Again he brings in the lamentation and entreaties of David and the prophets in limbo, but this theological introduction is not as long as it was in the previous song. The story of the birth differs also. Deleted are the decree of Caesar Augustus, the arrival of Mary and Joseph in Bethlehem, and the coming of the three kings. Instead the poet recounts the Annunciation, Conception, Birth, song of the angels, and the homage of the shepherds. Since the emphasis is upon Mary—nowhere is Joseph mentioned—it is not surprising to find a brief interpolation towards the end which declares that Christians are duty-bound to serve the Virgin, for it was she who bore the Savior, she who brought the "bright day." In the very last verse Hans Sachs returns to the motif of the "morning star" and thereby achieves a unified, artistic close.[2]

Wackernagel published the Meisterlied with the same title as No. 9, "Von der geburt Christi."[3]

In des zorens züg weis 3 lieder   24ᵛ
H S gedicht

1   A
           üe maris stella ich grüsse
           dich maria die lichtprehender morgen stern
           erleücht mein hercz vnd al mein sin
     5   das ich dich lob zw dissen weÿhenachten /ℇ̄

           Da
           mit ich hoch mit worten süsse
           dein lob aüs schreÿ / dar nach stet meines herczen gernn
           dw künigin aüs serafin
    10   hilff mir künstlich dein hohes lob betrachten /ℇ̄

           Von deiner frolichen gepürt   25ʳ
           da von die profetten haben geschriben
           pald ein steren aüf dringen würd
           von Jacob dar nach würd die nacht verdriben
    15   vnd wür aüf gen der helle dag
           des begerten sie al
           vnd lagen diff in der vorhelle qüal
           vnd schrien mit cleglicher stim
           kunig Daüit vnd her Isaias
    20   her reis entzweÿ vnd vns vernÿm

die trön sent vns dein sün der parmung vas
vn den vns nÿment helffen mag
zw dir her in den himelichen sal
o her vernÿm die vnser clag
25 hÿlff vns armen aus der varhele dal Ke̅

2 Ir
schreien wert fünf daüssent iare
vnd dennoch mer zw gott vatter in ewigkeit
pis in parmüng so hoch ermant
5 das er sein sün wolt lassen menschlich sterben Ke̅

Vÿr
der menschlichen grossen schare
des war gotter sün aüch gar williklich bereit
zw hant wart gabrihel gesant
10 zw Maria vnd det dÿ pothschafft werben Ke̅

Er sprach aüe vnd grüsset sÿ
vnd sprach dw solt ein kindelein geperen
ecce ancilla domini
nÿm war ich pin ein dinerin des heren
15 mir gesche nach den wortten dein
aügenplicklich geschwint
enpfjng die mait das himelische kint
von des heilligen geistes krafft
drüg sie neün monet vnd sechs dage me
20 vn czerdrenvng ir jünckfrawschafft
dar nach gepar sie keüschlich one we   25ᵛ
zw betlahem ir kindelein
in odem stal vor essel vnd vor rint
drang aüf des lichten dages schein
25 den vns her pracht der morgen steren lint Ke̅

3 Hoch
in dem lüfft die engel süngen
Gloria in exelcis deo also sÿs
lob seÿ got hoch in jerarcheÿ
5 der sein sün hat gesendet auf die erden Ke̅

Noch
et in terra pax erclüngen
ir stim hominibus bone volüntatis
dem menschen frid aüff erden seÿ
10 die sein des willens güt mit *herczen* gerden Ke̅

Das neü gesang war pald erhert
von den hirten wÿ cristus wer geporen
sie gingen dar in schneller fert
vnd petten on das kindlein aüserkoren
15 darvmb seÿ wir cristen verpflicht
zw dinst der maget clar
seit sie vns ÿe das hochste heil gepar
eüa pracht vns die vinster nacht
die nam dürch das rein aüe wider ent
20 wan es den lichten dag her pracht
dar vm maria pilich wirt genent
der prehent morgen steren licht
wan sie geit schein der cristen heit vür bar
zw lob schenck ich das new gedicht
25 dem morgensteren zw dem neüen iar /k̄e
1515 /k̄e

Two years elapsed before Hans Sachs composed his third Meisterlied on the
Nativity. Similarly to the second it was written at Christmas time, is dedicated to
the Virgin, and is just three strophes long. In this song, however, he omits the
theological introduction and merely says many wise sibyls and prophets foretold
that a Virgin would give birth to the Son of God and that this Son would take away
the curse brought upon us by Adam. From here on the narration in the main
follows the account in Luke 2:1-17, but again a few realistic details as well as some
of the traditional apocryphal particulars are interwoven. Skillfully the poet ties in
the mystic event with the present by inviting his Christian hearers to join in the
rejoicing of the angels and to go with the shepherds to Bethlehem, there to view the
child and to sing praises to Mary who bore Him. In one verse only, the second to
the last, Hans Sachs calls attention to the significance of Christ's coming into this
world, thereby again tying in the end of his poem with the first strophe. Just as
there was no plea to the Virgin at the beginning of the Meisterlied, so too it closes
without a prayer.

In dem lait don nachtigals   88ʳ
Hans Saxen gedicht
3 lieder

1   Menschlich vernünfft
         erheb dich heüt in freüde
         in deines heiles vresprüng
         mit iniger pedrachtüng frolock geüde
    5   seit das mon heüt den dag pegat
         das vns ein meit geporen hat
         menschlichen gottes süne /c͂

         Welches zw künfft
         vorlang verkündet hetten
    10   dürch die gotlichen ein sprechvng
         vil weisser sibella vnd vil profetten
         ein jünckfraw würd enpfahen schon
         vnd geperen ein sün so fron
         der würd den flüch ab düne /c͂

    15   Dar ein vns pracht adame
         die proffezeÿ ist da erfüllet worden
         wan die jünckfraw lobsame
         ir kint gepar wider natüres orden
         von dem heiligen geist so rein
    20   aügenplicklich got vnd mensch zwü natüre
         doch in einer person allein

63

menschlich gelidmassiret rein vnd pure
den sie drüge neün monat lang
in irem leib an allen zwang
25   in magetlicher wüne /℉

2   Da nün die zeit
irer gepürt erscheine
ein mechtig keisser war zw ram
Octaüianus was der namen seine
5   der lis peschreiben al dis welt
ein zinst pfenig war anctz gemelt
dem keisser da zw reichen /℉

Also die meit   88^v
vnd Josehp sich aüff machte
10 kamen gen petlahem mit nam
da heten sie nit herberg vber nachte
do bart ein altes vich haüs sten
dar ein der früm Joseph müst gen
vnd die meit ermikleichen /℉

15 In der nacht die meit ware
in pescheülicher süssikeit verstricket
vnd da on we gepare
recht sam der sünen glancz ein glas dürckh plicket
da sie ir kindt ersehen kündt
20 vormenschlich freüd ir reines hercz pebeget
in alte düchlein sie es wündt
vür esel rindt es in das kriplein leget
die nacht würdt liecht recht als der dag
auch geschah nach der lerern sag
25 die nacht vil wünderzeichen /℉

3   ein engel pal
den frümen hirtten saget
geporen wer messias fron
sie eÿlten dar da funden sie die maget
5   vnd aüch ir neü geporen kind
in dem kriplein vor essel rind
das günden sie gloriren /

In süssem hal
süngen die engel werde
10 lob seÿ got in der hohe dron
vnd dem menschen seÿ der frid ÿe aüf erde
geporen ist der ware crist

der aller welt erlosser ist
des sol wir jübÿliren /kͤ

15 Ir cristen lat vns freÿen
mit den engelen lat vns frolich singen
die hoch gepürt aus schreÿen
mit *geÿstlicher* frolockvng das verpringen
vnd lat vns mit den hirten gen
20 zw der krippen lat vns das kindlein schawen
mit iniger pedrachtüng schen
sprecht lob der jünckfraüen aller jünckfraüen
die vns geporen hat die frücht
die vns pracht aüs der helle sücht
25 der dv ich heüt hoffiren /kͤ
1517

No. 12, foll. 25ᵛ-26ᵛ (Unpublished)

The main topic of this three-stanza Meisterlied written in 1517 is the Annunciation to which, however, Hans Sachs devotes only a little more than half of his song. In the *Abgesang* of the second strophe he refers briefly to the Nativity, to its theological import, and to Mary's having been chosen from eternity for her role as mother. The last third of the poem, replete with metaphors, is an encomium for her. When the poet declares that she deserves the highest homage next to God and that she is the most exalted next to Him, he can go no further, hence merely adds that she will never desert a Christian.

In dem geschiden don Cünracz 25ᵛ
nachtigals 3 lider H· S· gedicht

1   Ein engel wart gesante
von der heilligen drinidat
gen Jüda Nasaret der stat
da er Mariam fante
5   er grüsset sie mit eren /℮   26ʳ

Aüe gracia plena
gegrüst seistw genaden vol
der her mit dir gar vnverhol
et sine omni pena
10   solt dw iünckfraw geperen /℮

Ein zartes kindeleine
Jessus so sol sein nom werden genenet
da sprach die iunckfraw reine
wie mag das sein ich hab kein mon erkennet
15   der engel sprach der heillig geist
wirt dich vmb schetten aller meist
mit dem gotlichen scheine /℮

2   Da disse wort verginge
da sprach die zarde iünckfraw rein
mir geschech nach den wortten dein
zw stünt die meit enpfinge
5   von dem heilligen geiste /℮

Rein vber die natüre
die iünckfrewlich enpfencknus was
recht sam die sün durch scheint das glas
an all zw prechvng püre
10   vns die geschrifft beweiste /℮

Sam sie dan aüch gepare
an alle we ann einem weÿnacht morgen
zw hilff der cristen schare
der ir frücht halff aus schwer dotlichen sorgen
15 zw mütter sie er wellet het
die hoch wirdige drinidet
von ewigkeit vür ware /c̄

3 Sie ist des heils vrsprünge
sie ist der gütikeit ein sarch
vnd ist der heiligkeit ein arch
vnd ein prün der parmünge
5 mer ein schrein vol genaden /c̄

Sie ist der zücht ein spigel
sie ist der reinigkeit ein gart   26ᵛ
sie ist der güldin aimer zart
dar inen lag das sigel
10 var ewiklichen schaden /c̄

In den vns pracht adame
aller dügent ist sie ein pluend reisse
die küngin lobesame
nach got hat sie das aller hochst preisse
15 sie ist nach got das hochste güt
kein cristen sie verlassen düt
wer erent iren name /c̄ 1517 /c̄

As Hans Sachs indicated in the superscription for this Meisterlied of 1517, it deals with the three conceptions of the Virgin Mary. To each of these he devotes one strophe: the first, her election by God from eternity to be the mother of the Eternal Word; the second, her earthly conception which took place in a natural manner, but about which the poet deems it wiser to maintain a chaste silence; and the third, the Immaculate Conception, which Hans Sachs defines as the infusion of Mary's pure soul into her pure body. Inherent in this last one are three Church doctrines which the poet notes in three consecutive verses, namely that Mary was preserved from all stain of original sin, that she was free from any inclination to sin, and that she was exempt from the dominion of death. He also alludes to the fact that he has heard criticism of the Immaculate Conception when he says that one should not argue against it because there is proof of it and because it has been confirmed by the Church. He then closes by urging Christians to honor the Feast Day set aside for it. Since that day was December 8 and since the poet speaks of "dem heutigen fest," this gives us the exact date for the composition of this Meisterlied, a date not supplied by the K-G Index.

In dem freÿen don Meister hans   26^V
volzen die dreÿ enpfencknus
3 lieder H S gedicht

1   O
            keisser dreÿer jerarcheÿ
            begab hercz müt mit künst der sin
            aüf das ich heut frölich aüs schreÿ
5   das lob der himel künigin
            von dreÿen entpfencknusen ir
            in welchen sie dreÿ hohe kir
            enpfing vber al menschen schar /℮

            Gotlich ist ir erst enpfencknüs
10   weliche was von ewigkeit
            wann got al creatür beschlüs
            in dem spigel seiner weisheit
            dar in er al geschopf vür sach
            die zw künfftig würden her nach
15   alda was auch Maria clar /℮

            Enpfangen von got ÿe vnd ÿ
            da von geschriben stet lobsam
            proverbiorüm octaüo nün hert
            hÿ nondüm erant abbissÿ
20   ego iam concepta eram

in der enpfencknüs wirt ir cür peclert
wan da mit wirdikeit die rein
vber draff alle creatür
englisch menschlich ir mercken selt
25 seit sie von der gotheit so pür
zw einer mütter wart gewelt
zw geperen das ewig wort   27^r
menschlich das dÿ sünt würt zw stort
so
30 adam würt verschülden sein /c̄

2 Dÿ
ander enpfencknus die ist
leiplich do maria dÿ zart
in mütter leib zeitlicher frist
5 natürlich nach menschlicher art
enpfangen wart von der geschicht
ist clerer hÿ zw künden nicht
ein zuchtig schweigen zimet pas /c̄

Hir in sol mon ir kür versten
10 ist das sie so zart was gezilt
das sie mit ir leip lichen schen
vber draff al weipliche pild
nemlichen nach Bernhardüs sag
das mon leicht lich probiren mag
15 dürch zwü vrsach so mercket das /c̄

Die erst sie was von edlem stam
von patrijarchen künig früm
Mateüs eigentlich melt ir geschlecht
nent ir zwen vnd virczig mit nam
20 in seinem ewangeliüm
züm andren die menscheit cristj an secht
welcher geporen wart von ir
der doch aüf erd der sch^eonest was
der ir er schon aüch zeücknüs git
25 ÿdoch sol mon hÿ mercken klar
das mon disser enpfencknus nit
beget in dem heütigen fest
aüch nit die erst allein die lest
wÿ
30 wol die zwu aüch eren wir /c̄

3 Her
nach die drit ich nen vnd czel

die genadreichen die becleib
do maria ir reine sel
5   enpfing in iren reinen leib
freÿ aller erbsünd ich verkündt
auch do zw neigvng aller sündt
dotlich deglich wardt sie qüitirt /c̄

Mit dysser kür sie vber hoch
10   vÿr draff al pur menschlich persan
so ÿe waren vnd werden noch
wider disse enpfencknüs man
mit nichte argwiren sol
seit sie ist vor beweret wol
15   vnd von der kirchen confirmirt /c̄

Aüs disser kür wirt sie erkent
speculum sine macüla
seit sie aügenplicklich nie sünt dürch büt
darvm wirt sie pillich genent
20   virgo mater purissima
wan sie ist ÿe nach got das hohest güt
mit im ein wil kür imer me
on dreffent die parmherczikeit
in not sie kein kristen verlat
25   pevor wer sie mont der freiheit
disser rein enpfencknüs verstat
des frolocket ir cristen al
eret das fest nit reichem schal
der
30   rein enpfencknus Marie /c̄ Deo gracias   1517 /c̄

27ᵛ

Wackernagel, who published this Meisterlied which Hans Sachs wrote in 1515, rightfully named it *Salve Regina*, for, if we discount minor variations in spelling, it contains the complete Latin text of that hymn, together with a German paraphrase, within the structure of its three strophes.[1] The poet interprets freely as he follows the dictates of syllable count and rhyme. Sometimes this enables him to adhere to the Latin construction, sometimes not; occasionally he even breaks up a sequence of Latin words and interpolates something of his own invention. Into each strophe he also works in an extra item or two relating to the Virgin. In the first he requests her to stand by us at death and uses the second *salve* to greet her as an empress and queen; in the second he inserts the comment that it was she who dispelled the curse and that, according to many a wise prophet, salvation was conceived in her; and in the third he asks that she keep us from sin and that she place her shield between us and the enemy.

In des Hans Saxen Silber weis vnd   37ʳ
sein gedicht 3 lieder

1   Sal
             ve ich grües dich schone
             reigina in dem drone
             seit das dw dregst die krone
      5   misericodie ƒℰ

             Al
             er parmherczikeite
             ein mütter man dich seite
             an vnser leczten zeite
      10   vns jünckfraw peÿ geste ƒℰ

             Vita dülcedo pist vürbar
             des lebens vresprüng
             et spes nostra wan an dir gar   37ᵛ
             leit al vnser hoffnüng
      15   salue jünckfraw wir grüssen dich
             ein keisserin gewaltiklich
             gar hoch in jerarcheÿe
             atte zw dir mareÿe
             clamamus wir stet schreÿe
      20   hilff vns aüss allem we ƒℰ

2   Eck
             xüles gar ellende
             filli kinder wir sende

dar in pracht vns behende
5   Eüe im paradeis ƙe̅

Weck
hast den flüch verdriben
peÿ dir ist heil becliben
als von dir hat geschriben
10   maniger proffet weis ƙe̅

Jünckfraw atte süspÿramus
zw dir so seüfczen wir
gementes ich auch melde süs
et flentes mit begir
15   wir weinen vnd clagen gar ser
in hac lacrimarvm er her
valle in drubsal früme
eia ergo darvme
advocata sa küme
20   nostra ich gib dir preis ƙe̅

3   Rein
e vürsprecherine
illos tüos mit sine
Maria künigine
5   misericordies ƙe̅

Dein
ocülos mit gere
ad nos conüertte kere
et Jesüm dein sun here
10   von sünden vns beles ƙe̅

Benedicktum gebenedeit
früchtum ventris tüi
seÿ diÿ frucht deines leibs geseit
nobis post hoc merck wÿ
15   exylliüm osstende nach
dem ellent o clemens enpfach
o pia gütigs pilde
o duldcÿs süs vnd milde
Maria secz dein schilde
20   vür vns dem veinde pes ƙe̅ 1515

A year after Hans Sachs produced his first paraphrase of the *Salve regina* (No. 14) he wrote a second one. It is quite unlike the first in that even though he again quotes the entire hymn, the Latin words seem more like stepping stones which give the poet pause to praise the Virgin by means of time honored imagery, or original variations thereof, and occasionally also to inject a remark of his own. Since this Meisterlied is longer than the first, five strophes to the earlier three, he can well afford to laud Mary extravagantly by two, three, five, once even by seven metaphors in a row, some thirty in all.[1] However, he weaves these into the paraphrase so ingeniously that they do not detract, but form a colorful tapestry. In closing, the poet calls upon Mary to come at the time of death and to lead us into the presence of her child.

In caspars singers schlechten don   23ʳ
5 lieder H S gedicht

1
       Sich freüt hercz müt vnd sine
       seit mein münt aber sol
       dich loben künigine
       aller genaden vol
   5   wie wol
       mein hercz dar zw ist vnpereit /ͤe

       Salüe nün pis gegrüsset
       tw celi reigina
       dein nam der ist dürch süsset
 10 vnd heisset Maria
       iunckfra
       vnd mütter der parmherczigkeit /ͤe

       Matter missericordie
       dw pist der würczel von iesse
 15 ein edler stam
       von künigklicher arte
       der cristen heit ein kron
       der himelfricht ein garte
       dw vel her Jedion
 20 da von
       vns wol vitta dülcedo kam /ͤe

2
       Des lebens süssikeite
       pistw ein vresprüng
       et spes nostra in leitte
       pistw vnser hoffnüng
   5   kein züng
       der lerer nie dein lob ergrint /ͤe

Salüe dw clarer spigel
die engelischen zir
atte der schom ein rigel
10 clamamus fraw zw dir
schreÿ wir
exulles fillÿ eüe kint /Ƈ

Atte zw dir dw fürstin clar
seüffczen wir armen sunder gar
15 süspiramus
gementes zw dir reinen
et flentes in fraw nün
clag wir zw dir vnd weinen
dw genadreiche sün
20 dw prün   23ᵛ
aller parmug ein vber flüs /Ƈ

3   Hac lacrimarüm valle
seit wir doch al gemein
in dissem jamerdale
in grossem dribsal sein
5 in pein
anfechtüng angst vnd grosser net /Ƈ

Er leücht in disser dünckel
ale die dein pegern
dw licht klarer karfünckel
10 dw heller meres steren
lw zern
eÿa ergo dw morgen ret /Ƈ

Advocata in seraffin
nostra vnser vürsprecherin
15 vür vnsser schüld
vor deinem liben kinde
dw miltes palsam vas
mach seinen zoren linde
dw gotlicher pallas
20 dw stras
die vns dreget in gottes hüld /Ƈ

4   Dw himelischer sarche
der drinidat ein schlos
küngin der patrijarche
on doren dw edle ros
5 jllos
tüos missericordies /Ƈ

Ocülos at noss wende
dein aügen zw vns her
conüertte ins allende
10   vnser drübsal vnd schwer
verker
dw prinender püsch moÿses /ꝑ̄

Et Jesüm benedictum sis
früctum ventris tüi nobis
15   dein edle frücht
die zeig vns dort in freiden
in seinem keissertum
wen wir von hinen scheiden
post hoc exilliüm
20   *soküm*
ostende vns dein keüsche zücht /ꝑ̄

5   *O clemens o maria*
dw senftmütiges pild
mon nenet dich o pia
den gülden aimer myld
5   dw schild
aller die stet hoffen in dich /ꝑ̄

O dulcis süesser daüe
dw süsses elpaümreis
der himel kor ein frawe
10   dw part des paradeis
peweis
die müter vns parmhercziklich /ꝑ̄

Wan wir sollen aus dem ellent   24ʳ
so küm zw vnsrem leczten ent
15   halt vns in pflicht
vnd dw vns meit beware
vor deuffelischem neit
hinan der engel schare
gib dw vns das geleit
20   in freit
vür deines kindes angesicht /ꝑ̄ 1516 /ꝑ̄

For his third poetic paraphrase of a Latin hymn Hans Sachs chose the *Ave, maris stella*, a hymn of seven stanzas made up of four verses each.[1] The poet follows this definite structure in this Meisterlied of 1516 by devoting one tri-partite strophe to each of the seven. Systematically he opens each *Stollen* and each *Abgesang* with one line of the Latin, then lets the fourth Latin verse constitute the beginning of the third verse in the *Abgesang*. The fourth strophe alone in the Meisterlied deviates from this regularity, for there Hans Sachs combined two Latin lines (except for one word), which normally would appear in the *Abgesang*, to form the whole last verse of the second *Stollen*, so that nothing is left for that particular *Abgesang* save that solitary word. For his interpretation he either gives the equivalent of the Latin, or he paraphrases it, in almost equal proportion; then, where the verse seems to demand it, he gives a reason for, or the result of, the Latin statement. Sometimes, too, he presents additional information. In order to show his love for the Virgin he addresses her throughout the song by numerous metaphors which serve to enrich the poem. Similarly to No. 14 the poet closes with the request that Mary place her shield of mercy before us.

In frawen Eren don das Aüe Maris   21^V
stellis 7 lieder H S gedicht

1   Aüe maris stella ich grües
         dich lichter meres steren
         maria himel dawe sües
         dw genadreiche süne
    5   dw morgenrot vnd wüniklicher dag /$\overline{k}$

         Deÿ mater alma dw pist
         ein mütter Gottes heren
         geheilliget zw aller frist
         der paremüng ein prunen
   10   dw palsam raüch vnd susser veiel hag /$\overline{k}$

         Atque semper virgo reine jünckfrawe
         pist tw ewig dw himelische aüe
         felix celi porta in hohem preisse
         pistw der seligkeit ein pfort
   15   dar dürch wir ein gen vnzw stort
         wol in des himelische paradeisse /$\overline{k}$

2   Sümens illüd aüe enpfach
         aüe das wort dürch süesset
         kein süsser wort vor vnde nach
         aüf erden nie erclange
    5   dan das aüe als manig lerer schreib /$\overline{k}$

76

Gabrihelis ore der mündt
Gabrihellis dich grüesset
aügenplicklich die selben stündt
hastw jünckfraw enpfange
10 war got vnd mensch in deinem keüschen leib /k͞e

Fünda nos in pace dw vns beschÿrmen
in stettem frid vor den helischen wÿrmen
mütans nomen Eüe hastw gar schone
verwandelt den nomen Eüa
15 in das aüe o maria
des dregstw wol von zwelff steren ein krone /k͞e   22ʳ

3   Solüe vincla reis los aüf
      den schüldigen ir pande
      das der helisch drack nit er laüf
      seit das dw pist alleine
5   virsprecherin der armen sünder schar /k͞e

      Profer lümen cecis gib licht
      den dis verloren hande
      vnd in sünden gesehen nicht
      lichter karfünckel steine
10   erleücht ir hercz dürch rew peichtpüsse gar /k͞e

      Malla nostra pelle dreib von vns gancze
      al missedat dw gottes monastrancze
      bona cüncta peste dw lilgen stengel
      erwirb vns cristen alles güt
15   das wir mit andechtigem müt
      got loben vnd dich künigen der engel /k͞e

4   Monstra te esse matrem zeig
      dich sein ein mütter milde
      der cristenheit dw rossenczweig
      dein mantel für vns schwinge
5   das vns gottes zoren nit pring in we /k͞e

      Sümat per te preces dürch dich
      dw senftmütiges pilde
      nempt got aüf vnser pet so rich
      dw pist des hails vrsprÿnge
10   qüi pro nobis natus tülit esse /k͞e

      Tüüs dem sün den dw vns hast geporen
      dar zw pistw von ewigkeit erkoren
      dar vm dir ale himlisch her wol sprichte
      dw pist der güldin aÿmer zart

77

15   dw gottes sarch vnd maien gart
       dw hast vns pracht die himelischen frichte /k͞e

5   Virgo singularis noch mer
       pist ein jünckfraw pesünder
       dir dint das engelische her
       al profetten mit sine
   5   die loben dich dü vel her gedion /k͞e

       Inter omnes mitis in zücht
       pistw warlichen vnder
       allen weiben die gütigst frücht
       dw himel keisserine   22ᵛ
10   dw pist der püsch der her moÿsem pron /k͞e

       Nos cülpis salütos al die sind freÿe
       von den sunden den ste dw hilfflich peÿe
       fac mittes et castos mach vns mit gire
       senfftmütig in dem iamer dal
15   seit dw der dügent pist ein sal
       der güet vnd keüscheit dw edler saphire /k͞e

6   Vitam presta püram vns gib
       jünckfraw ein reines leben
       das wir pleibe in gottes lib
       dw spigel one mackel
   5   dw pist die daüb die *her* Noe aüs sant /k͞e

       Iter para tütum vnd pfleg
       dw milt süsser wein reben
       das wir haben sicheren weg
       zünt vns die lichte fackel
10   aüf das wir kümen in das vatter lant /k͞e

       Vt videntes Jesüm das wir an sehen
       Jesüm dem wir ewiges lob veriehen
       semper coletem*ür* da wir an leite
       besiczen himelfreiden vil
15   mit engelischem seitten spil
       hillf vns da hin dw gottes herpffen seite /k͞e

7   Sit laüs deo patri lob seÿ
       got vatter alle friste
       der alle ding beschüff sso freÿ
       wie wol menschlich geschlechte
   5   verdamet wart vmb das einig gepot /k͞e

Sümo cristo decüs geleich
lob seÿ dir hochster criste
der vür vns starb gar willikleich
aüf das er wider prechte
10 menschlich geschlecht von dem ewigen dot $\bar{Xe}$

Spiritüi sancto dem heilling geiste
seÿ zir der vns mit sein genaden speiste 23^r
honor drinus et vnus sey gesünge
den dreÿen er in ainigkeit
15 maria keisserliche meit
secz wür vns deinen schilt der paremünge $\bar{Xe}$ 1516 $\bar{Xe}$

Among the earlier Meisterlieder dedicated to the Virgin Mary is this one of 1515 which consists almost entirely of metaphors, titles, and epithets descriptive of her. Interwoven are John's vision of her in The Revelation, a few Old Testament prophecies concerning her, and three doctrines which during the course of the centuries had become firmly established in the minds and hearts of the worshippers, namely: Mary is the fount of divine mercy, she is the source of salvation, and she is free from all sin. Hans Sachs declares that no tongue on earth can praise her sufficiently. He presents his song to her and prays that she will help him reach heaven.

Schnorr v. Carolsfeld published the Meisterlied, but from the Dresden manuscript M 8.[1]

In des frawenlobs gülden don   24ʳ
3 lieder Hans Sax gedicht

1   Mar
        ia künigine
        war
        lichen der driüalte
5   ein
        clar
        es spigel glase
        dar
        zw ein dochter frone
10   güt
        vetterlicher art /c̄

        Müt
        er des sünes criste
        ge
15   spons des hailling gaiste
        schwe
        ster der engel clare
        her
        liche fraw der welde
20   zw
        dir hon ich begir /c̄

        Zir
        liches palsam vase
        mit gnad pistw gespeiste
25   dw
        pist ein meisterine

der apostel gezelte
vnd der ewangeliste
sterck der marterer schare
30 mer
küngin mit gebalte
rein
patrijarchen zart
sal
35 aller keüsch ein krone
al
es heil kam von dir /c̄e

2 Her
Johannes beweÿsset
der
dich sach himel frawe
5 glancz
cler
lich als die süne
mer
sach er wol geziret
10 ob
deinem haübt ein kron /c̄e

lob
lichen hort er singe
vÿl
15 engelischer zünge
wil
ig vnd dar zw gerne
rich
schrib Johanes milde
20 wie
sie dich lobten meit /c̄e

Seit
das dw pist ein prüne
der gotlichen parmünge
25 die
deglich dürch dich fleÿsset
der gütikeit ein schilde
des heilles ein vrsprünge
dw lichter merres sterne
30 dich
jünckfraw figvriret
gancz

24^v

81

```
             das vel Jedeon
             das
   35        war von himel dawe
             nas
             das dich fraw bedeÿdt  /ħ

3            Part
             verschlossen gezirte
             gart
             himelischer frichte
    5        rein
             zart
             von dir geporen
             wart
             der künig der engel
   10        I
             saias das seit  /ħ
             Si
             meon das ercleret
             Wa
   15        Ilaam des geleichen
             da
             vit vnd Salamone
             zeig
             en sint deiner pürte
   20        dar
             in vns heil erschin  /ħ
             kin
             igin aüser koren
             kein züngen mag erreichen
   25        gar
             dein lob er vnd wirde
             kein sünd dich nie berürte
             als / himlisch her dich eret
             dort in der himel drone
   30        zweig
             susser lilgen stengel
             dein
             lob vnd er ist preit
             dir
   35        schenck ich das gedichte
             mir
             hilff in seraffin  /ħ  1515  /ħ
```

During the three years which had elapsed between the writing of the previous Meisterlied in 1515 and this one in 1518 Hans Sachs' store of imagery descriptive of the Virgin Mary seems to have grown apace, for he now creates a song of joy for her completely out of German and Latin metaphors and epithets. With two-thirds of its verses beginning with *Ave*, the Meisterlied might well be included among *Ave*-poems. Even though most of the figurative expressions are based on tradition, a surprising number are the poet's own variations, and a few could even be original in their entirety.

In vnser frauen gesanck weis   461ʳ
Hans Sachsen vnd sein
gedicht 3 lieder

1   A
        ue sponsa mater virgo
        sanctissima Maria
        o sedŭla deyidatis
    5   aŭe plena gracia
        et pia
        wenedicta aŭe soror angelorum /c̄̃ /c̄̃ /c̄̃

        Aŭe gloriosissima
        aue tŭ speciosa
   10   aŭe alma redemptoris
        aŭe pulchra vormosa
        tŭ rosa
        sine spina aue corona virginum /c̄̃ /c̄̃ /c̄̃

        Aŭe von daŭit sŭser mandel kerne
   15   aue grŭnende rŭt jesse
        aŭe von jacob heller meres sterne
        aŭe dŭ sŭn her Jossŭe
        aŭe
        von Israhell dŭ leŭchtende luzerne
   20   aŭe dw ros von Jericho
        aŭe arch noe frone
        aŭe dw vel Jedeonis
        aŭe dw pŭsch der prane
        vnd glane
   25   aŭe von Nasseret dw wol richende plŭm /c̄̃

2   A
        ŭe ancilla Domini

aůe des heils ein průne
aůe dw plůend olpaům reis
5 aůe du himel sůnne
freůd wůnne
aůe du morgen rot vnd wůniklicher dack K̄ K̄ K̄

Aůe virgo frůctiffara
aue peschosner garte
10 aůe gart himelischer speis
aůe versperte pfarte
rein arte
aůe důgranatapfel sůser palsam schmack K̄ K̄

Aůe des himel her ein keiserine
15 aůe ein kůngin der parmung
aůe der miltikeit ein herczogine
aůe ein greffin der hoffnůng
vrsprung
aůe der demůtikeit ein fůrstine
20 aůe porta paradisi
aůe der welt ein frawe
aůe vocktin des paradeis
aůe der genad awe
vnd dawe
25 aůe dw zelt dar in der hochste kůnig lack K̄ K̄

3   A
         ůe archa deidatis
         dw gottes tabernackel
         aůe důprůn der reinikeit   461ᵛ
5   aůe spigel an mackel
         licht fackel
         aůe dů drost aller pedrůbten herczen gar K̄

Aůe důsůasissima
aůe senft můtigs pilde
10 aůe dů grunt der cristenheit
aůe des frides schilde
zart milde
aůe vůrsprecherin der armen sůnder schar K̄ K̄ K̄

Aůe dw wol pegossner aimer půre
15 aůe aller důgent ein kron
aůe dw hochste aller creatůre
aůe der selikeit ein pon
gar fron
aůf nach got dregstů die hochsten kůre

84

20 aŭe dŭ edle jŭnckfraw sÿs
mein grŭs ich dir hie sende
ich pit dich so mein sel hie scheit
aŭs dissem dal ellende
so wende
25 zw mir dein aŭgen der parmŭng dŭ jŭnckfraŭ clar Ᵽe AM en
Ᵽe 1518 Ᵽe

Chapter III / Two Legends

Background

In his Mary-songs Hans Sachs revealed his love for the Virgin by honoring her name and by embellishing his verses with numerous metaphors glorifying her. Furthermore he showed his faith in the efficacy of her intercession through his petitions to her at the close of various songs. He had learned from his reading that she comes to the aid of those who love and serve her. To illustrate this the poet recounts, in the first of the two legends in this chapter, the story of a miracle which, he says, he found in "mirakŭlis beate marie." This is a storehouse of 100 miracles attributed to the Virgin which Johannes Herolt, a Dominican friar called Discipulus, had collected from various sources, probably between the years 1435 and 1440, and which he had named *Promptuarium Discipuli de Miraculis Beate Marie Virginis*. Herolt's book was published in Nuremberg in 1486 and may well have been the one which Hans Sachs read, especially since he quotes the essential portion of the title.[1] He chose No. 23, one of the lesser-known legends, for his Meisterlied.[2]

Alongside of the Mary-legends were those pertaining to saints in general. Among these, St. Catherine held an interest for Hans Sachs, for not only was there a convent dedicated to her in Nuremberg, but at every Mass he heard the priest intone her name among the few saints prominent enough to be in the *Confiteor*.[3] Although the poet does not mention the source for the second of his two legends, except to say "die schriefft anzeŭcht," he had apparently been reading *Der Heiligen Leben*, a compilation in prose of saints' tales made around 1400 in Nuremberg, but not published until 1471-1472 in Augsburg. This book was designed for the spiritual uplift of the laity and proved to be so very popular that from its first printing until 1521 it appeared frequently in Ulm, Straßburg, Basel, and Nuremberg.[4] Included in the collection are three legends about Catherine of Alexandria.[5] The primary one, which is the familiar account of her conversion, martyrdom, and death, is very long, but the other two, which attest to miracles wrought by her, are shorter and not so well known. Of these Hans Sachs selected the second for his retelling.

The central theme of both legends is the same, namely that devotion, be it to the Virgin or to St. Catherine, will assure unfailing help when one is in dire need. The two Meisterlieder were written in the same year, 1518.

In the legend upon which Hans Sachs based this Meisterlied we read that an adulterer plotted the death of his wife, a faithful devotee of the Virgin, by murdering a knight's child whom the wife was nursing in order to earn a living. After the dastardly deed was done, it was the woman who was accused and arraigned. Since there was no one in court who would listen to her plea of innocence, no one to defend her, she called upon the Virgin, who would know that she was not guilty, and placed herself under her protection. Almost immediately a beautiful lady with a child in her arms appeared and announced that her child would be the judge. Before the child-judge pronounced judgment, however, he demanded that the dead infant be brought into court. This done, the miracle came about: the dead infant was restored to life and pointed out the murderer, the woman's adulterous husband. As soon as his wife had been freed and he had been sentenced, the vision vanished. In retelling this legend Hans Sachs fills out the factual statements of the original by means of descriptive details which heighten the interest. For instance, he motivates Mary's help more clearly by stressing the woman's daily devotion to her; he makes the entrance of the lady more dramatic by having her appear in the midst of a supernatural radiance which silences the courtroom; he deletes bits of phraseology from the speeches of the child which are out of keeping with its age; he foreshadows the identity of the child by having the slain infant, who has been restored to life, bow to the child-judge; and at the end, where his source closes with the punishment meted out to the murderer, Hans Sachs rounds out the story by saying that as the lady and her child vanished, the people, realizing that this had been the Queen of Heaven, praised and thanked her, and that the miracle was proclaimed far and wide. To this he also adds his own tribute to Mary, and then with a fine technique he connects the legend with his plea to the Virgin that she act as intercessor for us when we face the judge in the hereafter.

> **In vnser frawen gesanck weis**   466^v
> **Hans sachsen vnd sein**
> **gedicht 5 lieder**

1   [O]
       küngin der parmherczikeit
       dŭ mir aŭf meinen mŭnde
       das ich dein hoches lob vnd preis
5   dŭrch ein wŭnder mach kŭnde
       das vŭnde
       ich in mirackŭlis beate marie $\widetilde{Re}$ $\widetilde{Re}$

       Von einem eprecher also
       der ein frŭm ebeib hette

10   die dinet maria mit fleis
      kein gůt er ir nit dette
      verstette
      die fraw dient Maria ẏe lenger vnd ẏe me   ꝛc ꝛc

      Vnd befalch sich alle dag in ir hŭtte
15   ir man drůg ir gros neid vnd has   467ʳ
      vnd verzert vnŭczlich ir peider gŭtte
      mit dem eprŭch so mercket das
      des was
      die fraw arme draŭrig vnd vngemŭtte
20   vnd seŭget vm lon etlich zeit
      einem ritter ein kinde
      da mit gewan die fraw ir speis
      des ir der man nit gẏnde
      geschbinde
25   er im gedacht wie er sie precht in dotes we   ꝛc ꝛc ꝛc

2   Vnd
      dŭrch deŭffelisch einplasŭng
      verporgen er zů nachte
      dem kindlein die kelen ab schnidt
5   vnd aŭs dem haŭs sich machte
      gedachte
      vm djs mort lest dotten mein beib der ritter freẏ   ꝛc

      Zů morgen frŭ die fraw aŭf stŭnd
      wolt das kind seŭgen drote
10   nach irem gewonlichen sidt
      da vandt sie das kindt dote
      gancz rote
      von plŭt die fraw erschrack vnd det ein lauten schreẏ   ꝛc ꝛc ꝛc

      Da von erwachet alles ingesinde
15   vnd lŭffen zů irer kamnet
      vonden sie allein ob dem dotten kinde
      vnd meinten sie het es erdet
      ir ret
      halff nit man saget dem ritter geschwinde
20   im het die fraw sein kindlein jŭng
      in ir kemnat ermorte
      der ritter sich nit lang periedt
      da er soliche worte
      erhorte
25   lẏs er die fraw fangen mit grosser rŭmoreẏ   ꝛc   ꝛc

88

3   Mort

lich vŭrt man sie vŭr gericht
mit hart gepŭnden hende
vil volckes da zŭ laŭffen war
5   die fraw stŭnd gar ellende
ein ende
het ir hoffnŭng petriebet waren all ir sin /c̄

Man wolt nit horen ire wort
nimant sie aŭch versprache
10 die fraw hŭb aŭf ir aŭgen dar
vnd gen dem himel sache
vnd jache
o Maria dŭ weist das ich vnschŭldig pin /c̄

Darŭm dŭ kŭngin der parmherczikeite
15 ich gib mich in die parmŭng dein
so pald die fraw weinet die wort geseite
kam gar ein vberlichter schein
gemein
in gegenwŭrtikeit da aller leÿtte
20 vnd erschein in dem claren liecht
ein schones frawen pilde
het ein kind an dem arme clar
das gericht wardt gestilde
die milde
25 sprach verziehent mein kint mŭs richter sein darin /c̄

4   Noch

der red alles volck geschwig
stŭnden in grossem wŭnder
soliches war der horet nÿe
5   vnd erschracken pesŭnder
darŭnder
stŭnd in forcht der eprecher vnd mordisch pŏswicht /c̄

Zŭ hant der frawen kint da sprach
ee das ich vrteill velle
10 so sol man den ermorten hie
her vŭr gerichte stelle
gar schnelle
pracht man des ritters dottes kint vŭr das gericht /c̄

Das kint sprach zŭ dem dotten kindlein dratte
15 ste aŭf zeig mir den morder an
aŭf das die vnschŭldig fraw kŭm aŭs nate
zŭ hant das dote kindlein schan

aůf stan
offenlich do vor richter vnd vor ratte
20 ret gar frisch gesůnd lebentig
vnd sich dem kindlein naiget
\ vnd aůf den falschen morder ẙe
mit einem finger zeiget
geschweiget
25 wart der mörder das kint sprach da zů angesicht /ℇ

5 Das
ist der mich der mordet hat
ein gericht fahen liesse 468ʳ
den morder vnd ein vrteil velt
5 das man im hent vnd fiesse
abstiesse
mit einem rad die frůmen frawen lis man hin /ℇ

Paldt dis vrteil gefellet was
die schone fraw verschwante
10 mit irem kindlein auserwelt
dar peẙ das volck alssante
erkante
das es gewessen war dẙ himel kůnigin /ℇ

Der sageten gros lob alt vnde jůnge
15 dis wůnder werck gar weit der dos
o reigirende kůngin der parmůnge
dein milte parmůng ist so gros
gruntlos
wirt aůs gesprochen hie von keiner zůngen
20 das alhie wol peweret stat
peẙ dem grossen mirackel
so wir dort werden vůr gestelt
dů gottes tabernackel
on mackel
25 so seẙ vnser parmherczige vůrsprecherin /ℇ
1518

90

The legend which Hans Sachs selected for this Meisterlied concerns a young count who was so very devoted to St. Catherine that he chose her for his betrothed. When he was at length compelled, against his wishes, to take unto himself a real wife, he did not give up his daily visits to the church of St. Catherine, but did not tell his wife about them. As a consequence she became suspicious, readily believed the lie concocted by her maid that the count was having an affair with the daughter of the man who lived beside the church, and, in spite of her pregnancy, killed herself. The count blamed himself for not having refuted the lie, and, on the assumption that this sorrow had come upon him for having broken his promise to St. Catherine, hastened to her church to pray. In a vision she appeared to him, reprimanded him, but declared that she would never desert him since he had served her so faithfully. She bade him return home where he would find that his wife was alive and that she had given birth to a daughter whom he was to name *Katharina*. In the end the count and his wife, after some thirty years of virtuous living, received eternal blessedness.

For his introduction to this tale Hans Sachs draws upon a few details from the main legend. After that he follows his source quite closely, not, however, without making some changes here and there which contribute to a greater realism. Among other changes, he authenticates the miracle by remarking that the wreath which St. Catherine had placed upon the count's head is still preserved in a monastery; he motivates the real marriage of the count by the simple explanation that he had arrived at the proper age; he has the wife succumb to the temptation of the Devil before she angrily commits suicide in order to account for her being in his clutches after death; he also changes the method by which the wife kills herself from "falling into the sword" to piercing her throat with it. The poet appends the sequel that the daughter was carefully reared and became the abbess of a convent which the count and his wife had built in honor of St. Catherine. On the other hand, he deletes the number of years which his source had allotted to the young couple; he merely states that the two had a blessed death. As a kind of verbal "postlude" in the last *Abgesang* he reverts for a few verses to the primary legend by advising Christians to think about and to do honor to the martyrdom of St. Catherine, for in time of stress she can gain favor for them. Then, just as he had called upon her at the very beginning of his Meisterlied to direct his tongue in proclaiming her praise anew, he closes by presenting his poem to her (perhaps he wrote it on her Feast Day, November 25) and by requesting her to intercede for him in his last hour, all of which is a close parallel to statements in some of his Mary-songs.[1]

Wackernagel published this Meisterlied with the opening verses for its title.[2]

In vnser frawen gesanck weis hans 464ᵛ
Sachsen vnd sein gedicht
7 lieder

1   O
    Sancta katherina gŭt
    ich pit wollest mir leÿhen
    lencken mein vngelerte zŭng
5   dass ich heŭt mŭg aŭs schreÿen
    verneÿen
    dein lob des sint all cristenliche lant dŭrch leŭcht $\overline{/\!\!k}$

    Seit dŭ dein diner machest fro
    die dir dinen in drawe
10   des dŭt mein hercz in freŭden sprŭng
    seit ich dein lob sol paŭe
    jŭnckfrawe
    ein prŭn der siben freÿen kŭnst mein hercz befeucht $\overline{/\!\!k}$

    Dŭ edel reiche weisse one dadel
15   gesponst des heren Jesŭ crist
    der hat pegabet deinen hochen adel
    wer hie dein leiden eren ist   465ʳ
    dem pist
    von got genad erberben one zadel
20   des halb mon van dir lessen dŭt
    ein mercklich wŭnderzeichen
    von einem edlen graffen jŭng
    der dient andechtikleichen
    der reichen
25   jŭnckfrawen Sant katharina die schriefft anzeŭcht $\overline{/\!\!k}$

2   Der
    graff was vernüftig vnd clŭg
    warhafftig vnd gerechte
    zŭchtig demŭtig alle zeit
5   doch von hohem geschlechte
    nŭn sechte
    wie ein capel nit weit von seiner pŭrge lag $\overline{/\!\!k}$ $\overline{/\!\!k}$ $\overline{/\!\!k}$

    In Sancta katharina er
    nemlich geweichet warte
10   nŭn hat der graff ein gewonheit
    dass er ging vngesparte
    ein farte
    in die capel vnd pett mit andacht alle dag $\overline{/\!\!k}$ $\overline{/\!\!k}$ $\overline{/\!\!k}$

Aŭf einem dag wass er darin alleine
15 vnd entschlieff vor irem altar
ein wolgezirte jŭnckfraw im erscheine
mit zweÿen jŭnckfrawen virwar
gancz klar
ir schein was licht als der karfŭnckel steine
20 der graff sein aŭgen vnder schlŭg
erschrack ob dissem wŭnder
die schonste jŭnckfraw zw im seit
graff erwel dir pesŭnder
hie vnder
25 vns ein gemachel der graf da aŭf plicken pflag /℞ /℞

3   Nim
war das ist katharina
sprach ein jŭnckfraw damitte
vil der graff nider fur ir fÿs
5 mit demŭtigem sitte
gŭnd pitte
das sie in nem genediklich aŭf zŭ der frist /℞ /℞

Ein rossenkrancz aŭf seczet im
die schŏn mit irer hande
10 vnd sprach verlas mich nit das wÿs
vnd damit schnel verschwande   465ᵛ
pald vande
der graff den krancz der noch in einem kloster ist /℞

Darnach virt der graff gotfŭrchtig leben
15 do er nun zŭ den jaren kam
sein freŭnd gŭnten im ein gemahel geben
ein jŭnckfraw von edelem stam
die nam
er wie wol es im genczlich nit was eben
20 do nun sein fraŭ wŭrdt schwanger da
gewan sie heimlich sorgen
vnd vil in grosse ergernÿs
seit der graff ging al morgen
verporgen
25 von ir in die capel das selb die fraw nit wist /℞

4   Vnd
fraget ir dinstmait in kaim
weistŭ nit wŭ hin gatte
der edl graff al morgen frŭ
5 die meit antwŭrt aus fate

93

es hate
der pfarer ein dochter die pŭlet er warlich /ℓ̄

Zŭ morgen do der graff aŭf stŭndt
die fraw gŭnd in zŭ fragen
10   des pfarer dochter pŭllestŭ
der graff schimpflich verschlagen
gŭnd sagen
nit des pffarer dochter ein schonere pŭl ich /ℓ̄ /ℓ̄

Damit der graff zŭ der capellen ginge
15   der greffen det gar we die schmach
deŭffelisch anfechtŭng ir hercz vmfinge
vnd fŭr aŭf schnel in zornes rach
vnd stach
ir ab die kel mit eines schwertes klinge
20   do nŭn der graff kam wider heim
die greffÿn noch nit horte
er eillet seinem kemnat zw
vnd fandt in dem plŭt dorte
ermorte
25   die greffin da sanck er in amacht schnelliklich /ℓ̄

5   Schmercz
lich so sprach er manig mal
liebster gemahel meine
wie vbel hastŭ an dir dan
5   vnd an dem kindeleine
o reine
katherina an dir han ich verdint die not /ℓ̄ /ℓ̄

Er ging hin mÿt draurigem hercz   466ʳ
wider in die capelle
10   vnd hŭb cleglich zw weinen an
we meiner armer selle
die helle
han ver dint ich pin schŭldig an ir peider dot /ℓ̄

Der graff entschlieff in aller mas wie foren
15   sein katherina im erschein
vnd sprach dŭ hast ein andre aŭserkoren
doch ich nit gar verlassen pin
gehin
dein greffin hat ein dochterlein geporen
20   das selb mein namen haben sol
wirt ein eptasin frŭme
vnd wirt irem altvater schan

zŭ hilff in peinen kŭme
dar vme
25 ste aŭf geheim sag danck dem almechtigen got ꝛͤ ꝛͤ

6 Al
so verschwant im das gesicht
der graff erwacht in schwere
ein diner schnel gelaŭffen kam
5 vnd pracht im liebe mere
o here
din fraw geporen hat ein dochter vnd lebet ꝛͤ ꝛͤ ꝛͤ

Der graff kam heim mit freiden pal
vnd fand die recht warheitte
10 sein fraw er in die arme nam
vnd aŭch das kint gemeitte
vnd seite
al ding was er in der capel gesehen het ꝛͤ ꝛͤ

Die greffin sprach ich hab mich erstochen
15 der deŭffel kam ein grosse schar
fŭrten mein arme sel mit we vnd sochen
vŭr den gestrengen richter dar
do war
ich von Sancta Katharina versprochen
20 mein arme sell wardt am gericht
geŭrteilt zŭ dem leibe
des bŭrden frolich peidesam
der graff vnd auch sein weibe
verdreibe
25 ir zeit vnd dinten katharina stet ꝛͤ

7 Ir
kint aŭf er scham vnd zŭcht
sie gar fleisig aŭf zŭgent
die aŭch sant katherina her
5 dinet in ir jŭgent
in dŭgent
nam sie ser zŭ vnt wŭrt ein eptesine frŭm ꝛͤ ꝛͤ ꝛͤ

In einem closter lesen wir
das disser graff lies pawe
10 in Sancta Katharina er
der heiligen jŭnckfrawe
in drawe
der graff vnd aŭch sein fraw ein selig ende nŭm ꝛͤ ꝛͤ ꝛͤ

466ᵛ

95

Ir christen nemet das wŭnder zu sine
15 vnd die marter fleisig eret
der heiligen jŭnckfrawen katharine
wŭ ir dan seit in grosser net
sў let
eŭch nit sie kan eŭch gar wol hŭlt gewine
20 o Katherina edle frŭcht
dir schenck ich mein gedichte
vnd so ich lig in dodes schwer
vnd mein mŭnt nimer sprichte
gerichte
25 so pit vŭr mich deinen gesponss Jesŭm Cristum ⳡ
1518 jar

Chapter IV / Diverse Aspects of Love

Background

It is true that on the surface the first Meisterlied in this group of eight has nothing whatsoever to do with love, and yet in a way it seems to reveal an undercurrent of joyousness indicative of Hans Sachs' mood at the time that he found himself once more in Munich. Upon rereading this familiar Meisterlied on the "werck zeüg . . . vnd erbet" of a "schüknecht" one is inclined to join in with the laughter of the "mütter" as she handed back the coat which the young man had forfeited because he could not pay for his wine. From first to last the words come tumbling out in a good-natured way, for Hans Sachs was apparently pleased with the request to string such verses together. It was winter, cold and hard for many a journeyman on that "sant stefans dag" (December 26) in 1514. In all likelihood there had been no work during the past weeks so that he had arrived in Munich without any money. But why Munich, when he had just spent the spring and summer there? Possibly, as the largest city around, it would again afford work; possibly also, it was not too far away from wherever he happened to be, but most probably he was drawn there by thoughts of a girl whom he could not forget.[1] This last surmise is based on Hans Sachs' statement in a later poem in which he tells us about his overwhelming love for the girl in Munich: "Da wurd gefangen ich in lieb / Gehn eyner junckfrawen fürwar / Etwas fast auff ein gantzes jar."[2] If, according to his words, he was in love for almost a year, then he had to have known the young lady before he returned to Munich, since his second stay in that city extended only from December 26, 1514, to sometime in May 1515, when his father summoned him home:

> In solcher meyner strengen lieb
> Mein Vater mir gar ernstlich schrieb
> Das ich kemb eylend gehn Nürnberg
> . . .
> Ich von der liebsten urlob namb
> Mit grossem trawren also kam
> Hin nauß der stat mit grosser eyl
> . . .
> Es war gleich in deß mayen blüt.[3]

Thus, although this Meisterlied was composed more than a year (1516) after the incident occurred, its leaping verses seem to have brought back to Hans Sachs the anticipation he must have felt at the time, never dreaming of the unhappiness which lay in store for him. He had kept his love hidden, but when, as he later tells us, he became so deeply immersed that he feared he had been bewitched, he decided to propose to his chosen one. It was then that the blow fell, for she told him she was in love with another! When he perceived that his "lieb und gunst / Gen ir nit waβ gewest umb sunst," but that nevertheless he had to give her up to someone else, his suffering became intense.[4] The very fact that Hans Sachs had actually asked this girl to marry him shows how deeply he must have loved her, because from the laws of his guild he knew that marriage before the completion of the journeyman years barred an artisan from attaining the rank of master.[5] No doubt this was the prime reason for his father's summoning him to come home, knowing that a youth in love is often minded to act foolhardily. Whether at the time Hans Sachs hoped his father would be sorry that he had sent for him is a matter of conjecture. At all events, in a *Spruchgedicht* written on the first of May 1515, presumably just after the young man had received his father's letter, he has "der Alt," in imagination most probably his father, lament:

> Ein jüngeling bey zwaintzig jaren,
> Dem was ein kranckheyt wiederfaren,
> Die ihm von keynem artzt auff erden
> Mit nichte mocht gebüsset werden,
> . . .
> Das im sein hertz wart hart verhawen
> In strenger lieb gehn eynr junckfrawen;
> Des ich im doch nicht wolt verhengen,
> Das er sie nemb, thet das verlengen,
> . . .
> Das krencket meynen sun so fast
> Het darnach weder rhu noch rast.[6]

Thus the young journeyman's second stay in Munich, so auspiciously begun, ended abruptly and heartbreakingly. How very much he must have suffered seems indicated in the same poem:

> Wie bitter wirt dann da ihr leyden
> So hertzlieb von hertzlieb muβ scheyden,
> Etwan viel meyl in frembde land
> Und gentzlich kein hoffnung mehr handt,
> Zusam zu kummen nymmer meh!
> . . .
> Darumb von liebe mag ich jehen
> Es sey ein schmertz ob allem schmertz.[7]

His rationalization that "lieb ist nichts dann bitter leyden / Vermischet gar mit kleynen freuden" could not end his pain and longing, and therefore he very probably did not tarry long in Nuremberg, but restlessly turned his steps in a direction that took him farther and farther away from Munich and the girl he still loved.[8] And along with the loss of his love there seemingly went his desire to write, for we have nothing from his pen between May 15, 1515, and Ascension Day, 1516. Moreover, we know nothing definite with regard to his whereabouts until the Meisterlied, "Ir schükknecht güt," discloses that on Ash Wednesday of 1516 he had been in Würzburg.

The next Meisterlied in this group is a long allegory which, with its interpretation, can be construed as a graphic picturization of that obsessing love experience in Munich. The young poet's attempt to look upon the affair somewhat objectively is not too successful, in view of the fact that every time he thought of those pleasurable hours of making love his heart suffered anew.[9] The inner torment had not yet been stilled.

Even many years later Hans Sachs vividly recalled this love of his and tells us how, when in a dream he was an unwilling captive in the "buler kercker," the Muses once again came to him, but this time to castigate him verbally for not having written any poetry for so long. Upon pleading with them to help him escape from his prison they advised him:

> Heb an! mach etliche gedicht
> Vonn der lieb unnd darinn bericht,
> Was ubels darinn werd verborgen
> Trübsal, wemut, forcht, angst und sorgen,
> Eyfer, sehnen, klagn und meyden,
> Unruh, seufftzen, senckn und leyden,
> Der-gleich lieb pitter-herbe frucht.
> Weyl du es zum thayl yetzt hast versucht,
> Wirdst du es wissen herauß zu streichen,
> Zu eynr artzney dir und deins gleichen,
> Fürbaß zu hüten vor der lieb.[10]

He took their advice. During the year which had been barren of poetry he had evidently been doing a great deal of reading. Among the books was a translation of the *Decameron* which had been published in 1472.[11] Since all of the stories told in the Fourth Day end unhappily, they were no doubt attuned to Hans Sachs' own state of mind; hence he chose three of them, "Gismonda vnd Guisgardüs," "Constancia vnd Gerbino," and "Andreola vnd Gabrioto" to versify as Meisterlieder. At the same time that he was reading the *Decameron,* or shortly thereafter, he must also have become acquainted with Eyb's *Ehebüchlein*, which appeared in Nuremberg in 1472. Evidence of this is the fact that he borrowed Eyb's advice to parents from the first of the three tales retold also in the *Ehebüchlein*. Steinhöwel in his translation had deduced no lessons from these three stories; therefore it was Eyb who led Hans Sachs along this path which he then continued to pursue on his own in the two following tales. However, he also found precepts here and there in other books which he was reading, for instance, in Wyle's *Translationen* and Steinhöwel's translation of Boccaccio's *De claris mulieribus*.[13] Nowhere does Hans

Sachs dwell on the bliss of love in these poems, instead, probably because of his own mood, he emphasizes the cruel consequences thereof. To judge from slight discrepancies *passim* he undoubtedly wrote his verses without ever referring to his source again. On the whole it is remarkable with what craftsmanship he reduces each tale to just about one third its original length. Indeed he re-creates in so far as his own unerring instinct for telling a good story leads him to make changes by deleting nonessential details, by slightly varying or altering the sequence of others, by occasionally inserting a bit of needful motivation, and by substantially abridging the long speeches.[14] Bound as he was by his metrical pattern, he nevertheless carries the reader along at a rapid pace, keeps him in suspense where the story demands it, and holds his interest to the end.

It could be said that these three tales from the *Decameron* proved to be the final catharsis for his unhappy heart so that he was again free to view life in a more normal manner. Seemingly, however, the subject of love still engrossed him, for after a brief interval devoted to other topics, he returned once more to it, but this time to the concept of love in its wider aspects in a trilogy which would delineate the characteristics of love in a descending order: divine, fraternal, carnal, all three songs to be of equal length and all set to the same *Ton*. With the word "güldin" in the overall title, "die güldin tablatür der dreÿer lib," Hans Sachs bestows a high accolade upon love and with the word "tablatür" embraces the attributes of love, more particularly those of the first two, in an idealistic roster. Divine love, the first of the three, is pre-eminent and generates all the virtues. Without it, he declares, even faith and hope fall into despair. Conceivably, therefore, it had also proved to be of help to him in placing his own love experience into proper perspective. Whereas he calls divine love the fountainhead of all good actions, brotherly love, the subject of the next song, is for him the firm bond which holds such actions together. Unlike these two kinds of love with their inherent quintessence of good, the third, carnal love, seems to operate only in a negative and bad manner. But after the young poet finishes with his enumeration of the harmful effects, the Meisterlied becomes colorful with its array of famous love pairs, one or the other person of which, or even both, met with a tragic end. It must have been brought home to him over and over again in the stories he was reading, that the words he had written as early as 1513, "der liebe lon ist traurig ent / herzleit nachfolget großer freut," were borne out in both prose and poetry.[15] Not just in the *Decameron*, but in romances and *Volksbücher*, in Boccaccio's *De claris mulieribus* with its references to Ovid and Virgil, in Niklas v. Wyle's *Translationen*, in Eyb's *Ehebüchlein*, in Hartlieb's translation of the treatises on love by Capellanus, in Virgil's *Aeneid*, yes, even in the Old Testament Hans Sachs found what happens when sensuous love holds sway.[16] And when he came to his strict conclusion that such love is forbidden in the Commandments and that it has its origin in the counsel of the Devil, he may have made his observation also from submission to Church authority. Mainly, however, he most probably wanted this Meisterlied to serve as a warning against love outside the bonds of marriage, for the whole song intimates that which he said at the close of his *Spruchgedicht* of the first of May 1515:

100

. . . wer lieb im hertzen hab,
Der laß zu rechter zeytte ab
Und spar sein lieb biß inn die ee
Dann halt ein lieb und keyne meh,[17]

Hans Sachs was delighted at the easy task the innkeeper's wife gave him when she suggested that, in order to retrieve his coat, he put into rhyme the tools of trade together with the work which a journeyman does in making shoes. Possibly he jotted down some verses at the time and sang them, verses whose substance is contained in stanzas two, three, and four of the Meisterlied as it stands, for it was written even more than a year after the occurrence took place. He recaptures the mood of that happy day as he begins in narrative manner to state the time, the place, and the incident which prompted the original rhymes. Then he spins out the details which the "mother" had requested so many months ago. She laughed, he said, when there was nothing more to tell, and brought him his coat which he still has. In fact, he continues, he took it with him to Würzburg, where he had gone because he had heard about the fine group of Meistersinger there. On Ash Wednesday, he informs his listeners, the Würzburg *Gesellschaft* made him a member and conferred upon him the name of "Hans rossengart." After weaving his name into the rhyme, the first time in a Meisterlied, the poet closes with the wish that praise for the Würzburg Society might continue to increase.

When Goedeke published the Meisterlied, he called it *Der Rock*; Goetze-Drescher also published the song, but from the Dresden MS. M 195.[1]

In des Müscaplücz langen don   35^r
5 lieder Hans Saxen gedicht

1   Ir schükknecht güt
           seit wolgemüt
           sant stefans dag
           pracht manchem clag
   5   dort in dem winter kalte /c̄

           Dar vmb ich sing   35^v
           wie es mir ging
           ich het kein gelt
           müst vbers velt
  10   kam gen Münichen palde /c̄

           Zw vnsrem vatter züg ich ein
           ich wart gar schon entpfangen
           ich het kein gelt / er gab mir wein
           mein rock pleib peÿ im hangen
  15   die mütter sach
           mich an vnd sprach
           sün kanstw reimen eben
           den werck zeüg den ein schüknecht hat
           in der werckstat

20   vnd aüch dar peÿ
      sein erbet freÿ
      den rock wil ich dir geben /Æ

2   Der rede do
      der was ich fro
      jch sprach hort zw
      am mentag frw
5   stet aüf der maister schnelle /Æ

      Wie pald er laüfft
      vnd leder kaüfft
      paczen pock heüt
      ich eüch bedeüt
10   rintleder vnd kalpvelle /Æ

      Wie pald er das hin heine dreckt
      sein gelt das düt in schmerczen
      wie palt der knecht das leder streckt
      pstost es vnd düt es schwerczen
15   drücknetes pas
      so reipt er das
      er welcz vnd schlecht das schmere
      dan streicht es an dÿ maisterein
      so reipt ers nein
20   dar nach er spat
      get in das pat
      dar nach so seüfft er sere /Æ

3   Am dinstag frw
      rüst er sich zw
      wan er aüf stet
      wie pald er get
5   hinab wol in die stüben /Æ

      Er wescht die hent
      vnd sich pald went
      nempt den knÿ rim
      vom filcz vernim
10   ein clein al vnd ein schüben /Æ

      Dar nach so macht er im ein drat
      von pech porsten vnd garen
      die schü er peÿ im ligen hat
      ein hauffen peÿ sechs paren
15   wan er sticht zw
      stiffel vnd schw

so wichst er den ein zwiren
dan spinet man aüs hanf vnd flachs
mit einem wachs
20 ein nadel güt
vnd finger hüt
die mus er dar nach viren /$\overline{k}$

4   Haüeissen mer
stahel vnd scher
becz stein vernempt
wan er gestempt
5   wil ich eüch weiter weissen /$\overline{k}$

Er sücht die zweck
vnd den streich fleck
hantleder freÿ
deimling darpeÿ
10 schwamen vnd koder eissen /$\overline{k}$

Gneib reisser dapel vnd ne al
so net er dan behende
vnd zücket den went stecken pal
vnd düt die schw vmb benden
15 vnd ein aüf züg
ist wol sein füg
schin vnd die vnterschlagen
zw pantoffelen müs man han
pülczmesser schan
20 lang zweck stempfeis
raspen ich preis
nit mer wais ich zw sagen /$\overline{k}$

5   Das dreiben wir
vir vnde vir
vnd drincken wein
mercket das sein
5   al vnsser erbeit hartte /$\overline{k}$

Die mütter lacht
mein rock mir pracht
den ich hab noch
da mit ich zoch
10 gen wirczpürck aüf der vartte /$\overline{k}$

Da ich dÿ pest geschelschafft vant
die ich offt horen preissen
weil ich was in dem paerlant

das hilff ich nün beweissen
15 wan sie mich han
gedaüffet schan
an dem asschen mit wochen
da mir der nam gegeben wart
Hans rossengart
20 den wünscht Hans sachs
das ir lob wachs
gancz ewig vnzw prochen $\overline{R}$
$\overline{R}$ 1516 Jar $\overline{R}$

This allegory may well have been an outgrowth of Hans Sachs' *Spruchgedicht*, "Kampff-Gesprech von der lieb," written May 1, 1515, judging from various similarities in the two. Something portended sorrow in 1515; one year later, however, the poet knew what it meant to suffer a lost love, and hence could write about it more realistically. Since a deep hurt still lingered within him, he may have hoped that others would be forewarned by his words to break off an affair in time. Briefly the story of the knight, whom Hans Sachs says he had encountered on his walk, is that he had heeded the call of Venus only to have his heart pierced by an arrow in her garden, that he had been healed and made happy by a little bird, but that a dragon had soon frightened it away with the result that the wound again burst open and he was banished from the garden. His tale told, the knight rode off and soon passed from view in a "gruesome" lake. At this point, the exact middle of the seven stanza poem, the transition from narration to interpretation occurs. The parallel is well carried out, except for one small detail: the knight represents both man and woman. This may have been Hans Sachs' device for deflecting attention from the specific (his own situation) to the lot of lovers in general, for it seems to me that the explanation of the allegory is only camouflage for its real meaning.

A reinterpretation might be the following: the willingness of the knight to be led to Venus (Hans Sachs' return to Munich because of his ardent attachment to a girl there); the horse's resistance to crossing the bridge (his desire for her even against all reason); led by "fraw dreÿ" (his honorable intentions); the knight's heart pierced by an arrow (his almost overwhelming love for the girl); the little bird (his brief spell of happiness); appearance of the dragon (envious gossipers); loss of the bird and the reopening of the wound (his despair when he learned the truth of her engagement to another); banished from the garden by an old knight (ordered home by his father); the stumbling of the horse (reason still enmeshed in sensuousness); and what may only be surmised, the arguments which his father used to bring him to his senses. These were, namely, that just as the knight's sword was broken into three pieces so persistence in this love would call down the wrath of God in a three-fold way; "an leib" (physically, in that he might become distraught even unto illness), "er" (damage to his honor, probably either if he transgressed in the relationship with his loved one, or if he continued to see her when everyone knew that she was betrothed to another), "an gutte" (he could never, as we have seen, attain to the position of master in his craft if he were married as a journeyman, hence could never acquire much in the way of wealth). Finally the cry of the knight could indicate that the young man was still obdurate and the knight's disappearance in the abysmal body of water could signify peril to his soul as the ultimate consequence of his conduct which so defied parental authority. From such an end, Hans Sachs concludes, may God preserve us!

1   An einem morgen fru was mir mein weil gar lang
    ich det ein gang
    dürch einen grünen walde
    dar dürch ich manig valde
5   was gangen an ein lüstig stat
    zw einem prinlein kalde
    dar peÿ ich alweg sus gedŏn
    von der nachtigal fünde /C̄

    Aüf einer linden der ich aber nahet kam
10   da peÿ vernam
    ich sten ein pferdlein weisse
    vnd gesattelt / mit fleisse
    dar ab ich grosses wünder hat
    ich ging hin zw gar leisse
15   da sas vnder der linden grün
    ein ritter zw der stünde /C̄

    Des harnisch was von plüt gar nas
    sein schwert lag peÿ im ein dem gras
    der ritter sas
20   gancz freüden los
    sein antlicz in verplichen was
    der linden drat ich neher pas
    vnd grüsset dissen ritter kün
    sprach wer hat eüch verwünde /C̄

2   Der ritter sprach das mach ich dir hie offenpar
    es sind zwaÿ jar
    da kam fraw drew mit sine
    vnd sprach die künigine
5   Venus hat mich zw dir gesant
    sicz aüf vnd reit von hine
    also schid ich von meinem schlos
    rit mit ir manig meile /C̄

    Sie viret mich vber ein prücken die was hoch
10   mein pfert verzoch
    wolt nit vurpas in zoren
    stach ich es mit den sporen
    es luff vber die prück zw hant
    zw venus aüs erkoren

15 in einen gartten der was gros
    dar in mit einem pfeille /ℓ̄

    Dürch schos ein kint das hercze mein
    zw hant gab mir die künigein
    ein fogelein
20 was rot guldein
    vnd sprach nün magstw pey mir sein
    in dem gartten vn alle pein
    weil der vogel ist dein genos
    zw hant mein wünt wart heille /ℓ̄

3   Also was ich in dem gartten in grosser freit
        in kürzer zeit
        da kam ein drack vernime
        schraÿ mit graüsamer stime
5   da von mein vogelein verschwant
        mein wünt ris aüf mit grime
        zw hant drib mich ein ritter alt
        aüs dem garten mit schmerczen /ℓ̄

        Also rit ich verwündet aüs dem gartten hin
10   also ich pin
        geritten hin vnd here
        in landen weit vnd verre
        mit offner wünt on alle pant
        küm aüch heim nÿmermere
15   also ich zw dein prünlein kalt
        pin kümen ane scherczen /ℓ̄

        Also mein wünt hat ein anfanck
        daran da pin ich alczeit kranck
        ich laid gros zwanck
20   weil ist mir lanck
        hin an dem rein stet mein gedanck
        der ritter sein harnisch an schwanck
        vnd sas da aüf sein rosslein palt
        mit hart verwüntem herczen /ℓ̄

4   Da nam vrlaüb vnd schid von mir der ritter wert
        vnd stach sein pfert
        mit seinen sporen kürcze
        es straücht vber ein würcze
5   das der ritter mit grossem we
        herab det einen stürcze
        so hart das im sein schwert zw prach
        vnd in dreÿ stuck zw füre /ℓ̄

Der ritter det ein schraÿ mit dimerlicher stim
10 dar nach in grim
er aüf sein pferdlein schreitte
vnd zorniklichen reitte
in einen grausamlichen se
der was gar tiff vnd weitte
15 dar in ich in lang schwimen sach
zw lecz ich in verlüre /k̄e

Zw hant eilt ich aüs dissem walt
zw einem weissen meister alt
dem ich er zalt
20 die red gar palt
des ritters peÿ dem prinlein kalt
sein ritt in den se vngestalt
der meister mir gar palt veriach
pedeütnüs der figüre /k̄e

5   Wiltw wissen wer disser wünde ritter seÿ
ja den fraw dreÿ
hat pracht zw solcher peine
frawen vnd man das seine
5   die rechte drew offt pringet hart
zw flaischlich lieb ich meine
das röslein das nit gen wolt virt
vber die prücken wilde /k̄e

Jist des menschen vernüft die alzeit wider rat
10 al missedat
wirt dürch die sporen zwüngen
der sinlikeit gedrüngen
zw verwilligvng ist der gart
der pfeil des kindes iüngen
15 ist die vnordenlich pegÿrt
so ist die küngin milde /k̄e

Die pedrachtüng der scharpffen list
flaischlicher lieb zw aller frist
der vogel wist
20 rot gültein ist
deüt das gelück ir mercken mist
dar von das draürig hercz genist
das dan in freüden jübilirt
man oder frawen pilde /k̄e

6   So kümet dan der drack das sint die falschen dick
dürch vngelick

der clafer mengerleÿe
die sie dürch neid beschreÿe
5 da von sie kümen in vnrw
ir alte wünt wirt neÿe
so düt sie dan der alt ritter
aüs dem gartten verdreibe /c̄

Das ist so es wirt offenlich an allem art
10 dan wirt zw stort
jr lieplich wün vnd freiden
mussen aneinder meiden
so mon im so hart seczet zw
mussen sie sich gar scheiden
15 so dencken sie dan hin vnd her
in ellent sie beleibe /c̄

Vnd werden nÿmer mer gesünt
sagen vns weisser maister münt
wen lieb entzünt
20 in rechtem grünt
wan der dencket der libe stünt
so offt wirt im sein hercz verwünt
vnd wirt recht frolich nÿmer mer
es seÿ mon oder weibe /c̄

7   Das straüchet ros des ritterss vnss bedeüten ist
vernüft das wist
die wirt so dieff versencket
dürch sinlikeit gekrencket
5 kan nit haben recht rew vnd leit
wan sie der freid gedencket
vergangner lib die sie vor hot
da ist das hercz noch peÿe /c̄

Das schwert das dem ritter da in dreÿ stück zw prach
10 das ist die rach
die got dem menschen dütte
an Ieib er vnd an gütte
dürch sein genad in disser zeit
mit seines straffes rütte
15 wan dan der mensch ret wider got
pedeüt des ritter schraie /c̄

So strafft dan in got an der sel
die müs dort leiden ewig qüel
pey dem deüffel
20 die diffe hel

35ʳ

110

pedeüt den se ich eüch erczel
dar ein ritt disser ritter schnel
deüt al die sterben ewig dot
dar vor vns got mach freÿe $\overline{K}$ 1516 $\overline{K}$

Although Hans Sachs had versified a tale from the *Decameron* for his very first *Spruchgedicht* (April 7, 1515), this is the first Meisterlied based on that collection.[1] It was written in 1516. He begins by giving the title and author of the book in which he says he found the tale, then proceeds to relate the story of "Gismonda vnd Güisgardüs," but restricts himself to the most significant and interesting points. In doing so he deletes detailed descriptions, materially reduces the long speeches, and rearranges some particulars in order to create greater plausibility. Furthermore, he says nothing about the inequality of the social position of the two lovers, which is so emphasized in his source along with the implication that if Gismonda had taken a man of equal rank her father might have condoned her transgression. At the end of the tale Hans Sachs appends the lesson which Eyb in his translation drew from it.[2] He closes with a proverb and, as he had done once before in a Meisterlied, he signs his name in rhyme, but now for the first time he also adds the name of his native city, Nuremberg.[3]

Goedeke published this poem under the title *Guiscardus und Gismonda*, and Goetze-Drescher with the title *Gismonda mit Guigardo*.[4]

In frawen Eren don 3 xiii par nach   12ᵛ
ein ander vnd heissen die 3 neuen
historj H S gedicht

1   Ein puch Cento nonella heist
         hat ein poet geschriben
         hündert histori es aüs weist
         mir saget mein memori
     5   dis püch sey Johanes pocaciüs /ℯ̄

         Als noch ist mengem weissen kündt
         dem solich künst düt liÿben
         in dem gemelten püch ich fundt
         gar ein schone histori
    10   von einem fürsten der hies concretus /ℯ̄

         Der was in der stat Salerrno gessessen
         sein hocher adel der was vngemessen
         was doch dar peÿ ein demütiger mone
         als in disser histori stet
    15   allein er einen erben hett
         das was ein minikliche dochter schone /ℯ̄

2   Die was züchtig vnd dar zw weis
         die het er lieb vnmasse
         er züg sie aüf mit ganczem fleis

wolt ir lang kein mon geben
5   Gismonda so was die dachter genant /꜀

Ein reicher herczog het ein sün
der zw Capüa sasse
dem gab der fürst sein dochter nün
er daücht in dar zw eben
10   der selbig fürt sÿ mit im in sein lant /꜀

Sein leben doch kürczlich ein ende name
die dochter wider zw dem vatter kame
in mitler zeit was ir müter gestorben
mit dem vatter sie lang reigirt
15   mit dügent so was gezirt
von manchem ritter wart vmb sie geworben /꜀

3   Ir vatter het sie herczlich holt
zw ir er sich gesellet
keim mon er sie mer geben wolt
des det sich hart bedriben
5   die fraw vnd offenwart es nit vor scham /꜀

Dar vm sie ir gar heimeleich
ein jüngling aüsserwellet
schon jüng gerad vnd sinen reich
den det sie herczlich liben
10   an irem hoff Qüisgardus was sin nam /꜀

Sie schrib ein prieff vnd det den in ein rore
da mit macht sie dem jüngling offenpore
das sie im drüeg soliche lieb vnd günste
pald der jüngling den prieff gelas
15   zw stünd sein hercz entczündet was
mÿt flamendem feür der liebe prünste /꜀

4   In dissem prieff bart er gelert
wie er balt kümen mechte
in ir kamer vnder der ert
dürch ein heimlichen gange
5   der dürch ein fels den seinen ein gang het /꜀

in einer doren hecken gros
der iüngling das aüs spechte
pald im wart geben disses los
er saümet sich nit lange
10   sein leib mit leder er becleiden det /꜀

113

Vnd lies sich hinab in den hollen steine
da stünd dÿ fraw vnd wart mit freüden seine
firt in dürch den perck in ir kammer weitte
da nossen sie der libe prün
15 in honig süsser freüd vnd wun   13^V
das driben sie dar nach ein lange zeite /$\widehat{e}$

5   Darnach eins mals on einem dag
         det sie im aber künde
         des er kem vnd die weil ich sag
         ging sie in iren gartten
5   die weil ir vatter in ir kamer lieff /$\widehat{e}$

         Vnd wolt mit ir reden etwas
         vnd da er sie nit fünde
         hinder ein firhang er do sas
         wolt seiner dochter wartten
10   pis das sie kem in dem der her entschliff /$\widehat{e}$

         Der jungling kam dürch denn ein gang mit eille
         sach seinen herren nit inn zw vnheille
         die fraw sich haim pald in ir kamer machet
         do sie iren liebhaber fandt
15   sie hetten grosse freüd zw handt
         der her hinder dem virhang aüf erwachet /$\widehat{e}$

6   er alle ding da hort vnd sach
         sein hercz in zoren qualle
         idoch er da kein wort nit sprach
         da ir freüd het ein ende
5   der iüngling widerein den ein gang schloff /$\widehat{e}$

         Die fraw beschlos die selben dir
         vnd ging hin aüf den salle
         da sie dan vand ir jünckfraw schir
         der her schaich gar behende
10   aüs der kamer vnd pot an seinem hoff /$\widehat{e}$

         Zwaien das sie zw disser holen gingen
         vnd wer dar aüs schlüff das sie im den fingen
         vnd zwen gingen hin zw der doren hecken
         vnd warten lang peÿ dissem loch
15   pis der iüngling her aüsser kroch   14^r
         do er sie sach wie hart günt er verschrecken /$\widehat{e}$

7   Sie fingen in pünden in hart
         virtten in vür den herren

der weinet vnd bedriebet wart
we das dw pist geporen
5 in meinem flaisch vnd plüet hast mich geschmecht /Ꝓ

Der jüngling sprach das mein gemüt
det die streng lieb verkerren
der herr in grossem zoren wüt
sprach werfft in ein den doren
10 vnd hüt sein wol pis das der dag her necht /Ꝓ

Zw morgen kam er zw der dochter gangen
sein hercz das was mit schmerczen vmefangen
Gissmonda dochter ich hab dich erzogen
in eren vnd in grosser zücht
15 dügent het ich peÿ dir gesücht
eÿ bie felschlichen hastw mich berdrogen /Ꝓ

8 Dw pflagst mit Gwisgardo der lib
sach ich mit meinen aügen
dar vmb so müs der falsche dieb
mir lan sein jünges leben
5 aüch gewinest dw nÿmer mer mein hüld /Ꝓ

Die fraw erschrack was vngemüt
dach stündt sie one laügen
vatter wir sint doch flaisch vnd plüt
als wol dw vnd merck eben
10 darüm hab wir den dot gar nit verschuld /Ꝓ

Da dw mir wolltest geben keinen mane
Gwisgardüm ich mir aüsser welte hanne
in rechter lib dar vmb wil ich nit werben   14ᵛ
vmb dein hüld oder dein genadt
15 mit dem mein hercz gelebet hat
in freüd mit dem wil es in leit aüch sterben /Ꝓ

9 Da der herr horret disse wort
da ging er also alte
schüff das der jüngling würd ermort
haimlich vnd nam sein hercze
5 vnd leit das in ein kopff von clarem goldt /Ꝓ

Vnd rüffet ein ritter vür sich
vnd sprach pring hin gar palte
den gülden kopff gar kosparlich
meiner dochter an schercze
10 sagt im dar peÿ was er ir sagen soldt /Ꝓ

Der ritter ging hin zw der frawen clüge
vnd west doch nit was er verdecket drüge
er grüst die frawen vnd sprach vnerschrecket
hÿ schikt dir dein vatter den drost
15   den dw herczlich gelibet host
dÿ fraw nam den kopff vnd den pald aüff decket /$\overline{R}$

10   Dar in vand sie das hercz vnd seit
nün pis mir got wilkumen
ein herberg meiner wün vnd freÿt
dw pist mein leczte gabe
5   von meinem vatter doch dürch falsche list /$\overline{R}$

O dw freüntlich wünsames hercz
hastw dein ent genümen
aüf disser welt mit grossem schmercz
in einem gülden grabe
10   leistw des dw aüch gar wirdig pist /$\overline{R}$

Den kopff drüeg sie gar freüntlich on ir prüste
das dotte hercz sie gar freüntlichen kuste
sie sprach kein zeher wart vmb dich vergossen
die wil ich auch mit daillen dir
15   mÿt dem druckt sÿe den kopff zw ir
weint das dÿ zeher in den kopff vmb flossen /$\overline{R}$

15^{r}

11   Ir jünckfraw lüffen hin vnd dar
vor angsten mange schweiste
westen nit bes des hercze war
dar vm die fraw het laide
5   Gwisgardüs dot der was noch vngemelt /$\overline{R}$

Da sie nün lang geweinet het
sprach sie dein edler geiste
der wart an mich aüf disser stet
pis das mein geist auch scheide
10   vnd mit dir var aüs der betrubten welt /$\overline{R}$

Sie machet ir ein tranck von herbem giffte
saget vns warlich von ir die geschriffte
das selb sie gar pald aüf das hercze güsse
vnd das gar vnerschrocken dranck
15   darnach sie aüf das pet hin sanck
sein dottes hercz sie in ir arme schlüsse /$\overline{R}$

12   Vnd lag da in grosser amacht
zw hant lüff ein iünckfrawe

vnd da den edlen fürsten pracht
der günt gar heisser weine
5 do er sein dochter fünd in dodes zil /R̄

Ir aügen keret sie zw im
det in senlich anschaüe
vnd sprach gar mit senlicher stim
pehalt die zeher deine
10 des zw geschehen war dein freÿer wil /R̄

Congkrette zw dir hon ich noch ein pette
den meinen leib zw Gwisgardo bestette
den dw mir lebendig nÿt woltest gine
mit dem der dot vast mit ir ranck
15 das hercz ir aüs den armen sanck
da mit so schid ir arme sel von hine /R̄

13   Dem fürsten grosse reüe kam
doch war es vil zw spatte
mon leget in ein grab zw sam
ir paider dotter leibe   15ᵛ
5 zw Salerno / vns die historÿ seit /R̄

Dar peÿ wirt vns clerlich pestimpt
Wie solche lieb zw gatte
vnd ein drawriges ende nÿmpt
das merck dw man vnd weibe
10 gib deinem kint ein mon zw rechter zeit /R̄

E das in strenge liebe angesiget
ein dochter ist ein abs das nit lang liget
dar aüs maniger vnglick ist erwachse
das sie ist kümen vmb ir er
15 die sie gewinet nÿmer mer
zeit pringt rossen spricht von Nürnberg Hans Sachse /R̄ 1516 /R̄

After the merest mention of his source in the first verse of this second
Meisterlied based on the *Decameron*, and written also in 1516, Hans Sachs begins to
retell the story of "Constancia" and "Gerbino."[1] On the whole the poet follows
Steinhöwel's translation closely, making only infrequent changes. For instance, he
bestows a name upon the heroine, who in his source is only the lady or the king's
daughter; he supplies a few details with regard to the early training of Gerbino; he
has Constancia's father himself go to the King of Sicily to request a free conduct
for her instead of having him send an envoy; and when the ship bearing Constancia
is sighted, he deletes the speech Gerbino makes to his men in which he promises
them all of the rich booty to be found aboard. At the end of his tale he points out
that this tragedy would not have happened if Constancia's father had not insisted
upon her marrying an old king. Wedlock, he adds, is bitter poison for the person
forced into it; therefore it is advisable to give an offspring someone pleasing to him,
for at best it is clear that honey may very well turn into gall. In this Meisterlied he
signs his name by weaving it into the last verse.

Goetze-Drescher published the poem with the title *Constancia und Gerbino.*[2]

Die ander histori in dem vorgmelten   15ᵛ
don H S gedicht 13 lieder

1   Mon list in cento nevella
          wie das vor zeiten sasse
          ein künig in cecillia
          des nam wilhalmus hisse
     5   der selbig künig der het einen sün /c̄

          Rügire was des sünes nam
          der aüch ein künig wasse
          da sein leben ein ende nam
          ein sün er nach im lisse
     10   des nam hies Gerbino das mercket nün /c̄

          Der würt von sein onherren aüff erczogen
          saget vns die histori vngelogen
          do er aüf wuchs wart er ein küner degen
          mit renen fechten springen vil
     15   in allen ritterlichen spil
          was er der künest alczeit vnerlegen /c̄

2   Dar vmb sein nam wart weit vnd preit
          in den landen erkennet
          nün sas ein küng zw der zeit

dort in der haidenscheffte
5 in einem lant das heisset Tünici /t̄e

Der selb ein schone dochter het
Constancia genenet
die horet wÿ mon preissen det
des jüngen ritters kreffte
10 dar vmb gedacht sie alle zeit wie sÿ /t̄e

Aüch disen strengen ritter sehen kündte
ir hercz würt gegen im in lieb entczündte
des geleichen der ritter von ir heret
wie Constancia vorgemelt
15 dÿ schonest wer der ganczen welt
dar vm er sie zw sehen aüch begeret /t̄e

3 Vor lieb sein hercz prant in dem leib
wie wol er ir nit kante
heimlich er ir ein ein priefflein schreib
er wer in lib verstricket
5 mit freüd die iünckfraw dissen prieff entpfing /t̄e

Sie schreib her wider haimelich
das er kem in ir lande
vnd da mit nit lang saümet sich
dar peÿ sie im aüch schicket
10 in rechter lieb von clarem gold ein ring /t̄e

Der ritter disse mer mit freid vername
idoch er nit pald zw der iünckfraw kame
die weil da warb ein künig wol vm die zarten
der selbig was von Gramata
15 do das vernom Constancia
sie pat iren vatter lenger zw wartten /t̄e

4 Ir vatter ernstlich haben wolt
das sie den wilden haiden
zw einem mane haben solt
das war ir wider zeme
5 idoch gab sie iren willen darein /t̄e

Dem ritter sie haimlich verschrib
wie sie sich müsset scheiden
sie ermant in der grossen lib
das er zw hilff ir keme
10 vnd mit im nem die pesten ritter sein /t̄e

Das er sie aüf dem mer nem mit gewalte
wan mon sie schicken wolt dem künig alte

det er des nit er sech ir nÿmer mere
pald der ritter die mer er hert
15 sein hercz in draüren wart versert
er rüstet zw sein harnisch vnd sein were /Ā

5 Der iünckfraw vatter das vernam
das sich Gerbino rÿste
dar vm er zw wilhelmo kam
pat im geleit zw geben
5 das sein dochter mocht ffaren dürch sein reich /Ā

Des was wilhelmüs wol zw müt
vmb die sach er nit wÿste
er sprach wer sie bedrieben düt
der müs mir lon sein leben
10 dar vmb mag sie wol varen sicherleich /Ā

Da der heiden het solich freÿ geleitte
sein dochter er gar zirlichen bereite
mit grossem schal sie aüf dem mer hin füre
der ritter macht sich aüf dÿ fart
15 wie wol es hert verpotten wart
zw helffen im maniger ritter schwüre /Ā

6 Zw nacht er aüs der stat hin reit
mit seiner ritterschaffte
gen Missina in kürczer zeit
da samlet er die schare
5 vnd rüstet zw grosser galleien zwü /Ā

Dar ein sacz er mit ganczer macht
mit ganczer heres kraffte
vur gen Sardini peÿ der nacht
da solt die praüt vür vare
10 vnd solt peÿ disser jnsel lenten zw /Ā   17ʳ

An einem morgen da der dag aüf prache
das haidenisch schiff mon her varen sache
gar sitiklich mit einem senfften winde
da zogen sie ir segel aüf
15 driben ir schiff mit schnellen laüf
hin gen dem heidenischen schiff geschwinde /Ā

7 Da sie nün kamen zw in schir
da günd der ritter riffe
gebet heraüs die jünckfraw mir

eüch mag nit pas geschehen
5   sie sprachen al ein freÿ geleit wir han /k͞e

Der ritter stant aüf seinem port
sach in der haiden schiffe
Canstancia den edlen hort
sie künt in aüch ersehen
10 vor strenger lieb ir paider hercze pran /k͞e

Das doch ir paider erst anplicken wasse
der ritter aller seinen sin vergasse
da er an sach das minikliche pilde
er sprach gent mir die iünckfraw wert
15 sie sprachen nem sie mit dem schwert
zw hant zücket gerbino seinen schilde /k͞e

8   Vnd stach aüf sie mit zornes gral
sein diner zw im drongen
manige püchse da er qüal
dÿ wilden haiden stünden
5   vnd werten sich do lag maniger dot /k͞e

Von schissen werffen mangerleÿ
die schwert gar laüt erklongen
von in wart gar ein gros geschraÿ
sie hieben diffe wünden
10 das wilde mer das war von plüt gar rot /k͞e

Die schiff würden genaw sw sam gestossen
den heiden wart ir güttes schiff zw schossen   17ᵛ
da von das wasser wart gar ser ein prechen
da wart ir wer gar schwach vnd mat
15 dar vmb hetten sie schnellen rat
wie sie sich om Gerbino mochten rechen /k͞e

9   Sie nomen do die schon jünckfraw
der was ir hercz gar schwere
vnd sprachen zw Gerbino schaw
vor seinem angesichte
5   so schniten sie ir ab die kelen weis /k͞e

Dar nach die vngedrewen hünd
würffen sie ein das mere
dem ritter do vor leidt geschwünt
idoch er sich aüf richte
10 vor grossem zoren drang im aüs der schweis /k͞e

Er sprang do in des haidnisch schiff mit zoren
wen er vrgrüeff der het sein leib verloren

121

in irem schiff so wüt mon in dem plüte
da mon der haiden vil er schlüg
15   zw stünd aüs irem schifft mon drueg
edelgestein perlein vnd grosses gütte /c̄

10
Der haiden schieff er da verprent
dar nach er drauriklichen
wider hin zw der ȳnsel lent
er hies die iünckfraw pringe
5   die wart dotlich vür den ritter gepracht /c̄

Sie lag vor im cleglich ermort
ir antlicz was verplichen
kein mon hat grosser klag er hort
dan von dem jüngelinge
10   er sanck zw der jünckfrawen in amacht /c̄

Gestrecket er do aüf der erden lage
seim herczen gab er gar manigen schlage
sein ritterschafft det inn mit droste laben
do er die clag nün lang getrieb
15   da lissen irer dotten leib
nach küniklicher wirdikeit begraben /c̄

11
Dar nach er wider heim hin reist
dar nach etlichen dagen
würd den heiden die dat beweist
von im komen geritten
5   in zecillia ein herlich potschafft /c̄

Die waren al in schwarcz becleit
detten dem künig clagen
in wer geprochen ir geleit
wan sie waren pestritten
10   von Gerbino mit ganczer heres krafft /c̄

Aüf wildem mer hat er vns angerenet
vnd hat vnser güttes schiff verprennet
ritter knecht die hat er al erstochen
dar peȳ des künigs dochter wist
15   aüch vm ir leben kümen ist
das let vnser künig nȳt vngerochen /c̄

12
Do Wilhelmus dȳ mer er hert
zw Gerbino er sprache
wee dir das dw ie kamst aüf ert
nün müstw ie verderben
5   dw weist das ich in freȳ geleite gab /c̄

18ʳ

Do antwert im der ritter iung
anherr zw disser sache
die strenge lib mein hercz pezwüng
müs ich den dar vmb sterben
10 so küm ich meins betrüeptes lebens ab /ʀͤ

Der edel ritter wart gefangen dratte
maniger fürst vm dissen ritter patte
sein anher müst dem seinen pot gennüge
vnd vor des heiden potschafft do
15 dem strengen ritter Gerbino
sein ritterliches haubet abeschlüge /ʀͤ

13 Sein anher schüff das mon pegrüeb
sein leib merck disses morte
dürch die jünckfrawen sich erhüeb
da sie ir vatter drünge
5 das sie den alten künig haben müst /ʀͤ

Vns meldet warlich die geschrifft
clerlich on mengem ortte
der ellich stant sey herbes gifft
wer dar zw wirt bezwünge
10 der hat weder gelück freüd oder lüst /ʀͤ

Pezwüngen eˊselten zw gütem kümen   18ᵛ
als ir in der histori hant vernümen
dar vm lad aüf dein kind nit solche perge
gib im einen der im gefal
15 aüs honig wirt dennoch wol gal
es leit am dag spricht Hans sachs von Nürmberge /ʀͤ
1516

123

This last one of the three tales from the *Decameron* was written the same
year as the other two.[1] Hans Sachs omits the preliminary discourse on dreams
which he found in his source and proceeds at once to the introduction of his
characters: a high-born knight, Messer Negro, his daughter, Andreola, and Gabrioto,
a youth of lowly estate, whom Andreola, unbeknown to her father, had chosen for
her lover. This concealment, the poet interpolates, was the beginning of Andreola's
sorrow. He adheres to his source in recounting the fateful dreams of the two lovers,
but substitutes a dragon for the greyhound which in Gabrioto's dream tore out his
heart. When the youth dies, the poet skips over the fact that because of her
overwhelming grief Andreola wants to take her own life and is only dissuaded
therefrom by her maid. Where his source merely states that Gabrioto, as though he
were a prince, was carried to his burial by several powerful burghers, the poet
makes this more colorful by having a procession, including priests, carry him into
the church amidst the tolling of bells. His source ends with Andreola's entering a
convent, but Hans Sachs adds a few more vivid details of his own invention, among
them that each night during that very hour in which Gabrioto had died Andreola
lies unconscious. He ends by quoting two proverbs of which the first lends weight
in an oblique way to his transference of the import of the tale from the supposition
that dreams may come true to his superimposed theme of the heartbreak inherent
in secret marriages, and the second reveals, perhaps unconsciously, that his own
love-wound had not yet completely healed.

Goetze-Drescher published the poem with the title *Andreola mit Gabrioto*.[2]

Hernach volget die drit histori in dem	18ᵛ
vorgemelten don 13 lieder H S gedicht	

1   In Cento Novella mon list
          wie das vor mangem iare
          in perssia gessessen ist
          ein ritter hoch geporen
   5   des nam geheissen was misser nigro /c̄

          Der hat ein dochter miniklich
          his Andreola clare
          disse iünckfraw het haimelich
          ein jüngling aus erkoren
   10   in strenger lieb der hies Gabrioto /c̄

          Disser jüngling wart nit von edlem stame
          idoch in disse edle jünckfraw name
          gar heimelich das ir vatter nit beste
          dar zw die pitter lieb sie zwang

15   das war irs laides ane fang
       als ir wol horen wert noch in der leste /k̄e

2   Sie gab dem jüngling ein bescheit
       wie sie sein wolte warten
       in ires vatters gartten weit
       dar ein so lobt er kümen
5   zw nacht wen ÿ der mon entschlaffen wer /k̄e

       Da nün der dag verginge schir
       da schlaich sie in den gartten
       da kam der jüngeling zw ir
       da prachen sie die plümen
10   der süssen lib nach ires herczen ger /k̄e

       Gegen dem dag sie sich wider haim machte
       das driben sÿ darnach manige nachte
       gar heimelich das es nÿmant würd inen   19ʳ
       allein die meit in irem haüs
15   die richt ir alle potschafft aüs
       hin vnd wider gar mit listigen sinen /k̄e

3   Eins nachcz het die jüng fraw ein draüm
       in dem schlaff ir erscheine
       wie sie wer vnter einem paüm
       vnd het liplich vmbfangen
5   ir herczen lieb dar nach daücht sie graüsam /k̄e

       Wie das im ging aüs seinem münt
       ein schwarczer geist vnreine
       gros erschrocklich der sich zw stündt
       an seinen hals det hangen
10   in mit gewalt aüs iren armen nam /k̄e

       Vnd vürt in schnelliklich vnder die erden
       das er von ir nim mocht gesehen werden
       in dissem aügenplick sie aüf erwachte
       zw morgen kam ir mait zw ir
15   sprach der jüngling der saget mir
       tas ir zw im solt kümen disse nachte /k̄e

4   Die fraw sprach laüff sag wider vmb
       wie ich nit kümen müge
       die meit luff vnd pald wider küm
       vnd sprach der jüngelinge
5   der pit eüch vast das ir heint kumen selt /k̄e

Zw nacht die fraw sich vngemüt
det in den gartten füge
da fand sie iren jüngling güt
der sie freüntlich enpfinge
10 fragt warvmb sie von erst nit kümen welt *Ke*

Sie sprach im schlaff het ich ein schwer gesichte
dar vmb wolt ich zw dir sein kümen nichte
er sprach solt ich dürch schwer draüm dich meiden
so kem ich gar selten zw dir
15 *wan erst hat gedraümet mir*
ein schwerer draüm des wil ich dich bescheiden *Ke*

5 Mir draümt wie ich mit hünden wech
jaget in grünem walde
vnd fing do ein schne weisses rech
dem was sein hals wmb schlosse
5 ein pant das war gemacht von rottem goldt *Ke*

Mit dissem rech ich rüen kam
vnder ein linden pallde
das wart mir haimlich wnd gancz zam
es leit mir in meinn schosse
10 sein haüpt von mir es nÿmer weichen woldt *Ke*

In dem daücht mich wie ein graüsamer würme
zw mir her schos in eines dracken fürme
fiel mir mit seinen zenen in mein prüste
nam mir das schone rech zw hant
15 in einem aügenplick verschwant
das er schrack ich das ich erwachen müste *Ke*

6 Die fraw der red erschrack gar hart
ir hercz das war ir schwere
das lacht der edel jüngling zart
er günt mit ir zw scherczen
5 in süsser lib sein hercz was freüden vol *Ke*

Das was der frawen wider zem
sie sach offt hin vnd here
ob nÿchte vngefieges kem
das sie da precht in schmerczen
10 sie sach allein ir meit dÿ sa sÿ wol *Ke*

Da dÿ fraw stünt in solchen schweren dencken
det der jüngling ein diffen seuffczen sencken
vnd sprach o we a we mit laütter stime
hilff mir dw aüser weltes weib

mit dem er pidnet al sein leib
      vnd saück dar nider ein das wort mit grime /ƫ̄

7   Die fraw vnmenschlich hart erschrack
      aüf ir prüst sie in züket
      dar aüf er vnpeweglich lag
      sein hercz begünet lechczen   20^r
5   vor grosser not verkeret er sein varb /ƫ̄

      sie sprach o lieb wü ist dir we
      ir hant er ir do drücket
      mocht ir kein antbort geben me
      mit seüffczen vnde echczen
10   er seinem hercz lieb in den armen starb /ƫ̄

      Ir hent vor leit ob dem haüpt *si* zam schlüge
      in dem do kam zw ir die meit gar clüge
      den dotten jüngling sie gar palt erplicket
      dar peÿ ir fraw lag in amacht
15   die mait pal küles wasser pracht
      da mit sie die edlenn frawen erqüicket /ƫ̄

8   Der clag so gar cleglichen was
      das es mich düt bedribe
      sie sanck dar nider ein das gras
      an sein hent sÿ im stisse
5   den ring damit er sie vermahelt het /ƫ̄

      Sie sprach nÿm hin mein leczte gab
      dw herczen libes libe
      die drag mit dir pis in dein grab
      mit irem mündlein sisse
10   sie in ob hündert malen küssen det /ƫ̄

      Sie seczt im aüf ein rossen krenczeleine
      vnd fing von neüem cleglich on zw weine
      das drib sie schir bis es beginet dagen
      da würden alle peid zw rat
15   vnd namen dissen iüngling drat
      wolten vür seines vatters haüsse dragen /ƫ̄

9   Sie drügen aüs dem gartten her
      gancz plos vnd vnbedecket
      in dem der wachter vngefer
      pekamen in entgegen
5   vnd fingen sie paid mit dem dotten man /ƫ̄

Fürten sie vür den richter hin
der wart pald aüf gewecket
da er vernam den fremden sin
er pegünt sie zw fregen
10 Andreola verantwort sie gar schan /ꝛ̄

Der richter glaübet nit den iren worte
er meint sie hette im mit gift ermorte
er hiss im ein gelertten doctor pringen
der schaüet den jüngling behent
15 wie er genümen hab ein ent
er begriff seinen leib an alles zwingen /ꝛ̄

10 Dar nach sprach er mit clügem sin
dem jüngling ist zw prochen
peÿ seinem herczen ein pastin
dar an ist er vrsticket
5 die fraw ist vnschüldig an seinem dot /ꝛ̄

Von dem richter sie aüf der fart
wart freÿ ledig gesprochen
doch heimlich er pegeren wart
das sie sein hercz erqüicket
10 vnd peÿ im schliff seit er ir hülff aüs not /ꝛ̄

Dar zw wolt er sie czwingen mit gebalte
die fraw erwert sich kaüm des richters alte
in dem wart disses mort weit kümen aüsse
das aüch vür iren vatter kam
15 sein peste freündt er zw im nam
vnd kam dar mit hin vür des richters haüsse /ꝛ̄

11 Der richter da die fraw lies
der ritter da ein ginge
sein dochter vil im vür die fÿes
vnd pat in vmgenaden
5 das er ir wider geb verlorne hüld /ꝛ̄

Sie sprach ich hab dein rot verschmecht
vnd hab den jüngelinge
genümen von nÿdtrem geschlecht
der hat genümen schaden
10 an seinem dot hab ich aber kein schüld /ꝛ̄

Der ritter sprach es müt mich gar faste
den clein verdrawen den dw̌ zw mir haste
hestw mich vmb dissen jüngling gepetten
vür bar so het ich dich gewert

15   nün so las ich in zw der ert
als meinen liben aiden ÿe pestetten /c̄

12   Er lies in legen aüf ein par
vnd lies in herlich dragen
mit der proces vnd priester schar
mit der glocken gedo̊ne
5   in die kirchen nach adelichem sit /c̄

Da man in nün pegraben het
darnach etlichen dagen
der richter da pegeren det
der jüngen frawen scho̊ne
10   zw rechter e´ aber sie wolt sein nit /c̄

Sie det sich wilig in ein closter geben
dar in da fürt sie gar ein strenges leben
das selb sie als gedültiklich lide
dar zw lag sie aüch alle nacht
15   ein gancze stünde in amacht
darin ir hercze lib verschide /c̄

13   Sie wart aüch fralich nÿmer mer
sie het kein freüd kein wüne
sie war alczeit bedriebet ser
deglichen sie beweinte
5   pis an ir ent irs herczen liebes dot /c̄

Peÿ der historÿ mercke mich
dw dochter vnd dw süne
greiff nit zw der e· heimelich
vnwissen deiner freÿnte
10   dir wür stünst zw dem schaden aüch der spot /c̄

Haimliche e· gar selten wol geratten
man sicht ir vil in vngelick vmbwatten
dar von ist disses spricht wort aüf erwachse
wer im wil schaffen ach vnd we
15   der nem sein püllen zw der ee
nah lieb kumpt leit spricht von Nürnberg Hans Saxe /c̄
1516 /c̄

In 1516 Hans Sachs began a triad of seven-strophic Meisterlieder on the subject of love, divine, brotherly, and carnal, but only this first one, in which he announces his purpose, was finished that year.[1] He petitions God the Father for counsel in his undertaking and says that he will begin with divine love, for it is fundamental. As he delineates the many characteristics of this love of God, it takes on a form for him, is an entity and not just an abstraction. He shows how all of the virtues emanate from it and how it helps us to shun various vices. In the *Abgesang* of the sixth strophe, however, he speaks of it as a quality which is so powerful that it imbues our entire being, so powerful that it enabled martyrs to endure torture and to go joyfully to their death. To prove his point he names five saints as examples. For emphasis he repeats that man should love God with his whole heart, then lets this first commandment serve as a transition to brotherly love, a subject which he intends to elucidate in the next Meisterlied.

> **In dem langen marner ein parat** 1^r
> **von dreÿerleÿ lieb Hans**
> **Saxen gedicht**
> **Die güldin tablatür der dreÿer lib**

1		[O] Got vatter aüs jerarcheÿ
		sent mir gotlichen rat
		das ich die eigenschaffte freÿ
		von dreÿer lÿeb bewere drat
	5	des ersten von gotlicher lieb
		die ander nachvolgent süptil /℮
		Von prüederlicher lÿeb vnd dreÿ
		die dritten von dem stat
		fleischlicher lieb vnd pülereÿ
	10	nün heb ich on aüff dein genat
		den zweÿen ich icz rüe gieb
		in dissem par allein ich wil /℮
		Ercleren die erst aigenschaft
		gotlicher lib penent
	15	dÿ ist der ganczen cristenheit ein fundament
		sie leüchtet sam die sün
		vür alle ander dügent gar
		sie ist aüch ein qüelender prün
		da von al cristenlich düget
	20	nemen iren vrsprüng
		gelaüb hoffnüng
		köm gar pald in verzweiffelüng

so sie gotliche lib nit zwüng
das sie beliben stet vnd fest
25   heiliger geist lenck mir mein züng
das ich bie Aügustinus schrib
ercler ir eigenschafft vnd hil /c̄

2   Ir erste eigenschafft nün her
da mit sie ist bewart
sie ist alzeit demütig ser
vnd ist gancz wider die hochfart
5   sie allein got die er zw zelt
sie helt gehorsam wer sie strafft /c̄

Zw miltigkeit stet ir beger
sie fleücht geiczige art
almüs geben ist ir nit schwer
10   gros schecz sie nit zw samen spart   1ᵛ
willig armüt sie aüs erwelt
parmherczikeit die git ir krafft /c̄

Gotliche lie ist keüsch vnd rein
in wort werck vnd gedanck
15   vnkeüsche lib ist peÿ ir ein vbel gestanck
prüderlich lieb sy dreit
gar nÿmant sy nit arges düt
sie dreget nÿmant has noch neit
sie ist senfftmütig wie ein lam
20   lebet stet in dem frit
sie zürnet nit
gotliche lib ist ein gelit
daman den zoren stÿllet mit
den got mvb vnsser sünde hat
25   so man in lib genade pit
so wirt sein zoren hin gestelt
nün hor vür pas mer aigenschafft /c̄

3   Gotliche lib helt messikeit
in dranck vnd aüch in speis
sie ist gancz wider die frassheit
der drünckenheit git sie nit preis
5   sie priechet ir ab alle frist
vnd claget stet ir sünt vnd schüld /c̄

Weltlich lüst ir nit freüde geit
merck in aller leÿ weis
sie hoffet aüf ewige freit
10   des himelischen paradeis

von got sie geren hort vnd list
strebet alzeit nach seiner hüld /Ɛ̄

Gotliche lieb die ist nit dreg
müssigkeit sie verschmacht
15 dag vnd nacht das leiden cristi sie bedracht
sie ret nit wider got
sie benedeiet seinen nom
vnd helt mit fleÿs seine gepot
vnd was gepeüt die kristlich kirch
20 das sie nit vber get
frw vnde spet
opffert sie got ir rein gepet
ob sie von disser welt on wet
widertigkeit schant vnd schmach
25 freflich dar wider sie nit ret
ob sie geleich vnschüldig ist
so leit sÿ das vnd helt gedüld /Ɛ̄

4 Gotliche lieb helt schom vnd zücht
das sÿ reiczvng nit ricz
vor vnschamheit so geit sie flücht
vnd meidet alle werck vnnicz
5 ir hercz das wachet degeleich
das sÿ nit fach der sünde seil /Ɛ̄

Vil heilliger stet sie heim sücht
sie schiucht nit kelt noch hicz
sie geit manige edle frücht
10 sie scherpffet vernünfft vnde wicz
sie samlet vil der dügent reich
vnd wirbet vmb das ebÿg heil /Ɛ̄

Gotliche liebe dinet got
aüs in hicziger prünst
15 gotlicher dinst aüs forcht vndie lib ist vm sünst
zw dem ebigen licht
wan lib die werck aüf pringen müs
merck für das gotlich ongesicht
gotliche lieb ein fackel ist
20 dar dürch mon got erkent
nimant sie plent
sie leüchtet ewigklich on ent
ist sie schon in trübsal ellent
das macht sie alles honig süs
25 ob sie in prünstigkligchen prent

got wonet peÿ ir ewigkleich
der deüfel hat on ir kein deil /ℯ̄

5   Gotliche lib die ist ein schilt
vür onfechtüng verstat
wü ein hercz nit ist mÿt dürch zilt
das des feindes ein plassvng hat
5   so wirt es aügenplicklich wünt
merck von dem gifftigen geschos /ℯ̄

Ww sie ist aber ein gepilt
da ist gotlich genat
die stat ist dem deüffel gar wilt
10 wie offt er gibet falschen rat
so wider stet es im al stünt
das er wirt flüchtig sigelos /ℯ̄

Gotliche lib ist mechtig gancz
krefftig vnd darzw starck   2ᵛ
15 das sie dürch dringet sel leib hercz gepein vnd marck
sie ist kleinmutig nit
so ich dürch such dÿ heillig schrifft
manig lerer mir zeücknüs git
der ich ein deil wol nennen wolt
20 ÿdoch die red ich spar
schaw on die schar
aller heilligen mertrer gar
die in gotlicher liebe clar
stürben frolich vnd dürsttigklich
25 der ich ein deil wil nennen zwar
aüf das ich vor der meister münt
müg hÿ sten aller straffe plos /ℯ̄

6   Hor wÿ sanctus laürencius
lag aüf gluendem rost
recht wÿ in küllem dawe süs
das schafft das er im het genost
5   so in prünstiklich gotlich lib
das er des feüres nit entpfant /ℯ̄

Hor bie seit vns Sanctus paülus
hicz hünger dürst vnd frost
von got mich nit ab benaden müs
10 durch gotlich lib hab ich den drost
dar von er manigfaltig schrib
vnd vns mit fleis dar zw vermant /ℯ̄

133

Sanctus petrüs ging in den dot
wider hin ein gen ram
15 her wie sanctüs andreas von des creüczes stam
nit ledig werden wolt
aüch wÿ Sanctüs johannes sas
in heissem ol dw mercken solt
das im doch alles schadet nÿt
20 des geleich aüch das gifft
dar beÿ so brifft
was stercke gotlich libe stifft
hor was gepeüt die heillig schrifft
das mon ein got lib haben sol
25 das selb vns alle sammt andrifft
her nach ich dir zw kennen gib
die vrsach nach meinem verstant /̅c̅

7 Ein ÿder das vernemen mag
seit das der mensch enpfing
von got vernüftig selich sag
nach seiner pildnüs vnd al ding
5 leib güt freÿ willen vnd gedanck
vür al ander geschopffe gar /̅c̅

Der dürch deuffelischen rat schlag
ein gepot vber ging
dar vmb er in vngenad lag
10 pis das got auff der erden ring
sein sün her sant on allenn zwanck
das er onnom die menscheit clar /̅c̅

Dar in er starb vür vnsser schüld
mit dem herbesten dot
15 her ber dan nÿ kein kreatür er liden hot
darpeÿ merckest tw wol
das in herczlichen widervmb
ein itlich mensch lib haben sol
wan es ist das erst gepot merck
20 die ewangelisch ler
o mensch nün hor
lieb einen got mit ganczer ger
deinen nachsten sam dich selber
verste in prüderlicher lieb
25 weliche ich hernach ercler
ob ich on künsten nit wür kranck
clerlichen in dem andren par /̅c̅ 1516 jar

3ʳ

134

For the second Meisterlied in the trilogy of love, written in 1517, Hans Sachs fittingly calls upon the second person in the Trinity to invigorate his mind so that he may explain the nature of brotherly love clearly and wisely. He places the first example of it, or rather of its opposite, in Genesis when Cain killed Abel. This fratricide shows what happens when a person is so devoid of brotherly love, the prime law of nature, that he is not willing to grant to another that which he himself does not want. From Genesis the poet turns to Plato, who, he says, taught his pupils that fraternal love, if not carried to excess, is the root of all virtues. Beginning with the second strophe the Meisterlied is an account of what this love is and is not, drawn in part from observation, in part from the reading he had been doing. He seems also to have incorporated some of his own ideals and, unconsciously perhaps, traits of his own character. Similarly to St. Paul in I Cor. 13:4-8 he personifies brotherly love on through to the last *Abgesang*. To some extent this love coincides with divine love, but on the whole it is earthly. More than that, certain qualities which Hans Sachs says are an integral part of it show him to possess a surprisingly comprehensive social conscience, for he mentions such practical goals as looking after the common weal, giving medicine to the ill, feeding the poor, seeing that a person is buried respectfully, granting a request for a loan, and paying good wages. The strength of brotherly love, he asserts, can be seen in the story of Titus and Gisippus each of whom was willing to die for the other.[1] In closing the poet warns not to overstep the bounds, because that might carry a person into the realm of sensual love which, God willing, he will describe in the last song of this trio.

      In dem langen marner das   3ʳ
      ander par H S gedicht

1   Her Jesü crist aüs seraffin
          deiner hilff ich beger
          dein gotlich krafft sterck mir mein sin
          das ich das ander par ercler
5   mit borten verstentlich vnd clüg
          von art der prüederlichen lieb /ℓ̃

          Die von der welte anbegin
          hat iren vrsprüng her
          in Genesis ich finden pin
10   dar dürch ich den vrsprüng bewer
          wan pabl caim abel erschlüg
          vil jar adam an frücht verdrieb /ℓ̃

          Prüderlib lib wart die vrsach
          grüntlich disser figür

15 prüderlich lieb war das erst gesecz der natür
was ein mensch nit wolt hon
das selbig es aüch williklich
solt einen anderen verlon
peÿ dem hastw entlichen grünt
20 das es ÿder verstet
der weis poet
plato sein iünger leren det
welicher disse libe het
der het aller dügent ein würcz
25 so er die mas nit vber dret
vür pas der eigenschafft genüg
disser lib ich zw kenen gieb /c̄

2 Prüderlich lib ist früm vnd schlecht
hochmüt ir hercz nit qüelt
nach keinem hohen stant sie specht
kein eigenlob sie ir zw zelt
5 sÿ zeicht sich nach irem geleich
vber nÿmant sie sich nit pricht /c̄

Sie ist gehorsam wie ein knecht
nach irem stant erwelt
den armen sie gar nit verschmecht
10 den alten sie aüch erlich helt
den dümen macht sie künsten reich
kein straff sie aüch verachtet nicht /c̄

Prüderlich liebe die ist milt
so sÿ ist reich on hab
15 so geit sie reÿlichen aüs ir schenck oder gab
wer hilff an sie begert
dürch lehen der wirt pald van ir
mit frolichem herczen gebert
sie begeret an iren schacz
20 aüch keines fremden güt
in irem müt
sie nÿmant nit betriegen düt
gefünden güt beÿ ir nit rüt
raübereÿ wücher vnd dibstal
25 ist nit in disser libe glüt
gemeinen nücz sie festÿgkleich
mit irem münt drewlich vür spricht /c̄

3 Der brüderlichen libe wert
die keüscheit ich zw schreib

zw vnkeüscheit sie nit begert
keines dochter schwester noch weib

5 aüsser halb dem elichen stant
aüf das sie nÿmant schmehet mit *ſc*   4ͬ

In zoren sie nÿmant versert
sein er güt oder leib
vil schnoder wort sie vberhert

10 das sie ir zeit mit frid verdreib
sie hebet nÿmant aüf sein schant
sie wünschet nimant arges nÿt *ſc*

Doch wer ir frefflich schaden düt
wider die pillikeit

15 so zürnet sie vnd helt doch darin vnderscheit
ir zorenn pald zw gat
so reüet sie von herczen dan
das sie also gezürnet hat
zw zoren geit sÿ nit vrsach

20 irer red hat sie acht
hort sie zwitracht
da van so wirt ir freüd geschbacht
in herczlicher dreÿ sie erwacht
al ding sie zw dem pesten went

25 aüf das wer wider frid gemacht
peÿ keinem zoren sie nit want
sie hat kein rw dan peÿ dem fritt *ſc*

4 Prüderlich lib dreget kein neit
sie hat herczlichen holt
den neben menschen alle zeit
ist er reich an küst oder golt

5 dem dreget sie kein neid ich sag
sie ginet im das vnd vil me *ſc*

Nimant sie aüch dÿ er abschneit
dar peÿ dw mercken solt
weis sie schon grüntlich die warheit

10 ir dreües hercz doch nit verdolt
das sie es pringe an den dag
es schmilczet peÿ ir als der schne *ſc*

So prüderliche lieb dan hort
von ander leütten das

15 sÿ einem nachreden etwan aüs neid vnd has
vnwarhafft drogenlich
das selb sie nit verdulden mag

ir dreües hercz bedrüebet sich
die vnwarheit sie wider spricht
20 vnd dem sein er bewart
das ist ir art
hort sie einen noch reden hart
dar an aller neid wird gespart
das es ist offen vnd warhafft
25 doch sie es ze dem pesten kart
kein nach red sie nit horen mag
des fremden schant düt dir aüch we /ƛ

5 Prüderlich lieb warhafftig ist
sie treibet keinen spot
sie praüchet keinen hinterlist
sie warnet manigen vor not
5 geferlich sie nÿmant nach grÿnt
sie geit kein ergernüs dar peÿ /ƛ

Sie ist gedreÿ zw aller frist
sie gibet dreÿen rot
sie ist aüch dreg vnd loncksam wist
10 zw rach wen sie zw straffen hot
ir straff ist aüch gar senfft vnd lind
peÿ ir ist aüch kein schmeichlereÿ /ƛ

Prüderlich lib ist parmherczig
ist itlichem verpflicht
15 in mit leiden wan sie einen in notten sicht
manigen sie erlost
aüs drübsal vnd aüs anfechtüng
sie geit hoffnüng vnd gütten drost
sie speisset aüch der armen vil
20 die dotten sie gar wert
pestet zw ert
ir vil sie von dem dot ernert
das recht sie zw parmünge kert
witwen vnd waissen geit sie schücz
25 die krancken erczeneÿ sie leyt
sie neret vil der cleinen kint
sie meret müterliche dreÿ /ƛ

6 Prüderlich lieb ist clüg vnd weis
sie geit aüch gutten lan
sie ist danckpar mit ganczem fleis
wü mon ir gütheit hat gedan

138

5   zw widergelt ist sie verpflicht
gelihen ding bezalt sie schen /℞

Sie ist senftmütig vnd aüch leis
sie zanet nÿmant an
sie geit dem güten lob vnd preis
10   bües mit warheit mag bestan
den possen schendet sie doch nicht
let in beÿ seinem berd besten /℞

Prüderlich lib ist aüch dinsthafft
al ir arbeit sind sÿes
15   mit willen düt sie nÿmant keinen widerdries
sie mag wol leiden schimpff
sie scherczet aüch her wider vm
vn allen schaden mit gelimpff
peÿ frolichen sie freüdreich ist
20   sie dreibet kürczweil vil
mit seiten spil
mit singen fechten gar süptil
dach vber get sie nit das zil
aüf das kein schaden volg hernach
25   schimpffen on schaden ist ir wil
des fremden schaden sie vür sicht
dar vm ich disse dügent kren /℞

7   Prüderlib lib dreget den krancz
der zücht vnd scham gewant
in dem gericht geit sie gelancz
keisserlich recht sie nit aüf spant
5   sie ist so gar holt selig gar
die frümen dragen ir al günst /℞

Prüederlich lieb ist starck vnd gancz
in dem elichen stant
ist sie ein kett an alle schrancz
10   dar zw ist sie ein festes pant
aller sitlichen dügent gar
der keine künt beleiben sünst /℞

Von prüderliche liebe sterck
schreibt perobaldus do
15   von zweÿen jünglingen Dito vnd gisipo
hetten sich also holt
das ir itweder williklich
vür den anderen sterben wolt
der geschicht zw erzelen mer

20 von kürczwegen ich las
o mensch merck das
dw nit vber geest die mas
das dich nit disser libe strass
hin drag zw der fleischlichen lib
25 die ich hernach erczelle pas
ob got wil in dem dritten par
zw rint mir nit künstlicher künst /k̄e 1517 /k̄e

Hans Sachs opens the last Meisterlied of his trilogy on love, written also in 1517, with a plea to the third member of the Trinity, the Holy Spirit, to send him grace in carrying out his undertaking of explaining the characteristics of carnal love. Although he cites Ovid, whose conception of love was essentially sensual, as his main source, and refers briefly to Virgil, he actually gathered most of his material from a number of books. Whereas the qualities inherent in divine and brotherly love were idealistic, those of carnal love are just the opposite. The poet sets these down at random, perhaps as they came to mind. After enumerating the negative effects engendered by sensual love, he proceeds to show by example how personages throughout the ages have borne out what he has just said. First of all he mentions two figures in the Old Testament, then turns to profane literature and cites one character after another who has been betrayed by erotic love. The details connected with his illustrations do not always conform to his source material, possibly because he had been reading so many tales that some of the particulars got slightly mixed up. After viewing the array of tragic endings which he had found Hans Sachs may well have been thankful that in his own experience with love he had suffered only mental anguish.

With this Meisterlied he has accomplished two things: he has warned again in no uncertain terms of the consequences of unbridled sensual love, as the Muses had bidden him do, and he has completed his threefold praise of the Trinity, to Whom he gives all honor.

In dem langen Marner das drit par   5ᵛ
H S gedicht

1   Heilliger geist genad mir sent
              heraüs der himeldron
              das ich das dritte par vollent
              dar in ich vür genümen hon
      5   zw ercleren die eigenschafft
              fleischlicher lieb vnd irer art /ℓͤ

              Ovidiüs gar wol bekent
              was die lib fügen kon
              wü sie in hiczigklichen prent
     10   da geit sie entlich possen lon
              sie nÿmet vernünft vnd krafft
              vnsinikeit ist sie ein gart /ℓͤ

              Die lib ist plint vnd hat gros sczmercz
              von wegen kleiner freit
     15   vnd endet sich alweg in grossem herczen leit
              vil eigen schafft sie hat

die lib sich nit verpergen mag
dar vm cüpidus nacket stat
vnd hat ein pogen in der hant
20   seit der proffetten deil
mit seinem pfeil
scheüset er manig hündert meil
die selbig wünt wirt selten heil
ww sie ein hercz verseren ist
25   das zeuhet an fraw Venus seil
vnd wÿrt mit disser lib behafft
dar van ich sing ze disser vart /℮

2   Fleischlich lieb hat nit zal noch mas
sencket vil seüftzen schwer
sie wüttet stet an vnterlas
sie trachtet hin vnd wider her
5   sie vber windet alle ding
vnd leret clüge list süptil /℮

Kein arbeit ist der lib zw gras
sie hat selczsam geper
süchet verporgen weg vnd stras
10   vnd geit sich offt in gros gefer
das wiget sie gar leicht gering
dürch freud vnd minnikliches spil /℮

Vnmassen ser wechset dÿ lÿb
deglich nacht vnde dag
15   vor schwerem müt sie nit essen noch drincken mag
sie mag aüch schlaffen nicht
schlaffet sie dan in draümes weis
kümet ir vor selczsam gesicht
sie ist gar starck dar zw behent
20   scharpff in irer sübstancz
wer dissen krancz
dreget dem dũt erpleichen gancz
gotlicher genaden gelancz
er lebet in der finsternis
25   vnd springet in des flüches dancz
vnd acht nit ob im misseling
noch hor ir aigenschaffte vil /℮

3   Flaischlich lieb schneit al freüd enczweÿ
keiner kürczweil sie acht
sie dät manig cleglichen schreÿ
manig freÿ hercz sie draurig macht

6^r

5   lib weinet oft ist drawrikleich
    zeit vnde weil die ist ir lang /℮

    Fleischliche lieb pringet vndrew
    vil lügen sie petracht
    sie pfleget vil der zaübereÿ
10 dar dürch maniger wirt geschwacht
    sie macht manch schones antlicz pleich
    lieb ist des leides anefang /℮

    Fleischliche lieb dÿ nÿmet hÿn
    er güt schon vnd aüch zücht
15 dar vür geit sie vnd dügent vnd helesche frücht
    raübereÿ vnd diebstal
    got schwervng meinaid krieg vnd streit
    vnd aüch der dot schlag ane zal
    sich selb dettvng frawen vnd man
20 junckfraw schwechvng eprüch
    so ich dürch süch
    Ovidiüm das künstreich püch
    aus Virgilio manchen sprüch
    so vind ich der lib haber vil
25 die al drucket vnseles schüch
    der ich her nach ein dail / eÿn zeÿch
    zw zeügen in meinem gesang /℮   6ᵛ

4   Der weisse künig Salamon
    dürch lieb bedrogen war
    des geleichen der starck Samson
    dürch grosse lieb kom vm sein har
5   vnd sterck das in sein feint gezbüng
    vnd im peide aügen aüs prach /℮

    Von Jason sollest dw verston
    dürch lib media clar
    in wildem feüre er ver pran
10 dürch zaüber list gemachet zwar
    vnd pÿramus der ritter iüng
    dürch lib Tisbe zw dot sich stach /℮

    Achilles kam dürch lib in leit
    der edel ritter wert
15 do er die schön jünckfraw Polixena pegert
    zw ir in tempel kam
    ir prüder sich verporgen het
    vnd im sein iünges leben nam
    dürch lib kam Paris aüch in not

                                    143

20   da in sein vatter sant
in krichen lant
da er die schon hellena fant
füret sie mit im heim ze hant
der edel keisser Menel*as*
25   im zorniklichen nache rant
seinen herfanen er auf schwüng
vnd pracht Troia in vngemach /c͞

5   Mit dem ich aber beiter ker
hÿ mit dÿssem gedicht
Demonovm solt zihen ver
gen Athenis was er vür pflicht
5   da er nit kam vor grossem leit
hing sich Phillis an einen stranck /c͞

Mon lisset aüch von leander
von libe das gesicht
schwam al nacht vber ein wasser
10   zw Ero die zünt im ein licht
an ein zinen doch kam die zeit
das er in dem wasser ertranck /c͞

Man lisset aüch da Eneas
schid von Dido da stündt
15   sie aüf ein düren da sie in nÿm sehen künt
ir schwert stach sie dürch sich
von Porkris ich auch melde die
parck sich in koren heimelich
wolt sehen ob Zeffalo lib
20   het fraw aürora zir
er fant dÿ spir
meinet es wer ein wildes dir
vnd schos mit einem sper zw ir
von Herckůle / ich melden dw
25   het lib deonira mit gir
dar vm Jole ein hem bereit
dar ine in der dot bezwanck /c͞

6   Herzog Bilhalm von osterreich
dürch fleischlich liebe gros
vür er vber des meres deich
vngelück war offt sein genos
5   pis er die schon Agleÿ erbarb
dar vm mon in zw lecz er stach /c͞

Canis bart der sein geleich
dürch list ein pürck auf schlos
vnd zw fraw gardoleÿe schleich
10 dar vm in nampecenis schos
das er ellendikklichen starb
dürch fleischlich lieb im das geschach /ℓ̄

Her Dristrant ist aüch in dem spil
fleischlich lib in enzündt
15 gegen fraw Isalden ist mir wol worden künt
dürch sie litt er offt not
wan er gar offt ver huettet wart
solt kissen da den grimen dot
dürch liste kam er doch dar von
20 wie mon es lessen hert
sein kleit verkert
damit er seinen leib ernert
zw pülereÿ was er gelert
zw lecz kam vngeluckes vil
25 er würd pÿs jn den dot versert
vnd da er lag in dodes farb
zw stünd Isald ir hercz zw prach /ℓ̄

7 Vnd auch der schone jüngeling   7ᵛ
genenet Quisgardüs
in ein loch durch die erden ging
in ein kamer dürch libe süs
5 zw Gismünda der frawen fein
dar dürch er vmb sein leben kam /ℓ̄

Fillius in dem korbe hing
dürch lib das wart sein püs
Prenberger drug der lib ein ring
10 sein hercz man im aus schneiden lüs
dis as die edel Herczogein
dar dürch sie aüch ir ende nam /ℓ̄

Darqinus aüch verdriben wart
des keisser sün alda
15 dar vmb das er ab zbüngen het lükreczia
vor grosser lib ir er
ir sint noch vil an disser schar
die fleischlich bedroge ser
fleischliche lib verpotten ist
20 am sibenden gepat
fleischlich lib hat

145

vrsprünge dürch des deüffel rat
sie prinet in der helle pfat
da mit ent ich das dritte par
25 zw lob der hohen drinidat
o herre got die er seÿ dein
behüet vns for der helle flam /k̄e Deo gracias 1517 /k̄e

Chapter V / On Meistergesang

Background

Just when a *Singschule* was established in Nuremberg is not certain, although it may have been shortly after the middle of the fifteenth century.[1] Hans Folz seems to point to this when he says in a Meisterlied, "Die weil ich was von joren jung / Do dacht ich wie der urespring / Mitt kunst allein zu Nurmberg wer."[2] Hans Sachs recounts the founding—he does not say when—, renown, and decline of the *Singschule* in an allegorical Meisterlied of 1527.[3] Some of the imagery for this he borrowed from his allegory on the origin of Meistergesang written in the year 1516 (No. 32); for example, he transfers the symbolism of the garden from Meistergesang to the Nuremberg *Singschule*. In both poems twelve men cultivate the ground, and in both poems these represent twelve Masters, in the one the Twelve Masters of Meistergesang, in the other those of the Nuremberg Society. The assiduous work of the Nuremberg Masters, Hans Sachs declares, brought about the flowering of their *Singschule* so that visiting Meistersinger praised it above all others and disseminated its *Kunst* throughout Germany. In contradistinction to the revered Twelve Masters of Meistergesang, however, the Nuremberg Masters were all artisans who plied a variety of trades: one was a baker, another a nailsmith, two fashioned clasps and hooks for garments; there were also a tailor, an illuminator, a measurer of wood, a barber, and a weaver.[4] The barber, of course, is Hans Folz, whom Hans Sachs further designated as "der durchleuchtig deutsch poet" and for whom he showed his great admiration by including more than fifty of his Meisterlieder in Berlin 414.[5] In like manner he honored the weaver, his teacher Lienhart Nunnenbeck, by copying forty-two of his songs into the manuscript-book.[6] But the rest of the Masters did not fare this well, for the poet entered Meisterlieder by only five of them, four for one, two for another, and one each for three.[7] On the other hand, ten of the twelve are represented by from one to ten *Töne* each.[8] Even though just four of Master Fritz Zorn's *Töne* appear in Berlin 414, they were apparently extremely popular, for seventy-three Meisterlieder were set to them![9] Not even the *Töne* of such old Masters as Frauenlob, Der Marner, and Regenbogen come close to this number.[10] Aside from Zorn eight others of the Nuremberg Masters find their *Töne* used from one to thirty-three times; to this may be added the fragment for one other.[11] The names of the twelve Nuremberg Masters, which Hans Sachs recorded in his allegorical Meisterlied, did not remain constant; over the years from one to three substitutions are to be found.[12] Two of these might not have mattered very much to him because there is not a single *Ton* or Meisterlied for either one in Berlin 414, but the replacement for the third would have sorrowed him.[13] That Master was Lienhart Nunnenbeck!

The decline of the Nuremberg *Singschule* seems to have come about gradually, due perhaps to two factors. One of these may have been mediocrity to which Folz alludes in the Meisterlied cited above. He had come to Nuremberg with great expectations of the *kunst* he would find among the Meistersinger, only to voice his disappointment with the words, "Nun kum ich auß eym dorff von Francken here / Und meint mit frag weyßheit von euch zu lere, / So sint euch vil zu schwere / Drey kindisch frag von grobenn knecht."[14] Hans Sachs, too, found mediocrity to be the order of the day among Meistersinger when he says in a Meisterlied of 1516, "Sie hetten gar cleinen verstandt / vnd daüchten sich doch meister sein / gar clein / was da ir künst / gen rechter kunst ein schercze."[15] The second factor, however, was the real cause which undermined the *Singschule*; this is the beast in Hans Sachs' allegory which laid waste the garden so that only thistles and thorns remained. The beast, according to the poet, is envy, and in its wake came dissension and prejudice. To a greater or lesser degree envy had no doubt always been present in a *Singschule* because Folz had already warned against it in the fifteenth century: "Dar umb, ir meister frut / Seit strefflich mit der kunsten rut / Senfftmutiglich an neides mut / Verschmecht nit ander meister kunst."[16] And Hans Sachs, too, must have encountered envy as he journeyed about, for the word recurs in these early Meisterlieder. In 4,1,31 it is one of the sins for which man will have to account before God; in 5,4,19-22 the tenth joy in heaven is the absence of envy; in 15,5,16-17 the poet requests the Virgin Mary to protect us "vor deuffelischem neit"; in 26,2,18 he finds that a person who loves God does not envy anyone; and in 27,4,1, and 4-5 he states, then repeats, that brotherly love is free of envy. Thus it would seem that the rivalry which usually existed among the trades, as well as between members of the same guild, seeped into the *Singschulen* and contributed to the feeling of ill will and discontent, and that this rivalry may have been engendered to a great extent by the cantankerousness of human nature itself inasmuch as envy is one of the Seven Deadly Sins.[17] The Twelve Masters of the Nuremberg *Singschule* presumably had worked hard to bring eminence to their organization, but when one after another died, including Hans Folz in 1515, the cankers of vainglory and malice probably festered unchecked.

That such pettiness existed among those who practiced the "noble art" of Meistergesang may not have entered the head of the seventeen-year-old Hans Sachs as he started out with high heart on his journeyman years to learn more about life and shoemaking and, hopefully perhaps, about Meistergesang. Uncritical though he may have been at first, as time went on perchance he began to wonder at the little talent abroad in the various *Singschulen* and at his inability to find a great master.[18] Yet he had high praise for the *Singschule* at Würzburg where he was so well received; he was pleased, no doubt, to help in the School in Munich, and even more so in being asked to conduct the one at Frankfurt.[19] For his fellow Meistersinger to so honor him, a young man, they must have heard and approved of songs of his own making. And the willingness with which apparently they gave him the many Meisterlieder for his collection points also to the good impression he must have made upon them. It is no wonder, therefore, that when he arrived home after his five years away, he may have been elated with anticipation for the part he would now be able to play in his Nuremberg *Singschule*.[20] Unfortunately such an unalloyed gratification seems not to have been in store for him in the immediate

148

future, for to judge from the content of some of the songs on Meistergesang Hans Sachs seemingly found the *Singschule* of Nuremberg at a low ebb.

His twelve songs which center on various phases of Meistergesang do not convey the joyousness of those to the Virgin Mary, for instance. In fact, several of them, written during the years 1517 and 1518, after he had returned to Nuremberg, reveal a definite dissatisfaction, a deep hurt at the apparent slighting of his own Meisterlieder, and at the same time a kind of anger directed at his fellow Meistersinger. Whereas his religious Meisterlieder disclose that he conformed to and recognized the authority of the Church and its dogma, in matters of Meistergesang he seems to be asserting an independence, and he lets his Meisterlieder speak of his discontent with existing conditions. They convey also his belief in himself and in his own poetic gift.

The first of these twelve, all of which are just three strophes long, suggests that a singer suit his subject matter to the audience before which he is appearing; the next two are extremely important for the history of Meistergesang in that in the first one Hans Sachs not only mentions five kinds of songs which were forbidden as well as three kinds of *Töne* which were to be avoided, but also enumerates some thirty specific items which he says were penalized. The second of the two takes up seven of the aforementioned points and defines them in detail. These two Meisterlieder of 1516 thus present the earliest comprehensive listing extant of matters which later were incorporated in the *Schulzettel* and *Tabulaturen*, and the first definitions extant of seven items of the "scherpff." Following these there is an allegory of the origin of Meistergesang, towards the end of which Hans Sachs criticizes in no uncertain terms those who scoff at and mock the art of Meistergesang. The fifth song depicts the ideal Master whom the young poet had sought in vain throughout the length and breadth of the land; the sixth, ironical in character, is a song without rhymes. After this Hans Sachs praises the poet, symbolized by a bubbling spring. over and above the singer, represented by a pond, for when the singer dies, his art perishes with him, but not so for the poet: his art lives on and becomes greater after death. The eighth Meisterlied is both ironical and satirical; ironical in that he says he can never be equal to the Masters whom he is addressing, and satirical in that he invites them to be his guests and to accept all that his home has to offer. He is of course speaking figuratively. In the next one the poet intimates that he has been criticized, no doubt unjustly, belittles his own ability, and mockingly acclaims that of his fellow Meistersinger. At the close of the tenth poem he reveals his troubled state of mind when he says that his heart would be joyful if it were not for one matter. Since this Meisterlied was written in 1518, these words, it seems to me, can only refer to the lack of rapport between himself and his fellow Meistersinger. The last two songs deride the *Singschule* and the *Merker* respectively by means of allegories. Again reading between the lines one surmises that these reflect unhappy experiences encountered in the *Singschule* after his return home and shed light on conditions therein. Thus three things stand out in Hans Sachs' criticism: the restrictiveness of minor rules, the dearth of talent among the singers, and the besetting sin of envy. Had he not loved Meistergesang so much, he might have been less concerned about the way matters stood in the *Singschule*. Knowing, however, that the art itself was greater than the singers who practiced it, he was undaunted and composed two new melodies during the year 1518, his "morgen weis" and his "vnser frauen gesanck weis."[21] Unwaveringly he faced the task before him of revitalizing the *Singschule* of Nuremberg.

The very first Meisterlied which Hans Sachs devoted to a phase of Meistergesang was written in 1515.[1] Notwithstanding the fact that his father had summoned him on or before the first of May to come home, he may have tarried in Munich long enough to take part in the meeting of the Meistersinger at Pentecost. This was a high festival and may have been held in the open, since the poet speaks of singing on the "plan."[2] Emotionally upset as he was, it is no wonder that he begins by stating that his heart knows no peace. He has come to sing, even though he knows he cannot give pleasure to everyone. A singer, he thinks, should be versed in sundry subjects so that he will present what people like to hear. It is to no purpose, he points out, to sing only of the art of music, because just about one tenth of the listeners can understand this matter and hence tends to ridicule what is being sung. Rather one should suit the subject matter to the audience. In the suggestions which follow Hans Sachs goes beyond the scope of Meistergesang, for when would a Meistersinger sing before audiences made up exclusively of priests, or nobles, or lovely ladies, or merchants, peasants, soldiers, drinkers, gamblers, lovers? Persons interested in Meistergesang were no doubt invited to various meetings of the *Singschule*, and one or several from the categories which Hans Sachs mentions might be present, but certainly never in sufficient numbers to constitute a homogeneous whole.[3] It could be that he is here expressing a wish with regard to the role he would like to have Meistergesang play culturally in the life of the community, i.e., actually living up to the term *kunst* which its members applied to it, or, and this seems more probable in view of the fact that the pronoun "ich" slips into the second *Stollen* of the first strophe instead of the required *er*, he may have been giving voice to dreams of what he himself would like to do in the future.

Goedeke published the Meisterlied under the heading "Eine schone schulkunst, was ein singer soll singen" and Lützelberger-Fromman with the simple title of "Ein schulkunst."[4] Weddigen's publication is a reprint from Goedeke.[5]

In des wolferams langen don   31ʳ
3 lieder H S gedicht

1   Mein hercz das mag nit rüe han
        dar vm so wil ich heben an
        zw singen hÿ auf dissen plan
        wie wol ich nit kan iderman
5   hÿ singen das in freüden geit
        das ist mit leit
        seit
        ichs nit kan verpringen /ℰ   31ᵛ

        Das doch zimet eim singer freÿ
10   das er sol künen mangerleÿ

aüf das wü ich pey leüten seÿ
das er mit süsser melodeÿ
den leuten sing was mon beger
vnd geren her
15 der
mag wol preis gewingen /ᴄᵉ

Maniger düt desselben nicht
vnd singt allein von müsica der künste
dar mit er sich her fire pricht
20 vnd ist doch solich materÿ vm sünste
wan der czehent sein nit verstat
dar vmb hat mon sein nit genat
die leüt dreiben daraüs den spat
dar vm so wer der peste rat
25 ein singer las sein künst nit rw
pis er küm zw
wü
maister singers singen /ᴄᵉ

2 Peÿ den sing er von maisterschafft
vnd von der siben künsten krafft
ist er mit rechter künst behafft
so pleibt er von in vngestrafft
5 peÿ andren leutten zimet pas
zw singen das
was
ich hernach wil sagen /ᴄᵉ

Dis nem ein ÿder singer war
10 ob er ist peÿ der prister schar
so sing er von der gotheit clar
vnd von der hohen himel kar
vnd von der heilligen geschrifft
was ssie on drifft
15 prifft
er es vnverschlagen /ᴄᵉ

Ist er peÿ edel leütten güt
so sing er nit von solchem dispütiren
sünder sing in aüs freiem müt
20 von renen stechen kempfen vnd dürniren
von springen fechten ringen vil
vnd iagen paissen wÿ mon wil
von solchem ritterlichen spil
manige histori süptil

32ʳ

25 kan er das meisterlichen do
sein hercz wirt fro
so
er düt preis eriagen /℞

3 Weÿtter gib ich dem singer ler
ob er beÿ schonen frawen wer
der sing von scham zücht vnd achch er
sein lob wirt im geprissen mer
5 den paüeren sing von dem pflüeg
das ist ir füg
clüg
von der erden frichte /℞

Vnd von der liechten maien zeit
10 den kriegs leütten seÿ er bereit
zw singen von krieg vnd aüch streit
den kaüf leuten von landen weit
von merck vnd stetten ane zal
von perg vnd dal
15 al
les lob mon im gichte /℞

Dem drincker sing von gütem wein
dem spiller sing von wurffel vnd von kartte
so mag sein hercz wol frolich sein
20 dem püler sing von schonen frawen zartte
also han ich ein clein erzelt
wie sich ein singer halten solt
wü er das sein gesang erschelt
da mit gros preis eriagen welt
25 der sing was idem zw gehert
wes er begert
lert
in das mein gedichte /℞
/℞   1515 /℞

From what Hans Sachs said at the close of the Meisterlied on the tools of his trade (No. 21) we know that he was in Würzburg on Ash Wednesday, 1516. Shortly after that he may have left there to go to Frankfurt for the Easter Fair.[1] It was in Frankfurt that he conducted a *Singschule* for the first time, and it was there that he wrote this song on Ascension Day.[2] Its opening verses with their all-inclusive welcoming words to the Masters skilled in the art of Meistergesang, to the learned singers, to the honored *Merker,* and to all those who, because of their interest in Meistergesang, had come to hear the songs, lead one to think that this may just possibly have been his initial appearance before the Meistersinger of Frankfurt. Since technical skill is necessary in the production of a good song, Hans Sachs proposes to give a summary of the items which were forbidden both in the construction of a song and in the singing of it.[3] To begin with he eliminates certain kinds of songs and meters, then registers in and out of rhyme the errors which no competent singer dare make. A few times he offers a positive suggestion: let the four principal melodies resound, sing slowly and in a moderate tone of voice, and always finish a song. He closes by affirming that whosoever will follow the course which he has pointed out in his song will have a foundation for the art of Meistergesang. This Meisterlied contains the earliest comprehensive list extant of the errors which were penalized.

In des frawenlobs langen don 3 lieder   29ᵛ
H S gedicht

1   Seit mir got wilkümen ir maister künstenreich
          vnd des geleich
          die singer wol gelerete
          ir mercker hoch geerette
    5   vnd wer hie hat gesanges günst
          vnd von herczen begerte
          das er gesang zw horen wel
          der seÿ mir gewilkümen /℮

          Seit ir dürch gesanges willen seit algemein
    10   kümen herein
          wer singen wil ist notte
          das er nit werd zw spotte
          das er sing aüs gerechter künst
          vnd meid was seÿ verpotte
    15   dar vmb bil ich mit wortten schnel
          al straff kürcz vbersümen /℮

          Straffer vnd reiczer solt ir lonn
          loÿca aüiüoca seit on

dencz reÿen schon
20 al vberkron
vber kürcz vber lange don
die sollen hÿ kein vür geng hon
sein münd die vier haüpton erschel
die mügen im wol frümen /℞

2 Hüt sich ÿder das im al hie nit pring sein züng
falsche meinvng
meit falsche melodeÿe
mit falsch gemes da peÿe
5 falsche latein ist aüch vnicz
die in congrüa seÿe
zw kurcz zw lanck ist lesterlich
wir merck es mit der kreiden /℞

Hüt eüch dar pey das keiner pring eqüiboca
10 mercket alsa
halb vnd aüch schiller ande
meit plos reimen am pande   30ͬ
schiller reimen paüs vnd die sticz
ist aüch ein grosse schande
15 greuf nit her für noch hinter sich
wer die straff wil vermeiden /℞

Wer ir wirt von dem stül nit spring
ein itlicher sein lid aüssing
kein laster *sch*bing
20 kein reimen zwing
das er nit vnpequemlich cling
keiner hÿ differencze pring
meit die gespalten mercke mich
weitter wil ich bescheiden /℞

3 Haimlich eqüifoca solt ir aüch pringen nit
meidet aüch mit
al reimen die do riren
wü es nit düt gepiren
5 vnd pring aüch keiner hÿ cleb silb
las sich keiner verviren
das er hÿ precht einen anhang
strefflich wirt er sünst funde /℞

Meidet plinte meinvng vnd dar zw plinte wort
10 an allen ort
düt halbe wort verdreiben

155

die wir aüch strefflich schreiben
noch ist ein straff heisset ein milb
die las keiner becleiben
15 welcher wil das er vrlang
das preis der maister münde /c̄

Singet lancksam wan ich rat das
man eüch mag mercken dester pas
nit hoch on mas
20 fein senft an has
keiner sich nit veriren las
welicher get die rechte stras
wie in leret das mein gesang
der hat der künst ein grunde /c̄
    1516 /c̄

Although this Meisterlied may very probably have been written months after the preceding one in the year 1516, I am placing it immediately after it, because of its related subject matter. Whereas in the former Hans Sachs had set down the infractions of the basic rules, which incurred penalties, here he deals with items of the "scherpff," a register of points which were more strictly judged. His restless mood of a year ago is seemingly gone, supplanted now by a joyous frame of mind. The young poet begins by invoking the grace of the Holy Spirit for help in proving his skill as he sings about these stringent rules. Many a singer, he declares, has inquired about them, wherefore he intends to clarify them briefly. Although he had already included all of the items, which he now enumerates in the first *Abgesang,* in his catalogue of common errors in the previous Meisterlied in exactly the same sequence, he now defines them.[1] Strophes two and three, except for the last five verses, contain the explanations which, Hans Sachs says, he has given penetratingly, precisely, and clearly.

These inhibiting rules which took no account of dialect, might well serve the untalented, but surely could not be expected in their entirety to restrict Hans Sachs, whose verses flowed along in a seemingly effortless manner. As one pursues the items subject to penalization in this and the previous Meisterlied, one has the impression that the young singer had indeed memorized the list without, however, deeming it worth putting into over-all practice for himself.

| | **In dem verhollen don 3 lieder Hans** | 30^r |
| | **saxen gedicht** | |

1	Mein jünges hercz ist freüdenreich	
	seit mein mündt aber singen sol	30^v
	heilliger geist genad mir leich	
	das ich mein künst bewere wol	
5	zw singen von scherpff vnd gelet /$\overline{e}$	

	Maniger singer fragen dut	
	was in der scherpff zw straffen wer	
	das zw ercleren han ich müt	
	mit kürczen worten gib ich ler	
10	ein künstreicher mich vol verstet /$\overline{e}$	

	Was in gemein zw straffen ist	
	al frist	
	das wirt hÿ nit gemelt	
	wan ider singer wais wol was	
15	man in gemein straffet gar dick	
	das straffet aüch die scherpff merck das	
	vnd dar zw aüch noch siben stick	

157

werden hernach kürczlich erczelt
heimlich eqüifoca merck vort
20   rurende reimen vnd clebsilb
anhenck plint mainvng plinte wort
halbe wort vnd dar zw die milb
hernach die stück ich pas ercler /c̄

2   Haimlich eqüifoca verstan
so sich zwen reimen pinden zw
die pede in dem ein gang
·b· vnd aüch ·p· oder zweÿ ·v·
5   ·j· ·g· ·z· ·s· geleich den sein /c̄

Rürende reimen mercke mich
so raimen oder waissen mit
anderen raimen pinden sich
dar zw sie doch gehoren nit
10   das ist in die scherpff gar vnrein /c̄

Die clebsilben die merck also
ist wo
man krefftigklich zwinget
zbw silben in ein silben hart
15   die paid sollen sten nach dem grünt
vnd der ein vocal wirt erspart
clebet heimelich in dem mündt
hinden oder vor an verstet
das ist ein anhang mercke pal
20   so ·l· ·n· ·r· oder ·s· hang
an einem wort vn ein vocal
da von das wort hat ein nach clang
das ist der scherpff ein vber drit /c̄

3   Von plinter mainvng ich dir sag
vnd plintem wort ist wü man nicht
wort oder meinvng mercken mag
das es ist dünckel vnd vnlicht
5   das ist strefflich vm argen list /c̄

Die halben wort sin bw mon ab
prech einem wort an seinem schwancz
ein silben oder ein püstab
das es wür vnüerstentlich gancz
10   ist in der scherpff strefflich al frist /c̄

Die milben aigentlich merck dw
ist wü

31ʳ

gencztlich verschwigen wir
der vocal ·i· oder das ·e·
15 dar dürch verkürchet wirt ein silb
miten inn einem wort verste
des geleichen ist aüch ein milb
so ein vocal zweÿ wort reigir
also han ich erclert süptÿl
20 die straff der scherpff laüder vnd clar
welicher dar in singet vil
vnd alle straff vermaidet gar
der dreit pillich der künst ein krancz /̄e 1516 /̄e

The fourth song in this group, composed also in the year 1516, is an allegory, original with Hans Sachs, pertaining to the origin of Meistergesang.[1] For this he uses the symbol of a beautiful garden which he describes in detail throughout most of the first strophe. To his depiction he adds that people came from far and near to partake of the fruits of this garden until some powerful enemies of the king to whom it belonged prevented their doing so by beleaguering it. Beginning with the second strophe Hans Sachs then gives his interpretation: the garden represents Meistergesang; the king is the Holy Ghost, the source of this noble art; his twelve servants are the Twelve Masters; the golden fence is Holy Writ; the seven portals stand for the Seven Liberal Arts; the grapevines and flowers are various kinds of poems; and the spring with its rivulets denotes the melody without which a Meisterlied could not exist. In the third stanza he explains that the enemies of the king are those persons who war against God with their sins. Since they do not have His grace to learn the art of Meistergesang, they deride the songs of a Master and hold only that person to be artistic who thinks up new poetic creations. Wisdom and art, Hans Sachs declares, are scorned, wherefore the world is destitute. These last statements may perhaps voice his indignation at the lack of attention paid to Meistergesang; it is possible he encountered such neglect as he traversed the land. Yet in spite of this state of affairs he maintains that the "garden" will be preserved by those imbued with art who will work constantly therein.

Wackernagel published this Meisterlied under the title, "Der heilige vrspring des meistergesanges."[2]

In Regenpogens langen don 3 lieder   32^r
H S gedicht

1   Ein edler gartten wart gepaüen
                 von einem künig het zwelff diner wol behüt
                 dar vm da ging von golt ein zaün
                 dar an da waren siben guldin pforten ℞

       5   Zwelff weinstock waren wol gehaüen
                 in mitten stant ein paüm der het dreÿ este güt   32^v
                 dar peÿ ein lilgen zweÿg was praün
                 veÿel rossen stünden an allen orten ℞

                 Miten in dissem gartten qüal
      10   ein prinlein was geleit mit meisterscheffte
                 in dissem gartten vberall
                 da von enpfingen alle fricht jr kreffte
                 wer zw dem gartten kam gemein
                 vnd disser fricht begert
      15   von den zwelffen dem würden sie peschert

der fricht hollet man weit vnd ver
nün het der küng gros feintschafft ich melt
die kamen dar mit einem her
schlügen vor dem gartten aüf ire zelt
20 verschrancketen al weg vnd steg
nossen doch selber nit der frichte wert
vnd lissen nÿmant dar zw ein
wen sie ergriffen wart von in peschwert /ͤ

2 Hort was bedeüt vns disser garte
er deüt meister gesang die hoch süptille künst
der künig ist der heillig geist
von dem die künst hat iren vrespringe /ͤ

5 Zwelff diner die zwelff maÿster zarte
der gülde zaün ist die heillig geschrifft mit günst
siben pfortten werden beweist
das sein die siben freÿen künst ich singe /ͤ

Dar dürch mon in den gartten gät
10 die wein stock sind vns die gedicht pedeÿte
von dem gelaüben mich verstet
der paüm bedeüt von der driüalttikÿte
alle gedicht süptil vnd hach
die lilgen ich pericht
15 das lob das von maria wirt gedicht
feÿel vnd rossen manger leÿ
sin al hofflich gedicht der meister vil
der prün pedeüt die melodeÿ
vnd alle meisterliche don süptil
20 vn die kein frucht becliben kan
wer sich dan zw dissem garten verpflicht
vnd disser kunst ringet nach
dem werden pald zw deil der edlen fricht /ͤ

3 Die feind die vmb denn gartten ligen
vnd aüf geschlagen han ir czelt weit vnde preit
vnd han verschrancket weg vndt stras
das selbÿg sind al menschen die ich melde /ͤ

5 Die in sinden wider got krigen
mit hoffart geicz fülereÿ vnd vnlaüterheit
mit mordereÿ neid vnde has
gotschwervng spil ist vol al disse welde /ͤ

Die han der genad nit von got
10 das sie soliche kunst mochten gelernen

33ͬ

sie dreiben aüch dar aus den spot
wü sie gesang von einem meister heren
sÿ sind in sünden hart verwünt
vnd kein aüf merckvng han
15   der frücht die in dem edlen gartten stan
wer posheit vnd neü fünt bedracht
den halten disse leüt vür künsten reich
weisheit vnd künst wirt gar veracht
dar vm stet es in der welt kümerleich
20   idoch der gart enthalten wirt
aüf erdt von mangem künsten reichem man
der dar in erbeit alle stünt
dem gab der künig dort ewigen lan /e̅
/e̅ 1516 /e̅

This Meisterlied seems almost a corollary to the song written a year earlier (No. 29, wherein Hans Sachs advocated that singers adapt their themes to their audiences) in that it shows what an illimitable field of subject matter he envisioned for Meistergesang. As he plied his trade over the length and breadth of the land, he tells us, he sought in vain among the many singers whom he heard for a gifted Master who with honor before all men was wearing a crown of this art. How gladly would he have bowed before him, listened to him, and learned from him! And that which the young journeyman desired to learn encompasses the universe. Not only did he want to know about the art of Meistergesang, about courtly poetry, songs of all kinds, and unusual melodies, but also about the mysteries appertaining to God and to the celestial hierarchy; about his fellow human beings, from those in the ecclesiastical ranks on down to the lower stations of life; about Turks, Jews, and the heathen. As if this were not enough, there then come pouring out from his pen in kaleidoscopic fashion further innumerable things on, in, and above the earth, concerning which he fain would have knowledge. After that breathless recital it is no wonder that he closes with the few brief words that whosoever will teach him about all of the aforementioned may joyfully begin, for he himself will be silent. With this Meisterlied Hans Sachs reveals his own insatiable thirst for knowledge (and perhaps even his secret wish for more education), and, already dimly conscious of what he himself would accomplish, gives us a forecast of his own creativeness. No one besides himself in the field of Meistergesang ever ranged over so much diverse material as he did, and no one could teach him all that he had outlined, for it is he who is the Master whom he envisions.

Schnorr von Carolsfeld published this Meisterlied from the Dresden MS. M 100, there labeled "Schulkunst."[1] Mummenhof printed the first two *Stollen* and the last six verses of the poem in a more modern German.[2]

       In der vberhohen perck weis Hans Saxen   38^V
       vnd sein gedicht 3 lieder

1   Ich
         pin geczogen ver vnd weit
         lang zeit
         allenthalb ich vil singer vandt
5   der hort ich singen ane zil
         vil
         mit worten grob vnd nit süptil
         sie hetten gar cleinen verstandt
         vnd daüchten sich doch meister sein
10   gar clein
         was da ir künst
         gen rechter künst ein schercze /ẽ

Dar
vmb han ich begeret lang
15 gesang
von einem künstenreichen münd
der disser künste drüg ein kron
schon
mit eren wol vor ider man
20 wü ich ein solchen meister fünd
gen dem wolt ich mich naigen ser
ob er
mir zaigt dürch günst
der rechten künsten strasse /ℓ̃

25 War
lich kein straff solt mich von im verdrisse
ob ich mocht leren disse künst so sÿsse
det er sein künsten reichen mündt aüf schlisse
so
30 wolt ich von im leren
geren
der siben künsten keren
süs
in scherpff zal vnd masse
35 mercken lert ich mit fleisse   40ʳ
schen
hofflich sprich da peÿe
ach
gesang manger leÿe
40 freÿe
neÿe
mit süsser melodeÿe
den
die fremd selczam seÿe
45 dem meister gib ich preisse
güs
er mir aüff mein hercze
do
von das ich lert dichten
50 schlichten
von mangerleÿ geschichten
nach
den offt hat verlanget mich /ℓ̃

2   Das
er von erst mich leren det

164

```
        verstet
        von dem wessen der gotheit freÿ
  5     vnd wÿ mensch worden ist der sun
        vün
        Maria der parmüng prün
        vnd von der engel jerracheÿ
        vnd von dem himelischen sal
 10     an czal
        vnd von der schar
        aller heilligen gancze /k̄c

        Vnd
        von dem geistlichen stant wert
 15     auf ert
        von pebsten vnd aüch von der süm
        cardinel vnd pischoff mit ler
        mer
        von epten vnd von probsten her
 20     von minich closter frawen früm
        vnd von der werden pristerschafft
        pehafft
        vnd laütter clar
        von der heiligen schriffte /k̄c

 25     künt
        er mich leren dichten adeleichen
        von keisser künigen in allen reichen
        von fürsten herzogen graffen des gleichen
        hoch
 30     von edlen geschlechten
        rechten
        von ritteren von knechten
        schon
        was sie hon gestiffte
 35     vnd von iren reigiren
        vil
        von hofflichen dingen
        wie
        man die mag verpringen
 40     springen
        singen
        von saiten spil *erclingen*
        [*zil*
        *laufen fechten ringen*]
 45     *von stechen* vnd dürniren
        von
```

essen drincken dancze
och
von stürmen vnd streitten
50 reitten
lert er mich das bezeiten
nÿ
lies ich ab ich lert vurpas /c̅

3 Von
allen stenden vnderzelt
der welt
von pürger pawer aüch dapeÿ
5 von frawen vnd jünckfrewelein
fein
von dürck jud heiden ich aüch mein
von kaufmonscheffte mangerleÿ
von kranckheiten von lieb vnd leit
10 von freit
vnd manig valt
von dügenden von sünden /c̅

Vÿr
pas von allem das do lept
15 vnd schwept
in lüft wasser ert vnde feur
von allerleÿ diren geschlecht
recht
wie mon sie ein der wildnüs specht
20 von mangem würme vngeheür
von mer wünderen gar selczam
der nam
ist vnerzalt
von vo̊gel vnd von vischen /c̅

25 Zir
lich von allem das aüf erd ÿe wasse
von früchten würczen kreütten laub vnd grasse
von gold silber küpfer perlein vnd glasse
vnd
30 von merck stetten alle
zalle
von welden pergen dalle
saüs
von wasseren frischen
35 vnd wie das mer vmfange
gar

```
       hat der welt vmkreisse
       me
       von dem paradeisse
40     weisse
       leisse
       vnd von der helle heise
       dar
       zw von reiff schne eisse
45     des firmamentes gange
       aüs
       den planeten zünden
       künt
       seÿ wer mich süptille
50     wille
       leren so schweig ich stille
       fre
       lich heb disser meister an /ſ̄e̅ 1516 /ſ̄e̅
```

Hans Sachs labels this Meisterlied "ein plos gedicht," a song without rhymes, which with an undertone of mockery he may have written as a challenge to the Masters to supply the proper substitutes for his unrhymed words. Unlike the traditional greeting addressed to all of the Masters he singles out the one who, like unto a treasure chest, is filled with "art," and commends him to the care of God, then shifts to the plural in the second *Stollen*. Ironically he decries his own lack of talent and says that he has come to hear singing so that he might transmute his inadequate skill into "art," an inclination he has had since he was young (he is now twenty-three). Through exaggerated praise of the artistry of the Masters, repeated references to "art," three times modified by the word precise, and the use of the verbs "grinding" and "digging," Hans Sachs veils his derision of those who deem themselves Masters because of their strict observance of the minutiae of the rules.

     Schnorr von Carolsfeld published this Meisterlied from the Dresden MS M 8 under the title "Ein Ploss gedicht von H. Sachs."[1]

In dem kürczen don Müglings   28ᵛ
ein plŏs H S gedicht

1   Got grües den meister güt
     got hab in schon in seiner pfleg
     seit das er get der künsten stras
     vnd ist der künst ein voller schrein /c̄

   5   Ir habt der künsten schacz
     dar vmb so küm ich aüf den plan
     wie wol ich nit vil künste hab
     das pringet meinem herczen we /c̄

     Darvmb so wolt ich geren horen singen   29ʳ
  10   ob ich mein plosse reimen mocht beczwicke
     vnkünst in künst verwandlen
     dar zw het ich von jügent günst /c̄

2   Meister mit künsten scharpff
     erclünget ir gesanges geig
     recht sam ein meüslein ich stil ses
     ob ich die künst erkennen kent /c̄

   5   scharpf künst die sin so wech
     ob ich nit eben dar auf schawt
     so wür die stras mir pal verpont
     das ich nit keme zw dem ort /c̄

     Wan scharpffer künste der sind alss mengerleÿe
  10   wol dem meister dem sie al wonen mite

aüs seines herczen mille
so melt er manig schone rank /rc̄

3   Dar vmb meister lobsam
seit das ir habet maister werck
vnd grabet in der künste hol
lat schawen ewer gülde ercz /rc̄

5 Wan ich grüntlich wol weis
da ir gewinet hÿ das lob
wan eüer künst die ist nit schwach
new künst habt ir in ewrem sin /rc̄

Die wolt ich von eüch also geren heren
10 ob ich der aüch ein dail hÿ mecht gemercken
ich pit eüch düt hÿ nemen
in eÿttel gut mein plos gedicht /rc̄
/rc̄ 1517 /rc̄

While Hans Sachs was listening to one Meistersinger after another in the *Singschulen* which he visited, it must have been brought home to him how unequal these Masters were in the practice of their art and how lacking some of them were in poetic gifts. Perhaps it was then that he conceived this allegory, a simple one, but did not write it down until 1517. He begins by praising a cool, bubbling spring over and above a large pond which is without a source, because the latter, subject to the heat of the day, becomes stagnant, useless, and unpleasantly odorous, whereas the former, constantly freshened by its own underground waters, is unaffected by the sun's rays. The interpretation is sketchy, for only the spring is definitely identified as the poet who creates songs from out of his poetic imagination; it is simply inferred that the pond represents the singer who receives his verses from another. Because of the fact that the singer has blazed no new trails and that his art perishes with him, Hans Sachs bestows upon him a green wreath, but he awards the poet a crown of gold, since it is through him that new art arises and lives on even after his death. With such a one Hans Sachs could identify himself. Here once again we find affirmation of his strong belief in his own calling.

Goedeke published the Meisterlied under the appropriate title "Dichter und Singer"; Lützelmann-Frommann and Weddigen have taken their copy of the poem from Goedeke.[1]

      In der silber weis Hans Saxen   37^V
      vnd sein gedicht 3 lieder

1   Ich
         lob ein prünlein küle
         mit vrsprünges aüf wülle   38^r
         vür ein gros wasser hülle
    5   die keinen vrsprüng hat /$\overline{\kappa e}$

         Sich
         allein müs besechen
         mit zw flissenden pechen
         der prünlein mag ich sprechen
  10   die hül nit lang bestat /$\overline{\kappa e}$

         Wan von der sünen grosse hicz
         im sümer langen dag
         die hul wirt faul vnd gar vnicz
         gewinnt possen geschmack
  15   sie drücknet ein wirt grün vnd gelb
         so frischet sich das prünlein selb
         mit seinem vresprünge
         beleibet vnpezwunge
         von der sünen scheinvnge
  20   es wirt nit faul noch mat /$\overline{\kappa e}$

2 Das
  prünlein ich geleiche
  einem dichter künstreiche
  der gesanck anfenckleiche
5 dichtet aüs künsten gründt /℥

  Pas
  lob ich den mit rechte
  vür einen singer schlechte
  der sein gesang enpfechte
10 aüs eines fremden mündt /℥

  Wan so enspringet neüe künst
  noch scherpffer dan die alt
  des singers gesang ist vm sünst
  er wirt geschweiget palt
15 er kon nit gen neüe gespor
  sie seÿ im dan geponet vor
  durch dem dichter on scherczen
  der aüs künstreichem herczen
  kan dichten ane schmerczen
20 neü gesang alle stündt /℥

3 Wan
  alle künst aüf erden
  deglich gescherpffet werden
  von grobheit vnd geferden
5 die man vor dar in vant /℥

  Van
  gesang ich eüch sage
  das es von dag zw dage
  noch scherpffer werden mage
10 durch den dichter verstant /℥   38ᵛ

  Dar vmb gib ich dem dichter gancz
  ein kron van rottem golt
  vnd dem singer ein grünen krancz
  dar peÿ ir mercken solt
15 kem der singer aüf dotes par
  sein künst mit im ab stirbet gar
  wirt der dichter begraben
  sein künst wirt erst erhaben
  müntlich vnd in pustaben
20 gar weit in mengem lant /℥
  /℥ 1517 /℥

Among the forbidden songs which Hans Sachs listed in his Meisterlied on "al straff" (No. 30) is the "loica," and yet here in defiance of the rules, he has written one and so labels it. Although it carries no date, it was entered into Berlin 414 when the poet was still writing the vowel *u* as *ü*. Furthermore, since it precedes nine other Meisterlieder written in 1518, that year may perhaps also be assigned to it.[1] The opening verses voice the author's consternation at the fact that his sharp skill has been cut to pieces; that he can never be like the Masters who are so rich in this exact art. Accordingly he requests them to continue with their songs because they sing with such mastery that they are never penalized, whereas he seldom appears before the *Singschule* with his art. He says that he grants them the Master's chair with pleasure and crowns their art above his own, asserting at the same time that he is not speaking mockingly. And yet that is exactly what he is doing. One senses his deep chagrin at the treatment accorded himself in contrast to that given the other Masters. The mockery is even more pronounced where he speaks figuratively. The invitation to his house, there to partake of food and drink, to spend the night, and to borrow money, may mean that he is offering them his own poetic work, no matter what the cost to himself. Everything is nicely laid out for them; nothing is wanting. They may take without giving him credit. Possibly this had already occurred, just as we have seen how Holtzmann somewhat later virtually appropriated one of these early Meisterlieder (No. 32).

In zwingers rottem don ein loi   437ᵛ
ca 3 lieder hans Saxen
gedicht

1   Hercz sine mut ist mir worden erschrecket
      nie weitter wart mir vor ein zil gestecket
      das ist mein scharpffe kunst al hÿ verschniten /̃℮

      Mit nichte mag ich eüch meister geleiche
5   wan ir on scharpffer kunst seit also reiche
      dar vmb meister so dw ich eüch hÿ pitten /̃℮

      Nit lasset von eurem gesang
      wan ir singet aüs reicher meister schaffte
      gar wenig zw kürcz vnd zw lang
10   aüf der künsten schul seit ir vngestraffte
      gar selten ich mit künste
      küm aüf der singer schul
      der meister stül
      wÿrt euch von mir mit günste
15   nÿe valet ir in spottes pfül /̃℮

2 Dar vmb ich eüer künst vür die mein kröne
 gar nit in spottes weis ich euch hie höne
 ich spot hie nit seÿet zw mir geladen /ꝛ̄

 Mercket meister heim in mein haüs zw mire
5 schmecket eich wein nit hol ich malvasire
 ich las es nit precht es mir grose schaden /ꝛ̄

 Einen placz mon euch pachen sol
 in schwarczer prw gib ich euch vorhen aschen
 vnd ein pretlein gesalczen wol
10 dar aüf maget ir eüren goder waschen
 dar zw auch ein geschlagen   438ʳ
 oxen augen ich gib
 ir seit mir lib
 nit weitter solt ir fragen
15 das eüch ein kelt peÿ mir bedrib /ꝛ̄

3 Wan mein offen der hat vnholcz kein note
 vnd auch mein disch on weissem kes vnd prote
 vnd ob ir aüch peÿ mir penachtet wÿrte /ꝛ̄

 So lis ich eüch die nacht peÿ mir peleibe
5 mit nichte wolt ich euch von mir aüs dreibe
 wan mein haüs ist on petstat wol gezirte /ꝛ̄

 Meister dar vmb so kümet pal
 hat ir gelt nit on pfant wil ich euch porgen
 achtent nit wer die vrten zal
10 was ich verheis dar vmb dürfft ir nit sorgen
 in künsten wol wir scherczen
 vnd leben in dem saüs
 in meinem haüs
 meister aüs ganczem herczen
15 pitt ich eüch nit beleibet aüs /ꝛ̄   [s.d.]

173

This Meisterlied is seemingly a companion piece to the preceding one in that Hans Sachs designates it also as a "loica." Although no date is affixed to the poem in Berlin 414, the Keller-Goetze Index supplies it, namely "1518 März 13." There, too, we find the information that the song is directed "wider ein hoffertigen singer."[1] The tone of the poem is derisive. Without any greeting the poet declares that a Master has taken a thrust at his own technical skill and that, therefore, he will no longer fence with him. In order not to increase his own shame, he would like to learn the Master's art of which he himself possesses but little. From this point on by means of exaggeration, innuendo, ambiguity, and now and then a direct attack, Hans Sachs delivers blow after blow to his opponent. A discerning Meistersinger could well have called out "touché" upon hearing this song.

In der grünt weÿs frawen   438ʳ
lobs 3 lieder Hans
Saxen gedicht loica

1   Ein meister hat on künsten mich gestochen
        des las ich hie mein pochen
        nit mer wil ich wÿder in fechten sein /℞

        Aüf das ich nit mein grosse schant dw mere
5   mocht ich sein künst gelere
        der ist gar wenig in dem herczen mein /℞

        Zw rechter künst
        so drag ich günst
        wü ich dÿe hör
10   von eüch hab ich gehort eüer gedichte
        das ist zw straffen nichte
        gib ich eüch hÿ vor ÿder mon dÿ ör /℞

2   Wan ir seit ÿe ein meister lobesane
        der er ich euch wol gane
        nie scharpffe künst ich in mein hercz peschlüs /℞

        Ir seit in künst gar scharpff sübtil nit grobe   438ᵛ
5   geleichet frawen lobe
        ia hinter dem offen ich siczen müss /℞

        Vnd haber rw
        euch horen zw
        gar künstlichen ir seit
10   ein grober essel künt das nit gemercken
        eüer lob wil ich stercken
        nit mein ich das in künst der drogenheit /℞

3   Was ir eüch rümet hant ir hie verprachte
mit nichte ich gedachte
wie hoche künst in eüch verporgen leg /c̄e

Nü ist es nichs was ich hie hab gesüngen
5   zw schar der meister züngen
so nemet meister von mir ewren weg /c̄e

Zw andren nar
en ich auch var
da ich mein geleich vant
10   zw lecz meister secz ich eüch auf dÿ krone
der schande seit ir one
der rechten künst ein dürch varer der lant /c̄e   [s.d.]

I have included this particular Meisterlied of 1518 in the group of songs treating of Meistergesang because it has an indirect bearing thereon in its third strophe.[1] The poem is a tabulation of the distinguishing attributes by which one may recognize matter of one kind or another. After a brief mention of day and night and the stars, Hans Sachs devotes the rest of the first strophe to the animal kingdom ending with the feature which characterizes the human substance. This then serves as a natural transition to the second stanza in which man appears in specific walks of life, each of which in turn can be recognized by one particular item. At the close of that strophe the poet says one can also deduce man's heart and mind by means of signs, a statement which carries us on to the abstract qualities of man, the subject of the third and last stanza. The conclusions which Hans Sachs has drawn from human nature in its numerous aspects of life show how keenly perceptive he was even at this early age. But here and there among the observations in the third stanza are also a few which, one may surmise, intimate the state of his own mind at that precise time: when he says that fellowship can be recognized by loyalty (9), that one notes goodwill if a person speaks well of someone (13), that the work itself reveals its art (14), and that friendship is apparent in time of necessity (22). Perhaps it was the absence of such positive values in the *Singschule* in Nuremberg that troubled the young poet and caused him to close with the remark that his heart would rejoice if it were not for one thing. Moreover, the appended words "Nit on vrsach," borrowed as they were, seem to underscore the inference that he had a reason for his disappointment: the attitude of his fellow Nuremberg-Meistersinger toward himself.

Goedeke published this Meisterlied under the title "Kennzeichen."[2]

In der hohen dag weis Hans Sach   462ᵛ
sen vnd sein gedicht 3 lieder

1   Mon kent den hohen dage
           pey der sǔnen ich sage
           die nacht man kennen kan
           peÿ dem driglichen schein der man
    5   die steren peÿ dem glancze /ℓ /ℓ /ℓ

           Den krenich peÿ dem krage
           den straŭs peÿ seinem mage
           vnd peÿ dem kam den han
           peÿ weiser far kent man den schwan
    10   den pfaben peÿ dem schwancze /ℓ

           Mon kent die nachtigale
           peÿ irem sǔsen hale
           die lerch peÿ dem gesang

den storch peÿ seinem schnabel lang
15 den widhopff peÿ der gŭpffen
den Igel pey dem stŭpffen
vnd an dem laůf das rĕch
das kamel dir peÿ seiner hŏch
die schlangen peÿ dem schlŭpffen
20 den frosch peÿ seinem hŭpffen
an dem springen die flŏch
den fŭchs peÿ seinen listen spĕch
den hŭnt peÿ seinem kale
den esel peÿ dem vale
25 den krebs peÿ seinem gang
peÿ dem antlicz kent man an zwang
art menschlicher sŭbstancze /ē

2   Den ritter peÿ den sporen
den jeger peÿ dem horen
den reŭter an dem drab
den waller kent mann peÿ dem stab
5 den kŭnig peÿ der krane /ē

Peÿ den schellen den doren
vnd peÿ der schwercz den moren
den reichen peÿ der hab
das weib peÿ den prŭsten gelab
10 vnd peÿ dem part den mane /ē

Am carmen den poeten
denn weissen peÿ den retten
den mŭnich peÿ der kŭt
den wŭnden kent man peÿ dem plŭt
15 den plinten peÿ dem gange
den meistter peÿ dem gsange
den fechter am parat
die jŭnckfraů peÿ dem krancz verstat
vnd den dip peÿ dem strange
20 denn schmidt peÿ hamer zange
den paůren peÿ der watt
den mader kent man an dem matt
den pfeŭfer peÿ der fletten
den gfangen peÿ der ketten
25 also man kennen dŭt
des menschen hercz vnd seinen mŭt
peÿ den zeichen verstane /ē

Peÿ lachen kent man freyden
peÿ weinen kent man leiden
dorheit peÿ fanthaseÿ
peÿ achiczen do kent man reÿ
5   peÿ seüfczen kent man schwere /℗

Hoffart kent man peÿ geiden
feintschafft kent man von meiden
pedrüg mit schmaichlareÿ
geselschafft kent man peÿ der dreÿ
10   peÿ zücht do kent man ere /℗

lieb peÿ den aügen plicken
holtschafft peÿ hentlein drÿcken
peÿ wol sprechvng die günst
vnd peÿ dem werck kent man die künst
15   vn vernünft peÿ dem krigen
vorcht kent man peÿ dem schmigen
scham kent man on der rĕtt
schwacheit kent man peÿ gilb verstett
peÿ vil geschwecz das ligen
20   geicz kent man peÿ pedrigen
verachtung peÿ gespett
freüntschafft kent man in grosser nett
vndrew peÿ hinder dicken   463ᵛ
wol dem der sich kan schicken
25   aüs kantnüs der vernünst
des stet stünd mein hercz in freüden prünst
wen nür ein sach nit were /℗
      Nit on vrsach 1518

In this Meisterlied, written in 1518, Hans Sachs seems to be depicting matters related to the Nuremberg *Singschule*. He employs Latin abstract nouns as personifications to build up an allegory, but does not interpret it. This he leaves to his hearers. To introduce his story he again avails himself of the convention of a walk, but motivates it by stating that common sense told him to do so in order to refresh his mind. During the course of his stroll, he says, he lay down in the shade of a linden tree, fell asleep, and dreamed that he saw a wondrously beautiful young woman hastening toward him. Even before she greeted him he noticed that her right hand had been wounded, and that she was pregnant. Since she seemed so sad, he politely inquired her name and the cause of her distress. Her reply furnishes the allegory. When Hans Sachs copied the poem into the first book of his Meisterlieder he provided a clue to its meaning by entitling it "Die falsch geselschaft."[1] This precludes an interpretation (to which at a first reading one might have been inclined) in which the vices of pride, envy, and disloyalty are arrayed against virtuous tradition and naturalness, etc. The alignment of the vices and virtues remains the same, but their abstractions are now subordinated to the concrete, namely to a picturization of the Nuremberg *Gesellschaft*, the *Singschule*, at the time that Hans Sachs returned from his journeyman travels.

Mindful then of the title in Mg. 1, "Die falsch geselschaft," my interpretation runs thus: "societas," the name of the lovely lady with the voice of a nightingale, would symbolize the Nuremberg *Singschule*, and her mother, "fraw dreÿe," its tradition. "societas" tells the poet that she once entered the garden, which would be Meistergesang, of "fraw sciencie," who perhaps represents the Seven Liberal Arts, a knowledge of which the Meistersinger deemed essential for the writing of their Meisterlieder. There she partook of the fruit "superbia," pride, which caused her to become pregnant with "invidia," that is, filled with envy. Shortly thereafter "perfidia," faithlessness, wounded the right hand of "societas"; by this the poet may mean that the *Singschule*, because of its betrayal of the trust which had been placed in it, was no longer able to produce fine songs as heretofore. It wasn't long until "societas" was expelled from the garden, signifying perhaps that the *Singschule* was disrupted. Her penitent return to "fraw dreÿe" may imply that the *Singschule* decided to go back to tradition, but since envy and the lack of ability to write (the wounded hand) were still present, "fraw dreÿe" drove her daughter out of the land, in other words, one no longer heard of the Nuremberg *Singschule*. More deeply grieved than ever, "societas" sought out Queen "simplicitas," which perhaps denotes that as a last resort the *Singschule* thought a return to simplicity (artlessness), might help the situation. However, when the queen discovered "societas' " impaired condition (pregnancy and wounded hand) which "societas" had tried to conceal, she banished her from court. Now the Nuremberg *Singschule*, in so far as fame was concerned, ceased to exist.

At this point Hans Sachs identifies himself with the situation, for upon "societas' " statement that she is completely miserable, he tells her he feels sorry for her and will give her his unswerving loyalty provided she will love him always. The two plight their troth, but at that moment he awakens and finds himself deluded. This, it seems to me, is revelatory of his wish to revive the Nuremberg *Singschule* and of his joy that a union between it and himself might be consumated. But it was only a dream, and the awakening was rude. Fulfillment still lay in the future.

In der hohen dagweis Hans sachsen vnd sein gedicht

1
    Ein mal wolt ich stŭdiren
    da schwindlet mir mein hiren
    dar von wardt mein gedicht
    vnd inmaiginacz gar entwicht
5   scharpff kŭnst die ward mir zanger /ℰ̄

    Mein vernŭfft gŭnt mich riren
    ich solt ein weil spaciren
    vnd frischen mein gesicht
    also ich meinen gang hie richt
10 aŭf einen grŭnen anger /ℰ̄

    Vnder ein grŭne linde
    da ich wardt schaten vinde
    ich leit mich in das gras
    dar dŭrch ein kleines pechlein flas
15 von einem kŭlen prŭne
    ein schlaff kam mir gerŭnne
    aus fraw zithera sal
    ich er plicket in schlaffes qŭal
    ein fraŭen pild mit wune
20 ir antlicz als die sŭne
    dŭrch glenczet perg vnd dal
    ir stim hel als der nachtigal
    ir gang schnel als der winde
    ir kleid pŭrpŭr ich kinde
25 wŭnd ir rechte hant was
    ir aŭgen voller zeher nas
    vnd was von leib gros schwanger /ℰ̄

2
    Das wŭnderliche pilde
    kert zw mir aŭs der wilde
    grŭset mich zw der zeit
    darnach in groser draŭrikeit
5   zw meinem haŭbet stŭnde /ℰ̄

Ich sprach důrch eůer milde
ob es eůch nit pefilde
saget mir wer ir seit
vnd aůch von eůer schwangerheit
10   vnd wer eůch hab verwůnde /ℇ

Sie sprach mein nam der iste
fraw societas wiste
mein můter heist fraw dreÿ
hort wie ich schwanger worden seÿ
15   ich kam eins in den garte
fraw sciencie zarte
do as ich armes weib
der frůcht sůperbia die dreib
wider natůrlich arte
20   das ich geschwengert warte
der frůcht in meinem leib
heist in vidia also pleib
ich da ein kůrcze friste
pervidia mit liste
25   kam mit grosem geschreÿ
hib mir mein rechte hant entzweÿ
vnd mich aůs dreiben gůnde /ℇ

3   Also kert ich in reÿe
wider hin ze fraw dreÿe
zw handt sie da mein frůcht
vnd auch mein wůnde handt verflůcht
5   vnd drib mich aůs dem lande /ℇ

Do wůrd mein leid erst neÿe
die edlen kůngin freÿe
simplicitas ich sůcht
vnd verparg da mit groser zůcht
10   mein frůcht vnd wůnde hande /ℇ

Also es mir gelicket
pis die kingin er plicket
das mein er wardt geschmacht
vnd aůch mein rechte hant geschwacht   464ᵛ
15   zw hant sie mir abschribe
den hoff vnd mich verdribe
nůn pin gancz ellent ich
do sprach ich fraw ir daůret mich
mein dreÿ ich eůch hie gibe
20   wolt ir in rechter libe

181

mich liben stetiklich
mein dreÿ ich ÿ an eŭch nit prich
vnser dreŭ wŭrd verstricket
in freŭd wŭrd wir er qŭicket
25 ir rottes mŭndlein lacht
in dem aŭgenplick ich erwacht
vnd mich pedrogen fande /Ꞓ
1518

This is the last one of Hans Sachs' own Meisterlieder which he copied into Berlin 414. It was written in 1518. Again he uses the device of taking a walk to present an allegory, although a modified one, forasmuch as the fishermen whom he observed do not represent certain persons, merely remind him of them, and the meaning of their torn net and of the fish which they caught is simply implied, not stated. Most likely the poet drew upon his own experience in creating this allegorical incident, for it is directed primarily at the *Merker*. Just as the fishermen ensnared small fish but let large ones escape, so the *Merker* perhaps chalked up minute errors against Hans Sachs at the same time that they failed to penalize the gross errors committed by other singers. He must have been extremely irritated at this in the same way that he was vexed at the fishermen for having a net with large holes in it. Such carelessness caused him to lose interest in their fishing, he says, signifying, it may be, that he no longer found joy in singing before his fellow Meistersinger. His closing words of advice for those who would fish to have untorn nets intimate a need for betterment in the Nuremberg *Singschule*, a matter which in time he himself was to bring about.

      In dem lieben don Caspar   468^r
      singers von eger Hans
      Sachsen gedicht 3 lieder

1   Ein mal was mir mein weil gar lang
                ich det durch kŭrczweil einen gang
                da ich hort der vogel gesang
                in feihel kle
     5   peÿ einem prŭnlein frischen /ℓ̄

                Dar aŭs flos gar ein schoner pach
                dem selbigen ging ich lang nach
                pis ich dŭrch ein staŭden ersach
                ein grossen se
    10   ˏ dar auf sah ich wol fischen /ℓ̄

                Drey fischer daŭchten sich gar klŭg
                gŭnden ir necz ein deichen
                der ein pald in den wage schlŭg
                die fischlein gŭnden streichen   468^v
    15   klein vnde gros an mas vnd zal
                da ward ich stan
                mit ganczem schwal
                gŭnden dem necz zw schleichen /ℓ̄

2   Jir necz was eng vnd gar sŭbtil
           fingen der kleinen fischlein fil
           sengel steinpeis grŭndel vnd pfril
           die fischer dreÿ
  5   günden in freuden praŭssen /c̄

           Jch sach ein ding das mich verdros
           das necz het vil der locher gros
           das dŭrch manig gros fisch aus schos
           hechten vnd schleÿ
10   karpfen hŭchen vnd haŭssen /c̄

           Da dacht ich in dem herczen mein
           der vnfleisigen sachen
           das mŭgen wol los fischer sein
           das sie ir necz nit machen
15   vnd grosse visch auch fahen dan
           da ward ich stan
           vnd ir gar spötlich lachet /c̄

3   Jch dacht der fischer mich ermant
           der dŭmen mercker die da hant
           reigister nach irem verstant
           scharpff vnd gelat
  5   mercken kleb vnd die milben /c̄

           Vnd vber horen doch darpeÿ
           gancz stŭcz mŭtirte melodeÿ
           plose laster vnd wie dem seÿ
           vŭr solich dat
10   seczen sie keinen silben /c̄

           Also kert jch von dissem se
           vnd lies die fischer faren
           irs fischen lŭstet mich nit mer
           wan sie los fischer waren
15   dar vm rat ich wer fischen welt
           das er pestelt   469^r
           ein vnzŭrissen garen /c̄   1518 jar /c̄

Linguistic Summary

These early Meisterlieder in large measure reflect not only the state of flux existent in the German language during the decade which ushered in the Reformation, but also Hans Sachs' Nuremberg-Bavarian dialect (Weinhold, *Bairische Grammatik*—cited henceforth W. *BGr.*—, p. 11, note, declares that the Nuremberg dialect is *bairisch*, but that, p. 12, it occupies *eine besondere Stellung*). To a lesser degree they give evidence of possible borrowings from the speech of fellow Meistersinger or of other persons with whom he came into contact as he journeyed about working at his trade (see, for instance, the Middle German forms here and there), and occasionally from the books he was reading (see the Background for Chapters III and IV). In addition they refute the assumption that Hans Sachs used any expedient to fill the pattern of Meistergesang, for, with the exception of a small percentage, his deviations from Middle High or Early New High German are legitimate forms of his Nuremberg-Bavarian dialect. The exceedingly few fragmentary studies of the poet's language have been based on his printed works. According to Drescher (*Studien zu Hans Sachs*, p. 101) "Die Untersuchung über die Sprache, die Hans Sachs schrieb . . . ist noch zu liefern." For this reason I have recorded exactly what I have found in the manuscript.

The data below summarize the findings with regard to orthography, phonology, and morphology, and give examples of some syntax and usage. Unless something special warrants it, therefore, I shall not call attention to individual instances in the Notes.

1. Orthography, Phonology, and Morphology

Vowels, diphthongs, and consonants

For purposes of listing I have arranged these in alphabetical order. I shall give the letter which Hans Sachs uses, the equivalent in modern orthography, the Middle High German in parentheses, and then the verse in which the word illustrating the letter is to be found. Where relevant the Medieval or the Classical Latin letter (abbrev. ML., CL.) will also be indicated. Vowels and consonants for which Hans Sachs makes no substitutions are not listed. He does not distinguish between long and short vowels. At this point I should like to call attention to the fact that he uses the letter $\ddot{u}$ for the vowel u (inclusive of the Latin u) in all except eight of these Meisterlieder. In those eight, which begin on foll. 460^r, he employs the u-hook ($\breve{u}$). Infrequently he omits one or the other superscript and in a very, very few negligible instances he reverts to writing $\ddot{u}$ for $\breve{u}$. The consonantal use of i and $\ddot{u}$ is entered under the consonants and the vocalic use of the consonants j, v, w, and of the character $\ddot{y}$ under the vowels. Documentation for almost all of Hans Sachs' substitutions will be found in W. *BGr., passim.*

185

Vowels

a

a = ä (MHG. *a*): Es růft ein *wachter* faste, 7,1,1.

a = e (MHG. *e*): zw *petlahem* die meit gepar, 9,3,17.

a = o (MHG. o and ô): *lab* er seÿ dem heilligen geist, 1,1,5.

    ein mechtig keisser war zw *ram*, 11,2,3.

a = CL. *ae*; ML. *e*: loÿca *aüiüoca* seit on, 30,1,18 (once).

e

e = a (MHG. *â*): die hoch wirdige *drinidet*, 12,2,16 (once).

e = a (MHG. *a*): an sein *hent* (Hand) sÿ im stisse, 25,8,4 (see the note on this verse).

e = ä (MHG. *e*): der aüser welten *geste*, 5,5,6.

    sie *helt* gehorsam wer sie strafft, 26,2,6.

e = ä (MHG. *æ*): ob sie bedriebet *were*, 3,3,16.

    vnd aüch mein disch on weissem *kes* vnd prote, 36,3,2.

e = e (MHG. *æ*): pistw der *seligkeit* ein pfort, 16,1,14.

e = e (MHG. *î*): in einem *gülden* grabe, 23,10,9.

e = i (MHG. *i*): *wer* erent iren name, 12,3,17 (see the note on this vs.)

e = i (MHG. *î*): der *greffen* det gar we die schmach, 20,4,15 (once).

e = i (MHG. *ei*): on alle schüld *led* er dÿ pein, 8,3,12 (see note 3,1,26).

e = ö (MHG. *ö*): ir nit entrinen *mecht*, 7,1,21.

e = ö (MHG. *oe*): dar vm ich disse dügent *kren*, 27,6,27.

e = ö (MHG. *oi, öu*): den pfeüfer peÿ der *fletten*, 38,2,23 (once).

e = äu (MHG. *öu*): dem zarten *frewenlein*, 7,2,3.

e = CL. *ae*; ML. *e*: in *secüla* . . . / *secülor vm* . . . , 1,1,10-11.

e = CL. and ML. *oe*: sine omni *pena*, 12,1,9.

i

i = ei (MHG. *î*): *din* fraw geporen hat ein dochter vnd lebet, 20,6,7.

i = ie (MHG. *ie*): so *lis* ich eüch die nacht peÿ mir peleibe, 36,3,4.

    das günden sie *gloriren*, 11,3,7 (Hans Sachs spells all verbs ending in *ieren* with an i).

i = je (MHG. *ie*): der sing was *idem* zw gehert, 29,3,25.

i = o (MHG. *ü*): hinder ein *firhang* er do sas, 23,5,8.

i = ö (MHG. *ü*): sie *ginet* im das vnd vil me, 27,4,6.

i = ü (MHG. *ü*): peÿ dem *prinlein* kalt, 22,4,21.

i = ü (MHG. *üe*): *misen* wir alle sterben, 4,3,24.

j

j = i (MHG. *i*): mit schmerczen *jch* vmbfangen pin, 4,1,5.

    enpfjng die mait das himelische kint, 10,2,17.

ji = i (MGH. *i*): *Jist* des menschen vernüft . . . , 22,5,9.

ÿ

Hans Sachs often uses this character in place of the MHG. vowels *i*, *î*, and occasionally *ü*, alone and in a diphthong; also now and then for CL. *i*.

ÿ = i (MHG. *i*): *ÿn* jemerlicher not, 4,1,4.

ÿ = CL. *i:* Gloria *patrÿ* lob vnd er, 1,1,1.

ÿ = ö (MHG. *ü*): des ir der man nit *gÿnde*, 19,1,23.

ÿ = ü (MHG. *ü*): wan es keinem nit zw *gepÿrt*, 1,3,22.

ÿ = ü (MHG. *üe*): dǔ edle jǔnckfraw *sÿs*, 18,3,20.

ÿ = ie (MHG. ie): *lÿs* er die fraw fangen, 19,2,25.

ÿ = ie (MHG. *iu*): *dÿ* hel die stet mir offen, 4,2,45.

ÿ = je (MHG. *ie*): mein dreÿ ich *ÿ* an eǔch nit prich, 39,3,22.

ÿe = ü (MHG. *üe*): sein dochter vil im vür die *fÿes*, 25,11,3.

ÿe = ie (MHG. *ie*): soliches war derhoret *nÿe*, 19,4,4.

ÿe = je (MHG. *ie*): *ÿe* lenger vnd *ÿe* me, 19,1,13.

eÿ = ei (MHG. *î*): . . . zw dissen *weÿhenachten,* 10,1,5.

eÿ = ei (MHG. *ei*): feÿel vnd rossen *manger leÿ*, 32,2,16.

eÿ = ie (MHG. *îe*): mit irer süssen *melodeÿ* (Early NHG. *ei*), 1,1,25.

eÿ = ei (MHG. *îo*): *feÿel* vnd rossen . . ., 32,2,16.

eÿ = eu (MHG. *iu*): das dich fraw *pedeÿdt*, 17,2,37.

aÿ = ei (MHG. ei): du pist der güldin *aÿmer* zart, 16,4,14.

o

o = a (MHG. *a* and *â*): darnach betracht wie *mon* in schlüg, 3,2,11.
     in fleisch vnd plüt gar *drot*, 2,3,2.

o = e (MHG. *ë*): gros *erschrocklich* der sich zw stündt, 25,3,8 (see the note on this verse).

o = ö (MHG. *e*): mag *schopffen* in das grübl klein, 1,3,10.

o = ǒ (MHG. *œ*): vil *schnoder* wort sie vberhort, 27,3,9.

ü (Hans Sachs' *u*)

ü = e (MHG. *e*): gen Athenis was er *vür pflicht*, 28,5,4 (see the note on this verse).

ü = ie (MHG. *ie*): sein hercz man im aüs schneiden *lüs*, 28,7,10 (see the note on this verse).

ü = o (MHG. *ô* and *o*): *wǔ* ir dan seit in grosser net, 20,7,17.
     man *vün* der andren aǔch verstet, 6,1,21.

ü = ö (MHG. *ü*): wan alle ding got *müglich* sent, 2,3,23.

ü = ü (MHG. *üe*): Sie ist *senftmütig* vnd aüch leis, 27,6,7.
     von einem *kǔlen* prǔne, 39,1,15.

ü = u (MHG. *uo*): wü mon ir *gütheit* hat gedan, 27,6,4.

ü = CL. *u:* et *spiritüi* sancto fron, 1,1,4.

v

v = e (MHG. *e*): welcher wil das er *vrlang*, 30,3,15.

v = o (MHG. *â*): *vn* den vns nÿmant helffen mag, 10,1,22.

v = u (MHG. *u* and *û*): . . . lob *vnd* er, 1,1,1.
  dich / jünckfraw *figvriret*, 17,2,30-31.

v = ü (MHG. *ü*): kam gar ein *vberlichter* schein, 19,3,17.

w

w = ei (MHG. *ô*): *zbw* silben in ein silben hart, 31,2,14.

w = o (MHG. *â, ô*): *Ww* sie ist aber ein gepilt, 26,5,7.

w = u (MHG. *û*): aŭe *dw* hochste aller creatŭre, 18,3,16.

w = ü (MHG. *üe*): in schwarczer *prw* gib ich eüch vorhen aschen, 36, 2,8.

w = u (MHG. *uo*): sie hat kein *rw* dan peÿ dem fritt, 27,3,27.

w = ü (MHG. *uo*): ging *frw* vnd spet, 3,1,30.

Diphthongs, exclusive of those with ÿ
ai = ei (MHG. *ei*): dw pist des *hails* vrsprÿnge, 16,4,9.

aü

aü = au (MHG. *û*): Dreÿ fischer *daŭchten* sich gar klŭg, 40,1,11.

aü = au (MHG. *ou*): sein ritterliches *haubet* abeschlüge, 24,12,16.

aw

aw = au (MHG. *ou*): *schaw* ich vnder mich gen dal, 4,2,14.

ei

ei = e (MHG. *e*): got vatters der ewig *reigirt*, 1,3,25 (see the note on this verse).

ei = i (MHG. *î*): Dar vmb sie ir gar *heimeleich*, 23,3,6.

ei = ei (MHG. *î*): het ir den *leib* verloren, 7,1,19.

ei = ie (MHG. *î*): vnd schlos mit aüff das *paradeis*, 2,1,12.

ei = au (MHG. *iu*): gŭnden ir necz *ein deichen*, 40,1,12.

ei = eu (MHG. *iu*): schmecket *eich* wein nit hol ich malvasire, 36,2,5.

ei = eu (MHG. *öu*): Der graff kam heim mit *freiden* pal, 20,6,8.

eü

eü = ei (MHG. *î*): den *reüter* an dem drab, 38,2,3 (see note 30,2,15).

eü = eu (MHG. *iu*): dem kümet es zw *steür*, 2,1,16.

eü = ie (MHG. iu): dw *verleüsest* das ewig heil, 4,3,9 (see the note on this verse).

eü = äu (MHG. *iu*): paczen pock *heüt*, 21,2,8.

eü = äu (MHG. *öu*): das *freülein* aŭserwelde, 7,2,7.

ie

ie = i (MHG. *ie*): die nacht würdt *liecht* recht als der dag, 11,2,23.

ie = i (MHG. *i*): . . . die *schrieff*t anzeücht, 20,1,25.

ie = ei (MHG. *î*): sprach *verziehent* mein kint müs . . ., 19,3,25.

ie = ü (MHG. *üe*): der weinet vnd *bedriebet* wart, 23,7,3.

je = Hie (Greek *hie*): küngin der *jerarcheÿ*, 8,7,20.

üe

üe = i (MHG. *ie*): wen er *vrgrüeff* der het sein leib verloren, 24,9,12 (once; see
　　the note on this verse).

üe = u (MHG. *uo*): das *plüet* vber sein antlicz ran, 8,1,23 (see the note on this
　　verse).

üe = ü (MHG. *üe*): wie jemerlich dein . . . *fües* durch graben sint, 8,6,15.

Consonants

b

b = w (MHG. *w*): vm djs mort lest dotten mein *beib* der ritter freÿ, 19,2,7.
　　da van so wirt ir freüd *geschbacht*, 27,3,22.

b = ML. *v*: das keiner pring *eqüiboca*, 30,2,9 (once).

c

c = k (MHG. *k*): *clag* wir zw dir vnd weinen, 15,2,18.

ch = g (MHG. *c*): von got vernüftig *selich* sag, 26,7,3.

ch = g (MHG. *g*): mit *reüichem* müt, 4,3,16.

ch = h (MHG. *h*): der hat pegabet deinen *hochen* adel, 20,1,16.

ch = ch (MHG. *h*): darvm zw rew peicht pus dich *pflicht*, 7,2,22.

ch = CL. *c*: *früchtum* vertris tüi, 14,3,12 (once; see the note on this verse).

ck = g (MHG. *c*): gen *wirczpürck* aüf der vartte, 21,5,10.

ck = g (MHG. *g*): mit dem der dot vast mit ir *ranck*, 23,12,14.

ck = k (MHG. *c*): daran da pin ich alczeit *kranck*, 22,3,18.

ck = k (MHG. *k*): mit dem eprüch so *mercket* das, 19,1,17.

ck = ck (MHG. *c*): gesicht *geschmack* felt daran gar, 2,3,6.

ckh = ch (MHG. *ch*): recht sam der sünen glancz ein glas *dürckh plicket*,
　　11,2,18 (once).

cz = ts (MHG. *ts*): die fremd *selczam* seÿe, 33,1,44.

cz = β (MHG. *ȝ*): Dar ein *sacz* er mit ganczer macht, 24,6,6.

cz = z (MHG. *z*): Her / nach die drit ich nen vnd *czel*, 13,3,1-2.

cz = tz (MHG. *tz*): Ein rossenkrancz *aüf seczet* im, 20,3,8.

d

d = t (MHG. *t*): sie samlet viel der *dügent* reich, 26,4,11.
    da sprach die *zarde* iünckfraw rein, 12,2,2.
d = ML. *t*: archa *deidatis*, 18,3,2.
dt = d (MHG. *d*): Dar vm dŭ *frembdter* gaste, 7,1,6.
dt = d (MHG. *t*): da *vandt* sie das *kindt* dote, 19,2,11.
dt = t (MHG. *t*): der ritter sich nit lang *periedt*, 19,2,22.

f

f = f (MHG. *v*): ob nÿchte *vngefieges* kem, 25,6,8.
f = v (MHG. *v*): in *feihel* kle, 40,1,4.
f = ph (MHG. *ph*): da von die *profetten* haben geschriben, 10,1,12.
f = CL. *v*: *eqüifoca*, 30,3,1.
ff = f (MHG. *f*): *seüffczen* wir armen sunder gar, 15,2,14.
ff = f (MHG. *v*): *deüffel*, 20,6,15.
ff = pf (MHG. *pf*): vnd wer dar aüs *schlüff* . . ., 23,6,12 (once).
ff = ph (MHG. *ph*): maniger *proffet* weis, 14,2,10.
ff = Cl. *ph*: wolt sehen ob *Zeffalo* lib, 28,5,19.

g

g = g (MHG. *c*): ein czins *pfenig* gar schon, 9,3,14.
g = i (MHG. *j*): dar peÿ ein *lilgen* zweÿg was praün, 32,1,7.
g = k (MHG. *k*): *Gneib* reisser dapel vnd ne al, 21,4,11 (once).
gc = g (MHG. *c*): dem deüffel *ewigcleichen*, 4,1,24 (once).
gk = g (MHG. *c*): stürben frolich vnd *dürsttigklich*, 26,5,24.
gk = gk (MHG. *c+h*): Zw *miltigkeit* stet ir beger, 26,2,7 (once).

h

h = ch (MHG. *ch*): *nah* lieb kumpt leit, 25,13,16.

i

i = j (MHG. *j*): wie das vor mangem *iare*, 25,1,2.

j

j = g (MHG. *g*): dw vel her *Jedion*, 15,1,19 (see the note on this verse).

k

k = ck (MHG. *ck*): hÿ *schikt* dir dein vatter den drost, 23,9,14 (once).
k = g (MHG. *c*): vnd da *ellentiklichen* stünd, 8,3,26.
k = h (MHG. *ch*): Ir *schükknecht* güt, 21,1,1 (once).
k = gk (MHG. *c+h*): nach *küniklicher wirdikeit* begraben, 24,10,16.
kk = g (MHG. *c*): das er *elenndikklichen* starb, 28,6,11 (once).

l

l = ll (MHG. *ll*): dar vür geit sie vnd dügent vnd *helesche* frücht, 28,3,15.
ll = l (MHG. *l*): von dem *heilligen* geiste, 12,2,5.

m

m = n (MHG. *n*): wan . . . *caim* abel erschlüg, 27,1,11 (see note 24,3,14).
mm = m (MHG. *m*): dreÿ *nommen* vnd ein got genent, 1,1,6 (once).

n

n = m (MHG. *m*): mit dem *er pidnet* al sein leib, 25,6,15 (see note 18,1,24).
n = m (MHG. *n*): davon *enpfingen* alle fricht jr kreffte, 32,1,12.
n = nn (MHG. *nn*): dar dŭrch magstŭ *entrinen*, 7,2,23.
nn = n (MHG. *n*): vnd beleibet wessenlich ein der himel *dronn*, 2,2,15.
ng = nn (MHG. *nn*): mag wol preis *gewingen*, 29,1,16 (see the note on this).

p

p = b (MHG. *b*): mein rock *pleib peÿ* im hangen, 21,1,14.
pf = f (MHG. *ph, v*): dar dürch vns würt / gros leit *enpfürt*, 9,3,5-6.
pf = pf (MHG. *ph*): nÿe valet ir in spottes *pfül*, 36,1,15.
pff = f (MHG. *f, pf, ph*): nie *scharpffe* künst ich in mein hercz peschlüs,
   37,2,3.
pff = pf (MHG. *pf*): meister mag man dŭrch dÿ *schopffvng*, 6,3,19.

r

rr = r (MHG. *r*): zerspilten sich die *herrten* stein, 8,5,25 (once).

s

s = β (MHG *ʒ*): *das* ich dich lob zw dissen weÿhenachten, 10,1,5.
s = z (MHG. *z*): Die schiff würden genaw *sw* sam gestossen, 24,8,11 (once; see
   the note on this verse).
ss = s (MHG. *s*): das es *gewessen* war dÿ himel kŭnigin, 19,5,13.
   der alle ding beschŭff *sso* freÿ, 16,7,3 (initially only once).
ss = CL. *s*: at *noss*, 15,4,7.
ss = β (MHG. *ʒ*): er *grüsset* sie mit eren, 12,1,5.
ss = z (ML. *z*): aŭe von *Nasseret* dw wol richende plŭm, 18,1,25.
sch = s (MHG. *s*): Da ich dÿ pest *geschelschafft* vant, 21,5,11 (once; see the
   note on this verse).
scz = sch (MHG. *s*): Die lib ist plint vnd hat gros *sczmercz*, 28,1,13.

t

t = d (MHG. *d*): dar peÿ merckest *tw* wol, 26,7,16 (initially only twice; see
   note 25,3,16).
   dw *miltes* palsam vas, 15,3,17.

t = CL. *d:at* noss, 15,4,7.

t = tt (MHG. *tt*): das ist mein scharpffe künst al hÿ *verschniten*, 36,1,3.

tt = d (MHG. *d*): et spes nostra in *leitte*, 15,2,3 (once).

tt = t (MHG. *t*): er schreÿ *vatter* mit *laütter* stim, 8,5,5.

tt = tt (MHG. *t*): wirt dich *vmb schetten* aller meist, 12,1,16 (once).

ü

ü = f (MHG. *v*): von der hohen *driüaltikeit*, 1,2,27.

ü = v (MHG. *v*): das es wür *vnüerstentlich* gancz, 31,3,9.

ü = CL. *v*: proberbioriüm *octaüo* nün hert, 13,1,18.

v

v = f (MHG. *v*): vor grosser not verkeret er sein *varb*, 25,7,5.

w

w = b (MHG. *b*): die fraw . . . *offenwart* es nit vor scham, 23,3,5 (once).

w = f (MHG. *v*): secz *wür* vns deinen schilt.

x

x = chs (MHG. *ch+s*): Hans *Sax* gedicht, Heading No. 1.

z

z = CL. *c*: wolt sehen ob *Zeffalo* lib, 28,5,19.

z = z (MHG. *t*): ich laid gros *zwanck*, 22,3,19.

Umlaut

For the umlauts *e, ä,* and *ae* Hans Sachs uses the vowel *e*:
Das ich *bewer* die heimlikeit, 2,1,4.
Er *wescht* die *hent*, 21,3,6.
ob nÿchte vngefieges *kem* / das sie da *precht* in schmerczen, 25,6,8-9.
von *welden* pergen dalle, 33,3,32.

In addition *a* appears twice with two little dots over it:
sie *dät* manig cleglichen schreÿ, 28,3,3 (see the note on this).
Dar dürch mon in den gartten *gät*, 32,2,9 (see the note on this).

For the umlauts of *ö* and *oe* Hans Sachs also uses the vowel *e*:
ir nit entrinen *mecht*, 7,1,21.
Das neü gesang war pald *erhert*, 10,3,11.
dw süsses *elpaümreis*, 15,5,8.
mit iniger petrachtüng *schen*, 11,3,21.

There are also twenty-eight instances in sixteen of the forty Meisterlieder where a superscript appears over an *o*. The difficulty is that there is no way of knowing whether Hans Sachs himself or someone else who may have had access to Berlin 414 added the superscripts. To illustrate the existent confusion a few examples will suffice: In 9,2,15-16 we find "Irer entpfencknüs vnzw stŏrt / nün hŏrt esechielis wŏrt." These superscripts were most surely added at a later date by someone other than Hans Sachs, because they destroy his series of six rhymes, of which the other four are "port:fort:hort:dort"; furthermore in 13,1,27-28 we have the same rhyme-pair in inverse order, "wort: stort" and in 22,6,10 "stort" rhymes with "art" (Ort) in vs. 9; also in 27,3,9 the poet writes "vil schnoder wort sie vberhort." – Twice the *o* in the substantive *schön* is modified by a superscript, once in the positive degree, "die schŏn mit irer hande," 20,3,9 and once in the superlative, "der doch aüf erd der schŏnest was," 13,2,23, but not in the comparative, "ein schonere pŭl ich," 20,4,13, nor in the superlative of the adjective, "die schonste jŭnckfraw ...," 20,2,23. – In 13,1,4 "frŏlich" appears within the verse, but in 10,1,11; 11,3,16; 22,6,22, etc. the word "frolich." And so on. Further details are in the Notes.

Again and again Hans Sachs uses the *o* without umlaut:
in *odem* stal vor essel vnd vor rint, 10,2,23.
dotlich deglich wardt sie qüitirt, 13,3,8.
lob seÿ dir *hochster* criste, 16,7,7.
Aüe dw plüend *olpaümreis*, 18,2,4.
die *horet* wÿ man preissen det, 24,2,8.
manigen sie *erlost*, 27,5,16.

For the umlaut *ü* and *üe* Hans Sachs uses the vowel i:
vnd die zwelff *fricht*, 5,2,4.
vir iren eingebornen sün, 8,3,18.
... peÿ dem *prinlein* kalt, 22,4,21.
Also es mir *gelicket*, 39,3,11.
misen wir alle sterben, 4,3,24.

More often than not he does not umlaut the vowel *u*:
also wenig *dürch gründen* mag, 1,3,11.
sie in ob hündert malen *küssen* det, 25,8,10.
Mort / lich *vŭrt* man sie *vŭr* gericht, 19,3,1-2.
vns *vŭr pas* me, 6,1,3.
der *würd* den flüch ab düne, 11,1,14.
dan *wŭrdt* eüer freüdt schmale, 7,1,24.
vnd befalch sich alle dag in ir *hŭtte*, 19,1,14.
peÿ einem *prŭnlein* frischen, 40,1,5.

Linguistic Summary

Loss of vowels and consonants

Weinhold (*BGr.*, §3) says, "Charakteristisch ist für das bairische im allgemeinen die Kürzung oder der völlige Abstoß der Suffixe und Flexionen, wobei selbst der Stamm zuweilen leidet . . . ." For the most part such dialectal practice provided Hans Sachs with a great deal of flexibility in the matter of rhyme and syllable count. Here and there, however, it does not serve him in one way or another. In order to show more clearly the manner in which he deleted certain vowels and consonants I have cited examples under specific headings with the letters under each in alphabetical order, and have indicated Weinhold as authority.

Loss in final position

b (W. *BGr.*, § 126,a):
Gotliche *lie* ist keüsch vnd rein, 26,2,13 (once).

ch (W. *BGr.*, § 188):
müntlich vnd in *püstaben*, 35,3,19.

d (Weinhold, *Mittelhochdeutsche Grammatik*—cited simply as Weinhold—, § 373, and W. *BGr.*, § 149)
vnd zücket den went stecken *pal*, 21,4,13.
so wür die stras mir *pal* verpont, 34,2,7.
ir herczenlibes *kin*, 8,2,2.
dar vm Jole ein *hem* bereit, 28,5,26.
vnwissen deiner freÿnte, 25,13,9.
(See also the loss of *de* in the 1. sg. pres. ind. and in the 3. sg. pres. and pret. subj. of the verb *werden*.)

e
May disappear from all cases of feminine nouns in the singular and from the nominative and accusative plural (Weinhold, § § 451-452):
kein *sünd* dich berürte, 17,3,27.
. . . ein sal / der *güet* . . ., 16,5,15-16.
aüs rechter *lib* vnd warer *min*, 2,1,9.
die im kein *hilff* mocht dün, 8,3,16.
da von enpfingen alle *fricht* jr kreffte, 32,1,12.
dar vmb Johannes in dein *hent*, 8,4,9.

From the nominative and accusative singular of weak masculine nouns and in the nominative and accusative plural of strong ones (Weinhold, § § 448-449, and 458):
vnd ein *prün* der parmünge, 12,3,4.

194

das der helisch *drack* nit er laüf, 16,3,3.
Gar schnel dreÿ edel *küng* vür bar, 9,5,8.

From the nominative and accusative singular of some neuter nouns (W. *BGr.*, § 455):
von welt zw welt ewig vn *ent*, 1,1,12.

From the 1. singular present indicative of both weak and strong verbs (Weinhold, §§ 367 and 395: W. *BGr.*, §§ 280 and 307):
das ich *bewer* die heimlikeit, 2,1,4.
ich *pit* dich so mein sel hie scheit, 18,3,22.

From the 1. and 3. singular present subjunctive of weak and strong verbs (Weinhold, §§ 370 and 397; W. *BGr.*, §§ 286 and 309):
dar vor vns got *mach* freÿe, 22,7,24.
der *helff* vns hie aüs aller clag, 1,3,26.

From the imperative of weak verbs (Weinhold, § 398; W. *BGr.*, § 310):
mit inniger pedrachtüng *frolock* geüde, 11,1,4.

From the 1. and 3. singular preterit ending of weak verbs, both indicative and subjunctive (W. *BGr.*, §§ 313 and 316):
Aügüstinus *müst* lassen ab, 1,3,13.
er im *gedacht* wie er sie *precht* in dotes we, 19,1,25.

From the 3. singular preterit subjunctive of strong verbs (W. *BGr.*, § 293; for lack of umlaut see ibid., § 267):
so er die *fünd* geschmecht, 7,1,17.

n, en
Dropped from nouns (Weinhold, §§ 449, 454, 458, and 463; W. *BGr.*, §§ 167, 347, 348, and 351; Weinhold disapproves of some of the examples he cites):
den straüs peÿ seinem *mage*, 38,1,7.
vÿl / engelischer *zünge*, 17,2,14-15.
Des schallen / der engelischen *stim*, 5,5,1-2.
Er ging hin mÿt draurigem *hercz*, 20,5,8.
vÿr draff al pur menschlich *persan*, 13,3,10.
von *merck* vnd stetten ane zal, 29,3,13.

From an infinitive and from inflectional endings (Weinhold, §§ 215 and 372; W. *BGr.*, §§ 167 and 288):
Sein anher müst dem seinen pot *gennüge*, 24,12,13.

wir *merk* es mit der kreiden, 30,2,8.
das wir *pleibe* in gottes lib, 16,6,3.
Da disse wort *verginge,* 12,2,1.
da ich wardt schaten *vinde*, 39,1,12.

From the 1. plural present indicative of both weak and strong verbs, as well as from the 1. plural preterit of strong verbs, when the pronoun follows (Weinhold, § § 369 and 396; W. *BGr.,* § § 283 and 292):
in künsten *wol* wir scherczen, 36,3,11.
schreÿ wir, 15,2,11.
in freüd *würd* wir erqüicket, 39,3,24.

From the past participle of strong verbs (W. *BGr.,* § 294, after *m, n, ng.*):
ein schlaff kam mir *gerünne*, 39,1,16.

s

Dropped from the genitive singular of strong masculine and neuter nouns (Weinhold, § § 448 and 454; W. *BGr.,* § § 338 and 342):
des *pfarer* dochter püllestü, 20,3,10.
der zehenn stent / des himelÿschen *here,* 5,4,15-16.

t, et

Dropped from inflectional endings (Weinhold, § § 194 and 200; W. *BGr.,* § § 143, 282, 284, 293, 308, and 316):
er *welcz* vnd schlecht das schmere, 21,2,17.
pis er *küm* zw, 29,1,26.
vnd wer eüch hab *verwünde*, 39,2,10.
hort was *bedeüt* vns disser garte, 32,2,1.
Flaischlich lieb *schneit* al freüd enczweÿ, 28,3,1.
als ir wol horen *wert* noch in der leste, 25,1,16.
het ir den leib verloren, 7,1,19.
Sie lag vor im cleglich *ermort*, 24,10,6.
dw vnd Johannes . . . / *halt* mein sel in eüer hüt, 8,7,25-26.

Sometimes the whole preterit ending *ete* of weak verbs disappears (Weinhold, § 382; W. *BGr.,* § 313):
also ich meinen gang hie *richt*, 39,1,9.
er ging. . . / in die capel vnd *pett* mit andacht . . ., 20,2,11 and 13.

Loss of vowel or consonant medially

ch (W. *BGr.*, § 188):
vil *heimlikeit* wart in bekünt, 1,2,5.

d
From the pronoun *du* when it is enclitic (Paul-Gierach, *Mittelhochdeutsche Grammatik* – cited P-G–, § 88):
pistŭ in hoher kŭnst gelart, 6,1,38.

e
In inflections, prefixes, suffixes (Weinhold, § 79; W. *BGr.*, § 14; P-G., § 60,2,b):
pstost es vnd dŭt es schwerczen, 21,2,14.
den *gfangen* peÿ der ketten, 38,2,24.
mag schopfen in das *grübl* klein, 1,3,10.
vnd *petten* on das kindlein aüserkoren, 10,3,14.
Eins nachcz het die jüng fraw ein draüm, 25,3,1.
irs herczen liebes dot, 25,13,5.

g (W. *BGr.*, § 177)
die al drucket *vnseles* schüch, 28,3,25.

h
From the suffix *heit* (Weinhold, § 245; W. *BGr.*, § 194):
seit die *menscheit* cristi, 6,1,25.

i
From the suffix *ic* (W. *BGr.*, § 14):
Erhor vns *küng* sabaotht, 9,1,15.
Als noch ist *mengem* weissen kündt, 23,1,6.

n (W. *BGr.*, § 166):
wan meines *lebes* nÿmer seÿ, 8,7,23.
aller *parmug* ein vber flüs, 15,2,21.
vnd verzert *vnŭczlich* ir peider gŭtte, 19,1,16.
Das *straüchet* ros des ritters. . ., 22,7,1.

t (W. *BGr.*, § 142):
den gülden kopff gar *kosparlich*, 23,9,8.

Spurious consonants and vowels

In contrast to the deletion of vowels and consonants, spurious ones are sometimes added or inserted into words. The vowels served to create extra syllables in a verse, and an appended *e* enabled Hans Sachs to make a feminine rhyme-word out of a masculine word. As for the consonants, only the *t*, attached to a word, was of use a few times in making a rhyme.

a

Inserted into one word only:

. . . dw gottes *monastrancze* (ML. monstrantia), 16,3,12.

b

Inserted (W. *BGr.*, § 126):

Dar vm dǔ *frembdter* gaste, 7,1,6.

d

Prefixed, inserted, and attached (W. *BGr.*, § § 145, 148, and 149):

Das / ist der mich *der mordet* hat, 19,5,1-2.

Von / allen stenden *vnderzelt*, 33,3,1-2.

o *duldcÿs* (CL. dulcis) süs vnd milde, 14,3,18.

in solcher *wünd* (MHG. wunne) / sie ÿmer ebig leben, 5,2,18 and 20.

e

Inserted and added (Weinhold, § § 85, 374, 448, 452, and 454; W. *BGr.*, § § 17, 290, 338, and 342):

von got sie *geren* hort vnd list, 26,3,11.

scharpff vnd *gelat*, 40,3,4.

der *paremüng* ein prunen, 16,1,9.

mach seinen *zoren* linde, 15,3,18.

von den die künst hat iren *vrespringe*, 32,2,4.

beib schaw das ist der *süne* dein, 8,4,5.

ein zartes *kindeleine*, 12,1,11.

. . . spricht von Nürnberg Hans *Sachse*, 23,13,16.

den sie *drüge* neün monat lang, 11,1,23.

mit gnad pistw *gespeiste*, 17,1,24.

sein leib was nacket *vnde* plos, 8,2,6.

im zorniklichen *nache* rant, 28,4,25.

merk so in sünden *diche*, 7,3,1.

g

Inserted (W. *BGr.*, § 177):

ob sie *in prünstigkligchen* prent, 26,4,25.

h

Inserted (W. *BGr.*, § 197):
Gabriheilis ore der mündt / *Gabrihellis* dich grüesset, 16,2,6-7.
verneÿhen (erneuen), 20,1,6.

i

Inserted (W. *BGr.*, § 20):
peÿ *achiczen* do kent man reÿ, 38,3,4.

j

Prefixed and inserted:
Jist des menschen vernüft . . ., 22,5,9.
von *patrijarchen* künig früm, 13,2,17.

n

Prefixed, inserted and attached (Weinhold, § § 395 and 460:
W. *BGr.*, § § 165, 168, and 307):
so reipt ers *nein*, 21,2,19.
dem zarten *frewenlein*, 7,2,3.
. . . dem *heilling* geiste / seÿ zir . . ., 16,7,11-12.
nach der *lerern* sag, 11,2,24.
kein *züngen* mag erreichen, 17,3,24.
die ich offt *horen* preissen, 21,5,12.

p

Inserted (W. *BGr.*, § 122):
nah lieb *kumpt* leit . . ., 25,13,16.
becz stein *vernempt*, 21,4,3.

r

Inserted (W. *BGr.*, § 163):
eÿ bie felschlichen hastw mich *berdrogen*, 23,7,16.

s

Attached (W. *BGr.*, § 155):
wü / maister *singers* singen, 29,1,27.

t

Infrequently inserted, but often attached (W. *BGr.*, § § 142,143, and 292;
Weinhold, § 396):
die wür *stünst* (MHG. sunst) zw dem schaden aüch der spot, 25,13,10.
ein *zinst* pfenig war anctz gemelt, 11,2,6.
dar peÿ ist clerlich zw *verstent*, 2,1,26.
wer (wir) *erent* iren name, 12,3,17.

Verb Forms

Along with early New High German forms for his verbs Hans Sachs uses many Middle High German ones plus a few Middle German forms. I shall give a sampling of strong verbs, partly in accordance with the MHG. grouping of the seven classes; of some irregular verbs including *sein*; and of a few weak verbs inclusive of *haben*.

STRONG VERBS

I. Not only in this class, but in all verbs which have an unaccented *e* in the ending of the 3. sg. pres. ind. Hans Sachs sometimes retains the *e*; sometimes not:
    vnd *beleibet* wessenlich ein der himel dron, 2,2,15.
    peschlossen ist vnd *pleibt* die port, 9,2,17.

The 3. sg. pres. subj. of MHG. *grîfen:*
greuf nit her vür noch hinter sich, 30,2,15 (see the note on this verse).

For the pret. ind. of this class Hans Sachs employs the MHG. form in the singular somewhat more frequently than the NHG. one:
Da nün die zeit / irer gepürt *erscheine*, 11,2,1-2.
vnd *erschein* in dem claren liecht, 19,3,20.
in aremüt *erschin*, 8,2,8.
er *schreÿ* vatter mit laütter stim, 8,5,5.
rit mit ir manig meile, 22,2,8.
Zw nacht er aüs der stat hin *reit*, 24,6,1.
der her *schaich* gar behende, 23,6,9.
vnd zw fraw gardoleÿe *schleich*, 28,6,9.

For the MHG. verb *lîden* there are three different forms in the 3. sg. pret. ind.:
dar vür es an dem creücze *leit*, 9,5,16.
das mort / *lit* cristus nach der menscheit hie, 6,2,18-19.
on alle schüld *led* er dÿ pein, 8,3,12 (1514); and the same form in rhyme:
hicz frost *erlet*, 3,1,26 (1517); (see the note on this verse).

II. In the pres. sg. of this class Hans Sachs uses the diphthong *eu*:
    dw *verleüsest* das ewig heil, 4,3,9.
    sie *fleücht* geiczige art, 26,2,8.

In the preterit indicative both the vowel *u* and the vowel *o* are to be found in the singular and in the very few instances of the plural:

das selb sie gar pald aüf das hercze *güsse*, 23,11,13.

die manigen zeher *vergos*, 8,6,5.

wann got al creatür *beschlüs*, 13,1,11.

Die fraw *beschlos* die selben dir, 23,6,6.

drei edel küng . . . / . . . *zügen* in gir, 9,5,8 and 11.

da *nossen* sie der libe prün, 23,4,14.

III,1. In this division the vowels *a* and *u* are to be found in both the singular and plural preterit:

kein meil *gewün*, 9,2,13.

gewan sie heimlich sorgen, 20,3,21.

wü ich ein solchen meister *fünd*, 33,1,20.

da ich mein geleich *vant*, 37,3,9.

da *vandt* sie das kindt dote, 19,2,11.

sie eÿlten dar da *funden* sie die maget, 11,3,4.

vonden (fanden) sie allein ob dem dotten kinde, 19,2,16.

in dem lüfft die engel *süngen*, 10,3,2.

sein diner zw im *drongen*, 24,8,2.

The preterit subjunctive shows the vowel *u*:

vünd er eüch dan peflecket, 7,3,5.

erklünget ir gesanges geig, 34,2,2.

The verb *brinnen* usually has the vowel *a* in the preterit, but once the vowel *u*:

in wildem feüre er *verpran*, 28,4,9.

grün / der püsch vnd *prün*, 9,2,21-22.

For the verb *beginnen* Hans Sachs uses the weak forms in the preterit:

Mein vernüfft *günt* mich riren, 39,1,6.

sein hercz *begünet* lechczen, 25,7,4.

die fischlein *günden* streichen, 40,1,14.

III,2. In the 1.sg. pres. ind. of this division the MHG. vowel *i* is still present:

das *hilff* ich nün beweisen, 21,5,14.

In the pret. sg. ind. Hans Sachs uses the vowel *a*; in the pl. *u*:

da cristus *starb* auf ert, 6,2,17.

manige püchse da *er qüal*, 24,8,3.
würffen sie ein das mere, 24,9,7.
stürben frolich vnd dürsttigklich, 26,5,24.

The pret. subj. shows the vowel *u*:
seit er ir *hülff* aüs not, 25,10,10.

MHG. *werden* (I shall call the various forms of this verb present and preterit, even though they may be part of a future tense, or of the passive.)

Present indicative:
das ich *wir* aüf gewecket, 7,3,27.
der *wir* verirt, 1,3,21 (see the note on this verse).
das selb . . . / *wirt* ein eptasin früme, 20,5,20-21.
als ir wol horen *wert* noch in der leste, 25,1,16.

Present subjunctive:
nůn seit die schrifft dis voren / gottes sun *wert* geporen, 6,2,31-32.
aüf das *wer* wider frid gemacht, 27,3,25 (see the note on this vs.).

The pret. ind. shows both the vowel *a* and the vowel *u*:
Ein engel *wart* gesante, 12,1,1.
Do *würd* mein leid erst neÿe, 39,3,6.

Preterit subjunctive; no umlaut:
dan *würdt* eüer freüdt schmale, 7,1,24.
Der *würd* den flüch ab düne, 11,1,14.
das es *würr* vnüerstentlich gancz, 31,3,9 (see note 1,1,17).

IV. Similarly to the verbs in III, 2 the vowel *i* is to be found in the 1. sg. pres. ind.:
mein geist *befilch* ich in dein hent, 8,5,6.
mein dreÿ ich ÿ an eüch nit *prich*, 39,3,22.

MHG. *komen*
Hans Sachs uses the vowel *u* throughout the present:
gar selten ich mit künste / *küm* aüf der singer schul, 36,1,11-12.
nah lieb *kumpt* leit spricht von nürnberg Hans Saxe, 25,13,16.
das dw / aüch *kumest* zw / ewiger rw, 5,5,21-23.
so *küm* zw meinem leczten ent, 8,7,24.
Meister dar vmb so *kümet* pal, 36,3,7.
wie er balt *kümen* mechte, 23,4,2.

Also in the past part.:
pin *kümen* vne scherczen, 22,3,16.

The Preterit subjunctive shows umlaut:
so *kem* ich gar selten zw dir, 25,4,14.
ob nÿchte vngefieges *kem*, 25,6,8.

MHG. *nëmen*
Both the vowel *e* and the vowel *i* (more often *ÿ*) appear in the 3. sg. pres. ind.
and in the singular imperative:
sie *nÿmet* vernünft vnde krafft, 28,1,11.
nempt got aüf vnser pet so rich, 16,4,8.
Er . . . / *nempt* den knÿ rim / vom filcz *vernim*, 21,3,6 and 8-9.
nÿm geleichnůs herniden, 6,2,16.
dissen aüs züg / al hie *vernem*, 5,1,24.

The past participle:
dar in ich *vür genümen* hon, 28,1,4.

V. Hans Sachs also uses the MHG. vowel *i* in the 1. sg. pres. ind. of the verbs in
    this class:
    oxen augen ich *gib*, 36,2,12.
    Weÿtter *gib* ich dem singer ler, 29,3,1.
    ich *sÿ* vor mir den grimen dot, 4,1,8.
    sich ich verspert der himel dar, 4,2,4.

With very few exceptions the forms for the verb *sehen* are spelled with *ch*:
det er des nit er *sech* ir nÿmer mere, 24,4,13.
man *sicht* ir viel in vngelick vmbwatten, 25,13,12.
sie *sechen* plos, 5,3,19.
sehen sÿ nit ewick, 7,3,17.
nun *sich*, 3,2,36.
nun *sechte*, 20,2,6.
spricht ich *sach* ihn, 5,1,17.
die *sach* allein ir meit dÿ *sa* sÿ wol, 25,6,10. (Hans Sachs let euphony
determine the spelling.)

In identical sentences the 3. sg. pres. subj. of the verb *geschehen* is spelled
with and without *ch*:
mir *geschech* nach den wortten dein, 12,2,3 (1517).
mir *gesche* nach den wortten dein, 10,2,15 (1515).

For the MHG. verbs *gëben* and *ligen* contracted forms are common in the 3.
sg. pres. ind. and occur a few times in the 2. sg. for *ligen*:
Exempel *geit* die schrifft so vein, 2,3,7.
der ir er schon aüch zeücknüs *git*, 13,2,24.
parmherczikeit die *git* ir krafft, 26,2,12.
Mein her *leit* in dem sale, 7,1,11.
in einem gülden grabe / *leistw* . . . , 23,10,9-10.

Once Hans Sachs uses a contracted form in the imperative:
er sprach *gent* mir die iünckfraw wert, 24,7,14.

There are two examples of the longer form only for gëben:
wie offt er *gibet* falschen rat, 26,5,10.
sie *gibet* dreÿen rot, 27,5,8.

MHG. phlëgen (only two examples, both pret.)
Dw *pflagst* mit Gwisgardo der lib, 23,8,1.
der graf da aüfblicken *pflag*, 20,2,25.

VI.   The forms for the pres. indicative of this class vary; many show umlaut:
kein neit / nÿmand nit *dreit*, 5,4,21-22.
des *dregstw* wol . . . ein krone, 16,2,16.
die vns *dreget* in gottes hüld, 15,3,21.
Wie pald er das hin heine *dreckt*, 21,2,11.
palt *schlag* / dein hercz . . . , 4,3,15-16.
so *melt* er manig schone rank, 34,2,12.
Vnmassen ser *wechset* dÿ lÿb, 28,2,13.

The one example, an infinitive, of the MHG. verb *pachen* is still spelled with
ch:
Einen placz mon euch *pachen* sol, 36,2,7.

In the preterit indicative of this class we find the vowel *u*, although a few
times *ue* is substituted in the 3. singular for MHG. *uo*:
die fraw *hüb* aüf ir aügen dar, 19,3,10.
der alle ding *beschüff* sso freÿ, 16,7,3.
drügen in zü dem grab, 8,7,16.
Sein anher *schüff* das mon *pegrüeb*, 24,13,1.
das sie im *drüeg* soliche lieb vnd günste, 23,3,13.
da mon der haiden vil er *schlüg* / zw ztünd aüs irem schifft mon *drueg*,
24,9,14-15.

VII. I have not subdivided this class, but have simply arranged the verbs in the alphabetical order of the NHG. vowel/diphthong of the stem.

a

MHG. *halten*
sie *helt* gehorsam wer sie strafft, 26,2,6.
dw vnd Johannes . . . / vnd *halt* mein sel in eüer hüt, 8,7,25-26.

MHG. *lâ͟zen, lân*
Both forms occur in the infinitive:
das er sein sün wolt *lassen* menschlich sterben, 10,2,5.
. . . so müs der falsche dieb / mir *lan* mein jünges leben, 23,8,3-4.

The 3. singular present indicative shows three forms:
in not sie kein kristen *verlat*, 13,3,24.
let in beÿ seinem berd besten, 27,6,12.
vm djs mort *lest* dotten mein beib der ritter freÿ, 19,2,7.

Plural imperative: ir cristen *lat* vns freyen, 11,3,15.

Hans Sachs spells the preterit in three different ways:
der *lis* peschreiben, 11,2,5.
lÿs er die fraw fangen mit grosser rŭmoreÿ, 19,2,25.
Der früm keisser aügüstus *lies*, 9,3,8.

MHG. *râten*
Jist des menschen vernüft die alzeit *wider rat*, 22,5,9.

MHG. *vâhen*
Hans Sachs uses both the MHG. and the NHG. forms for the infinitive in the same Meisterlied:
ein gericht *fahen* liesse, 19,5,3.
lÿs er die fraw *fangen* mit grosser rŭmoreÿ, 19,2,25.

Two forms in the 3. singular present indicative are of interest because they occur just two verses apart and show how Hans Sachs takes advantage of forms for syllable count and rhyme:
wer das *enpfahet* wirdiklichen also schon, 2,1,15.
wer das vnwirdiklich *enpfecht*, 2,1,17.

Singular imperative: . . . o clemens *enpfach*, 14,3,16.

Present subjunctive:
ir hercz das wachet degeleich / das sÿ nit *fach* der sünde seil, 26,4,5-6.

au

MHG. *loufen*
Hans Sachs uses the vowel *u* in both the singular and the plural preterit
indicative:
es *lüff* vber die prück zu hant, 22,2,13.
vnd *lüffen* zŭ irer kamnet, 19,2,15.

The past participle shows both *o* and *au*:
dein freüd ist pald *verloffen*, 5,5,16.
ein diner schnell *gelaüffen* kam, 20,6,4.

MHG; *bouwen* and *houwen*
The only examples are the past participles:
Ein edler gartten wart *gepaüen*, 32,1,1.
zwelff weinstock waren wol *gehaüen*, 32,1,5.

ei
MHG. *hei𝕫en*
A few times Hans Sachs spells the preterit with an *i*:
his Andreola clare, 25,1,7.

o
MHG. *sto𝕫en*
The preterit may show the vowel *i*:
an sein hent sy im *stisse,* 25,8,4.

u
The few forms for the verb *rufen* point to both the strong and the weak
verbs, MHG. *ruofen* and *rüefen*:
vnd *rüffet* ein ritter vür sich, 23,9,6.
so ich in sŭnd entschliff / mit der genaden stim mir *riff*, 7,3,25-26.
da günd der ritter *riffe,* 24,7,2.

IRREGULAR VERBS

MHG. *gân, gên*
Hans Sachs uses this verb frequently in rhyme:

als er am firmamente *gat*, 2,2,12.
seit das mon heüt den dag *pegat*, 11,1,5.
das sie nit *vberget*, 26,3,20.
dar ein der früm Joseph müst *gen*, 11,2,13.
Der . . . keisser lies / . . . / aüs *gen* vnd melt, 9,3,8 and 11.

MHG. *stân, stên*
The vowels *a* and *e* are almost equally distributed in the present:
die hül nit lang *bestat* 35,1,10.
da von geschriben *stet* lobsam, 13,1,17.
dw *stest* in schweren sorgen, 7,1,27.
der frücht die in dem edlen garten *stan*, 32,3,15 (see the note on this).

Within the same strophe Hans Sachs uses both forms of the infinitive:
bües mit warheit mag *bestan*, 27,6,10.
let in beÿ seinem berd *besten*, 27,6,12.

Both the singular and the plural imperative serve as a kind of "fill-in":
wegen der schopfüng *verste*, 6,3,13.
kein güt er ir nit dette / *verstette*, 19,1,11-12.
dürch den dichter *verstant*, 35,3,10.
. . . die ist ein schilt / vür onfechtüng *verstat*, 26,5,1-2.

In the preterit the Middle German vowel *u* is common for both singular and plural; twice, however, the vowel *a* appears in the 3. singular without the final consonant:
die fraw *stünd* gar ellende, 19,3,5.
veÿel rossen *stünden* an allen orte, 32,1,8.
Sein libe müter *stan* vor im, 8,1,13 (see the note on this verse).
. . . das dote kindlein schan / *aüf stan*, 19,4,17-18.

The preterit subjunctive:
des stet *stünd* mein hercz in freüden prünst, 38,3,26.

MHG. *tuon*
With only one exception Hans Sachs uses the consonant *d* initially for this verb:
dürch worttes krafft die der priester da sprechen *dut*, 2,3,15.
dü mir aüf meinem münde, 19,1,3.
die im kein hilff mocht *dün*, 8,3,16.
Aüs dem ich mag / hie *ton* ein frag, 6,1,23-24 (see the note on this).
Ich *det* ein gang, 22,1,2.

det er des nit er sech ir nÿmer mere, 24,4,13.
wie vbel hastŭ an dir *dan,* 20,5,4.

MHG. *wiʓʓen*
The imperative sometimes serves as a "fill-in":
vnd sprach verlas mich nit das *wÿs,* 20,3,10.
der vogel *wist,* 22,5,19.

In the preterit Hans Sachs uses forms with both the vowel *e* and the vowel *i*
(ÿ):
vnd *west* doch nit was er verdecket drüge, 23,9,12.
. . . das selb die fraw nit *wist,* 20,3,25.
vmb die sach er nit *wÿste,* 24,5,7.
westen nit bes des hercze war, 23,11,3.
gar heimelich das ir vatter nit *beste,* 25,1,13.

MHG. *gunnen, günnen*
In three of the four examples for this verb Hans Sachs uses the umlauted
form:
der ich euch wol *gane,* 37,2,2.
sie *ginet* im das vnd vil me, 27,4,6.
den dw mir lebendig nÿt woltest *gine,* 23,12,13.
des ir der man nit *gÿnde,* 19,1,23.

MHG. *kunnen, künnen*
Preterit indicative: da sie ir kint ersehen *kündt,* 11,2,19.

Along with the vowel *u* in the preterit subjunctive there is one form with an
e:
. . . gedacht sie . . . wie sÿ / Aüch disen strengen ritter sehen *kündte,*
24,2,10-11.
künt / er mich leren dichten . . . , 33,2,25-26.
ob ich die künst erkennen *kent,* 34,2,4 (see the note on this verse).

MHG. *mugen, mügen*
Present indicative:
vn den vns nÿmant helfen *mag,* 10,1,22.
Mag sich verwandlen prot vnd wein, 2,3,1.
dar aüf *maget* ir eüren goder waschen, 36,2,10.
das *mügen* wol los fischer sein, 40,2,13.

Present subjunctive:
dass ich heŭt *müg* aŭs schreÿen, 20,1,5.

Preterit indicative:
das sie ihn kaüm erkennen *mocht*, 8,1,24.
die im kein hilff *mocht* dün, 8,3,16.

In the preterit subjunctive Hans Sachs uses both umlauted and unumlauted forms:
ob ich der aüch ain dail hÿ *mecht* gemercken, 34,3,10.
wie er balt kümen *mechte*, 23,4,2.
ir nit entrinen *mecht*, 7,1,21.
mocht ich sein künst gelere, 37,1,5.
. . . hetten sie schnellen rat / wie sie sich om Gerbino *mochten* rechen, 24,8,15-16.

MHG. *müeȥen*
Present indicative:
ich *müs* mich von ir scheiden zwar, 8,4,12.
misen wir alle sterben, 4,3,24.

Preterit indicative:
dar ein der früm Joseph *müst* gen, 11,2,13.

Preterit subjunctive:
misten sünst ewig kümer dol, 8,4,25.

MHG. *soln*
In the 2. singular present indicative Hans Sachs uses the MHG. form both in and out of rhyme:
dar peÿ dw mercken *solt*, 27,4,8.
vnd sprach dw *solt* ein kindelein geperen, 10,2,12.

In the 2. plural present indicative we find both the vowel *o* and the umlaut of *o*:
Straffer vnd reiczer *solt* ir lonn, 30,1,17.
. . . die rein / vberdraff alle creatür / . . . ir mercken *selt*, 13,1,22-24 (see the note on verse 24).

The preterit subjunctive shows both the umlauted and the unumlauted vowel:
man bringen *selt*, 9,3,13 (see the note on this verse).
er sprach *solt* ich durch schwer draüm dich meiden / so kem ich . . . , 25,4,13-14.
solt da nit pein, 8,5,21.

MHG. *wellen*
Present indicative:
Wiltw wissen wer disser wünde ritter seÿ, 22,5,1.
das er gesang zw horen *wel*, 30,1,7 (see the note on this verse).

The preterit subjunctive shows umlaut:
fragt warvmb sie von erst nit kümen *welt*, 25,4,10.

MHG. *sin*
The 1. and 3. plural present indicative are present in a variety of forms:
seit wir . . . / in grossem dribsal *sein*, 15,3,2 and 4.
darvmb *seÿ* wir cristen verpflicht, 10,3,15 (see the note on this verse).
scharff künst die *sin* so weck, 34,2,5 (see note 5,5,11).
das *sein* die siben freÿen künst, 32,2,8.
sÿ *sind* vn mie, 5,4,4.
Zwü / natür *sint* in cristo fron, 6,1,12-13.
wan alle ding got müglich *sent*, 2,3,23 (see the note on this verse).

Singular imperative
nün *pis* mir got wilkumen, 23,10,2.

For the 1. and 3. singular preterit indicative there are two forms, MHG. *was* and NHG. *war*, both used within the verse and in rhyme; sometimes a spurious *t* is added to *war:*
der ÿe *was* et nüncet semper, 1,1,9.
wünd ir rechte hant *was*, 39,1,25.
das / *war* von himel dawe / nas, 17,2,34-36.
Das da genczlich erfüllet *war*, 8,3,1.
Disser jüngling *wart* nit von edlem stame, 25,1,11.

The 3. singular preterit subjunctive is always umlauted:
dar vm so *wer* der peste rat, 29,1,24.

WEAK VERBS

MHG. *haben, hân* (Even though this verb is used more frequently as an auxiliary than as an independent verb, I shall simply refer to the tenses as present or preterit.) In the 1. singular present indicative and in the infinitive the contracted form is the usual one:
das zw ercleren *han* ich müt, 31,1,8.
dar in ich vür genümen *hon*, 28,1,4.

ich *hab* kein mon erkennet, 12,1,14 (once).
zw pantoffelen müs man *han*, 21,4,18.

The plural of the present indicative shows variety:
darüm *hab* wir den dot gar nit verschuld, 23,8,10.
hat ir gelt nit on pfant wil ich euch porgen, 36,3,8.
als ir in der histori *hant* vernümen, 24,13,12 (see the note on this verse).
Die feind die . . . / . . . aüf geschlagen *han* ir czelt / vnd *han* verschrancket weg
vndt stras, 32,3,1-2 (see note 21,5,15).
der dumen mercker die da *hant*, 40,3,2.

In the 1. and 3. singular preterit indicative both *hat* and *het*, mostly without
an ending, are used in and out of rhyme:
dar ab ich grosses wünder *hat*, 22,1,13.
Der *hat* ein dochter miniklich / hies Andreola clare, 25,1,6-7.
ich *het* kein gelt er gab mir wein, 21,1,13.
disse iünckfraw *het* haimelich / ein jüngling aüs erkoren, 25,1,8-9.
der ein früm ebeib *hette*, 19,1,9.

The 3. plural preterit indicative shows only the vowel *e*:
vorlang verkündet *hetten*, 11,1,9.
dar vmb *hetten* sie schnellen rat, 24,8,15.

The preterit subjunctive also has the vowel *e:*
hestw mich vmb dissen jüngling gepetten, 25,11,13.
plato . . . leren det / welicher disse libe *het* / der *het* aller dügent ein würcz,
27,1,22-24.
dürch sein vrteil . . . / *het* ir den leib verloren, 7,1,18-19.

MHG. *antwürten*
Present indicative:
die meit *antwürt* aus fate, 20,4,5.

MHG. *bringen*
Preterit subjunctive:
er im gedacht wie er sie *precht* in dotes we, 19,1,25.
aüf das er wider *prechte*, 16,7,9.

MHG. *dunken*
Present indicative:
wan sie *dünket* ein aügenplick, 7,3,18.

Preterit indicative:
In dem *daücht* mich wie ein graüsamer würme, 25,5,11.
Dreÿ fischer *daüchten* sich gar klüg, 40,1,11.

MHG. *hôeren, hôren*
Hans Sachs uses both forms of the verb, the first exclusively in rhyme, the second almost always within the verse.

Present indicative and infinitive:
der sing was idem zw *gehert*, 29,3,25.
lob / lichen *hort* er singe, 17,2,12-13.
dar zw sie doch *gehoren* nit, 31,2,9.
darvmb so wolt ich geren *horen* singen, 34,1,9.
Die wolt ich von eüch also geren *heren*, 34,3,9.

The imperative serves as a "fill-in":
Ir erste eigenschafft nün *her*, 26,2,1.
nün *hor* vür pas mer aigenschafft, 26,2,27.

Preterit indicative:
der *hort* ich singen ane zil, 33,1,5.
Do Wilhelmüs dÿ mer *er hert*, 24,12,1.
der graff . . . / die greffÿn (acc.) noch nit *horte*, 20,4,20-21.

The past participle:
Das neü gesang war pald *erhert*, 10,3,11.
soliches war *derhoret* nÿe, 19,4,4.

MHG. *kennen, nennen*
For the past participle Hans Sachs uses both the short and the longer form:
Aüs disser kür wirt sie *erkent*, 13,3,16.
Dreÿ nommen vnd ein got *genent*, 1,1,6.
sein nam wart . . . / in den landen *erkennet*, 24,2,1-2.
genenet Quisgardüs, 28,7,2.

MHG. *legen*
Two examples for the 3. singular present indicative show the contracted form; the third the longer:
den sin / der schopfvng man sitlich *aüs leit*, 6,3,9-10.
vür esel rindt es in das kriplein *leget*, 11,2,22.

For the 1. and 3. singular preterit indicative and for the past participle Hans
Sachs uses contracted forms:
ich *leit* mich in das gras, 39,1,13.
nam sein hercze / vnd *leit* das in ein kopff . . . , 23,9,4-5.
ein prinlein was *geleit* mit meisterscheffte, 32,1,10.

MHG. *sagen*
Most of the forms show contraction; only a few do not:
Hor bie *seit* vns Sanctus paülus, 26,6,7.
als vns apocalipsis *seit*, 1,2,6.
Ein engel pal / den frümen hirtten *saget*, 11,3,1-2 (once).
. . . *sag* danck dem almechtigen got, 20,5,25 (once).
dar vmb sein lob singt vnde *seit*, 9,5,17 (once).
Dar in vand sie das hercz vnd *seit*, 23,10,1.
Der *sageten* gros lob alt vnd jünge, 19,5,14 (once).
Her Simeon het weis *geseit*, 8,2,25.

MHG. *senden*
The past participle has two forms:
Ein engel wart *gesante,* 12,1,1.
der sein sün hat *gesendet* auf die erden, 10,3,5.

The infinitive without zu:

das drib sie schir bis es beginet *dagen*, 25,8,13.
das günden sie *gloriren*, 11,3,7.
dar ein so lobt er *kümen*, 25,2,4.
vnd daüchten sich doch meister *sein*, 33,1,9.
. . . der graf da *aüf blicken* pflag, 20,2,25.

The past participle without the prefix ge:

wie vbel hastü an dir *dan*, 20,5,4.
dw hast vns *pracht* die himelischen frichte, 16,4,16.
Do das gepot *aüs gangen* war, 9,3,15.
pin *kümen* ane scherczen, 22,3,16.
wirt dürch die sporen *zwüngen*, 22,5,11.

The prefix zer

Hans Sachs uses a Middle German form *zu* for this:
vnd beleibet doch *vnzwdrent*, 2,2,10 (see the note on this verse).

zw schmilczet gar / dein freüd . . . , 5,5,15-16.
ein *vnzürissen* garen, 40,3,17.

Circumlocution

In order to produce the present or preterit of a verb in a roundabout way, Hans Sachs combines its infinitive with the present or preterit of one of the three verbs *sein, tun,* and *werden.* Of these he uses *tun* most frequently (see P-G § § 287 and note 1, as well as 295, note, and Weinhold, § § 428-429).
ein schlang *verlissen ist* ir gifft, 2,3,17.
Aüf das ich nit mein grosse schant *dw mere,* 37,1,4.
der richter da *pegeren det,* 25,12,8.
Die . . . / *detten* dem künig *clagen,* 24,11,6-7.
do *bart* ein altes vich haüs *sten,* 11,2,12.
da ich *wardt* schaten *vinde,* 39,1,12.

Personal pronouns

For the genitive and dative plural of the third person Hans Sachs makes use of the MHG. forms:
man sicht *ir* vil in vngelick vmbwatten, 25,13,12.
der dot / düt *in* kein not, 5,2,21-22.

For the dative singular of the reflexive he also employs MHG. forms:
die er *im* hat erkoren, 7,1,16.
Sic machet *ir* ein tranck von herbem giffte, 23,11,11.

Enclitic *du* and *es*
zwelff ze fellig freid *herste,* 5,2,6.
gegrüst *seistw* genaden vol, 12,1,7.
wie vbel *hastü* an dir dan, 20,5,4.
den *dis* verloren hande, 16,3,7.
so reipt *ers* nein, 21,2,19.
seit / *ichs* nit kann verpringen, 29,1,7-8.

The cardinal *zwei*

For this Hans Sachs uses the MHG. form:
so sich *zwen* reimen pinden zw, 31,2,2.
Zwü / *natür* sint in cristo fron, 6,1,12-13.
mit *zweÿen* junckfrawen virwar, 20,2,18.

ADVERBS

As a rule Hans Sachs uses the ending *en* for an adverb ending in *lich:*
Meitlichen rein on alle mon, 9,2,1.
nemlichen nach Bernhardüs sag, 13,2,13.
wü sie *in hiczigklichen* prent, 28,1,9.

dar and *da*
dar is used not only before propositions beginning with a vowel, but also before those beginning with a consonant; *da* is used once with *bei*, twice with *von*, but always with *mit*; once before a vowel:
dar peÿ ich kein wercke, 4,1,49.
dar dürch magstŭ entrinen, 7,2,23.
darnach so merck, 3,1,23.
dar von er manigfaltig schrib, 26,6,11.
vnd das ein mensch *dar vüre* ging, 2,2,23.
dar zw ist sie ein festes pant, 27,7,10.
da in doch ist ewige wün, 4,2,5.

2. **Syntax and Usage**

Cases of nouns

GENITIVE
As a possessive it may precede the noun; come between a preposition and its noun; between an article or the attributive adjective and its noun:
als wenig ich *des wassers* flüs, 1,3,9.
dem dŭt erpleichen gancz / *gotlicher genaden* gelancz, 28,2,22-23.
in *deines heiles* vresprüng, 11,1,3.
aüf das ich vor *der meister* münt / müg hÿ sten . . . , 26,5,26-27.
pedeŭt das *dages* licht, 7,2,17.
menschlichen *Gottes* süne, 11,1,7.

Of measure:
vnd rüstet zw *grosser galleien zwü*, 24,6,5.
wie *gros* gewesen sint / *der schmercz* mein liebes kint, 8,6,13-14.

Of time; and with an adverb of time:
Eins nachcz het die jüng fraw ein draüm, 25,3,1.
wan *meines lebes nÿmer* seÿ, 8,7,23.

Linguistic Summary

With *nicht:*
nit / drostes mag mir werden, 4,1,46-47.
Maniger düt *desselben nicht,* 29,1,17.

With an adjective:
freÿ aller erbsünd ich verkündt, 13,3,6.
Der rede do / *der* was ich *fro,* 21,2,1-2.

With the substantive *vil:*
sie neret *vil der cleinen kint,* 27,5,26.

As a partitive:
do *as* ich . . . / *der frücht süperbia* . . . , 39,2,17-18.

The subject is attracted into the genitive:
Wan *scharpffer künste der* sind alss mengerleÿe, 34,2,9.

Above all as the object of a verb:
keiner kürczweil sie *acht,* 28,3,2.
vnd *disser fricht begert,* 32,1,14.
Dw *pflagst* mit Qwisgardo *der lib,* 23,8,1.
die fraw *der red erschrack,* 25,6,1.
so *küm* ich *meins betrüebtes lebens ab,* 24,12,10.
nÿm der straff ware, 7,3,20.
des dodes ich icz *wartte,* 4,2,42.
der ritter *aller seinen sin vergasse,* 24,7,12.
Da *dacht* ich . . . / *der vnfleisigen sachen,* 40,2,11-12.

DATIVE
With the prepositions *gen* and *ob* (meaning *über*):
gen im dich ieb / im werck der lieb, 5,1,4-5.
vnd *gen dem himel* sache, 19,3,11.
erschrack *ob dissem wünder,* 20,2,21.
Doch / sie ich *ob mir* gelenczen von veren, 4,2,25-26.

With the adverb *nahe:*
Aüf einer linden *der* ich *nahet* kam, 22,1,9.
der linden drat ich *neher* pas, 22,1,22.

With various verbs:
dem seinen schwinden zoren / ir nit *entrinen* mecht, 7,1,20-21.

mit der genaden stim *mir riff*, 7,3,26.
sein anher müst *dem seinen pot gennüge*, 24,12,13.
Der richter *glaübet* nit *den iren worte*, 25,9,11.
den armen (pl.) sie gar nit *verschmecht*, 27,2,9.

ACCUSATIVE

Occasionally a double accusative:
würd *den heiden* (sg.) *die dat* beweist, 24,11,3.
die krancken erczeneÿ sie leÿt, 27,5,25.

With prepositions denoting place where:
zw singen hÿ *aüf dissen plan*, 29,1,3.
das ist *in die scherpff* gar vnrein, 31,2,10 (but in 31,1,7 the dative case: was
in der scherpff zu straffen wer).

With an intransitive verb of motion:
er kon nit *gen neüe gespor,* 35,2,15 (once).

Economy of Expression

Subject lacking but can be supplied by the subject of the preceding
independent clause:
das röslein . . . / *Jist* des menschen vernüft . . . / *wirt* dürch die sporen
zwüngen, 22,5, 7,9, and 11.

Subject supplied by the subject of the preceding dependent clause:
seit das *sant Athanasius* / von got*het* solich gras genat / . . . / *hat* heimelich
vnd stil / *geschriben* vil, 1,2,17-21.

Subject supplied by the object of the main introductory clause:
ich *erplicket* in schlaffes qüal / *ein fraüen pild* mit wune / . . . / vnd *was* von
leib gros schwanger, 39,1,18-19 and 27.

Ἀπὸ κοινοῦ construction:
die helle / *han ver dint ich pin* schüldig an ir peider dot, 20,5,12-13.
. . . merck das *ist der leibe dein* / *ist* aüf der pürg entschlafen, 7,2,4-5.

The predicate noun of the preceding sentence serves for the person addressed
in the following one:
das / *ist* / *Maria* milde / bilde / *secz* deiner parmüng schilde, 4,2,29-32.

The object of the verb in the first main clause serves also as object in the two following independent clauses:
vnd *namen dissen iüngling* drat / *wolten* vür seines vatters haüsse *dragen* / Sie *drügen* aüs dem gartten her, 25,8,15-16 and 9,1.

Article omitted in prepositional phrase:
in freüd ewiger selikeit, 1,3,27.
nÿmet dar aüs ir speis *mit ler*, 2,1,22.
vor angsten mange schweiste, 23,11,2.
Zü morgen frü die fraw aüf stünd, 19,2,8.

PRONOMINAL ADJECTIVES AND SUBSTANTIVES (see Weinhold, §§ 485 and 508, and W. *BGr.,* § 365)

POSSESSIVES
Often uninflected as adjective:
mein müter heist fraw dreÿ, 39,2,13.
Vnd befalch sich alle dag in *ir* hütte, 19,1,14.
das er *sein* sün wolt lassen menschlich sterben, 10,2,5.
sein freünt günten im ein gemahel geben, 20,3,16.
. . . wende / *dein* aügen zw vns her, 15,4,7-8.
al *vnser* erbeit hartte, 21,5,5.

As substantive uninflected:
Dar vmb ich eüer künst vür die *mein* krone, 36,2,1 (once).

al
As substantive uninflected when preceded by a personal pronoun, or in post position:
wan sie *al* sent, 5,4,17.
. . . seit vns *al* / Adam / . . . zw vale pracht, 3,3,6-8.

As limiting adjective sometimes inflected, sometimes not:
aller parmüg ein vber flüs, 15,2,21.
an *alle* hindernüsse, 5,3,3.
die frümen dragen ir *al* günst, 27,7,6.
da mit *al* meister sind gespeist, 1,1,26.

Uninflected before demonstrative and possessive adjectives:
der lis beschreiben *al* dis welt, 11,2,5.

zw dir stet *al* mein hoffen, 4,2,35.
betrüebet waren *al* sein sin, 8,2,4.

ander
Inflected and uninflected as substantive; uninflected as adjective:
vnd sprach dů hast ein *andre* aůserkoren, 20,5,16.
züm *andren* die menscheit cristj ansecht, 13,2,21.
die *ander* ist, 5,2,13.
vnd *ander* lerer mer, 1,3,14.

der
For *der* as a demonstrative pronoun Hans Sachs uses the MHG. form of the
genitive singular, masculine and neuter, and of the dative plural:
ein schwerer draüm *des* wil ich dich bescheiden, 25,4,16.
kein mensch aüch *des* nie wirdig wür, 1,1,17.
den ste dw hilfflich peÿe, 16,5,12.

dis
Hans Sachs at times uses this short form of the demonstrative adjective in the
nominative and accusative singular:
Pald *dis* vrteil gefellet was, 19,5,8.
vm *djs* mort lest dotten . . . , 19,2,7.
der lis peschreiben al *dis* welt, 11,2,5.

ein, kein
For the most part uninflected as articles in the nominative and accusative
singular, masculine and feminine:
das was *ein* minikliche dochter schone, 23,1,16.
kein züng / der lerer nie dein lob ergrint, 15,2,5-6.
Da horet er *ein* stime süs, 1,3,7.
an seinem dot hab ich aber *kein* schüld, 25,11,10.
ich det *ein* gang, 22,1,2.
in not sie *kein* kristen verlat, 13,3,24.

Inflected as pronouns:
gib im *einen* der im gefal, 24,13,14.
keiner sol gründen vüre pas, 1,3,18.

manic
Sometimes uninflected as adjective in the nominative and accusative:
manig lerer mir zeücknüs git, 26,5,18.
vnd hat beweget *manig* frag, 1,3,5.
. . . so sprach er *manig* mal 20,5,2.

Inflected as pronoun:
Maniger düt desselben nicht, 29,1,17.
sie warnet *manigen* vor not, 27,5,4.

selp, selbic

Hans Sachs uses these two words only a few times; as adjective *selp* is inflected, *selbic* is not; neither is inflected as substantive:
Die fraw beschlos die *selben* dir, 23,6,6.
das *selb* mein namen haben sol, 20,5,20.
die *selbig* wünt wirt selten heil, 28,1,23.
das *selbig* es aüch williklich / solt einen anderen verlon, 27,1,17.

solich

The few examples of this word show the uninflected form for the adjective in the accusative singular, feminine and neuter, but the inflected form in the dative singular and the accusative plural; the substantive is inflected:
von gothet *solich* gras genat, 1,2,18.
dar ab sie *solich* leid gewan, 8,1,25.
von *solchem* ritterlichen spil, 29,2,23.
da er *soliche* worte / erhorte, 19,2,23-24.
solches war derhoret nÿe, 19,4,4.

welich

Hans Sachs uses this only as relative pronoun and always inflects it:
von dreÿen entpfencknusen ir / in *welchen* sie dreÿ hohe kir, 13,1,6-7.
ir erst enpfencknüs / *weliche* was von ewigkeit, 13,1,9-10.
Plato . . . leren det / *welicher* disse libe het, 27,1,22-23.

ATTRIBUTIVE ADJECTIVES (Weinhold, § § 509-514; 516-521; 523-525)

Hans Sachs leaves these uninflected about as often as he inflects them. I shall give a few examples only for the uninflected:
das der *helisch* drack nit er laüf, 16,3,3.
was gangen an ein *lüstig* stat, 22,1,5.
opfert sie got ir *rein* gepet, 26,3,22.
Darnach virt der graff *gotfürchtig* leben, 20,3,14.
das mügen wol *los* fischer sein, 40,2,13.
die sein des willen *güt* mit herczen gerden, 10,3,10.

Two examples show strong inflection after an inflected possessive:
we meiner *armer* selle, 20,5,11.
so küm ich meins *betrüeptes* lebens ab, 24,12,10.

When more adjectives than one modify a noun, one or another may be uninflected:

der verleÿch vns rÿ . . . / dar nach ein *güt seliges* ent, 2,3,24-25.
Du *edel reiche* weisse, 20,1,14.
die fraw *arme draŭrig* vnd *vngemŭtte*, 19,1,19.

For the feminine accusative singular Hans Sachs always uses the MHG. weak ending for the attributive adjective:

ich sÿ vor mir den grimen dot / dar zw die *vngewissen* zeit, 4,1,8-9.
die *edlen* kŭngin freÿe / . . . ich sŭcht, 39,3,7-8.

THE CONJUNCTION wan

This may mean *denn, weil, wenn,* and a few times *als:*

wan so enspringet neüe künst, 35,2,11.
wan es den lichten dag her pracht, 10,3,20.
wan er aüf stet, 21,3,3.
wann got al creatür beschlüs, 13,1,11.

THE DOUBLE NEGATIVE

This is frequent usage for Hans Sachs:

kein / güt dat volget mir *nit* nach, 4,1,52-53.
kein hilffe het von *nÿmant nicht,* 8,3,10.
gar *nÿmant* sÿ *nit* arges düt, 26,2,17.

CONGRUENCE

A verb in the singular with more than one subject:
weisheit vnd künst wirt gar veracht, 32,3,18.

A verb in the plural with a collective noun as subject:
der engel *schar / süngen* schon zw der fart, 9,4,23-24.

A neuter singular referring to a definite antecedent in the plural:
Die feind die vmb denn gartten ligen / *das selbÿg* sind al menschen die ich melde, 32,3,1 and 4.
A singular pronoun, but plural antecedent:
dürch wortes crafft *der priester* rein / so *er* ob dem altare stot, 2,3,3-4.

A pronoun has the natural gender instead of the grammatical gender of its antecedent:

dar mit vmb geben wart *das müeterliche hercz / die* im kein hilff mocht dün, 8,3,15-16.

Notes

Introduction

1. A *Spruchgedicht* is a non-strophic poem written in rhyme-pairs; for a list of his twelve summaries see Ellis, *Das Walt got*, p. 8. To conserve space only the title of a work will be quoted the first time, since further information is in the Bibliography. After the first reference to a work abbreviations indicated in that first reference will be used. Where the reference is to an article the name and volume of the periodical will also be given the first time.

2. See Goetze, *Sämmtliche Fastnachtspiele von Hans Sachs*, II, No. 13, vss. 327-336.

3. Possibly Hans Sachs' father sped him on his way with the words which the father of Fortunatus spoke as his son was starting out to make his way in the world. See the *Tragedia*, "Fortunatus mit dem wunschseckel," (Keller-Goetze, eds., *Hans Sachs* 12, 189, 25-31) written in 1553:

> "Mein son, ich will dirs gleid nauβ geben.
> Sey frumb! thu Gott vor augen hon
> Und sey getrew bey iedermon!
> Red wenig und hör aber vil!
> Meid fürwitz, böβ gselschaft und spil,
> Füllerey sambt allen bösen stücken!
> So mag es dir noch wol gelücken! "

(The Keller-Goetze edition of *Hans Sachs* will be cited henceforth simply as *H. S.;* the first number after that will be the volume, the second the page, and the third the verse; Keller edited the first twelve volumes, Keller and Goetze vols. 13-14; Goetze 15-26; the Index is volume 26 which will be cited simply K-G Index.) For customs to be followed and for rules prescribed by the Guild of Shoemakers see Berlepsch, *Chronik vom ehrbaren Schumacherwerk* (cited Berlepsch), *passim.*

4. See *H. S.* 3, 95, 2-24; 7, 202, 11-22; and 21, 338, 16-20.

5. *H. S.* 7, 202, 3-10 and 24; 205, 17-21; and 209, 10-14 and 21-31. According to Holter-Trathnigg, *Wels von der Urzeit bis zur Gegenwart*, p. 86, the place in which Hans Sachs received his call to be a poet was in Emperor Maximilian's *Tiergarten*, in the area of the Reinberg, south of the Traun River.

6. See note 24 of the Background for Chapter I for Hans Sachs' own words with regard to his love of reading.

7. Hans Sachs actually wrote forty-two Meisterlieder, but did not copy two of these into Berlin 414; for references to these two songs see the K-G Index Nos. 24 and 54; for the former see also the Preliminary to No. 1 of this study. (The Meisterlieder in this study will be cited by number only with the addition of stanza and verse where such is necessary.) For the *Spruchgedichte* see the K-G Index Nos. 32, 33, 58a, and 61; and Nos. 47 and 59 for the Shrovetide plays.

8. See No. 27, *passim* for evidence of Hans Sachs' awareness.

9.   See Nos. 30 and 31.

10.   See the facsimile of Hans Sachs' Preface (the frontispiece of this study); also my "Analysis of Berlin 414," *PMLA*, Vol. LXI, pp. 947-996 (cited henceforth Ellis, "Anal. of Berlin 414"). In making this analysis I found that the total number of Hans Sachs' own Meisterlieder in the manuscript was *forty*, not thirty-nine as scholars through the years had been repeating.

11.   Wackernagel, *Das deutsche Kirchenlied*, Vol. II (cited henceforth *WKL*. II), Nos. 1403-1410.

12.   Goetze and Drescher, eds., say, for instance, in the Introduction to *Fabeln und Schwänke* 3, p. iii: "Zweifelhafte Lesungen zu klären, die Lücken zu ergänzen und hie und da auch des Dichters Niederschrift zu verbessern, dazu haben wir seine eigenhändigen Abschriften, die in verschiedenen Bibliotheken aufbewahrt werden, herangezogen." (This edition will be cited G-D, *Fab. u. Schw.*) Comparison with copies in later manuscripts show how Hans Sachs himself varied his own phraseology.

13.   The quotation is from the second act of the opera; Hans Sachs makes the observation, an indirect reference to Walther.

Chapter I / Meisterlieder of a General Religious Nature

Background

1.   See among others Heerwagen, *Zur Geschichte der Nürnberger Gelehrtenschulen* (cited Heerwagen), pp. 6 and 10; Specht, *Geschichte des Unterrichtwesens in Deutschland* (cited Specht), pp. 73 and 139; and Goetze, *Hans Sachs*, p. 4.

2.   Diesenberg, *Studien zur religiösen Gedankenwelt in der Spruchdichtung des 13. Jahrhunderts* (cited Diesenberg), p. 10.

3.   Liliencron (*Über den Inhalt der allgemeinen Bildung in der Zeit der Scholastik*–cited Liliencron), pp. 5-22 and 26-28, speaks of the influence which Vincenz v. Beauvais' cyclopaedic *Speculum universale* had from the 13th to the 17th cent. on the common man. However there is no proof that it, or a small book based on it by Bartholomaeus Anglicus, was translated into German (there were translations into French, English, Dutch, and Spanish by the end of the 15th cent.) until the end of the 16th cent. when Aegidius Albertinus made use of the *Speculum* for counter-Reformation purposes.

4.   For questions and answers see, for example, Mayer, ed., *Die Meisterlieder des Hans Folz* (cited Mayer, ed., *Folz*), No. 24; for refuting criticism and unbelief, Nos. 72 and 75; for a translation from the Latin, No. 35, vss. 1-2, and No. 56, vss. 1-2; sometimes, as in No. 34, Folz does not translate or even paraphrase the Latin. There are numerous songs among the Meistersinger which make use of analogies. Examples for each one of the points mentioned can also be found in WKL. II, *passim,* in Bartsch, *Meisterlieder der Kolmarer Handschrift* (cited Bartsch), *passim,* and in the Meisterlieder under consideration by Hans Sachs.

5. See Lütcke, *Studien zur Philosophie der Meistersänger* (cited Lütcke), pp. 26-27.

6. Hans Sachs (26,6,27) expresses this with the words: "nach meinem verstant."–The numbers in parentheses refer to a Hans Sachs Meisterlied in this study in the order: number of the song, strophe, verse. This pattern will be followed throughout the study.

7. See 4,3,20.

8. In 26,2,25-26 Hans Sachs offers the helpful suggestion: "so man in lib genade pit / so wirt sein zoren hingestelt." Cf. Diesenberg, pp. 57-58.

9. See the Background for Chapter II.

10. See 1,3,17; also Mayer, ed., *Folz*, No. 72, 185-189 (since the verses in the Folz Meisterlieder are numbered consecutively throughout a poem, the second number will always refer to a verse; the strophe will never be indicated. This procedure will also hold for the songs of other Meistersinger whose verses are numbered consecutively). Cf. Schwiebert, *Luther and his Times*, p. 166.

11. See 1,3,18-22 and Mayer, ed., *Folz*, No. 17, 126-128.

12. See 13,3,12-13.

13. Cf. Lütcke, p. 141.

14. See Heerwagen (p. 3) who says there were four Latin schools in Nuremberg, "bei St. Sebald, St. Lorenz, beim neuen Spital und im Schottenkloster bei St. Aegidien." Hans Sachs, according to Goedeke, *Dichtungen von Hans Sachs* I (cited Goedeke, *H. S.* I), p. xviii, most probably attended the one "beim neuen Spital zum heiligen Geist"; cf. Mummenhof, *Hans Sachs*, p. 7; for the number of years which Hans Sachs attended the school see his own words, *H. S.* 21, 337, 15-19 and 23.

15. For the account of the school day, the three divisions, and the subjects taught see Heerwagen, pp. 8-10. Hans Sachs' schooling falls into the period after the Nuremberg Council undertook the reform of the four schools in 1485. It was not until after the Reformation, however, that fundamental changes were made; for the discussion of the schools in Nuremberg from 1485-1526 see the whole article by Heerwagen; cf. Siebenkees, *Materialien zur Nürnbergischen Geschichte* I (cited Siebenkees), pp. 278-300.

16. The subjects which Hans Sachs says he studied are (*H. S.* 15, 550, 9-12 and 15-23):

> Der grammatica, rhetorica,
> Der logica und musica,
> Arithmetica, astronomia,
> Poetrey und philosophia
>
> Da ich lehrt griechisch und latein,
> Artlich wol reden, war und rein;
> Rechnen auch lehrt ich mit verstandt,
> Die außmessung mancherley land;

> Auch lehrt ich die kunst der gestirn,
> Der menschen geburt judicirn,
> Auch die erkentnuβ der natur
> Auff erden, mancher creatur
> Im lufft, fewer, wasser und erden;

17. Heerwagen, p. 10. In 1563 Hans Sachs remembered (*H. S.*, 15, 550,27 and 551,1-2) that he "Lehrt auch endtlich die poetrey / Darinn an tag zu geben frey / Manniches höfliches gedicht."

18. See Heerwagen, p. 8; religion was taken for granted; in none of his twelve summaries (see Ellis, *Das Walt got*, p. 8, note 19, for the list of these) does Hans Sachs mention having learned its basic tenets.

19. See Specht, p. 139; Siebenkees (p. 282) states that "Die Schüler wurden bey dem Choral- und Figuralgesang in den Gottesdiensten gebraucht, und die Leichen in jeder Pfarre durch sie besungen."

20. Specht, p. 73.

21. Messenger, *The Medieval Latin Hymn* (cited Messenger), pp. 32, 44, and 71.

22. G-D, *H. S. Fab. u. Schw.* 6, No. 1010, vss. 13-18.

23. *H. S.* 15, 550, 24-25.

24. Hans Sachs refers to his love of reading in this wise (*H. S.* 23, 107, 13-18):

> Mein kurzweil aber ist gewesen
> Von jugent auf puecher zw lesen,
> Gaistlich und weltlich auch darpey,
> Histori und auch mancherley
> Schön artlich poetische fabel,
> Schimpflich geleichnus und parabel:

and again (ibid., 133, 16-25):

> Und erwelt mir puecher zu lesen.
> Darin ich mancherley erfuer,
> Darfon klueg und geschicket wuer.
> Dis pfanczet ich fleissig in memori,
> Fing an und las manche histori
> In deutschen puechern allerley,
> Gaistlich und weltlich, auch darpey
> Schön artlich poetische fabel,
> Verporgen gleichnus und parabel.
> Das mich herczlich erfrewen thet.

Added to such generalizations as Hans Sachs makes are the books he had in his own library, the vast number of classical books whose titles have been compiled by Abele (*Die antiken Quellen des Hans Sachs*—cited Abele), and the yet untabulated books mentioned as source material in various studies (including this one) on the poet.

25. Hans Sachs refers to his *sinnreich ingenium* in *H. S.* 15, 550, 13. For the prerequisites of an apprentice and for the hard life entailed in those years of learning a trade see Mummenhof, *Handwerker*, pp. 48-60.

26. For the reference to Nunnenbeck see *H. S.* 23, 107, 22-23, and for the phrase *mit hohem fleiß* see *H. S.* 15, 550, 14.

27. Hans Sachs probably left Nuremberg in the spring of the year 1512 and returned in the fall of 1516 according to Windolph, *Der Reiseweg Hans Sachsens in seiner Handwerks-burschenzeit* (cited Windolph), pp. 13, 29, and 59-63. For the length of time required for an apprentice to learn the trade of shoemaking, see Berlepsch, pp. 62-64; see Krebs, *Alte Handwerksbräuche*, pp. 39-67, for a discussion of journeymen, rites, rules, etc., and cf. Mummenhof, *Handwerker*, pp. 61-74.

28. See *H. S.* 15, 550, 4-7, and 21, 338, 20-22 and 26-28.

29. For the subject matter of all of the Meisterlieder in Berlin 414 see Schroeder, "Topical Outline of Subject Matter in the Berlin MS. *Germ. Quart.* 414," *PMLA*, Vol. LXI (cited Schroeder, "Top. Outline"), pp. 997-1017.

30. See Note 1 to this Meisterlied and cf. the K-G Index, No. 26.

No. 1, foll. 10ʳ-11ʳ   Orig. 5

Preliminary:

1. The three Summaries were written in 1556, 1557, and 1567; for the first two see *H. S.* 23, 107, 27-29; 133, 29-30, and 134, 1; for the third, ibid. 21, 338, 29-33, and 339, 1-3; the quotation from the Dresden MS is cited K-G Index, No. 25. During the two previous years, while journeying from place to place intent upon acquiring an ever greater skill in his trade, Hans Sachs had been storing up knowledge about Meistergesang as well, and as early as 1513 had actually composed two melodies, the *silberweis* and the *gülden don* (see Nos. 14 and 9 respectively). To the latter he set original verses apparently in honor of the Virgin Mary (see the K-G Index, No. 24). He had also been no exception to the rule that boys in their teens tend to fall in love, and, in accord with his nature, had expressed his feelings in songs for which he had made up his own tunes (ibid., Nos. 1-23). With this measure of literary and musical activity behind him it seems strange that he should call the *Gloria patri* his *erst gedicht*. Perhaps the answer lies in the supposition that he considered the twenty-three love ditties to be practice verse which didn't count; perhaps also that the supposed Mary-song had faded in its significance by the time he wrote the three Summaries and entered the *Gloria patri* into the Dresden MS. Moreover he may have deemed it more seemly for his first appearance before the Meistersinger to write a Meisterlied which would show that he had sufficient knowledge of theological problems to use one as subject, and more proper also to set it to the *Ton* of one of the Twelve Masters, rather than to parade a melody of his own composition.

Notes for page 21

2. Hans Sachs seems to have been drawn to the subject of the mystery of the Trinity, for he copied more than fifty Meisterlieder dealing with it into Berlin 414; see Schroeder, "Top. Outline," pp. 1016-1017.

3. See Goedeke, *H. S.* I, No. 2, and Arnold, *Hans Sachs Werke* I (cited Arnold, *H. S.*), pp. 39-41.

Heading: "Marners langer don" is one of the four *gedrönten Töne* (see Taylor, *The Literary History of Meistergesang* (cited Taylor, *Lit. Hist. Mg.*), pp. 70-71, and Taylor-Ellis, *A Bibliography of Meistergesang* (cited Taylor-Ellis, *Biblio.*), pp. 60-61. To this *Ton* Hans Sachs set six Meisterlieder in Berlin 414, two more than to any other *Ton*. Its metric pattern was changed considerably during the course of the years by splitting seven long verses, which ranged from fourteen to seventeen syllables, into two each, so that from the original twenty verses, five in each *Stollen* and fifteen in the *Abgesang*, the strophe became lengthened to six in each *Stollen* and fifteen in the *Abgesang.* —For the structure of the Meisterlied I shall use only the technical terminology which was current at the time that Hans Sachs wrote these songs. Hans Folz mentions *Stollen* and *Abgesang* in one of his poems in Berlin 414 (foll. 474^V-475^V, and Mayer, ed., No. 93, 100 and 104); see also Plate, *Die Kunstausdrücke der Meistersinger* (cited Plate), p. 192. —For the variant forms of the *Ton* see v. d. Hagen, *Minnesinger* (cited v. d. Hagen) IV, pp. 533; 923-924; and 934; Bartsch, Nos. 8 and 93-100; Runge, *Die Sangesweisen der Colmarer Handschrift und die . . .* (cited Runge), Nos. 64a and 64b; Wagenseil, *Buch von der Meistersinger Holdseligen Kunst* (cited Wagenseil), n. pag., [558-559]; Mey, *Der Meistergesang in Geschichte und Kunst* (cited Mey), pp. 169-170 (Mey follows Wagenseil); and Mayer, ed., *Folz*, Nos. 35, 70, 75, and p. 404. For comment on the *Ton* see Münzer, *Das Singebuch des Adam Puschmann* (cited Münzer, *Singebuch*), p. 15, No. 31. Runge, v. d. Hagen, Wagenseil, and Mey print the music along with the text. For his own Meisterlieder Hans Sachs followed the pattern used by Folz with one exception: verse twenty-two in each *Abgesang* has eight syllables to Folz's six. Marner's *langer Ton* has only masculine rhymes. —Goedeke ran vss. 21 and 22, as well as 24 and 25, together, so that each of his strophes has only twenty-five verses instead of twenty-seven. He also made other minor changes here and there. —See Appendix C for the rhyme scheme which Hans Sachs used. —lieder: this is Hans Sachs' word for strophes, the only one he uses in these early Meisterlieder. Sax: Hans Sachs uses the consonant *x* for *chs* in the spelling of his name frequently; see W. *BGr.*, § 177 for the substitution. During the years 1514 through 1517 the poet writes *Hans Sax gedicht* twice, *Hans Saxen gedicht* fourteen times in the Headings of his songs, and uses *Hans Saxe* once in rhyme; in sixteen Headings he makes use of his initials, *H. S;* only three times during those four years does he spell his name with *ch*: once within the verse and twice in rhyme, all in the year 1516. However, in the year 1518 he writes *Hans Sachsen gedicht* in the Headings for all eight of his Meisterlieder.

1, 1 Gloria patrÿ: this canticle is based on Matt. 28:19, a paraphrase of which has, in part, been in use since the 1st cent. Hans Sachs was very familiar with it, because it is an integral part of the Mass (see Jungmann, *The Mass of the Roman Rite*, pp. 218 and 221). vnd: the regular spelling in these songs for *und*. Hans Sachs paraphrases the Latin as he goes along. er: *Ehre*; when Hans Sachs drops an *e* for the sake of the rhyme or syllable count, it is to be expected, since this is common practice in the Bavarian dialect (see W. *BGr.*, § 15 and *passim*).

2 dron: for this use of *Thron* see the apocryphal book *Die Weisheit Solomonis* 9:10 and 18:15 (my Biblical references and quotations are from the German translation by Luther,

a Bible in which some of the apocryphal books are included; when the Vulgate Bible is quoted, it will be so stated.)

3 her: (MHG. *her*, adj.) *herrlich.*

4 fron: (MHG. *vrône*, adj.) *heilig.*

5 lab: *Lob*; Weinhold (*BGr.*, § 6) states that he found irrefutable evidence that the substitution of *a* for *o*, so common in the Bavarian dialect, rests not on "Verdumpfung des *a*, sondern auf Öffnung des *o*." This substitution is common practice for Hans Sachs.

6 nommen: *Namen*; on the other hand, Weinhold (*BGr.*, § 22) says with regard to the substitution of *o* for *a*, "Eine reiche Quelle des unechten *o* ist die Neigung des bairischen *a* sich zu verdumpfen."

7 mer: this word has been crossed out in the manuscript and the word *aǔch* written above the line between "vnd" and "ÿmer"; I am keeping the original, because the writing of the emendation is that of a later hand.

9 ÿe: (MHG. *ie*, adv.) *immer*; was: more often than not Hans Sachs uses this MHG. form of the pret.; nüncet: (CL. *nunc et*).

10 on abelon: (MHG. *âne abe lân*) *ohne Ablassen.*

11 secülor vm: (CL. *saeculorum*) Hans Sachs uses the vowel *e* for the diphthong *ae* in accordance with Medieval Latin orthography.

12 vn: (MHG. *ân*, prep.) *ohne*; a virgule inserted between "welt" and "ewig" is a scribal error.

13 seinen sün gepirt: the Meistersinger frequently referred to this article of faith; for theological references see 2,24 below.

17 des: the MHG. gen. of the demonstrative pronoun with the adj. "wirdig"; wür: *würde*; see W. *BGr.*, § 149 for the form; Shumway (*Das ablautende Verbum bei Hans Sachs*, p. 69) cites this form, in rhyme as late as the year 1558. It is suggested that the reader consult Shumway for Hans Sachs' later usage of particular forms, and that he compare James, *Die starken Praeterita in den Werken von Hans Sachs*. Shumway's study is based on the works of the poet which have been published; see his Introduction for the list of those he used. James also used published works.–The thought in this and the following verse may have had its origin in Rev. 5:1-3.

20 den siben künsten: Hans Sachs lists these at random in vss. 21-24; see Notes 15 and 16 to the Background for Chapter I for the Liberal Arts which were taught in the Nuremberg schools and for those which Hans Sachs says he studied. The Meistersinger stressed a knowledge of these Arts; see Schroeder, "Top. Outline," p. 1014, for a list of five Meisterlieder on the subject in Berlin 414, and see a Meisterlied by Folz which Hans Sachs copied in Berlin 414 (foll. 272^V-274^r), published by Ellis, "The Solution for the Enigmatic Concluding Lines of the Munich Codex Germanicus 6353," *PMLA*, Vol. 67, pp. 446-472 (cited Ellis, "Solution . . ."). This song treats the Seven Liberal Arts, their masters, planets, colors, and metals. For a brief discussion of the Arts and Meistergesang see Taylor, *Lit. Hist. Mg.*, pp. 92-93.

21 geamatreÿ: (CL. *geōmetria*) Hans Sachs uses the ending *eÿ* in analogy, perhaps, with that of "melodeÿ" (25) and for the sake of his rhyme with "freÿ" (29).

23 loica: this second art of the trivium was more commonly called *dialectica*; Folz in his Meisterlied (see Ellis, "Solution . . .," p. 450, strophe II, vs. 4) used the term *loice* for CL. *logica.*

24 gramatia: the omission of the *c* is a scribal error.

25 süssen: this may be either the MHG. variant *suoӡ*, adj., or the Middle German form *sûӡe*; melodeÿ: the Early NHG. form. The very fact that Hans Sachs makes an additional statement with regard to music alone of all the Arts might well imply his great love for it.

26 al meister: here with the meaning of *Gelehrte*; sind gespeist: an apt, original figure of speech.

2, 1 adelar: (MHG. *adelar*, wkm.). The eagle is commonly recognized as the symbol for St. John. The origin of the symbolism, which became the basis for the representation of the four evangelists, is to be found in Ezekiel 1:5 and 10 (cf. Rev. 4:7). On the basis of Ezekiel's vision Irenaeus of Lyons (ca. 115-200) declared there had to be four gospels, thereby giving rise to the symbolism of the winged man for Matthew, the lion for Mark, the ox for Luke, and the soaring eagle for John (see also Hulme, *Symbolism in Christian Art,* pp. 132-134 and 190). The Meistersinger frequently alluded to John as *Adler;* see among others Frauchiger, *Dresden M 13,* XXVII, p. 41 and XLI, p. 50 (cited Frauchiger).

3 ein wessen clar: Hans Sachs may mean *das Wesen Gottes,* i. e., the substance of the Deity of which the "dreÿ person" are part, so that St. John would be seeing the Trinity at the same time that he would be seeing the One; cf. Mechthild von Magdeburg, *Das fliessende Licht der Gottheit,* p. 126.

4 ein maget: the Virgin Mary; see also Frauchiger, XXVII, 2, 5-9.

5 bekünt: (MHG. *bekunden,* wkv.) p. part. *bekundet.*

7 der himel: gen. pl.; Hans Sachs consistently uses the plural; there are a number of instances of this in the Old Testament, so, for example, Isa. 44:23 and 49:13; Job 41:2; Pss. 50:6, etc.; and in the New Testament among others, 2. Cor. 12:2; see Grimm, *DW.* 4, Pt. 2, col. 1333, I, 1, for comment. kar: (MHG. *kor,* stm.) here with the meaning of *himmlischer Raum als Wohnung für Gott.*

8 The concept of vss. 8-10, as well as of 3-4 above, is not to be found in the Apocalypse. I have not been able to find Hans Sachs' source.

10 pron: (MHG. *brinnen,* stv. III,1) pret. *brannte.*

11 nit: Hans Sachs uses this variant form of MHG. *niht* frequently both within the verse and in rhyme.

13 seit: conj. *da;* as in MHG. Hans Sachs uses this also for *weil.*

15 laÿ: (MHG. *leie,* stm., ML. *laicus*); Folz calls himself a *thumer ley* (Mayer, ed., No. 17, 1).

17 Athanasius: one of the outstanding Church Fathers (ca. 296-373); Hans Sachs praises him highly, perhaps because it was primarily due to him that the true deity of Christ was vindicated against Arianism.

18 von gothet: *von Gott hatte.*

19 ein sprechen: (MHG. *insprëchen,* stv. IV) inf. used substantively; des heilligen geist: see Weinhold, § 448, for comment on the uninflected gen. in the singular.

20 This may refer to the time when Athanasius lived as an exile in Rome; hat . . . geschriben (21): the subject is "Athanasius" (17).

24 des sünes ewiger gepürt: for a discussion of this theological point see Scheeben, *Handbuch der Katholischen Dogmatik, Fünftes Buch: Erlösungslehre* (cited Scheeben, *Erlösungslehre*) I, §§ 511-535 and 571-573.

26 münt: synecdoche; Hans Sachs often uses this particular figure.

3, 1 sant Aügüstinus: the greatest of the Church Fathers (354-430).

3 altissimus: CL. superlative.

6 vss. 6-12 refer to a well-known legend which Hans Sachs had perhaps read in *Der Heiligen Leben,* a prose collection of saints' tales; for comment on the collection see the Background for Chap. III.

9 als: adv. *so.*

10 schopffen: (MHG. *schepfen*, wkv.) *schöpfen*; see W. *BGr.*, § 23 for the vowel *o*; grubl: for the loss of the *e* before the *l* see W. *BGr.*, § 14, and for the syllabic value of *l* see ibid., § 158.
11 also: *ebenso*.
17 gelaüben: Folz (Mayer, ed., No. 79, 25-26) voices the same thought.
18 vüre pas: (MHG. *vürbaȝ*, comp. adv.) *weiter*.
20 berÿrt: *bezeichnet*.
21 wir: MHG. *wirt*; for the loss of the final *t* see W. *BGr.*, § 143.
22 zw gepÿrt: the prefix "zw" here has an intensifying effect; see Grimm, *DW*. 16, col. 150, 3,a.
25 reigirt: this is Hans Sachs' usual spelling for this verb; see W. *BGr.*, § 80, for the substitution of *ei* for *e*; see also Folz (Mayer, ed., No. 83, 79) for the same spelling.

1514: for all except two of these Meisterlieder Hans Sachs appends the year in which he wrote the song. Weber (*Zur geschichtlichen Entwicklung und Bedeutung d. dt. Meistergesangs*–cited Weber–, p. 44, note 2) made a scribal error in setting down 1513 for the year.

No. 2, foll. 11^r-12^r Orig. 6

Preliminary:

1. See *WKL*. II, No. 1403; Goedeke, *H. S.* I, No. 3; Arnold, *H. S.* I, pp. 41-43; and Friedman, *Prefigurations in Meistergesang* (cited Friedman), pp. 41 and 104.

Heading: "Marners langer don" is again the melodic pattern.

1, 1 himel keisserin: this is a traditional metaphor for the Virgin Mary, whom Hans Sachs is addressing, and not, as Friedman indicates in a note (p. 31), "an example of the use of prefiguration." The wording in this and in verse 3 is identical with that of the corresponding verses in a Meisterlied by Folz (Mayer, ed., No. 36, 1 and 3); the subject matter of the two poems is, however, quite different.
4 bewer: (MHG. *bewæren*, wkv.) *beweise*; in commenting on the substitution of the vowel *e* for *æ* Weinhold (*BGr.*, §307) says, "Es hängt das wahrscheinlich mit der sich verengenden Aussprache des *æ* zusammen . . . die am entschiedensten in der Nürnberger Mundart erscheint." The first three words in this verse are again identical with the first three in vs. 5 of the Meisterlied by Folz (see note 1 above).
7 der künig aüs seraffin: a metaphor for Christ. Isaiah (6:2) calls the sum total of angels around the throne of God seraphim; using the word to denote heaven is a convention of the Meistersinger; see among others Muscatblut, Groote, ed., *Lieder Muskatbluts* (cited Groote, ed.), p. 7, vss. 91-92.
9 mÿn: here with the meaning of *göttliche Liebe*.
10 e·: (MHG. variant *ê*, conj.) *ehe*; see also Schmeller, *Bayerisches Wörterbuch* (cited Schmeller) I, col. 4; possibly the dot midway up after the *e* signifies that the letter is a word; the *e* is capitalized in the manuscript.
11 ellent: (MHG. *ellende*, stn.) *Verbannung*.
12 paradeis: the early NHG. form.
16 steür: *Hilfe*; since this verse requires just six syllables and vs. 18 below just eight, Hans Sachs apparently pronounced the two rhyming words monosyllabically; see also Brant, *Das Narrenschiff*, p. 72, where the same rhyming words in inverse order are spelled

für:stür; Folz, too (Mayer, ed., Nos. 84, 101/3 and 85, 9/11), treats *fewr* and *stewr* as monosyllables: see also 33,3,16 for *feür* as monosyllable.

18   This and the preceding verse echo Church doctrine and 1 Cor. 11:29.

19   gelichnüs: here with the meaning of *Vergleichung* (cf. Friedman's comment pp. 41 and 103). Hans Sachs regularly uses the suffix *nüs.*

20   her: *herrlich.*

21   pin: (MHG. *bin,* stwkf.) *Biene*; ger: (MHG. *gër,* stf.) *Begehren.*

23   vnferffer: (MHG. *unvervære,* adj.) *ungefährlich*; I would not agree with Goedeke's meaning of *unwandelbar, stets* (*H. S.* I, p. 8, note 22), in view of the fact that two verses farther on Hans Sachs uses the positive "gefer" in contrast.

24   neüsset: (MHG. *niusen,* wkv.) pres. *erprobt*; note the enjambment.

26   verstent: inf. with a spurious *t* attached; see W. *BGr.* § 143.

27   fricht: pl. *Früchte.*

2, 1   Manigen nÿmet wünder: *mancher wundert sich*; cf. Curme, *A Grammar of the German Language* (cited Curme), p. 533, B,b.

3   fer: (MHG. *vër,* adv.) *weit.*

6   nÿndert: (MHG. *niendert,* adv.) *keineswegs.*

8   sün: (MHG. *sunne,* stwkf., stwkm.) *Sonne*; Hans Sachs uses the masc. gender; her: this word is doubtful, since the first and last letters are corrections.

10   vnzwdrent: *unzertrennt*; Hans Sachs regularly uses the Middle German prefix *zu* in place of *zer*; see Weinhold, § 303.

15   wessenlich: (MHG. *wesenlîche,* adv.) *wirklich*; ein: *in*; Weinhold (§ 333) says that during the 15th and 16th cents. *ein* was current in the Nuremberg dialect for *in*; Hans Sachs frequently uses it.

17   entpfa: here Hans Sachs splits a word, not for the rhyme, because this verse is always unrhymed, but for the syllable count!

18   mügen: the word was inserted above the line sometime later, hence the *u*-hook, instead of the regular *ü*; the handwriting is that of Hans Sachs.

20   ring: (MHG. *ring,* adv.) *leicht.*

21   ob: similarly to MHG. Hans Sachs uses this word for a conjunction, as here, or for a preposition, as in 3,4 below.

22   spigel: the analogy of a mirror, or mirrors, is traditional.

3, 2   drot: (MHG. *drâte,* adv.) *schnell.*

3   wortes: since the first and third letters in this word are corrections, Goedeke reads *gottes,* Wackernagel *wortes.* It could be either, however, *wortes* seems more logical, since Hans Sachs not only uses the phrase "dürch worttes krafft" in both vss. 15 and 16 below, but even narrows it in vs. 15 to "die der priester da sprechen dut."

5   wider wertig: Hans Sachs is critical of the remarks he has heard.

6   gesicht: *Gestalt*; geschmack: *Geruch.*

9   stein: Hans Sachs may have been thinking of rock salt for according to Gen. 19:26, Lot's wife was turned into a pillar of salt.

15   The virgule inserted after "krafft" is a clerical error, since the verse has to have twelve syllables.

17   verlissen ist: *verliert.* I have not been able to find Hans Sachs' source for his statement in this and the following verse about a snake's losing its poison through the power of the word. However, according to legend, the Egyptian snake charmers used, as incantation, a magic formula from the sun god Ra which gave them power over snakes; see Morris, *Men and Snakes,* pp. 138-139.

18 die: this refers to "gifft" (17) which for Hans Sachs is fem.; see also Schmeller I, col. 876.

23 sent: *sind*; see W. *BGr.*, § 296 for the form.

24 reÿ peicht vnd püs: *Reue, Beichte und Buße*, the three steps necessary for forgiveness of sins.

No. 3, foll. 27ᵛ-28ᵛ   Orig. 16

Heading: This is the first of two Meisterlieder which Hans Sachs set to "Six peckmessers korweis." Münzer (*Singebuch*, Nos. 224-226, pp. 23-24) rates this the best of three melodies by Beckmesser and adds "Der durch Wagner zu so unverdienter Verachtung gelangte Meister ist nicht besser oder schlechter als seine Umgebung." The "korweis" consists of thirty-eight verses, eleven in each *Stollen* and sixteen in the *Abgesang*. See Appendix C for the rhyme scheme.

1, 1 Pe: the prefix of "petracht" split off to make a verse. As Beckmesser's "korweis" shows, verses of one syllable had been in use for a long time, and Hans Sachs himself, as early as 1513, had incorporated such into the pattern of his "Silber weis" (see No. 14). In these early years no name was as yet attached to them, nor seemingly, had the rules pertaining to them been formulated. Hans Sachs frequently splits a word to make a verse of one syllable. See Plate, p. 204, for such verses. Folz also splits words for the sake of the rhyme; see, for example, Mayer, ed., Nos. 13, 24; 30, 1; 60, 1, etc.

7 nim war: a verse of two syllables is likewise nameless and rules with regard to it had not been stabilized; see Plate, p. 204, for details.

10 kelt: (MHG. *kelte*, adj.)

16 rinde: to make a rhyme pair with "kinde" (15) Hans Sachs substitutes this word for the usual *Ochs*; see the prophecy in Isaiah 1:3 and the apocryphal gospel of Pseudo-Matthew (*Apocryphal Gospels, Acts, and Revelations*, trans. A. Walker—cited, *Apocryphal Gospels*—), Chap. 14, which quotes Isaiah.

17 odem: (MHG. *ôede*, adj.)

21 Herodem: for the reference to Herod see Matt. 2:13-14; ermigklich: *elend*.

22 egipten: although this word has not been crossed out, the word *egiptinn* has been written above it by a later hand.

26 erlet: *erlitt*; for this Middle German form see Weinhold, § 354.

27 net: (MHG. *nôt*, stf.) for this form in the acc. sg. see Grimm, *Deutsches Wörterbuch*, 7, col. 905,3 (cited Grimm, *DW.*)

28 parvüs: CL. adj., *ärmlich, niedrig*.

30 frw: *früh*.

31 pet: *betet*; now and then, where there is narration, the poet makes use of the historical present.

38 des: *deshalb*.

2, 4 hertikleichen: *auf schmerzliche Weise*.

6 ret: *Rede*.

10 gezeiget: *angezeigt*.

14 bÿ: *wie*.

15 gekrŏnet: (MHG. *krœnen, krônen*, wkv.) p. part.; whether Hans Sachs or some one else modified the vowel *o* cannot be determined, nor do the three further examples ("kren" 27,6,27; "kron" 30,1,20; "krŏne" 36,2,1) shed any light on the matter, since in each case the vowel used can be attributed to the rhyme.

16 verhŏnet: (MHG. *verhœnen,* wkv.) p. part.; there is just one other example (hŏne) of this verb, again with a superscript and again in rhyme with the above verb "krŏne," namely 36,2,2.

19 schmehen: (MHG. *smæhe,* adj.) *schmälichen.*

21 velen: inf. used substantively, *Niederwerfen;* vnmacht: *Erschöpfung.*

24 schmit: (MHG. *smiden,* wkv.) *hämmerte.*

28 stündt: the meaning here is simply *war.*

38 dir: with this pronoun the poet reaches out to each person in his audience.

3, 5 einigen: *einzigen.*

8 zw vale pracht: *ins Verderben brachte,* vss. 8-11 reflect Rom. 5:18 and I Cor. 25:22.

9 alsam: (MHG. *alsam,* adv.) *ebenso.*

10 erlossen macht: this may be a kind of circumlocution for *erlöste,* or a transference of the ML. use of *facio* with an infinitive.

14 leit: pret. *litt.*

17 an: *ohne;* zw val: (MHG. *zuoval,* stm.) *Veränderlichkeit.*

19 vnleidenlich: *frei von Leiden;* for a theological discussion of this point see Scheeben, *Erlösungslehre* II, §§ 1164-1176, and cf. Wilhelm-Scannell, *Manual of Catholic Theology* (cited W-S *Man. Cath. Theol.*) II, p. 173,II.

21 sie: the antecedent of this is "gotheit" (13).

25 vür droffen: (MHG. *vürtreffen,* stv.IV) *übertroffen.*

26 dŏde: (MHG. *tôt,* stm.) acc. pl. *Todesarten;* the mark over the *o* is similar to that over the *o* in vss. 2,15 and 16 above.

31 The statement which Hans Sachs makes here is a superficial one; for the fundamental reasons see Scheeben, *Erlösungslehre* II, §§ 1194-1202, and cf. W-S, *Man. Cath. Theol.* II, Sec. 202, especially p. 176,IV.

No. 4, foll. 40ᵛ, 39ʳ-39ᵛ, 41ʳ   Orig. 28

Preliminary:

1. See the translation of the *Gesta Romanorum* into modern Greman by Gräße, chap. 143.

2. See Ehrismann, *Geschichte der deutschen Literatur bis zum Ausgang des Mittelalters* (cited Ehrismann) II, 2,2, p. 479 and note 1. The *Gesta Romanorum* is one of the books in Hans Sachs' library. For the complete list of books see *H. S.* 26, pp. 151-156.

3. *WKL.* II, No. 1408.

Heading: for the discussion of the "vberhohe perckweis," Hans Sachs' third original melody, see No. 33, for that is the first Meisterlied which he set to it a year before he wrote this one. Wackernagel shortened the strophes considerably by incorporating the one-syllabled verses into each following verse and by combining some of the verses of two syllables into one.

1, 1 Ach: there are thirteen verses of one syllable in each strophe.

5 schmerczen: the *m* has only two strokes; a capital *B* in the lower right-hand margin of this folio, 40ᵛ, after the prefix "vmb=" and another capital *B* at the top of the left-hand margin of folio 39ʳ, before "fangen," indicate the proper sequence of these folios which are numbered out of order.

7 frecher: (MHG. *vrëch*, adj.) *lebhafter.* See 33,1,7 for comment on the pattern of this verse.
9 die vngewissen zeit: Hans Sachs uses the MHG. ending for the acc. sg. fem. attributive adj.; see P-G § 136.
10 scheit: *scheidet.*
17 parmung: (MHG. *barmunge*, stf.) *Erbarmung.*
18 hert: (MHG. *hert*, adv.) *streng.*
21 mort: (MHG. *mort*, stm.) *der Tod*; das ewig mort: a metaphor for *die Hölle.*
30 hochfart: (MHG. *hochvart*, stf.) *Hoffart*; geitikeite: (MHG. *gîtecheit*, stf.) *Geiz.*
31 In vss. 30-34 Hans Sachs touches upon five of the Seven Mortal Sins: pride, envy, anger, gluttony, and lust.
33 This and the following verse were omitted at the time Hans Sachs copied the Meisterlied into Berlin 414, but were written in, in vertical position, into the right hand margin by a later hand; their position is indicated by means of two crosses, one within the verse and one in the margin.
40 schwere: (MHG. *swære*, wkm.) *Kummer.*
41 mere: *noch dazu.*
43 wa: (MHG. *wâ*, adv.) *wo auch.*
48 wan: (variant of MHG. *wande*, conj.) *weil*; cf. Schmeller II, col. 916, for the use of this conjunction.
53 güt dat: (MHG. *guotat*, stf.)

2, 4 dar: *Tor*, i. e. *das Tor der Himmel.*
5 wün: (MHG. *wunne*, stf.) *Wonne.*
6 vün: *von*; Weinhold *(BGr.,* § 28) says there was a tendency over the whole Bavarian dialect area "*o* in *u* zu verdumpfen."
7 der gotlichen sün: a metaphor for Christ.
12 mŏcht: *möchte*; the superscript over the *o* may have been added later, for in other poems in which Hans Sachs uses the pret. subj. he either does not umlaut the vowel at all (24,8,16: 34,1,10; 36,1,5), or he substitutes the vowel *e* (7,1,21; 23,4,2; 34,5,10).
13 Och: (MHG. *och*, conj.) *überdies.*
16 hel: (MHG. *helle*, stwkf.) *Hölle.*
17 be: *Weh.*
18 rach: (MHG. *râch*, stf.) *Strafe.*
21 got doch: these two words are crossed out in the manuscript and the word *cristus* has been written above them by a later hand. I am keeping the original.
27 The whole verse is a variant of a traditional metaphor for the Virgin.
28 In this and through vs. 41 the poet expresses both the comfort which he has in being able to turn to the Virgin Mary and his reliance on her for help. These verses also reflect the manner in which Christ as an angry God recedes into the background and Mary, mild and tender, is the one whom sinners can approach.
31 pilde: a reference to the metaphor for Mary in vs. 27 above.
32 secz: the person addressed, Mary, has to be supplied from the predicate noun in vs. 30 above.
33 vir: MHG. *vür*, i. e. *vor.*
36 cle: *Klee.*
37 gartte: together with the preceding verse this forms a traditional metaphor for the Virgin.
38 heil: *Beistand*; this epithet is frequently applied to Mary, but adding "der petripten harte" (*der schwer Betrübten*) may be attributed to Hans Sachs, for Salzer (*Sinnbilder u.*

Notes for pages 33-36

Beiworte Mariens in der deutschen Literatur und lateinischen Hymnenpoesie des Mittelalters–cited Salzer) does not list such a metaphor.

42 icz: (MHG. *iez*, adv.) *jetzt*; Grimm (*DW*. 4,2, col. 2317) says that this form was common in Bavaria during the 15th and 16th cents.
44 hine fartte: euphemistic for *Tod*.
50 sisse: *Süße*; here used substantively; a traditional epithet for Mary.
51 sunt: (MHG. *sunte*, stf.) *Sünde*; pisse: *büße*.

3, 2 gedenck: (MHG. *gedenken*, stn.) *Denken*.
3 wenck: imp. *wende*!
7 alle: according to Weinhold, § 508, this is simply an expanded *al* and, similarly to it, is not inflected. zw gencklich: (MHG. *zergenclich*, adj.) *vergänglich*.
9 verleüsest: *verlierst*; Weinhold (*BGr.*, § 84) states, "Im bairischen Wald erscheint überhaupt eu=ie."
12 Inadvertently, no doubt, Hans Sachs used a virgule instead of a partite sign at the end of the *Stollen*.
15 schlag: *schlägt*.
16 reüichem: for the substitution of *ch* for medial *g* see Weinhold, § 235.
19 A capital *C* in the right-hand margin at the bottom of this folio, 39^V, after *dein*, and the same letter at the top of folio 41^r in the left hand margin, before *lecztes*, indicate the place for the continuation of this verse.
26 reÿe: *reuen*.
33 wolt: pret. subj.
38 gilff: (MHG. *gëlfen*, stv. III,2) imp. *schrei*!
39 drawe: this may either be an infinitive used substantively, or a dialect variant of *Treue* for which see Grimm, *DW*. 11,1, col. 1284.
42 der parmüng aüe: although Salzer lists *Aue* for Mary, he does not cite this particular metaphor, which may be original with Hans Sachs.
50 here: *höre*!
51 küngin: Hans Sachs should have written *künigin*, for the verse is short one syllable.

No. 5, foll. 84^V-85^V Orig. 29

Heading: When Hans Sachs recorded one of Nunnenbeck's own Meisterlieder set to this *Ton* in Berlin 414 (foll. 83^V-84^V), he called it the *gülden schlag weis*, but then omitted the *gülden* for this song. Münzer listed it (*Singebuch*, p. 25, No. 268) as *Gulden Schlagweis*, with the laconic comment "etwas monoton." For that reason, perhaps, he did not publish the music. There are twenty-five verses to a strophe, six in each *Stollen* and thirteen in the *Abgesang*. Hans Sachs set only this one Meisterlied to it. See Appendix C for the rhyme scheme.

1, 2 zünfft: (MHG. *zunft*, stf.) *Gesellschaft*.
4 gen: (MHG. *gên*, prep.) *gegen*; used with the dat. as in MHG.; ieb: (MHG. *üeben*, wkv.) imp. *erweise dich tätig*! Weinhold (*BGr.*, § 89) says, "In Folge ungenauer Aussprache wird ie auch für üe geschrieben."
9 gütte: (MHG. *guot*, stn.) here with the meaning of *Güte*.
11 zwelff: the MHG. num. card.; freit: pl. *Freuden*.
13 clÿg: the stem-syllable of "clÿglich" (MHG. variant *klüegeliche*, adv., *auf schöne Weise*) split off to make a rhyme with the suffix of "lebentig" (19).
16 lesten: (MHG. superl. *lest*) i. e. the last chapter of The Revelation of St. John.

20 holcz: Weinhold (*BGr.*, § 152) says "... *cz* [for *z*] wird im 14. und 15. Jahr. sehr beliebt." i. e., medially, but says nothing about *cz* in final position; see, however, Weinhold, §§ 204 and 205.

22 frische: most probably a scribal error for *frichte*; klug: *fein.*

24 vernem: for the Middle German vowel *e* in the sg. imper. see Weinhold, § 349.

2, 2 ierüsalem: the new Jerusalem mentioned in Rev. 21:2; pedeit: *bedeutet*: for the diphthong see W. *BGr.*, § 79; here Hans Sachs uses prefiguration.

6 zwelff ... freid: the twelve joys symbolized by the twelve fruits are not to be found in The Revelation. However, in 1496 a little work, *Diaeta salutis*, appeared at Lyons under the name of Bonaventura, which in its tenth division, *gloria paradise*, named the twelve glories of heaven collected from various passages in the Bible (see the critical edition of Bonaventura's *Opera Omnia, Tomus X*, p. 24, Sec. 35, for a reference to the *opusculum* – the work itself is not included in the critical edition, since its authorship is now considered to be dubious – ; and see the list of the twelve joys which Bonaventura had named later set down by Gerhard, *Loci Theologici* XX, p. 321, § XXIV). Hans Sachs cites seven of these particular joys among his own twelve. Attention may have been called to these in the upper level in school, and the poet with his fine memory may have recalled most of them, or he might have come across the Bonaventura book itself. He could also have heard or read some exegesis (which I have not been able to find) of Rev. 22:2. (I am indebted to the Rev. L. Poellot of Concordia Publishing House, St. Louis, Mo. for the reference to Bonaventura.)

9 an: *ohne.*

14 gesünd: (MHG. *gesunde*, stf.) *Gesundheit*, i. e. of "der seligen" (16).

18 wund: *Wonne*; Schmeller (II, col. 933) cites *Wund* as a variant for *Wunne.*

20 sie: this refers to "seligen" (16); Hans Sachs uses "sie" throughout the poem without repeating its original antecedent.

22 not: *Schaden.*

24 fünd: (MHG. *vunt*, stm.) *das Gefundene.*

25 geben: p. part.

3, 3 lebent: the MHG. 3. pl. pres. ind.

8 er settigung: *Sättigung.*

17 Hans Sachs may have met doubters of scriptural passages.

18 wort lob wort: this may have been suggested by John 1:1.

23 kein vnwil: this is the subject of both "wont mit" (22) in the dep. clause and "ist" (24) in the independent clause, a rare ἀπὸ κοινοῦ construction: see Paul-Gierach, Mittelhochdeutsche Grammatik (cited P-G), § 385, note 2.

4, 4 vn mie: *ohne Mühe.*

6 an mü: Lexer cites a Middle German form *mû*; note the difference in spelling for the same phrase in this and vs. 4 above.

13 zehent: the MHG. num. ord.; the tenth joy.

15 der zehenn stent: just what Hans Sachs had in mind for this is not entirely clear, unless perhaps he meant (vss. 13-16) that the tenth joy consists in being in the company of all those who after a blessed death now constitute the tenth order in heaven. According to both Büchner (*Hand-Konkordanz* – cited Büchner) p. 1116 and Hopper (*Medieval Number Symbolism*) pp. 11, 117, and 144 the number ten symbolizes completeness and perfection.

22 dreit: *trägt.*

5, 1 Des: *das.*
   3 hoffirenn: *musizieren.*
   4 eilfft: the MHG. ord. num. elfte; the vowel *a* has faded.
   5 seligkeit: this and the next verse may be an allusion to Matt. 20:16.
  11 sein: *sind*; Hans Sachs uses the Middle German form *sîn (sein)* more than a few times for the 3. pl. pres.; see both Weinhold § 364 and W. *BGr.*, § 296 for the form.
  20 der himelpfort: *die Pforte der Himmel.*

No. 6, fol. 460ʳ-460ᵛ   Orig. 33

Heading: "six peckmessers kor weis" served Hans Sachs once before (No. 3) for a song of three stanzas. The strophes of this Meisterlied are not numbered. The numbering is mine.

1, 1 Sŭ: the first syllable of "sŭrexit" (ML. *subrigere*).
   2 The Latin of these first two verses was undoubtedly so familiar to Hans Sachs that he did not deem it necessary to translate, or even to paraphrase it.
  12 zwŭ: for this Middle German form see Weinhold, § 336, A.2.
  13 natŭr: for a detailed discussion of the divine and human natures of Christ see Scheeben, *Handbuch der katholischen Dogmatik* (cited Scheeben, *Dogmatik*) II, pp. 734-735 and 746-748; Scheeben, *Erlösungslehre* I, §§ 290, 612, 619, and 630-637; cf. W-S, *Man. Cath. Theol.* II, pp. 56-180, and see also the exhaustive work of 1578 by Chemnitz, *De duabus naturis in Christo,* translated by Preuss.
  17 aldo: (MHG. *aldâ,* adv.) a more emphatic *da*; schidvng: (MHG. *schidunge,* stf.).
  22 All of the points which Hans Sachs has made in this *Stollen* are to be found in the works cited in 13 above.
  24 ton: *tun*; Weinhold (§ 362) says, "Eine bairische junge Form des Inf. ist tan."
  25 menscheit: a MHG. variant form of *menschheit.*
  32 werdt: 3. sg. pres. subj. *werde.*
  34 ewick: the concept in this and the next verse Hans Sachs probably learned in school, based as it is on the Nicene Creed: *Ex Patre natum ante omnia saecula;* Folz also touches upon this mystery; see, for instance (Mayer, ed.), No. 12, 49-59 and No. 16, 1-5. See 1,2,24 for a theological reference.
  36 strick: *füge zusammen!*
  37 sehen: (MHG. *spæhe,* adj.) *unbegreiflichen*; gŭrt: (MHG. *gurt,* stm.) *Gürtel,* in the figurative sense of "circle."
  38 gelart: Middle German form for *gelehrt.*

2, 4 gepervng: (MHG. *gebërunge,* stf.) *das Gebären.*
  11 pescheid: *deute!*
  13 solt: the MHG. 2. sg. pres.
  16 geleichnŭs: here with the meaning of *Vergleichung.*
  21 leidlich: see 3,3,19 on this point.
  22 wart: for the spurious *t* see W. *BGr.* § 143.
  23 paŭlŭs: Paul only implies the statements in vss. 24-33 above (see Rom. 1:3-4).
  25 ein fart: (MHG. *învart,* stf.) *einfahrender Weg.*
  31 hÿe: a doubtful correction; voren: *vorher*; possibly a reference to John 1:1-2.
  33 This verse is a translation of the Latin *ex substantia Patris* from the Athanasian Creed with which Hans Sachs became familiar either in class or in church.
  34 wo: (MHG. *wô,* conj. for *swâ*) *wenn.* Up to this verse Hans Sachs has evinced a clear understanding that Christ's temporal birth was anteceded by his being begotten in

eternity, that Mary served as his entry into the world, and that his human body was formed *ex carne Virginis*. The difficulty for him now is the theological interpretation of the power of the Highest (see Luke 1:35) in the creation of the human Christ, which he sets out to explain from here on through strophe 3, vs. 16. For a thorough discussion of this difficult matter see Scheeben, *Dogmatik* II,2, pp. 918-941.

37 wŭr: *würde*; geseit: *genannt.*
38 nÿmancz: for the form see Schmeller I, col. 1604.

3, 10 schopfvng: see Grimm, *DW.* 9, col. 1558,2 for the form.
12 Vŭn / wegen (13): *mit Rücksicht auf.*
15 seÿe: to have the acc. "Cristŭm" used with this verb form might mean that Hans Sachs, under the influence of the Latin, was here thinking of the infinitive rather than the subjunctive, because of the familiar words: *dicit, Cristum natum esse.*
22 creatŭr: Hans Sachs may be using this word in the sense of ML. *creatura,* one of whose meanings is *Welt.*
27 franciscus: St. Francis of Assisi (ca. 1181-1226).
29 gericht: (MHG. *gerihte,* adv.) *geradeaus.*
30 an al geferdt: (MHG. *ane geværde,* adv.) *aufrichtig.*
37 erbe deil: (MHG. *erbeteil,* stmn.)
38 ewigen keisser dum: a metaphor invented perhaps by Hans Sachs for *Himmel.*

No. 7, foll. 461ᵛ-462ᵛ   Orig. 35

Preliminary:

1.   Kochs (*Das deutsche geistliche Tagelied*–cited Kochs, *Tagelied*–, pp. 111-115) is lavish in his praise of both Hans Sachs and of this *Tagelied.* He declares that of all the Meistersinger only Hans Sachs produced a religious dawn song in a pure form and adds that the danger of surprise and punishment by the rightful husband is an entirely original motif not to be found in any other religious *Tagelied,* a motif which even the worldly dawn song has only in a much more general form.

2.   See Goedeke, *H. S.* 1, No. 9; *WKL.* II, No. 1409; for the few verses which Kochs published see his *Tagelied,* pp. 113-114; and for part of the first strophe see Schweitzer, *Hans Sachs* (cited Schweitzer, *H. S.*), pp. 180-181.

Heading: "Die hohe dag weis," Hans Sachs' fourth original melody, was composed in Nuremberg in 1518. That same year the poet used it for three Meisterlieder; this is the first one. Ten years later he recorded it in MG. 2, foll. 269ʳ-269ᵛ as *die morgen weiß.* (One wonders if the use of the adjective *hoch* in his "vberhohe berckweise," composed in 1516, might have prompted the change in name of this *Ton.*) Set to the music in MG. 2 is the first strophe of a paraphrase of the ninety-second psalm (the textual reading "zwai vnd czwentzigisten" is clearly a scribal error, since the correct number of the psalm appears in the Meisterlied itself on fol. 182ᵛ and the content of the strophe is that of the ninety-second psalm). The rhyme scheme for the recorded strophe differs somewhat from that of the original in Berlin 414 in that it has a greater variety of rhyme-pairs. However, the number of verses to a stanza, five in each *Stollen* and seventeen in the *Abgesang,* as well as the syllable count for the respective verses, remains the same. The *morgen weiß* was *pewert,* i. e., recognized and accepted in the *Singschule* as a new and original composition (see Plate, p. 182), on the third Sunday after Easter in the year 1528. For a facsimile of the music as recorded in Mg. 2 see Appendix B. See also Münzer, *Singebuch*, p. 75, No. 275, for the music and p. 26, No. 275, for his comment. Münzer (p. 25) calls Hans Sachs "Unzweifelhaft auch einer der musicalischen Hauptmeister der Nürnberger Sänger." Cf. Mey, pp. 225-226, for music and words, and p. 128 for the later rhyme scheme found in MG. 2 (Mey's statement on that page that this is Hans Sachs' third melody composed in 1517 is clearly a misprint, since he correctly cites the *hohe Bergweise* as the third *Ton* and identifies the *Morgen- oder Hohe Tagweise* as the fourth on p. 225); see also Sommer, *Die Metrik des Hans Sachs* (cited Sommer), p. 134, for the later rhyme scheme. See Appendix C for the original pattern.—The strophes are not numbered in the manuscript. The numbering is mine.

1, 1 wachter: (MHG. *wahter*, stm.); faste: (MHG. *vaste*, adv.) *stark.* Since Hans Sachs used the courtly dawn song as model, he had perhaps become acquainted with this genre in school during that special hour set aside for exceptional pupils, for he declares later that he learned many a "höfliches gedicht" (see the Background for this chapter and Note 17 to it).

  2 glaste: (MHG. *glast*, stm.) *Glanz.*

  3 The terms "orient" and "occident" are traditional in the courtly *Tagelied.*

  4 lent: (MHG. *lënen*, wkv.) *neigt.*

  5 This verse is traditional; see, for instance, Graf Peter von Arberg, *WKL.* II, No. 496, 5.

  7 raste: *ruhe!*

  8 lib: (MHG. *liep*, subst. stn.) *Geliebte.*

  9 pŭrg: the whole milieu of the first strophe is courtly.

 12 quale: *Beklemmung.*

 17 so: conditional conj. *wenn*; geschmecht: (MHG. *smaehen*, wkv.) *entehrt.*

 20 schwinden: (MHG. *swinde*, adj.) *grimmigen.*

 22 schlecht: (MHG. *slëht*, adv.) *einfach.*

 23 das diffe dale: possibly Hans Sachs' invented metaphor for *Hölle.*

 24 schmale: (MHG. *smal*, adj.) *gering.*

 26 not: a scribal error for *net*, since it is the last of the rhyme-sequence "stet:det:pett" (13/14/25).

2, 4 der leibe dein: for this construction see P-G, § 385.

  7 aŭserwelde: p. part. used as adj. *auβerwählt.*

  9 pildnŭs: *Ebenbild*; for Hans Sachs the word is fem.; see also Grimm, *DW.* 2, col. 29.

 13 drat: (MHG. *drâte*, adv.) *schnell.*

 17 das dages licht: the gen. is between the art. and its noun.

 19 leite: *liegt.*

 25 dat: *Tod.*

3, 3 zw hant: (MHG. *zehant*, adv.) *sogleich.*

  6 riche: (MHG. *rëchen*, stv. IV) 3. sg. pres. with the loss of *t.*

 10 klecket: (MHG. *klecken*, wkv.) *genügt.*

 11 Sŭnder: (MHG. *sunder*, conj.) *vielmehr*; gefilde: (MHG. *gevilde*, stn.) *Feld.*

 12 wilde: *unbekannt.*

 20 sŭnder: *Sünder.*

 21 lös: this word, somewhat corrected, comes right after the prep. "von" which has been crossed out and may be an error in copying, since Hans Sachs uses the word "los" in the very next verse. Furthermore, the meaning of the verse would be clearer with "von."

 22 los dich: *befreie dich!*

 26 riff: (MHG. *rüefen*, wkv.) *ruf!* Here used with the dat. case.

Chapter II / Songs to the Virgin Mary

Background

1. For a discussion of the apocryphal gospels see Scheeben, *Erlösungslehre* II, § 1554.

2. Benrath, *Zur Geschichte der Marienverehrung* (cited Benrath), pp. 13-21.

3. See Scheeben, *Erlösungslehre* II, § 1550 (and for a discussion of prefigurations for Mary see §§ 1534-1552); also Salzer, pp. 111-120.

4. See Scheeben, *Erlösungslehre* II, §§ 1555-1558, and Benrath, pp. 21-27 and 39-78.

5. Beissel, *Geschichte der Verehrung Marias in Deutschland während des Mittelalters* (cited Beissel), pp. 57-70; see also Scheeben, *Erlösungslehre* II, § 1557.

6. Benrath, pp. 212-218.

7. Benrath (p. 217) says that it was Peter Damiani (1007-1072), a monk known for his holiness, who urged the dedication of Saturday to the Virgin; this became official with the *Officium beatae Mariae Virginis in Sabbato* in the 11th cent. (see Ehrismann II,1, p. 207); Beissel (p. 307) brings evidence that in the 9th cent. two masses were already being said for Mary every Saturday in Cologne, and (p. 308) supplies a possible reason for the choice of Saturday, in that Mary alone on that dismal day after the Crucifixion is supposed to have held fast to the belief in the divinity of Christ (in Hans Sachs' poem John, too, believed this; see 8,4,26-27); see also Scheeben, *Erlösungslehre* II, § 1803. A similar thought is to be found in the last of five reasons which Johann Herolt (*Promptuarium Discipuli de Miraculis Beate Marie Virginis—* cited Herolt, *Promptuarium,—*No. 94 of the Bland translation; see my Note 1 of Chapter III), gives for dedicating Saturday to the Virgin. According to a legend (Hans Georg Richert, ed., *Marienlegenden aus dem alten Passional,—*cited Richert, *Marienlegenden,—*No. XIII) Mary herself wanted to be honored especially on Saturday.

8. Beissel (pp. 195-228 and 266-269) informs us that the Cistercians and the Premonstratensians began to make Mary their patroness in the 12th cent., the Dominicans early in the 13th, and smaller orders, including some for women during the 13th and 14th.

9. See ibid., pp. 269-277 and 540-551 for details and *WKL.* II, Nos. 1063 and 1064 for two poems about Mary-brotherhoods. For a general discussion of the Virgin Mary in the Middle Ages see also Coulton, *Five Centuries of Religion* I, Chapters IX and X.

10. See Benrath, p. 220; for the greeting see Luke 1:28.

11. Benrath (p. 220) says the addition of the name *Maria* was all important, for thereby a kind of catchword was produced; for the excerpt from Elizabeth's welcome see Luke 1:42. Eisenhofer (*Grundriss der Liturgik des römischen Ritus*, p. 178) states that the *Ave* ended with the words *fructus ventris tui* in the 13th cent., and Beissel (pp. 231-232) thinks that *Jesus Christus* was probably added during that century also.

12. Even though the petition-part of the *Ave* was not incorporated in the prayer until late, the thought had been current for a long time, to judge from the closing verses of many

poems: see, among others, *WKL.* II, Nos. 37, 59, 60, 67, etc. Beissel (pp. 460-461) notes that one of the earliest versions of the wording of the petition is to be found as an inscription on a church bell in Schneeberg, Germany, from the year 1498; he adds (p. 652) that people began to attach the second part of the prayer at the end of the 15th cent. See Benrath, p. 222, for the statement about the last seven words.

13. Beissel (pp. 228-231) declares that synods, meeting during the 14th cent., continued to urge all Christians to pray the *Ave Maria* often, and that indulgences spanning a shorter or longer time interval were granted periodically for the praying of a stipulated number of *Aves.* See Joseph Baader, *Nürnberger Polizeiordnungen aus dem XIII. bis XV. Jahrhundert,* p. 318, for a Nuremberg ordinance of 1478 which even required nonresident beggars to give proof that they knew the *Pater Noster,* the *Ave Maria,* the *Credo,* and the Ten Commandments before permission to ask for alms was granted them. In the German *Fibeln* of the 15th and 16th cents. the *Ave* follows the abc and the *Pater Noster* as the earliest reading material.

14. See Benrath, pp. 223 and 226-237; also Beissel, pp. 235-236; for the legends see Pfeiffer, ed., *Marienlegenden,* and Richert, *Marienlegenden.* For a comprehensive study of the great collections of Mary-miracles see Mussafia, *Studien zu den mittelalterlichen Marienlegenden* I-IV (cited Mussafia, *Marienlegenden*).

15. The rose, according to Salzer (pp. 184-185) was a very common symbol of Mary. In Medieval Latin the classical Latin word *rosarium* (rose garden) has an added meaning of *Rosenkranz.* See Richert, *Marienlegenden,* No. 21, for a legend which gives an account of the purported origin of the *Rosenkranz.* For the early use of a prayer-chord and its later introduction into Western Europe see Benrath, p. 225 and Beissel, pp. 238-241 and 550-552.

16. For the various patterns employed in rosary devotions see Beissel, pp. 511-513 and 524-532, and for the Nuremberg pamphlet, ibid. pp. 532-533.

17. Salzer, p. 125; for poems containing examples of traditional and new metaphors see, among others, *WKL.* II, *passim* and Bartsch Nos. V and VI; see also Konrad von Würzburg's *Die goldene Schmiede* and Frauenlob's *Marienleich* for a great profusion of metaphors and epithets descriptive of the Virgin; likewise Hans Folz, Mayer, ed., No. 74.

18. See *WKL.* II, *passim,* for many poems illustrative of all of these topics.

19. Scheeben (*Erlösungslehre,* II, §§ 1630-1631) explains that, since Mary takes part in the transcendent and immanent position of Christ, she also, through divine grace, participates in His office as mediator, in an essentially different manner, however, in that she acts as mediatrix between man and her Son, and only through Him between man and God; for greater detail see §§ 1786-1842.

20. Popular belief in the efficacy of Mary's intercession grew apace, and from the many, many legends for which Mussafia (*Marienlegenden, passim*) gives the content it would seem that she almost had a predilection for great sinners. See Beissel, pp. 95-98, for the widespread use, for instance, of the story of Theophilus, and see Pfeiffer, *Marienlegenden,* No. XXIII, for the legend itself. For the plea that Mary stand by the poet *in hora mortis* see *WKL.* II, *passim,* and Frauenlob's confident words (No. 405, 3, 15): "Vnt bit vür uns den hochsten fogt, sint du sin hast gewalt."

Notes for pages 49-51

21. Beissel, pp. 379-402.

22. Ibid., *passim*; a few examples of outstanding works of art in some of the great churches in Nuremberg are, for instance: in the *Frauenkirche,* the Madonna and Child by Adam Kraft (1498/99); in the *Sebalduskirche,* the so-called *Strahlenkranz-Madonna* (ca. 1430), and, by Veit Stoβ, the crucifixion group with the figures of the sorrowing Mary and John under the cross (1506); in the *Jakobskirche,* the *Pieta* (1512); and in the *Lorenzkirche, Der englische Gruβ* by Veit Stoβ (1517).

23. Hans Sachs copied no less than ninety-five Mary-songs into Berlin 414; see Schroeder, "Top. Out.," No. 26, pp. 1006-1009, for a list of these.

24. See 17,2,31 and 37 for the two words. In 22,4,24 Hans Sachs uses the word "figüre" with the meaning of allegory, and in 27,1,14 to mean *Beispiel.*

No. 8, foll. 7ᵛ-10ʳ Orig. 4

Preliminary:

1. For the Latin hymn *Stabat mater* see Dreves-Blume, *Ein Jahrtausend Lateinischer Hymnen-Dichtung* I (cited Dreves-Blume), pp. 391-392, and for *Stabat iuxta Iesu crucem,* p. 391; for the German translation of the *Stabat mater* see Beissel, p. 254 and *WKL.* II, Nos. 602-604.

2. For the Meisterlied by Folz see Berlin 414, fol. 292ʳ-292ᵛ (Mayer, ed., No. 37, but from the Munich Ms. Cgm. 6353), and *WKL.* II, No. 1051.

3. Schroeder, *Mary-Verse in Meistergesang,* pp. 255-257.

Heading: For the third time Hans Sachs set a Meisterlied to "Marners langer don"; gülde: (MHG. *guldîn,* adj.) Schmeller (I, col. 896) cites both *gulden* and *guldin* for this adj.; in the Heading of No. 26 Hans Sachs uses the ending *in.* By calling his "clag" golden the poet may have wanted to set it apart as something beyond the lamentation of just any mortal.

1, 1 Except for the insertion of the word "fleissig" this verse is a duplicate of Folz' first verse (Mayer, ed., No. 37).
  3 verpracht: *vollbracht.*
  4 kar freitag: with this familiar term the poet brings the crucifixion closer to his hearers.
  5 This verse reflects vss. 4 and 5 of the Folz poem.
  7 amacht: (MHG. *âmaht,* stf.) *Ohnmacht;* cf. Folz, vs. 6.
  8 lerer: even though Hans Sachs does not name these, he wants to assure his listeners that what he is saying has its origin in authoritative works; sag: (MHG. *sag,* stf.) *Belehrung.*
  9 facht: (MHG. *vëhten,* stv. IV) *kämpfte.*
 13 stan: from the context this can only be the NHG. 3. sg. pret. with the loss of the final consonant; for such a loss in Middle German after an *n* see Weinhold, § 200; this may be the earliest example for Hans Sachs' use of the vowel *a* in the pret. of this verb; cf. Shumway, p. 117.
 16 gir: (MHG. *gir,* stf.) *Verlangen.*
 18 The last five words are identical with the last five of Folz's vs. 13.

243

21 dürne: (MHG. *durne*, stm.) *Dorn*; kran: *Krone.*
23 plüet: (MHG. *pluot*, stn.) *Blut;* Weinhold (*BGr.*, § 107) says that the substitution of *ue* for *uo* came to the fore in the 14th cent.; see also Schmeller I, col. 333, for the same spelling.
26 grosser schmerczen: nom. sg.; Schmeller (II, col. 557) gives *der Schmerzen* as the usual form; see also 6,10 and 7,18 below.

2, 15 die jüden: four times in this Meisterlied Hans Sachs mentions the Jews; in this verse they have no pity for Christ; in 3,3-4 they caused him to be crucified between two malefactors because of the ignominy attached thereto; in 3,22 they are called false and unworthy; and in 5,7 it is a blind Jew who pierces Christ's side. Since such sentiments are not restricted to Hans Sachs, but are also expressed in earlier Meisterlieder and in other poems (see, for instance, *WKL.* II, Nos. 421 and 523), they obviously reflect a widespread derogatory attitude towards the Jews in Germany. In the Gospels the Jews took no part in the actual Crucifixion, for that was carried out by the soldiers of the governor.
17 wonet: the historical pres.
20 gepreit: p. part.; this verse duplicates vs. 26 of the Folz Meisterlied, except for an *e* there attached to the participle.
21 on: *ohne.*
22 verschneÿt: the *eÿ* is a dubious correction; the rhyme requires the MHG. pret. This verse and the following one express the same thought as Folz's verses 134-135, but whereas Folz links this to a point in theology, namely the supreme martyrdom of Mary, Hans Sachs, much more effectively, simply reminds his hearers that what Simon had foretold has now come to pass.
23 Maria hercz: for the uninflected fem. name in the Gen. see Weinhold, § 468.
26 For the prophecy in this and the following verse see Luke 2:35.

3, 2 sant: (MHG. variant *sant,* adj.); Anshelmus: Anselm of Canterbury (1033-1109).
5 schweigendenn: Weinhold (§ 334) says that the acc. case with the prep. *mit* is used occasionally in Middle German.
7 weinet: the simplicity of this one word emphasizes the human nature of Christ; that He wept on the cross is however not Biblical. I have not been able to find Hans Sachs' "die schrifft" (8).
8 vergicht: (MHG. *verjëhen*, stv.V) *erzählt*; this is a correction made out of *pericht,* apparently at the time of copying.
10 This verse contains a fine example of negatives.
16 dün: *tun* in the sense of *geben.*
21 versert: (MHG. *versêren*, wkv.) *verwundet.*
23 verrert: (MHG. *verrêren*, wkv.) *vergossen.*
25 dar ab: (MHG. *dar abe*, adv.) *davon.*

4, 1 On allen drost: see also Folz, vs. 26.
3 This verse motivates the words which Christ speaks to Mary and to John whereby Hans Sachs increases the pathos of the situation.
5 This and vs. 6 approximate the brief statement in John 19:26-27.
8 nach: (MHG. *nâch*, adv.) *nahe.*
11 vor gesein: (MHG. *vorsîn*, anv.) *beschützen*; the prefix *ge* strengthens the concept of the verb.
13 See John 19:30.
14 erterich: Schmeller (I, col. 140) gives this as a variant spelling for *Erdreich.*

22 The substance of vss. 22-27 is to be found in Luke 24:26 and 46.
23 losset: *erlöset*; vnferhol: (MHG. *unverholn,* part. adv.) *unverborgen.*
24 dodes val: pleonastic for *Tod.*
25 dol: (MHG. *doln,* wkv.) *dulden.*
27 der sten: inf. *auferstehen*; see W. *BGr.,* § 145 for the prefix.

5, 5 In this and the following verse the poet paraphrases Luke 23:46.
8 Note the double acc.
9 There is no virgule at the end of the verse.
10 miltiklich: *auf reichliche Weise.*
11 vor: *vorher.*
12 verbent: (MHG. *verwenden,* wkv.) *verwandelt.*
15 dürch mas: *durch ging*; see the similar statement in 2,22-23 above.
17 gespan: the ending *en* of the p. part. has been cut off and pushed into the next verse for the sake of the syllable count (this verse is unrhymed).
23 See Luke 23:45.
25 zerspilten: (MHG. *zerspalten,* redv. 1) pret.; hertten: (MHG. *herte,* adj.) *harten.* Matthew (27:52) alone speaks of the rocks being rent.
27 vmehang: (MHG. *umbehanc,* stm.) *Vorhang*; Matthew (27:51), Mark (15:38), and Luke (23:45) all state, ". . . der Vorhang im Tempel zerriß in zwei Stücke . . . ."

6, 1 zw der vesper zeit: realistic as this is, it is not original with Hans Sachs, for in a poem of about 1470 (*WKL.* II, No. 1027) on the seven canonical hours for Mary, the sixth stanza begins: "Do nun kam die vesper zit / ward ihesus von dem crucz geleit."
4 aüf die erd: In the St. Jakobskirche in Nuremberg there is a woodcarving which depicts Mary kneeling on the ground beside the body of Christ. Since this *Pietà,* according to tradition, is said to have been presented to the church in 1512 by Hanns Murr (I am indebted to Dr. R. Kahsnitz of the Germanisches Museum for the date and the name of the donor), Hans Sachs may well have seen this group before he started out as a journeyman.
5 zeher: (MHG. *zeher,* stm.) *Träne.*
7 ÿm: dat. of possession, emphatic, since the poss. adj. is also employed in the next verse; mit pitterkeit: Hans Sachs offers a fine contrast to 2,21 above where Christ was pictured "on pitterkeit."
8 wünesam: (MHG. *wunnesam,* adj.) *wonniglich.*
12 küngin: this form may be analogous to the Middle German masc. form *kung* which Hans Sachs uses, for instance, in 9,1,15; die himelische küngin: a metaphor for the Virgin; up to this point in the poem she has been simply "mütter," and after her lament she is once more called "mütter," but at the close of the song, when Hans Sachs addresses her in prayer, he again exalts her. fran: *heilig.*
13 Mary begins her lament with this verse; it runs through the second *Stollen* of the seventh strophe, thus encompassing a whole stanza.
14 der schmercz: gen pl.; attracted into the gen. by the adj. "gros."
19 an: *ohne*; a somewhat blotted correction.

7, 1 Verses 1-4 are truly poetic.
2 The verse is a metaphor for Christ.
7 Jesw: CL. vocative case.
8 wün: *Wonne.*
9 künig aller engel: another metaphor for Christ.

15 Only the gospel of St. John (19:38-40) speaks of both Joseph of Arimathæa and of Nicodemus.

20 küngin der jerancheÿ: a metaphor for the Virgin; see 13,1,2 for comment on "jerancheÿ."

21 deÿ: CL. deī; when Hans Sachs rhymes this word of two syllables in a series with "jerancheÿ:freÿ:seÿ:peÿ" (20/22/23/25) it is clearly an eye-rhyme.

23 lebes: *Lebens*; the subject is attracted into the gen. by the adverb "nÿmer"; for the loss of the *n* see W. *BGr.*, § 166,b).

25 dw vnd Johannes: Wackernagel (*WKL.* II, p. XVIII) states that John seems to have been the first of the saints who was called upon for help and whose name, in the earliest times, was combined with that of Mary.

26 in eüer hüt: Weinhold (§ 480) quotes the same uninflected pron. adj. in a Middle German dat. sg.

No. 9, foll. 36ʳ-37ʳ   Orig. 24

Preliminary:

1. *WKL.* II, No. 1406.

Heading: This is Hans Sachs' only Meisterlied in Berlin 414 which he has set to his second original melody, the "güldin don," composed in Ried in 1513 (the date 1520 which Taylor, *Lit. Hist. of Mg.*, p. 57, gives, is erroneous). The very first song which the poet wrote for the *Ton* carries the same year as its composition, 1513, and begins "O musica dw werde kunst." See the K-G Index, No. 24, where it is called "Ein lob Marie," and see the first strophe which Michels published in his review of Drescher's *Studien zu Hans Sachs* in Anzeiger für deutsches Alterthum und deutsche Literatur, Vol. 18 (1892), p. 354. When the poet entered the music of the "güldin don" in Mg. 2, fol. 267ʳ, he chose neither the words of "Ein lob Marie," nor those of his Meisterlied in Berlin 414, to write down under the notes, but instead recorded the first strophe of a poem written in 1526. In it the first verse of each *Stollen*, originally made up of eight syllables, has been divided into two verses, of which the first is an unrhymed verse of one syllable. This alteration seems to have been a temporary one, for two years later, 1528, the first verse of the Meisterlied, "Marcus am zwelften vns fürwar" (cited K-G Index, No. 253), does not indicate such a verse. Furthermore, all subsequent Meisterlieder in this *Ton* have an eight-syllabled first verse. Drescher (*Studien* II, pp. 48-49) shows a later development of the *Ton*, namely the 1538-pattern and its final form of 1541. He also gives the rhyme scheme of 1520 which is essentially that of the original one, except that he does not designate the two one-syllabled verses in each *Stollen* and the three in the *Abgesang* as separate verses, but says (Note 1, p. 49), "Hier besteht der Vers aus zwei bezw. drei einsilbigen unter sich reimenden Worten." However, although Drescher mentions "das Gekünstelte und Unschöne der ersten Form" (p. 49) and the year of its invention and of its *Bewährung* (Note 1, p. 50), he does not give the original rhyme scheme, nor the 1526-version, of which he apparently was unaware, since for his facts about composition and recording of the *Ton* he quotes Ch. Schmidt (inaccurate for Schweitzer) *Étude sur . . . Hans Sachs*, instead of MG. 2. The final form reduced the length of the *Ton* from twenty-four to twenty-two verses (6-6-10), but increased the syllable count from ninety-one to one hundred and thirty-eight! As we learn from the notation beneath the score in Mg. 2, "Der gülden thon" was not *bewert* until 1541 "am suntag vor aller heilig tag" (Nov. 1). During the course of the years Hans Sachs also modified his early melody to suit the final draft of the metric structure. This can be seen from the three versions of the music which Mey published (pp. 214-217): the first from Mg. 2, where, however, he completely overlooked one virgule in the *Abgesang*, which indicated a verse of one syllable, and thus came out with nine instead of ten verses in the *Abgesang*; the other two melodies, an old one and a new one, from the Jena-manuscript. Set to the last named one is a Meisterlied of 1541, "Die jünckfraw Athalanta," which Drescher (*Studien* II, pp. XVII-XIX) printed. Mey's discussion of the three melodic patterns and his 1526 rhyme scheme are to be found on pp. 123-124, 213-214, and 217-219. The Puschmann version with one strophe of a Meisterlied of 1546, which Münzer (*Singebuch*, p. 80, No. 279) published, differs both from the original and from the two found in the Jena-manuscript! In addition to Drescher (*Studien* II, p. 49), Mey (pp. 123-124), Sommer (p. 132), Arnold (p. 31), and Goetze-Drescher (*Fab. u. Schw.* 6, p. 380) all record the form of the *gulden Ton* of 1541.—Wackernagel runs the two one-syllabled verses in each of the *Stollen* and the three in the *Abgesang* together with the result that his strophes are only twenty verses long, instead of twenty-four. All rhymes of the *Ton* are masculine. For the original rhyme scheme see Appendix C, and for a facsimile of the music from Mg. 2, Appendix B.

1, 1 zweÿ vnd fünfczig hündert iar: During the Middle Ages there was a controversy as to whether the time span between the creation of the world and the birth of Christ was 5199 years (according to Eusebius of Caesarea, 280-339 A.D., Christ was born in 5199 B.C.) or 5200, the figure which Hans Sachs gives and which Meistersinger before him used; see, for instance, Muscatblüt, Groote, ed., No. 17, vs. 37, and Nunnenbeck, Berlin 414, fol. 449^V; Folz, on the other hand, gives the rounded figure 5000 (Mayer, ed., No. 55, 44-45) which Hans Sachs also uses in the next Meisterlied.

7 varhelle: this is limbo which, according to the *Catechismus Romanus* I, 6,3, is the abode for the souls of the saints who lived before the coming of Christ. They were without pain and were sustained by the hope of redemption; see the prophecies in Isa. 9:2 and Luke 1:79. qüal: this is probably MHG. *twâl*, stf. m, which in Middle German is also *quâle*, because the meaning here is *Aufenthalt*.

14 zw dal: *hinab.*

15 küng: here Hans Sachs inadvertently wrote the Middle German form when he should have used *künig*, for, as it stands, the verse is short one syllable; küng sabaotht; in the New Testament Christ calls himself "ein Herr des Sabbaths" (Mark 2:28).

16 das himelische prot: a metaphor for Christ.

23 meit: the Bavarian form which evolved from *maget*. See P-G § 86,b.

24 keuschen sal: a metaphor for Mary's womb.

2, 1 on alle mon: see Luke 1:34-35.

4 kür: (MHG. *kur*, stf.) *Auswahl.*

6 vber natür: see Luke 1:35.

11 septimo: i.e. Isaiah 7:14.

15 irer entpfencknüs: gen. with the p. part. "vnzw stört." See the Linguistic Summary, under the umlaut of *o*, for the superscript.

16 esechielis wört: see Esechiel 44:1-2.

17 port: (MHG. *port*, wkstf.) *Pforte*; the two verses from Esechiel are prefigurations both for the Virgin birth of Christ and for Mary's constant virginity; see Scheeben, *Erlösungslehre* II, § 1552; but cf. Friedman, p. 76,2).

18 fort: *weiter.*

21 Moisem: possibly a contaminated dative; the reference in this and the next three verses is to Exodus 3:2 and is again a prefiguration for Mary as *virgō inviolāta;* but see Friedman, p. 76,3).

22 püsch: *Busch*; prün: *brannte.*
23 meil: (MHG. *meil*, stn.) *Fleck.*
24 pletlein: (MHG. *bletelîn*, stn.); ring: (MHG. *ring*, adj.) *klein.*

3, 7 schlos aüf: possibly "gepürt" is to be understood as subject; der himel: gen. pl.; pon: (MHG. *ban*, stfm.) *Bahn.*
8 früm: (MHG. *vrum*, adj.) *vornehm*; keisser aügüstus: Caius Julius Caesar Octavianus (B.C. 63-14 A.D.), the first Roman Emperor.
9 his: *hieß.*
11 melt: (MHG. *mëlden*, wkv.) *kündigte an.*
13 selt: 3. sg. pret. subj.; for the form see Weinhold, § 411.
14 czins: (MHG. *zins*, stm.) *Tribut.*
17 petlahem: this has been crossed out and what seems to be *watlaham* has been written at the bottom of the folio by a later hand. I am retaining the original spelling which is also in keeping with the word in 10,2,22 and 11,2,10.
22 freit: Hans Sachs transfers the joy of a young mother in her first born to the Virgin, a realistic detail.
24 einr: for this contraction see P-G, § 62,2: see also der Harder, *WKL.* II, No. 533, 1,19, and Folz (Mayer, ed.) Nos. 6,98; 49,30; etc.

4, 2 schan: *auf liebliche Weise.*
4 gerd: *Begierde.*
5 den fürsten: together with the next verse this is a metaphor for Christ.
6 himel vnd erd: gen. pl. plus gen. sg.
8 aüf zückt: (MHG. *ûfzucken*, wkv.) *hebt auf.*
13 This verse has one too many syllables.
14 In this second *Stollen* Hans Sachs has given a very realistic portrayal of a young mother's joy in her newborn child.
17 neigt in ein: *legt ihn nieder*; see Grimm *DW.* 7, col. 570 II, 2c, for this meaning.
23 der engel: gen. pl.
24 schon: see vs. 2 above, zw der fart: *zu der Gelegenheit.*

5, 1 steren: for the most part Hans Sachs uses this spelling; see W. *BGr.* § 17,b for the insertion of the second *e*; schein: pret.
6 benent: *verheißen.*
7 balaam: Balaam, a prophet of the city of Pethor; Hans Sachs may have had his prophecy in Num. 24:17 in mind. In the manuscript the word has been emended to *balae.* I have kept the original, for aside from the fact that the emendation was made by a later hand, "balaam" (spelled thus in the Vulgate Bible) is the actual name of the prophet, not the acc. case of the name, as the emendator may have thought. In 17,3,15 the word is spelled "Wallaam."
13 mir: (MHG. *mirre*, wkmf.) *Myrrhe*; this third gift for the infant Jesus, fragrant, yet with a bitter taste, was also brought by Nicodemus for His burial (John 19:39). Whether or not Hans Sachs thought of this, the word forms a fine transition to the brief theological reminder at the beginning of the *Abgesang.*
20 meit: i. e. Mary.
22 pflicht: *Obhut.*

No. 10, foll. 24ᵛ-25ᵛ   Orig. 11

Preliminary:

1. The presenting of a song as a New Year's gift to the Virgin may have been suggested by the closing words in one of the Folz-songs which Hans Sachs copied into Berlin 414, foll. 286ʳ-287ʳ (Mayer, ed., No. 78,104-5), "züm newen jar / Schenck ich der ausserwelten mein gedichte."

2. Kochs (*Tagelied*, pp. 108-109) affirms that this song, although not expressly designated as a *Tagelied*, is related to it because in all three strophes the day motif points most emphatically to the birth of Christ.

3. *WKL*. II, No. 1404.

Heading: "Zorens züg weis" is a melody with twenty-five verses, five in each *Stollen* and fifteen in the *Abgesang*. Münzer is somewhat derogatory in his evaluation of Zorn's music (*Singebuch*, p. 24, No. 238) when he says: ". . . ein sehr dürftiger offenbar von alten Mustern abhängiger Komponist." And yet this is the same Zorn whose *Töne* were used more frequently than those of any other Master in Berlin 414. Thirty-one Meisterlieder were set to the *Zugweise* alone (see Ellis, "Anal. of Berlin 414," p. 978), nevertheless Hans Sachs chose it for just this one Meisterlied. For the rhyme scheme see Appendix C, and cf. Folz (Mayer, ed., p. 406, No. 24,) where the first two verses are treated as one, although in a note Mayer acknowledges that the first syllable is a one-syllabled verse.

1, 2 *Ave maris stella*, the first verse of a famous Latin hymn serves Hans Sachs as introduction: see also No. 16.
  3   die: probably an oversight, for the verse originally read "die lichtprehenhen morgen steren." Possibly because it contained one too many syllables, "steren" was changed to "stern"; then the final *n* in "lichtprehenden" was converted into an *r*, but nothing was done about the "die" which should have been changed to *du*. lichtprehender: *hellfunkelnder*. The metaphor of the morning star has been transferred to Mary from Christ, for in Rev. 22:16 we read, "Ich, Jesus . . . bin . . . ein heller Morgenstern." See Hans Sachs' explanation of this metaphor in 3,23 below and cf. Salzer, p. 402.
  5   weÿhenachten: (MHG. *wîhenahten*, pl.) Dec. 24-Jan. 6.
  8   gernn: (MHG. *gërn*, wkv.) inf. used substantively, *Begehren*. A virgule after "schreÿ" is a scribal error.
  9   künigin aüs serafin: a metaphor for the Virgin paralleling the title for Christ in 2,1,7.
 13   steren: the star of the prophecy (Num. 24:17) symbolizes Christ.
 15   der helle dag: a metaphor for Christ.
 20   reis entzweÿ: the object of this is "vorhelle" understood.
 21   trön: (MHG. *trân*, stm., pl. *trêne*) *Tränen*; possibly the umlaut over the *o* did not originate with Hans Sachs; he may simply be using *o* for *a*, as he so frequently does; "tron" would thus be an older plural *trane* which Schmeller (I, col. 666) cites. der parmung vas: a metaphor for Christ.
 24   die vnser clag: a rare instance of an uninflected poss. adj. after a fem. def. art.
 25   dal: *Tal* with the meaning of *Tiefe*.

2, 2 fünf daüssent: see 9,1,1.
  4   in: *ihn*.

Notes for pages 61-63

7 der: the MHG. gen. pl. of the demon. pronoun referring to the "armen" (1,25 above) languishing in limbo. menschlichen grossen schare: acc. with the prep. "Vÿr" (6); see 4,1,9 for the adj. endings.
8 gotter: *Gott der.*
10 werben: *ausrichten.*
13 See Luke 1:38 in the Vulgate Bible.
18 krafft: a nice distinction; see Scheeben, *Erlösungslehre* I, §§ 547-550.
19 neün monet: the Meistersinger usually mentioned this length of time, so, for instance, Muscatblüt (Groote, ed., No. 26,105) and Folz (Mayer, ed., No. 82,105), but by adding "sechs dage me" Hans Sachs inserted a naively realistic human touch to his narration.
21 one we: poets liked to emphasize this detail, but see Scheeben, *Dogmatik* II,2, p. 939, as well as *Erlösungslehre* I, § 576, and the apocryphal gospel of Pseudo-Matthew, chap. 13.
24 des lichten dages schein: a metaphor for Christ.

3, 2 lüfft: note the masc. gender.
3 In this and in vss. 7 and 8 Hans Sachs inserts the song of the angels from the Vulgate Bible, Luke 2:14, and then paraphrases it. exelcis: (CL. *excelsus*, adj.) substantive in the dat. pl.; except for the High Mass at Christmas the Catholic Church has substituted this word for the *altissimis* of the Vulgate Bible. The *c* in "exelcis" is a blurred correction.
8 ir stim: *ihre Stimmen*; bone: ML. for CL. *bonae.*
9 dem: this may be a scribal error for the pl. *den*, since it refers to "hominibus" (8) and since Hans Sachs uses the plural of the relative in the next verse.
10 sein: see also 5,5,11; des willens gut: since this is within the verse it is a good example of the dialectal practice of placing an adjective in post position; herczen: this was added above the line by a later hand, which, however, is that of Hans Sachs; it is necessary for the syllable count.
13 fert: (MHG. *vart*, stf.) dat. case with the meaning of *Lauf.*
15 seÿ: 1. pl. pres. ind.; for the loss of the *n* see the Linguistic Summary, p. 126.
17 das hochste heil: a metaphor for Christ.
18 eüa: *Eva*; according to Benrath (pp. 13-17) it was Justin the Martyr (ca. 110-ca 165) who said that just as the curse of sin came into the world through the disobedience of Eve, so Mary was chosen as the instrument by which salvation was brought into the world; see also Scheeben, *Erlösungslehre* II, § 1551. As time went on this juxta position of the two women and of the consequences which resulted from the disobedience of the one and the obedience of the other gained favor, especially since the *Ave* which the angel spoke to Mary was the reverse of the name *Heva* in the Vulgate Bible, Gen. 3:20 (in the Luther translation this spelling was retained in Genesis, but in the New Testament the initial *H* was dropped). The Meistersinger adopted the conceit; see, for instance, Bartsch, p. 453, vss. 48-52, and *WKL.* II, Nos. 182, 224, and 311.
19 das rein aüe: Hans Sachs may have invented this metaphor for Mary.
22 licht: adj. *hell.*

No. 11, fol. 88ʳ-88ᵛ   Orig. 30

Heading: Hans Sachs set only this one Meisterlied to Nachtigal's "lait don" which is made up of twenty-five verses, seven in each *Stollen* and eleven in the *Abgesang.* Although Münzer (*Singebuch*, p. 24, No. 245) bestows words of praise upon Nachtigal as "einer der bedeutendsten Musiker unter den Nürnbergern," he considers his *Leid Ton* to be less noteworthy and calls it somewhat monotonous because of frequent repetitions. See Appendix C for the rhyme scheme.

Notes for pages 63-65

1, 4 geüde: *jubele!*
   5 pegat: pres. *feiert.*
   8 zw künfft: note the neut. gender.
   11 vil weisser sibella: in the ancient world these were divinely inspired women who foretold the future. The Sibyllene Books are a collection of apocryphal prophecies; for a discussion of the Sibyls and their books see Kurfess, *Sibyllinische Weissagungen,* pp. 5-22; for the Sibyllene tradition during the Middle Ages, pp. 33-203; and for prophecies concerning the Annunciation and the birth of Christ, to which Hans Sachs here refers, see the text, Book VIII, vss. 456-479.
   14 ab düne: *abschaffen.*
   16 proffezeÿ: (MHG. *prophêzîe,* stswf.)
   18 natüres: for the spurious *s* see W. *BGr.,* § 155, and cf. Grimm, *DW.* 7, col. 430,1,3. The Meistersinger stressed the fact that just as the Conception was supernatural, so also was the birth of Christ; see, among others, Folz (Mayer, ed., No. 35,168).
   22 gelidmassiret: *gestaltet.*
   24 zwang: (MHG. *twanc,* stm.) *Bedrängnis.*
   25 in magetlicher wüne: Hans Sachs provides a realistic detail.

2, 2 gepürt: here with the meaning of *Entbindung.*
   4 Octaüianus: see 9,3,8.
   5 peschreiben: *schriftlich auffordern zu kommen;* dis: for the shortened form see Weinhold, § 485, and W. *BGr.,* § 365.
   6 zinst: for the spurious *t* see W. *BGr.,* § 143; anctz gemelt: p. part. *angemeldet;* the *ctz* attached to the prefix may also be dialectal.
   9 Josehp: a scribal error for *Joseph.*
   10 nam: (MHG. *nam,* wkstm.) *Namen.*
   12 bart: *war* with a spurious *t;* bart ... sten: *stand;* vich haüs: (MHG. *vihe hûs,* stn.) *Viehstall.*
   16 pescheülicher: *scheuer,* a realistic detail.
   18 der sünen glancz: the analogy of the sun's shining through glass without breaking it was used for both the Conception and for the birth of Christ. Here it refers to the latter; see also Folz (Mayer, ed. No. 34,373-378); for examples referring to the Conception see Salzer, p. 72, and *WKL.* II, No. 1218, strophe 11; cf. Friedman, p. 93. dürckh: for *ckh = ch* see W. *BGr.,* § 182.
   20 pebeget: *beweget;* the verse conveys the joy of the young mother.
   21 alte düchlein: by means of this homely detail Hans Sachs creates what must have been for him a very real portrayal of the situation. wündt: (MHG. *winden,* stv. III, 1) *wickelte.*
   23 Vss. 23-25 contain details from the apocryphal gospel of Pseudo-Matthew, chap. 13.
   24 der lerern: gen. pl.; the reason for the attached *n* is not clear.

3, 7 A virgule, instead of the partite sign, here indicates the end of the *Stollen.*
   10 in der hohe dron: *in dem Thron der Höhe.*
   18 geÿstlicher: this word is doubtful, since all of the letters except the initial *g* and the ending *er* are corrections.
   23 die frücht: an epithet for Christ, which has its origin in Elizabeth's greeting to Mary in Luke 1:42.
   24 sückt: (MHG. *suht,* stf.) perhaps with the older meaning of *wirkung feindlicher geister* for which see Grimm, *DW.* 10, Sec. 4, col. 861,1; indirectly this points to Mary's role in helping overcome the devil; see, for instance, Benrath, p. 206, and Scheeben, *Erlösungslehre* II, § 1771.
   25 der: dat. with "hoffiren."

No. 12, foll. 25^V-26^V   Orig. 14

Heading: Again Hans Sachs has set a Meisterlied to a *Ton* by Nachtigal, this time to the "geschiden don," concerning which Münzer (*Singebuch*, p. 24, No. 249) says, ". . . wider eine ganz prächtige Melodie. Die schönste von N. und eine der besten überhaupt." For the music see ibid., p. 66, No. 249. The *Ton* has seventeen verses to a stanza, five in each *Stollen* and seven in the *Abgesang*. For its rhyme scheme see Appendix C.

1, 3   Jüda Nasaret: Hans Sachs may be using "Jüda" in the wider sense of the whole land of the Jews, for Nazareth was in Galilee, not in Judah; see Luke 1:26; Bethlehem was in Judah; see 1. Sam. 17:12.
    6   Aüe gracia plena: *Ave gratia plena*, the angel Gabriel's greeting to Mary; see the Vulgate Bible, Luke 1:28.
    7   The translation of the preceding verse.
    8   vnverhol: *unverborgen*.
    9   sine omni pena: one of the meanings of the ML. *poena (e* is substituted in ML. for *oe* as well as for *ae)* is *Schwierigkeit*; the phrase is comparable to the "one we" which Hans Sachs has used twice before (10,2,21 and 11,2,17) and which he again employs in 2,12 below; Folz (Mayer, ed., No. 36,68) also uses the Latin phrase.
   11   kindeleine: Hans Sachs substitutes this word for the Biblical *Sohn* (Luke 1:31).
   12   genenet: this reflects Luke 1:31.
   16   vmb schetten: (MHG. *umbeschetewen*, wkv.) *umschatten*.
   17   scheine: even though rhyme requirements may have necessitated changing the word *Kraft* of the Bible (Luke 1:35) to this word, the effect is nonetheless poetic.

2, 2   zarde: *zarte*; the *z* is a poorly made correction.
    9   zw prechvng: *Zerbrechung*; see 11,2,18; püre: refers to "enpfencknus" (7).
   10   geschrifft: (MHG. *geschrift*, stf.) Hans Sachs may be referring to something written by a Church Father.
   12   weÿnacht morgen: the poet brings the Biblical event closer to the hearts of his hearers by shifting it into a day of the present; this was not original with him, however, for a poet almost two centuries before had had the same thought; see Bartsch, No. 1,92-94, and p. 168, No. XIX, 1.
   14   der: a rel. pronoun referring to "schare" (13), in the dat. case the object of "halff"; ir frücht: this signifies Christ and is the subject of "halff." The verse brings a slight variant of the theological import of 11,3,23-24.
   15   er wellet het: *erwählt hatte*.
   16   drinidet: the subject of "erwellet het" (15); see W. *BGr.,* § 13 for e=â.
   17   von ewigkeit: Mary's having been chosen from eternity to become the mother of Jesus is a theological concept (see Scheeben, *Erlösungslehre* II, § 1619, and cf. W-S, *Man. of Cath. Theol.* II, pp. 212, 214) which the Meistersinger liked to weave into their songs; see, among others, Loufenberg (WKL. II, No. 745, 1-3), Michel Behem (ibid., No. 36, 8-11) and Folz (Mayer, ed., No. 21, 1-5).

3, 1   Almost the whole third strophe is a laud to the Virgin primarily by means of metaphors.
    3   arch: the ark of the covenant is a prefiguration for Mary; see Scheeben, *Erlösungslehre* II, § 1552; Salzer lists *Gottesarche*.
    7   gart: the term *Garten* is common for the Virgin, but Salzer does not include one of "der reinigkeit."
    9   das sigel: this is figurative for Christ.
   10   var: *vor*.

12 ein plüend reisse: a traditional epithet for Mary. In Isa. 53:2 *Reis* prefigures the Messiah.
14 preisse: (MHG. *pris,* stm.) *Lob*; the word is neut. for Hans Sachs; he might have been influenced in the gender by the CL. *pretium,* n.; The verse is one syllable short, for it should have eleven syllables. To accord Mary the highest praise of all, after God, and to bestow upon her the appellation of "das hochst güt" next to God (15) is theologically sound; see Scheeben, *Erlösungslehre* II, § § 1614 and 1626.
16 The many Mary-legends vividly bring home the point that the Virgin does not forsake a Christian in time of need.
17 wer: *wir*; see Weinhold, § 472, for the form; erent: for the appended *t* see ibid., § 396.

No. 13, foll. 26ᵛ-27ᵛ   Orig. 15

Heading: Hans Sachs set only this one Meisterlied to a *Ton* composed by Hans Folz, namely to his "freÿen don." Münzer (*Singebuch*, p. 24, No. 256) declares it to be a "Recht gute wenn auch einfache Melodie." It has thirty verses, eight in the first *Stollen* with the first of the eight a verse of one syllable, seven in the second, and fifteen in the *Abgesang.* See Appendix C for the rhyme scheme, and cf. Folz, Mayer, ed., p. 413, No. 4. Although Mayer calls attention to the verses of one syllable (1 and 28 in each strophe), he incorporates each into the next following verse, does not mention the fact that they form a rhyme-pair, and does not include their rhyme-words in the total pattern.—Schroeder (*Mary-Verse,* p. 79) quoted a few scattered verses from this Meisterlied.

1, 2 keisser dreÿer jerercheÿ: a metaphor for God. The three Celestial Hierarchies are three triads forming nine orders which, in descending order, are Seraphim, Cherubim, and Thrones; Dominions, Virtues, and Powers; Principalities, Archangels, and Angels. For a discussion see Scheeben, *Dogmatik* II,1, pp. 87-92; and Dionysius the Areopagite, *The Celestial Hierarchies,* pp. 45-58. Folz begins the last *Abgesang* of a Meisterlied (see Berlin 414, foll. 99ʳ-101ʳ and Mayer, ed., No. 72, 209) with the words, "O keisser dreyer jererchey."
4 frolich: this is the only time that the vowel *o* in this word has been modified by a superscript, possibly by a later hand.
7 kir: (MHG. *kür,* stf.) here with the meaning of *Gnadenprivilegien*; these are explained in 3,4-8 below.
9 The second *Stollen* expresses a poetically beautiful thought.
13 vür sach: *voraussah.*
16 ÿe vnd ÿ: *von Ewigkeit.*
18 proverbiorüm octaüo: in the eighth chapter of Proverbs.
19 Hans Sachs is quoting this and the next verse from Prov. 8:24 of the Vulgate Bible. The words actually refer to Wisdom, but are used by the Catholic Church to prefigure the Virgin; see Scheeben, *Erlösungslehre* II, § 1541. Although Folz cites "Proverbiorum octavo" in one of his Meisterlieder (Mayer, ed., No. 36, 73), he does not quote Prov. 8:24, merely gives a paraphrase in German.
21 peclert: *erklärt.*
22 die rein: the epithet refers to the Virgin.
24 selt: *sollt*; Weinhold (§ 411) says that the umlauted *o* for the plural of this verb was frequently used both in Alemannic and Bavarian during the 15th and 16th cents.; cf. W. *BGr.,* § 327.
27 das ewig wort: Christ, see John 1:1.
28 sünt: i. e. *die Erbsünde.*

29   so: this takes the place of a relative pronoun referring to "sünt" (28), with the meaning of *wodurch*; see Weinhold, § 327.
30   würt verschülden sein: *wurde verschuldet.*

2, 7   clerer: Hans Sachs umlauts the comparative degree of *klar.*
10   gezilt: *gemacht.*
11   schen: *Schönheit.*
12   pild: *Gestalten.*
13   Bernhardüs: St. Bernard, Abbot of Clairvaux (1091-1153); sag: *Bericht.*
14   probiren: (CL. *probāre*) *beweisen.*
15   vrsach: *Gründe.*
17   patrijarchen: these were more particularly the progenitors of the Israelites; künig: King David; früm: in the manuscript this word has been crossed out and the word *so* written above it by a later hand; similarly in vs. 20 below the second half of the rhyme-pair, "ewangeliüm," has been crossed out and what seems to be *awangalio* written above it. I am keeping the original words.
18   Mateüs: Matt. 1:1-17 records the genealogy of Joseph, not that of Mary, although she too was supposedly descended from King David.
23   was: inadvertently Hans Sachs must have written this word instead of *war* which is necessary for his rhyme with "klar" (25).
24   ir er schon: *ihrer Schönheit.*
26   disser enpfencknus: gen. with the negation "nit beget" (27).
27   beget: *feiert*; heutigen fest: the day set aside for the Feast of the Immaculate Conception was and still is Dec. 8.
28   lest: MHG. superlative degree.

3, 2   czel: *mitteile.*
3   die genadreichen: "enpfencknus" is understood; becleib: (MHG. *beklîben*, st. I, 1) 3. sg. pret., Schmeller (I, col. 1322) defines this as *concipi in utero* and says, "Mariä Empfängnis hieβ ehmals: unser Frauen Bekleibung, und dieser Tag der Kleibeltag."
4   In vss. 4-8 Hans Sachs is referring to three great privileges ("dreÿ hohe kir," 1,7) granted Mary: 1. complete freedom from original sin (this is the Immaculate Conception); 2. freedom from all inclination to sin, hence from all personal sin; and 3. freedom from the dominion of death, in which the incorruptibility of her body and corporeal assumption into heaven are implicit and which led to the doctrine of her assumption. It is the first of these which caused a great controversy from the 11th cent. on. Nevertheless, as early as the 12th a Feast Day was introduced honoring this grace. On and on the verbal battle continued until Pope Sixtus IV, by a decree on February 28, 1496, recognized and adopted the *festum Immaculatæ Conceptionis* for the entire Western Church. Apparently this did not end the dispute, for there was still opposition to the doctrine in the first half of the 16th cent. (Hans Sachs' words, vss. 12-15 below, refer to this), and it was not until 1854 that it was proclaimed a dogma. The second privilege granted Mary remains a doctrine, and the third, the Assumption of the Virgin, continued as such into the 20th cent., when in 1950 it too was pronounced a dogma. For a thorough discussion of these three privileges see Scheeben, *Erlösungslehre* II, §§ 1553 and 1691-1762; cf. the *Catholic Encyl.*, Vol. VII, pp. 674-680; and W-S. *Man. of Cath. Theol.* II, pp. 215-218.
6   freÿ aller erbsünd: the first grace.
8   dotlich: a reference to the third grace; deglich: a reference to the second grace; quitirt: *frei gesprochen.*

10 vȳr draff: *übertraf*; al pur: *gänzlich alle*; Schmeller (I, col. 403) says that the Latin *purus* had become very *volksüblich*.
13 argwiren: (CL. *arguere*); Hans Sachs takes a stand here in favor of the doctrine of the Immaculate Conception.
14 beweret: *bewiesen;* Hans Sachs may be referring to authoritative statements which he had either heard or read.
15 A reference to the Papal decree of 1496; see 4 above.
17 speculum sine macüla: one of the Latin metaphors for Mary; see 16,6,4 where the poet uses it in German.
18 büt: *wütete.*
19 pillich: *von rechts wegen.*
21 das hohest güt: see 12,3,14-15.
22 wil kür: *freie Einwilligung.*
23 on dreffent: *in Bezug auf*; this and the preceding verse perhaps refer to Mary's cooperation with Christ in the work of redemption; for a discussion of this point see Scheeben, *Erlösungslehre* II, §§ 1771-1845; cf. W-S, *Man. of Cath. Theol.* II, pp. 221-224.
24 See 12,3,16.
25 mont: *ermahnt*; freiheit: *Privilegium*; gen. with MHG. *manen.*
30 On the same line as the last verse Hans Sachs wrote "Deo gracias," a formula used repeatedly in the Mass, which, according to Jungmann (*The Mass of the Roman Rite*, pp. 274-275) has become "a part of everyday life." See also Franz, *Die Messe im dt. Mittelalter*, p. 752. Brant, too, added *Deo gratias* at the end of his *Narrenschiff* (1494), and Folz at the end of a long poem in Berlin 414 (foll. 92ʳ-94ᵛ; see also Mayer, ed., No. 71).

No. 14, fol. 37ʳ-37ᵛ   Orig. 25

Preliminary:

1.   See *WKL.* II, No. 1407 for the Meisterlied by Hans Sachs and Dreves-Blume II, p. 156 for the Latin hymn.

Heading: The "Silber weis" is the first melody which Hans Sachs composed. He was only eighteen at the time (1513) and was temporarily stopping and plying his trade in Braunau. Münzer (*Singebuch*, p. 26, No. 281) is lavish in his praise of it: "Wir haben in der Silberweise der Zwickauer Handschrift Sachsens musikalisches Meisterstück vor uns. Abgesehen von ihrer musikalischen Vollendung ist die Melodie wegen der Benutzung der Choralwendung S 3 beachtenswert ... an Schönheit und Kraft ... den besten Kirchengesängen ebenbürtig." With regard to Puschman's transcription of the Hans Sachs-melodies Münzer (p. 25) voices this criticism: "Wollte man aus der Verschieden-heit der Lesarten der Melodien by P ein Urteil auf die Glaubwürdigkeit des Autors ziehen, so würde dieses für den Verfasser des Singebuchs nicht eben günstig ausfallen, denn seine Überlieferung der Melodien Sachsens weicht von der Fassung, wie sie in den Zwickauer Handschriften vorliegen, oft erheblich ab und meist nicht vorteilhaft." Hans Sachs recorded the "Silber weis" in Mg. 2 (fol. 266ʳ-266ᵛ sometime between June 24, 1526 and June 24, 1528 (the dates for the beginning and end of Mg. 2). In the meantime, however, he had embraced the Reformation, whereupon a song to the Virgin Mary was no longer fitting, especially since two pastors in Nuremberg, Osiander in 1524 and Sebald Heid in 1525, had repeatedly referred to Luther's objection to the *Salve regina* (see Beissel, p. 19). Thus the strophe in Mg. 2 is now addressed to *Rex criste.* By transferring the Mary-epithets to those befitting Christ, and by a slight rewording here and there, Hans Sachs has deftly changed the whole tenor of the Meisterlied. Wackernagel published the original song, but all other scholars made use of the altered stanza in Mg. 2. See Puschmann's transcription, *Singebuch*, p. 81, No. 281, and cf. Mey, pp. 209-210, for the copy from Mg. 2, and pp. 210-211 for the version from the Jena-manuscript with the first strophe of a Meisterlied written in 1520 by Hans Sachs in seven of his *Töne*, as well as pp. 122-123 for the rhyme scheme with a 1555-song. On pp. 211-213 Mey discusses the "Silber weis" and calls attention to the great similarity in the melody of the third verse with that of the second verse of Luther's hymn *Ein feste Burg ist unser Gott* (1529). See also Genée, p. 398, and Schweitzer (*s. p.* but immediately preceding p. 455) who, however, misread 1532, the year in which the *Ton* was *bewert*, and printed 1552 instead. In view of the fact that Hans Sachs himself has given us the number of rhymes in the "Silber weis" by his notation directly under the superscription, "hat 20 reim vnd 125 silben," one would not expect anyone to suggest otherwise, yet, when Goedeke published a later Meisterlied in this *Ton* (*H. S.* I, pp. 24-26) he disregarded the two verses of one syllable in each strophe and showed only eighteen to a stanza. Sommer (pp. 131-132) followed Goedeke when he presented the rhyme scheme, but stated that Hertel, p. 18, and Wagenseil, p. 537, had listed 20. Wackernagel had the one-syllabled verses printed in blacker type, but did not set them off as separate verses, hence he, too, shows only eighteen. See Appendix C for the rhyme scheme and cf. G-D, *H. S. Fab. u. Schw.* III, p. XXVI, No. 49. For a facsimile of the music see Appendix B. One wonders why so many years elapsed between the composition of the melody and its final approval: 1513-1532.

1, 3   reigina: names and metaphors for Christ/God were very often transferred to Mary; here Hans Sachs parallels this one with "got vater in dem dron" (1,1,2); see W-S, *Man. of Cath. Theol.* II, p. 214.

   5   misericodie: (CL. *misericordiae*) Hans Sachs translates this in vs. 7; the omission of the *r* before the *d* is a scribal error.

   8   seite: pres. tense with the meaning of *nennt*.

 10   peÿ geste: (MHG. *gestên*, stv. VI) *steh uns bei!*

 11   Vita dülcedo: in the Latin hymn these are the first two words of three epithets (the third is *spes*, vs. 13) for the Virgin in the vocative case. Hans Sachs paraphrases "vita" by his effective phrasing "des lebens vresprüng" (12) which may be a metaphor of the poet's invention, for although Salzer cites Mary as the origin of various things, "des lebens" is not among them. "dülcedo" is not translated.

 16   keisserin: a common title for the Virgin, but adding the adjective "gewaltiklich" seems to have been Hans Sachs' idea.

 18   atte: this has been emended to the CL. *ad te* (the same spelling as here is to be found also in 2,11 below and in 15,2,9 and 13). zw dir mareÿe: these words have been crossed out and the words "du küngin freye" written above them. Apparently Hans Sachs himself made the corrections not only in this verse but also in strophe 3, vss. 5, 10, and 20 at a later date, for the handwriting is his. However, in spite of this and of the fact that the emendations are good, I am keeping the original in all instances, because that is what he set down in 1515.—Folz (Mayer, ed., No. 55,61) uses the spelling *Marey* within the verse.

 19   stet: (MHG. *staêt*, adv.) *stets*.

2, 2   ellende: *Verbannte*, the translation for "Eck/xules" (CL. *exsules*).

   3   filli: (CL. *filii*) *Söhne*, for which Hans Sachs uses the more general term "kinder"; sende: *sind*; see 2,3,23 for the form.

5   Eüe: ML. gen. sg., but Hans Sachs makes this the subject of "pracht" (4), in order to introduce the additional statement that it was Eve who brought about our banishment.

8   becliben: *gediehen.*

11   atte süspÿramus: the translation is in the next verse.

13   gementes: Hans Sachs paraphrases this and "flentes" (14) in inverse order in vs. 15.

16   er her: *erhöre!* the vowel in "her" is a correction.

17   drübsal: with this one word Hans Sachs paraphrases the Latin "in hac lacrimarvm (16) . . . valle" (*in diesem Tal der Tränen*); früme: (MHG. *vrumen*, wkv.) imp. *hilf!*

20   nostra: this modifies "advocata" (19).

3, 3   illos tüos: these are the first two words of the Latin verse, *Illos tuos misericordes oculos ad nos converte*, which is torn apart and distributed over vss. 3,5,7 and 8 below, with a German meaning for only two of the words, "tüos" in vs. 6 and "conüertte" in vs. 8; however, in 15,4,7-8 more of the vs. is translated.

5   misericordies: (CL. misercors, adj.) acc. pl. modifying "ocülos" (17); Hans Sachs seems to have carried the *i* found in the noun *misericordia* over into the adj. (see also 15,4,6 for the same spelling); in the manuscript the word has been emended to the CL. form *misericordes* and the adj. "gut" added after the partite sign to make up for the lost syllable. I am keeping the original.

9   Jesüm: the object of "osstende" (15); here: *heilig.*

10   von: the *n* is by abbreviation; later an *r* was added to "võ"; beles: (MHG. *beloêsen*, wkv.) imp. *befreie!* "-les" is the original syllable under the almost indecipherable emendation *hüt* to rhyme with the added "gut" in vs. 5 above. See my comment in 1,18 above.

11   Benedicktum: this word plus the next verse is in apposition to "Jesüm" (9); Hans Sachs' paraphrase is an independent clause composed of "gebenedeit" and vs. 13.

12   früchtum: (CL. *fructum*) the spelling may have been influenced by the noun "frucht" which Hans Sachs uses in the next verse.

15   osstende: *zeige!* this is the last word in the Latin verse, *Nobis post hoc exsilium ostende*, which Hans Sachs gives in this and the preceding verse, but does not translate, except for the phrase "nach / dem ellent" (15-16).

17   pia: Hans Sachs expands the adj. to make a metaphor "gütigs pilde."

18   duldcÿs: *süß;* for the insertion of a spurious *d* see W. *BGr.,* § 148; milde: the translation for "clemens" (16). In the Liebfrauenkirche in Nuremberg the words *O clemens, o pia, o dulcis Virgo Maria* are inscribed under the statue of St. Bernard.

19   secz dein schilde: figurative for *schütze uns!*

20   veinde pes: euphemistic for the Devil. This whole verse has been crossed out and a new one, *das vns der veind nichcz düt*, has been written into the left-hand margin, at right angles to the text; again I am keeping the original for the reason given in 1,18 above; pes: *bös'.*

No. 15, foll. 23^r-24^r Orig. 13

Preliminary:

1.   Koch's statement (*Tagelied*, p. 109) that there was a sharp decline among the Mary-Meisterlieder with regard to the concrete and sensuous figures of speech in favor of the more contrived and abstract metaphors closer to the theological concept does not hold true for the young Hans Sachs. In this poem, for example, poetic metaphors and epithets outweigh those which can be construed as bearing upon the Virgin's place in Church dogma.

Notes for pages 73-74

Heading: Münzer (*Singebuch*, p. 18, No. 82) labels Caspar Singer's "schlechten don," to which Hans Sachs set only this one Meisterlied, *unbedeutend*. For its rhyme scheme of twenty-one verses, five in each *Stollen* and seven in the *Abgesang*, see Appendix C, and cf. G-D, *H. S. Fab. u. Schw.* 5, p. 385, No. 18. – Schroeder (*Mary-Verse*, pp. 204-205) quotes the *Abgesang* of the third strophe and the two *Stollen* of the fourth.

1, 6 This and the preceding verse may imply that Hans Sachs feels himself unworthy and not in the proper mood because his thoughts are still dwelling on the unhappiness he experienced in Munich (see the Introduction to Chap. IV).

7 pis: MHG. sg. imp. *bis!*

8 celi: *des Himmels*; this word is not in the Latin hymn.

11 iunckfra: apparently Hans Sachs dropped the *w* with which he usually ends this word to make an eye rhyme with "reigina: Maria" (8/10); yet, according to Weinhold, § 125, there are rhymes in the Bavarian dialect of *au:a.*

13 Matter: CL. *mater*, a word not in the Latin hymn.

14 iesse: Jesse, the father of David (see I Sam. 16:1). This verse together with the next is a variant metaphor for Mary, a transference to her of the prefiguration for Christ in Isa. 11:1.

16 arte: *Herkunft.*

17 der cristen heit ein kron: a theological metaphor not listed by Salzer.

18 himelfricht: these are the fruits of the Mass; see W-S, *Man. of Cath. Theol.* II, p. 448, § VIII, Salzer does not cite the metaphor.

19 Jedion: Gideon; Weinhold (§ 198) says that the consonant *j* for *g* "erscheint bei den Nürnbergern des 15. und 16. Jhrh." The fleece of Gideon, a prefiguration for Mary has its origin in Judg. 6:36-38.

21 vitta dülcedo: again Hans Sachs throws aside the construction of these two epithets for Mary by saying that life and sweetness came to us from her, then emphasizes this in 2,1-2 below by declaring that she is the origin of the sweetness of life, a metaphor which Salzer does not cite.

2, 3 leitte: *Leid.*

6 lerer: probably Church Fathers; ergrint: pret. *ergründete.*

9 schom: *Keuschheit*; rigel: (MHG. *rigel*, stm.) *Art Kopfbedeckung, die man umwindet*; Schmeller (II, col. 74) gives the further definition of *Schleyer*, and says that among the relics in the monastery of Lorch (Württemberg) there is "Ain stück von dem rigel Maria." Salzer does not list this metaphor.

12 See 14,2,2-3.

15 süspiramus: the translation is in the previous verse.

16 reinen: this modifies "fraw" (17).

17 in: this Latin prep. is out of place; it belongs with 3,1 below.

18 clag . . . weinen: Hans Sachs paraphrases the Latin participles "gementes" and "flentes" (16 and 17 above) by means of the 1. pl. pres.

19 sün: the sun, figurative of Christ (see Scheeben, *Erlösungslehre* II, § 1551), is used frequently for Mary; see Salzer, pp. 391-392.

20 prün: (MHG. *brunne*, wkm.) *Quelle.*

21 aller parmug: these words complete the metaphor begun in the previous verse, a traditional one, but then Hans Sachs makes use of them to form a new metaphor in this verse. Salzer lists *Überfluß*, but not one of *Erbarmung.*

3, 1 The Latin preposition *in* of 2,17 above belongs with the phrase in this verse; the phrase is paraphrased in vs. 3.

4 Vss. 4-6 explain why this is a vale of tears for us.

6 net: the *e* has been made out of an *o*.

7 dünckel: (MHG. *tunkel*, stf.) *Dunkelheit*; Schmeller (I, col. 526) and Grimm (*DW.* 2, col. 1540) also cite *die dunkel.*

8 pegern: Hans Sachs uses the gen. of person with this verb.

9 licht: *strahlend*; karfünckel: a deep red gem.

10 steren: here this word should be monosyllabic both because of the rhyme with "pegern:lw zern" (8/11) and because the verse requires only six syllables.

11 lw zern: (CL. *lucerna*) *Leuchte*; Schmeller (I, col. 1550) cites the German spelling, *die Luzerne.* With fine stylistic effect Hans Sachs has shown in three consecutive verses by means of the poetic figures, gem, star, and beacon, how Mary illuminates the darkness for those who need her; for that reason she is the dawn in the next verse.

12 ret: the *e* has been made out of an *o*.

17 miltes: Hans Sachs may have been thinking of Mary, rather than of the vessel. Salzer does not list this adjective with *Gefäß.*

18 mach . . . linde: to mitigate Christ's anger was one of Mary's functions as mediatrix.

19 gotlicher pallas: (MHG. *palas*, stm.) *Palast*; a variant form of the metaphor *gotes palas* listed by Salzer.

20 stras: Salzer lists various streets, but not the one described in the next verse.

4, 1 himelischer sarche: Salzer does not list the adjective; cf. 12,3,2.

3 patrijarche: gen. pl.; Salzer does not list Mary as such a queen.

4 on doren: these two words, written below the verse by Hans Sachs somewhat later, contribute an extra syllable to the verse.

6 missericordies: see 14,3,5 for this word.

10 schwer: *Kummer.*

11 verker: imp. *verändere!*

12 dw . . . Moÿses: see 9,2,21 for the prefiguration.

16 zeig: sg. imp., the translation for "ostende" (21).

20 soküm: the "so," a correction by Hans Sachs, is hypothetical, justified by 5,14 below.

21 zücht: (MHG. *zuht*, stf.) *Kind.*

5, 1 O clemens o maria: these words have been written, probably later, over an indecipherable, partially erased verse.

2 senftmütiges: Salzer does not list this adjective with *Bild.*

3 pia: the voc. case, not the object of "nenet" which is "aimer" (4).

4 myld: the *y* has been made out of an *i.*

8 elpaümreis: *Ölbaumzweig.*

9 der himel kor ein frawe: the inclusion of "kor" creates a variant metaphor; see 1,2,7 for the meaning of this word.

10 part: *Pforte.*

15 pflicht: *Obhut.*

No. 16, foll. 21ᵛ-23ʳ   Orig. 10

Preliminary:

1. See Dreves-Blume II, p. 238.

Notes for pages 76-77

Heading: This is the first of four Meisterlieder which Hans Sachs set to Des Erenbots "frawen Eren don," but only this one is principally religious in character (for comment on Der Erenbote see Ellis, "Anal. of Berlin 414," p. 960). For the simple rhyme scheme of five verses in each *Stollen* and six in the *Abgesang* see Appendix C, and cf. G-D, *H. S. Fab. u. Schw.* 3, p. XIII; for further comment see Bartsch, pp. 159-160, Hertel, p. 16, and Münzer, *Singebuch*, p. 17, No. 69; for the music see Münzer (p. 44, No. 69) who, however, prints only a few bars, also v. d. Hagen IV, pp. 922-923. Schroeder (*Mary-Verse*, pp. 194-195) quotes the first two strophes.—stellis: a scribal error for *stella.*

1, 1 Similarly to No. 10 the Meisterlied begins with the first verse of the Latin hymn.
   4 süne: see 13,2,19 for comment on the metaphor.
   6 Deÿ: *deī*; alma: in ML. *gnädig* and *heilig.*
  10 raüch: (MHG. *rouch*, stm.) *Geruch*; susser veiel hag: Salzer lists *hag*, but not this kind.
  12 himelische aüe: the adjective seems to be original with Hans Sachs.
  13 felix: the poet paraphrases this adjective which modifies "porta" (14) more poetically by means of the gen. "der seligkeit" (14); the concept of "celi" (gen.) is also expanded by a new construction in vs. 16.

2, 1 Sümens: pres. part. becomes the imperative "enpfach."
   6 Gabrihelis: (CL. gen.) the angel Gabriel; see Luke 1:26; ore: abl. of CL. *ōs*; Hans Sachs changes the construction and makes the translation "mündt" the subject.
  11 dw vns beschÿrmen: this is a very free rendering of "funda nos" the meaning of which in ML. is *gründe uns.*
  12 helischen wÿrmen: figurative for *Teufel.*
  16 zwelff steren: this refers to Rev. 12:1, ". . . ein Weib mit der Sonne bekleidet, . . . und auf ihrem Haupt eine Krone von zwölf Sternen." Although *ein Weib* was interpreted to be the Church, the figure was very early carried over to mean Mary in that she is considered to be the prototype of the Church (see Scheeben, *Erlösungslehre* II, § 1531); the twelve stars are variously interpreted. The Meistersinger frequently alluded to this figure; see, among others, Bartsch, No. V, 72-75.

3, 1 Solüe: (CL. *solve*, imp.); vincla: acc. pl.; reis: (CL. *reus*, adj.) dat. pl. used substantively; the three preceding words are translated in this and the next verse; los aüf: *mache los!*
   3 der helisch drack: *der Teufel*; er laüf: pres. subj. *überhole; uns* is understood.
   7 In a fine way the verse expresses the one word "cecis" (CL. *caecīs*, dat. pl.) *den Verblendeten*, of vs. 6.
   8 This verse adds weight to the previous statement.
  11 Malla: (acc. pl. of CL. *malum*, n.); dreib: this begins the paraphrase of the three Latin words.
  12 monastrancze: *Monstranz* (a receptical in which the consecrated Host is exposed for veneration), a figure for Mary listed by Salzer, but not prefixed by "gottes."
  13 bona cüncta: this is translated in the next verse; peste: this may be a corruption of the sg. imper. *posce (bitte)* found in the Latin hymn.
  14 erwirb: the poet may be using this stronger term for *posce* in order to imply that whatever Mary requests will be granted.

4, 1 zeig: with this word and on through the word "mütter" of the following verse Hans Sachs translates the Latin literally, but adds the adjective "milde."
   3 der cristenheit: for the concept that Mary through Christ is also the mother of Christianity see Scheeben, *Erlösungslehre* II, §§ 1612-1613; Salzer also cites this theological metaphor for Mary.

4 dein mantel: very early it was a sign of protection and recognition to place a person under one's mantle, hence depictions in legend, song, carvings, and paintings of Mary in a voluminous cape under which she harbored those whom she loved were widespread beginning with the 14th cent. (cf. Beissel, p. 352 and *passim*). This verse, therefore, is evidence that Hans Sachs was familiar with such protrayals.—schwinge: this is the original word, but whoever tried to correct the spelling to make it conform with "vrsprÿnge" (9 below) made the ÿ out of the *n* instead of the *i*.

6 preces: Hans Sachs uses the plural where the Latin hymn has the singular *precem*, but then in his paraphrase he goes back to the sg. "pet" (MHG. *bët*, stn.) *Bitte*.

8 nempt: *nimmt*; the poet disregards the pres. subj. *Sumat* (CL. *sūmere*) of the Latin hymn in favor of the indicative; rich: (MHG. *rîch*, adv.) *auf herrliche Weise*; vss. 6-8 again refer to Mary's role of mediatrix.

10 Omitting only the word "tüüs," which Hans Sachs places at the beginning of vs. 11, he combines two lines of the Latin hymn to make this one verse.

11 dem sün: possibly dat. of ref. with "erkoren" (12). Although Hans Sachs in this and the following verse paraphrases the Latin freely, he indirectly expresses the factual Latin statement of vs. 10: who, born for us, tolerated to be yours.

16 die himelischen frichte: see 15,1,18.

5, 1 Virgo singularis: the translation is in the next verse.

2 pesünder: (MHG. *besunder*, adj.) *unvergleichlich*.

6 mitis: Hans Sachs heightens the concept of this word by his use of the superlative "gütigst" (8); zücht: *Abstammung*.

8 weiben: the MHG. dat. pl.; frücht: again a symbol for the Virgin which parallels that used for Christ.

11 Nos: the object of "fac" (13); cülpis salütos: (CL. *solutus, von Schuld befreit*) Hans Sachs' paraphrase is in this and the following verse.

13 mittes: the CL. *mites* (the translation is in the next verse) precedes *fac* in the hymn; castos: *rein*; there is no translation for this.

15 sal: *Saal*; this traditional symbol for Mary here becomes part of two different metaphors: "der dügent" in this verse, and "der güet vnd keüscheit" in the next one, neither of which Salzer lists.

6, 1 presta: (CL. imp.) among the meanings for this verb in ML. is *schenken* for which Hans Sachs uses the synonym "gib."

5 her: this is written below the line by a later hand (it could be that of Hans Sachs) between "die" and "Noe"; Noe: this is the spelling in the Vulgate Bible; the metaphor is traditional; for the source of the prefiguration see Gen. 8:8-12; see also Scheeben, *Erlösunngslehre* II, § 1551.

6 pfleg: imp. with the meaning of *versorge* which expresses the Latin *para*; the rest of the paraphrase is in vs. 8.

10 das vatter lant: figurative for *Himmel*.

11 videntes: Hans Sachs paraphrases this by means of a clause.

12 veriehen: (MHG. *verjёchen*, stv. V) *zugestehn*; the verse from "dem" on is a paraphrase of "semper coletemür" (13).

13 coletemür: (ML. *collaetari*, dep. inf. *sich freuen mit jem.*) 1. pl. pres. ind.; the ending *ür* is a later correction over an indecipherable letter; Hans Sachs expands the meaning to show, in vss. 14 and 15, where we rejoice with Christ. an leite: *ohne Leid*.

16 gottes herpffen seite: (MHG. *herphe*, wkstf.); the metaphor is partially original with Hans Sachs in that Salzer cites only David's harp.

7, 2 friste: *Zeit.*

6 Sümo: in the Latin hymn this is *summum*, an adj. modifying "decüs" *(Ehre)*; Hans Sachs changes its case to modify "cristo"; however, that may be the way he learned the hymn, for Loufenberg, a poet of the 15th cent., has the same form *Summo* untranslated (*WKL.* II, No. 778, strophe 7) in his paraphrase of the hymn. Aside from this word and *trinus* (13 below) Hans Sachs' poem has nothing in common with Loufenberg's.

7 criste: the voc. case.

12 zir: *Herrlichkeit.*

13 drinus: the distributive numeral adj. (ML. *trinus*) *dreifach*, instead of *tribus* in the Latin hymn; again this may have been the way Hans Sachs learned the hymn, since Loufenberg (see 6 above) also wrote *Honor trinus unus.*

14 er: *Ehre*; the verse is a pleasing paraphrase of Hans Sachs' "honor drinus et vnus" (13).

No. 17, fol. 24ʳ-24ᵛ   Orig. 12

Preliminary:

1.   Schnorr v. Carolsfeld, *Zur Geschichte d. dt. Mgs.*, pp. 41-42.

Heading: The *Ton* to which Hans Sachs set this Meisterlied, "frawenlobs gülden," is constructed in a most intricate manner. Not only do the rhyme-words of the two *Stollen* wander far afield, but the second *Stollen* has one less verse of one syllable than the first. See Münzer, *Singebuch*, p. 14, No. 2, where he comments on the inequality of the two *Stollen,* and p. 30, No. 2, where he gives the music of the *Ton* with words from a Meisterlied by Hans Sachs written Dec. 20, 1528. The rhyme scheme there duplicates the pattern of the first strophe of this one from Berlin 414. Cf. Bartch, pp. 293-300, for a variant pattern. In the version of this Meisterlied from the Dresden MS., M 8, Schnorr v. Carolsfeld set off the one-syllabled verses by spaces, but printed them as part of the following verse, so that the strophe has only twenty verses, five in each *Stollen* and ten in the *Abgesang,* instead of thirty-seven verses divided eleven, ten, sixteen. Schnorr's copy also shows two new verses of one syllable, one at the end of the second *Stollen,* the other at the end of the *Abgesang,* whereby, however, unrhymed verses are created. There are no unrhymed verses in Hans Sachs' song in Berlin 414. For its rhyme scheme see Appendix C.—Friedman (p. 35) quotes four verses from the Dresden MS.

1, 1 One-third of the one-syllabled verses in this Meisterlied are produced by splitting off the first syllable of a word.

4 drüalte: (MHG. *drivalte,* stf.) *Dreifaltigkeit*; the metaphor (2-4) seems to be original with Hans Sachs.

6 clar/es: Hans Sachs substitutes this for the usual *ohne Makel.*

9 dochter: a traditional name for Mary, but not modified by "frone," or designated as of "gut vetterlicher art" (10 and 11); for theological comment see Scheeben, *Erlösungs-lehre* II, §§ 1618-1619.

13 criste: here the Lat. gen. ending ī gives way to rhyme-requirements, but see W. *BGr.,* § 13, for the substitution of *e* for *i.*

15 ge/spons: (MHG. *spons,* stf.) *Braut*; see Scheeben, *Erlösungslehre* II, § 1527 for the relationship.

19 welde: (MHG. variant *wëlde,* stf.); note the rhyme with "gezelte" (27).

26 meisterine: Salzer lists this designation for Mary, but not with "apostel" (27) and "ewangeliste" (28).

29 sterck: *Stärke*; the theological metaphor in this verse may be original with Hans Sachs, since Salzer does not list it.

31 gebalte: *Gewalt.*

32 rein: *ohne Sünde.*

33 zart: *lieblich*; this modifies "sal" (34).

35 keüsch: *Keuschheit.*

37 Again a reference to Mary's role in the Redemption.

2, 2 Johannes: for St. John's vision see 16,2,16.

21 sie: this refers to "engelischer zünge" (15); the singing of the angels in praise of Mary, which John is supposed to have heard, is apocryphal.

27 der gütikeit: Salzer does not cite this with *Schild.*

28 vrsprünge: Hans Sachs overlooked the fact that he should have used the alternate form MHG. *urspringe* for his rhyme with "singe" (13), a form he uses in 32,2,4.

31 figvriret: by means of this word, which occurs only once in these early Meisterlieder, Hans Sachs calls attention to the fact that a happening in the Old Testament prefigures Mary.

36 nas: the poet not only refers to the traditional prefiguration for the Virgin, but adds the Biblical detail found in Judg. 6:38.

3, 9 künig der engel: a metaphor for Christ.

10 I/saias: Isa. 7:14.

12 Si/meon: a reference to Luke 2:29-32.

14 Wa/llaam: see 9,5,7.

16 da/vit vnd Salamone (17): Hans Sachs may be thinking of the prefigurations of Mary in the Psalms of David and in the Song of Solomon; see Scheeben, *Erlösungslehre* II, §§ 1536-1538 and 1960.

18 zeig/en: *Zeugen.*

19 pürte: (MHG. *burt*, stf.) *Geburt.*

22 kin/igin: the *k* is not capitalized; although the rhyme with vs. 37 here influenced the spelling of the first syllable, Hans Sachs uses the same spelling in 39,3,12 within the verse.

27 kein sünd: see 13,3,4 for this.

28 als: *alles*; the virgule after this word is a scribal error.

37 seraffin: for the concept of this word see 2,1,7.

No. 18, fol. 461ʳ-461ᵛ   Orig. 34

Heading: "vnser frauen gesanck weis" is the fifth melody composed by Hans Sachs, perhaps shortly after his "hohe dag weis" (see No. 7) in 1518 in Nuremberg. There are twenty-five verses in each strophe with the first *Stollen* one verse longer than the second because it alone has an introductory verse of one syllable. It is possible that both Folz's *freier Ton* and Frauenlob's *gülden Ton* (Nos. 13 and 17 respectively) may have influenced Hans Sachs in the uneven construction of his own *Stollen*. (Inequality in the metrical pattern would not be noticeable in singing, however, for the first verse of one syllable plus the second with seven syllables equals eight, and to balance this the first verse of the second *Stollen* has eight syllables.) The composer dedicated the melody to the Virgin by naming it after her, and further honored her by making this Meisterlied, the first one set to it, a glorification of her. But when the *Weise* was "bewert im 1528 jar am dritten Sontag nach ostern," ten years had passed, and Hans Sachs was no longer an adherent of the Catholic faith. Therefore, in recording it in Mg. 2, he cast aside the original Mary-song in favor of a paraphrase of the 94th Psalm, omitted the words "vnser frauen" from the *Ton*, and called it simply "Die gesanck weiß." As such it is known today. He also made another change in that he equalized the pattern of the two *Stollen* by supplying an introductory verse of one syllable for the second *Stollen* as well. However, this did not rectify the matter, for he failed to provide a rhyming word for it. (Inadvertently, perhaps, he also placed a virgule after "nicht" in vs. 20.) Münzer, who published both the music and the words (*Singebuch*, No. 277 pp. 77-78) from Mg. 2, makes the following comment on the melody (No. 277 p. 26): "Die Koloraturen sind zum Teil sehr schön, dies und der große Schwung einzelner Melodieteile und deren großer Umfang haben wohl der Melodie den Namen gegeben." He is referring here to the later name, "Die gesanck weiß," for apparently he knew nothing about its original one. See also Mey's transcription (pp. 229-231) of both music and words from Mg. 2, labeled *Zwickauer Fassung*, and the *Jenaer Fassung* of the music (pp. 231-233; the Meisterlied there printed is not listed in the *Register* of *H. S.* 26) together with his comments (p. 233). On p. 124 he set down the rhyme scheme of a Meisterlied by Hans Sachs from M 191 (in K-G Index this is No. 4870 with the date April 10, 1556) where there is no one-syllabled verse at all in the beginning of the first *Stollen*, so that the strophe has only twenty-four verses. Sommer, p. 133, likewise records a rhyme scheme with the same number, although in a footnote he calls attention to Hertel, who (p. 18) cites the original number, twenty-five, for "vnser frauen gesanck weis." See Appendix C for the original rhyme scheme of 1518 and Appendix B for a facsimile of the music as recorded in Mg. 2.

1, 2   sponsa mater virgo: the second of these names for the Virgin is to be found in Luke 2:51 and Acts 1:14; the third in Isa. 7:14 and in Luke 1:27 and 31 but the first is from the *Canticum Canticorum* (Vulgate Bible), especially chapter 4, which has been interpreted to refer to Mary (see Scheeben, *Erlösungslehre* II, §§ 1538-1540); see also 17,1,15 for comment on "sponsa." In Luke 1:27 and 2:5 Mary is designated as *desponsata.* –The first two *Stollen* are made up entirely of Latin metaphors and epithets.

4   sedŭla: (CL. *sedulus*, adj.) used as substantive with the meaning of *Eifrige*; deydatis: (gen. of ML. *deitas*) *Gottheit*; the metaphor seems to be original with Hans Sachs, for Salzer lists neither the Latin nor the German words.

7   wenedicta: (CL. *benedicta*) soror angelorum: the poet seems to have translated this metaphor into Latin from the German which he uses in 17,1,16/17. Salzer does not list the Latin.

9   tŭ speciosa: *du Glänzende.*

10   alma: adj. used here as substantive, *Ernährende*; redemptoris: gen., *des Heilands;* the metaphor is original with Hans Sachs.

11   vormosa: CL. *formosa, wohlgestaltet.*

14   sŭser mandel kerne: since, according to Salzer (p. 171), the almond, due to its early blossoming, was a figure for activity, fruitfulness, love, and loyalty, it was soon transferred to Mary; associating it with David, however, was Hans Sachs' idea. In the *Abgesang*, which begins with this verse, the poet combines every metaphor except one with the name of a Biblical person or place.

15   grŭnende rŭt jesse: it reflects the import of Isa. 11:1.

19   leŭchtende luzerne: Hans Sachs adds original variations to the "luzerne" (see also 15,3,11) by affixing the adjective "leŭchtende" and by relating the metaphor to Israel.

21   arch noe frone: Salzer (p. 472) states that Noah's ark is symbolical of Mary's great mercy, but see Scheeben, *Erlösungslehre* II, § 1551 for a different explanation of this prefiguration. Friedman mentions the ark on p. 80.

24 glane: (MHG. *glimmen*, stv. III, 1) pret. *glühte*; for the change of an *m* into an *n* see W. *BGr.*, § 169.

25 Nasseret: *Nazareth.*

2, 1 Both *Stollen* of this strophe begin with a Latin metaphor; the only other Latin in the stanza is in vs. 20 of the *Abgesang.*

4 plüend olpaům reis: both the adj. and the addition of "reis" are contributions by the poet to the figure of the *Ölbaum.*

5 himel sŭnne: for the figure of the sun, a transference from Christ to Mary, see 13,2,19.

7 morgen rot: Salzer (p. 387) says this metaphor was used for Mary because of the relationship of the dawn to the sun; see also Scheeben, *Erlösungslehre* II, § 1551.

8 frŭctiffara: CL. *fructifera, fruchtbringend*, a contribution to the long list of adjectives descriptive of the Virgin.

9 By grouping his metaphors around a garden and matters associated with it the poet achieves unity in this second *Stollen*; peschosner: either a scribal error for *beschloßner*; or the p. part. of the verb *beschießen*; see Schmeller II, col. 477, for this verb with the meaning of *ergiebig sein* which, when applied to a garden as here, would mean *fruchtbar.*

10 gart himelischer speis: an original metaphor.

13 granatapfel: see Salzer, p. 162, for a discussion of this symbol; palsam schmack: *Balsamgeruch.*

14 By means of nine verses (14-22) of this *Abgesang* which extol Mary by conferring upon her the titles of ladies of specific ranks, each of whom reigns over a particular domain—spiritual, temporal, or abstract—Hans Sachs achieves a fine stylistic effect; des himel her ein keiserine: this, an expansion of the popular metaphor *Himmelkeiserin*, is an innovation on the part of the poet.

16 der miltikeit: this specification is original with the poet.

17 der hoffnŭng: this seems to be part of two metaphors; Salzer lists both "greffin" and "vrsprung," but neither with "hoffnung."

19 der demŭtikeit ein fŭrstine: Salzer lists *Fürstin*, but not related to a virtue.

22 vocktin des paradeis: the MHG. *vogetinne* means *Herrin* with reference to Mary and as such Salzer lists it, but not in connection with "paradeis."

23 der genad awe: the *w* is a poorly made correction out of *ü.*

24 vnd: this seemingly was made out of the word *du*, for the *u*-hook remains; dawe: *Tau*; this may be part of the preceding metaphor; see 4,3,44.

25 zelt dar in ... lack: this metaphor is Hans Sachs' own invention, for only "zelt" is cited by Salzer.

3, 2 archa deidatis: Salzer does not list the Latin; see 12,3,3 for the prefiguration. Similarly to the second strophe both *Stollen* of this third one begin with a Latin metaphor.

3 gottes tabernackel: this is the translation for the previous verse; Salzer does not list "tabernackel."

7 drost aller pedrŭbten herczen: all except the "drost" is original with Hans Sachs.

8 sŭasissima: fem. superlative of CL. *suasus* used substantively, *höchste Zurednerin*, a title coined by the poet.

10 grunt der cristenheit: "grunt" is Hans Sachs' invention as variant for this common theological metaphor.

13 vŭrsprecherin ... schar: Hans Sachs has expanded a traditional metaphor by inserting "armen" and adding "schar"; this figure of speech refers to Mary's role as mediatrix.

14 wol pegossner aimer pŭre: this vessel is traditional for Mary, but to define it as one with purest content can be attributed to Hans Sachs.

18 fron: Salzer does not list this adj. for Mary, but Hans Sachs applies it to her also in
1,6,12 and 17,1,9.
19 See 12,3,14 for the theological concept of this verse. The verse is short one syllable.
22 From here on to the end of the song Hans Sachs poetically expresses the prayer to the
Virgin for help in *hora mortis nostrae.*

Chapter III / Two Legends

Background

1. Mussafia in his comprehensive study of Mary-legends says in a footnote on p. 45 of his
Marienlegenden III that he is using Herolt's *Promptuarium* published in 1486; and on pp.
45-52 he gives a brief summary of the legends in that book. I have not been able to find
out whether there was ever a German translation of Herolt's collection. Hans Sachs
probably used the original Latin edition, an assumption supported by his statement in
strophe 1, vs. 7. In 1926 Bland translated Herolt's whole collection into English with the
title *Miracles of the Blessed Virgin Mary*; see his Introduction for information of Herolt.

2. Mussafia's summary of this is on p. 47 of his *Marienlegenden* III, and Bland's translation
is on pp. 40-41 of his *Miracles.*

3. Priem (*Geschichte der Stadt Nürnberg*, p. 32) states that the building of a convent
dedicated to *der heil. Katharina* was begun in 1292; cf. Siebenkees, pp. 165-172. In a
reprint of the first edition of an interpretation of the Mass published in Nuremberg in
1481 (Franz, *Die Messe im dt. Mittelalter*, p. 751) we find the following in the
Confiteor: "... Ideo precor gloriosam virginem Mariam, sanctum Petrum, sanctum
Paulum, sanctam Barbaram, sanctam Katherinam, istos sanctos et . . . ."

4. The German prose collection, *Der Heiligen Leben*, was based on the poetic *Passional* (ca.
1300), the original source of which was the *Legenda aurea* by Jacobus de Voragine
(1230-1298); see Ehrismann, *Geschichte der deutschen Literatur bis zum Ausgang des
Mittelalters* II,2,2 (cited Ehrismann II), pp. 379-380 and 382; see also Rüttgers, *Der
Heiligen Leben und Leiden* (cited Rüttgers), pp. 464-469.

5. For the three legends about St. Catherine see Rüttgers, pp. 134-144.

No. 19, foll. 466ᵛ-468ʳ   Orig. 39

Heading: It seems fitting that Hans Sachs should set this legend also to his "vnser frawen
gesanck weis," since it concerns the Virgin. For comment on the *Ton* see No. 18.

1, 1 [o]: this letter is not present, but is necessary for the rhyme with "also" (8); it was
probably meant to be an ornamental letter, for a large block of space has been left for it.
7 in mirakŭlis beate marie: in the miracles of the Blessed Mary.
11 kein gŭt: *nichts Gutes.*
13 Hans Sachs repeats the import of vs. 10, because that is the key note of the story.
16 ir peider gŭtte: *das Gut von den beiden.*
19 vngemŭtte: *betrübt.*
23 gÿnde: *gönnte.*

2, 2 deüffelisch einplasŭng: Hans Sachs invents this detail.
    7 dotten: *töten*; freÿ: *adlig*.
  10 sidt: *Sitte*.
  15 lŭffen: for the vowel *u* in both the sg. and the pl. see Weinhold, § 361, and W. *BGr.,* §
      277; kamnet: (MHG. *kamenâte* and *kemenâte*, stwkf.) *Schlafgemach*; see 21 below for
      the spelling "kemnat."
  17 erdet: (MHG. *ertôeten*, wkv.) *getötet*.
  22 periedt: *bedachte*.
  25 rŭmoreÿ: *Lärm*; the suffix expresses prolongation of the noise.

3, 3 hart: *fest*
   9 versprache: *verteidigte*.
  12 jache: *sprach*.
  16 weinet: pres. part.; for the loss of the *n* see W. *BGr.,* §§ 166,b) and 312.
  17 vberlichter: (MHG. *überlicht*, adj.) *überaus glänzender*.
  19 gegenwŭrtikeit: (MHG. *gegenwürtikeit*, stf.) *Gegenwart*; leÿtte: *Leute*.
  21 ein . . . pilde: the Virgin Mary.
  22 ein kind: the infant Jesus; in the source this is a boy.
  23 gestilde: (MHG. *gestillen*, wkv.) p. part.
  25 verziehent: *abschlagend*.

4, 2 geschwig: the NHG. pret. spelled with an *i* instead of *ie*.
   4 derhoret: p. part. *erhört*; for the *d* in the prefix see 8,4,27.
   9 velle: (MHG. *vellen*, wkv.) *fälle*.
  10 ermorten: p. part. used as substantive, *Ermordeten*.
  16 nate: *Not*.
  17 schan: *schön*.
  18 aŭf stan: *stand auf*; see 8,1,13 where the same form is used within the verse.
  19 offenlich: (MHG. *offenlîche*, adv.); ratte: *städtische Behörde*.
  20 ret: Hans Sachs effectively uses the historical present.
  25 mŏrder: the superscript over the *o* seems strange in view of the fact that in vss. 15 and
      22 below and in 5,4 below the vowel *o* in "morder" is not modified, nor is it in
      "mordisch" and "ermorten," vss. 7 and 10 above; most probably the superscript here, as
      well as over the *o* in "pŏswicht" (7 above), was added by someone other than Hans
      Sachs.

5, 3 fahen: the MHG. inf., but see 2,25 above where the NHG. form is used.
   5 hent vnd fiesse: in Hans Sachs' source the murderer was punished by being tied to a
      horse's tail and so died.
  11 alssante: *allzusammen*; see also Schmeller I, col. 57.
  15 der dos: (MHG. *erdiezen*, stv. II, 2) pret. *erschallte*.
  23 dŭ gottes tabernackel: see 18,3,3 for the same metaphor and 12,3,3 for this
      prefiguration.

No. 20, foll. 464ᵛ-466ᵛ   Orig. 38

Preliminary:

  1.   See Haltaus, *Jahrzeitbuch*, p. 154, for the date of the Feast Day for *S. Catharine
       Virginis*.

Notes for pages 92-93

2. See *WKL.* II, No. 1410.

Heading: "vnser frawen gesanck weis" serves also as pattern for Hans Sachs' legend about St. Catherine. For comment on the *Ton* see No. 18. The strophes are not numbered. The numbering is mine. Here and there on the first two folios some letters have faded.

1, 2 katherina: according to the *Catholic Encyclopedia* Catherine of Alexandria died A. D. 305; Haltaus *(Jahrzeitbuch,* p. 154) gives the year 307; but in the legend we read, "Die heilige Jungfrau Sankt Katherina gab ihren Geist auf an einem Freitag, da man zählet nach Christi Geburt dreihundert und fünfzehen Jahr." Four times the poet spells the name with an *e* after the *th,* seven times with an *a;* the first spelling is that of his source, the second that of the convent in Nuremberg.

4 vngelerte: one wonders if this adjective might reveal a hidden wish for more education.

5 müg: pres. subj. *möge:* for the form see Weinhold, § 409.

6 verneÿen: *erneuen;* a very faint trace of an erased *h* after the *ÿ* remains.

8 According to the pattern of the *Ton* in Nos. 18 and 19 the faint virgule after "Seit" is a scribal error. The same would hold for the corresponding verse in strophes 2 and 4.

9 drawe: see 4,3,39 for this word.

10 sprŭng: inf. *springen;* Weinhold (§ 45) states that although it is rare to have an *i* turn into a *u,* it does occur in Alemannic and Bavarian.

13 ein prŭn . . . kŭnst: a metaphor for St. Catherine which Hans Sachs probably invented from the statement in the main legend, "man hieβ sie eine berühmte Meisterin der sieben freien Künste" (Rüttgers, p. 133).

14 weisse: adj. used substantively, *Weise.*

15 gesponst: for this metaphor Hans Sachs is again drawing upon the main legend where in a dream Catherine, through her faith, becomes the bride of Christ. For the spurious *t* see Weinhold, § 200 and W. *BGr.,* § 143.

16 This verse, together with vss. 19 and 20 below, reflects the promise which Christ made to Catherine when, in the basic legend, He appeared to her and told her He would never forsake her, nor anyone who through her believed in Him.

17 Hans Sachs extends the grace granted St. Catherine of gaining favor with God to the person who gives honor to her wounds.

18 pist . . . erberben (19): *erwirbst; du* is understood.

19 one zadel: (MHG. *zadel,* stm.) *ohne Unterlaβ.*

22 With this verse Hans Sachs begins the retelling of the third legend.

24 der reichen: in the basic legend Catherine was "edel und schön und weis und reich"; the first three of these are contained in vs. 15 above; here the fourth is woven into the rhyme.

25 Sant: variant form of MHG. *sancte;* schriefft: Hans Sachs' source; anzeŭcht: *bezeugt.*

2, 2 vernüftig: in this word the poet reverts to his former way of writing a *u;* see, for instance, 22,5,9, for the noun "vernüft." The characteristics of the Count enumerated in vss. 2-4 originated with Hans Sachs.

7 capel: (ML. *capella,* MHG. *kappel,* stwkf.); this is a *Kirche* in Hans Sachs' source.

9 geweichet: (MHG. *wîhen,* wkv.) *geweiht;* warte: *war.*

11 vngesparte: (MHG. *ungespart,* part. adj.) *ungesäumt.*

12 ein farte: *einmal;* this belongs with "alle dag" (14), *jeden Tag.*

19 ir schein: this and its description are the invention of Hans Sachs.

20 vnder schlŭg: *senkte.*

25 gemachel: see 3,16 below where Hans Sachs uses the MHG. spelling; aŭf plicken pflag: circumlocution for *blickte auf.*

3, 9 die schŏn: the superscript was probably added by a later hand, for note the superlative degree in 2,22 above and the comparative in 4,13 below.

10 verlas mich nit: with these words Hans Sachs has given the substance of St. Catherine's speech in his source in which she tells the Count that the wreath is to be the symbol of true love one for the other, and warns him not to take anyone in preference to her.

13 in einem kloster: this is an addition by Hans Sachs.

14 This verse is short one syllable.

19 eben: *paßlich.*

4, 2 in kaim: *in geheim*; see W. *BGr.,* § 14 for the contraction.

5 antwŭrt: (MHG. *antwürten,* wkv.); fate: (MHG. *vate,* stf.) *Schicksal*; Hans Sachs substitutes this statement for the not-too-plausible "Da beneidet die Maget den Grafen um seine Güte" in his source.

7 der pfarer ein dochter: in the source it is the daughter of a man living beside the church.

10 des pfarer: see 1,2,19 for the uninflected gen.

11 verschlagen: *verschmäht.*

15 greffen: as a rule Hans Sachs uses *i* in the ending; see 26 below.

16 deŭffelisch anfechtŭng: a detail invented by the poet.

22 seinem kemnat: Grimm (*DW.* 5, 1, col. 529, 3c) gives an example of a neuter "kemnat" with the meaning of *festes (Stein)haus*; one of Schmeller's examples (I, col. 1244) also shows a neuter word, "In einem alten ausgeprenten schlos und kemnat mit guten mauren."

5, 4 dan: p. part. *getan.*

11 meiner armer selle: gen. of thing with "we"; for the strong ending of the attributive adj. after the poss. see Weinhold, § 519.

13 ich: the subject of both "han ver dint" and of "pin"; see also 7,2,4. ir peider dot: see 19,1,16.

15 erschein: inadvertently, perhaps, Hans Sachs wrote the MHG. pret. instead of the NHG. one necessary for his rhyme with vss. 17 and 18.

17 The remark in this verse is the poet's invention; it implies that the baby daughter will be recompense for the count's defection.

21 Hans Sachs invented the details in vss. 21-23.

23 kŭme: see Weinhold, § 63, for this Middle German infinitive.

6, 3 schwere: *Bedrängnis.*

5 mere: *Kunde.*

11 gemeitte: (MHG. *gemeit,* adj.) *lieblich.*

14 This verse is short one syllable.

16 fŭrten: *führten*; sochen: (MHG. *sochen,* wkv.) used substantively with the meaning of *Anschein des Todes.*

19 versprochen: *verteidigt.*

25 This verse is two syllables short.

7, 2 This verse, as well as vs. 5 below, needs another syllable.

15 die marter: Hans Sachs assumes that his hearers are familiar with the martyrdom of St. Catherine.

16 katharine: the only instance where the name ends in *e.*

20 edle frŭcht: here Hans Sachs applies this epithet which is usually a symbol for Christ and which he used only once for the Virgin (16,5,8) to St. Catherine.

Chapter IV / Diverse Aspects of Love

Background:

1. According to Windolph, *Reiseweg*, p. 28, Hans Sachs may have been in Landshut just before he returned to Munich.

2. "Gesprech frau Ehr mit eynem jüngling, die wollust betreffend," written May 9, 1548, *H. S.* 3, 418, 6-8; for two other references to this early love affair, see also *H. S.* 4, 316, 1-15, and 322, 1-17.

3. See *H. S.* 3, 418, 9-11; 15-17; and 26.

4. "Der buler kercker" written June 19, 1544, *H. S.* 3, 389, 11, 24, and 27-30; and 390, 1, 6-7 (for the quotation), and 8-13.

5. See Krebs, *Alte Handwerksbräuche*, p. 147, and Ellis, *Das Walt got,* p. 21, note 54. According to Mummenhof (*Handwerker*, pp. 42-44) there were no guilds in Nuremberg, only trades (*Handwerke*). Even though these were forbidden to have organizations of their own, they most probably conformed to the rules set down by the guilds in other cities.

6. "Kampfgesprech von der lieb," *H. S.* 3, 408, 5-8, 21-24, and 27-28 (Hans Sachs treated the substance of this *Spruchgedicht* in a Shrovetide play written January 8, 1518, for which see *H. S.* 14, pp. 12-25, and Goetze, *Fastnachtspiele*, No. 1).

7. See *H. S.* 3, 414, 11-15 and 24-25.

8. For the quotation see ibid., 409, 16-17, and for his journeying on from Nuremberg see Windolph, *Reiseweg*, p. 58.

9. See No. 22,6,21-23.

10. *H. S.* 3, 392, 27-37.

11. For the reprint of the German translation of Boccaccio's *Decameron* see *Bibliothek d. Litterarischen Vereins in Stuttgart*, Vol. LI; originally attributed to Steinhöwel, Baeseke ("Arigo," *Zeitschrift f. dt. Altertum*, XLVII, p. 191) has now ascribed the translation to Heinrich Schlüsselfelder. I shall continue to use Steinhöwel's name.

12. See Vol. I of *Deutsche Schriften des Albrecht von Eyb*, edited by Max Herrmann, pp. 52-53.

13. For a reprint of Niclas von Wyle's *Translationen* (1478) see Keller, ed., *Biblio. d. Lit. Ver. in Stuttgart*, Vol LVII. N. v. Wyle was at one time a citizen of and *Rathschreiber* in Nuremberg. For Steinhöwel's translation of Boccaccio's *De claris mulieribus* see Drescher, ed., *Biblio. d. Lit. Ver. in Stuttgart*, Vol. CCV. Hans Sachs had a copy in his library with the title, "Johannes Boccaciy die 99 durchleuchting frauen."

14. Weber (pp. 56-57) criticizes Hans Sachs, because he thinks that the artistic effect is impaired by the drastic cutting of the speeches. Hans Sachs, however, had a far different

audience for the tales which he retold from that of Boccaccio's seven ladies and three young men, all of noble birth, who, to pass the time, told the stories to each other. It is doubtful that the Meistersinger would have appreciated the lengthy remarks which delayed action in the tales.

15. "Ein bul scheidlied," September 1, 1513; See Goedeke, *H. S.* I, No. 1, vss. 12-13.

16. Details on these in No. 28.

17. *H. S.* 3, 417, 28-31.

No. 21, foll. 35ʳ-36ʳ   Orig. 23

Preliminary:

1. See Goedeke, *H. S.* I, No. 6; and Goetze-Drescher, *Fab. u. Schw.* 3, No. 1; G-D changed the title found in the Dresden MS., *Der schueknecht handel*, to *Der schwknecht werckzewg.*

Heading: This is the only Meisterlied in Berlin 414 which Hans Sachs set to "des Müscaplücz langen don," a *Ton* of twenty-two verses, five in each *Stollen* and twelve in the *Abgesang*. For the rhyme scheme see Appendix C, and cf. G-D, *Fab. u. Schw.* 3, p. XXI, No. 34; see also the note on that page "Heißt auch langer Hofton." Münzer (*Singebuch*, p. 18, No. 83; music, p. 46) lists it under the name *Hofton*. Goedeke in his transcription combined various verses, whereby he reduced the stanza to sixteen verses. Windolph (*Reiseweg*, pp. 26-27) quoted a few verses of strophes 1 and 5 from the Dresden MS.—Dreyer, in his article "Hans Sachs in München und die gleichzeitigen Münchener Meistersänger," p. 326, states incorrectly, "Das Gedicht von Hans Sachs ist vom 1. Januar 1567 datiert." Where he found that date is not clear, for he cites the K-G Index, No. 37, as well as Goedeke, *H. S.* I, p. 15, in his note on p. 326. Both of these carry the correct date 1516. Furthermore, the erroneous date lead him to the conclusion that Hans Sachs took the incident from Wickram's *Rollwagenbüchlein* which, he says, appeared in 1557 (that was a later edition; the first was published in 1555). Rather it should be the other way around, for Jörg Wickram, the founder of the *Singschule* in *Colmar* and the author of its first book of rules (*Gemerckbuch*, 1549), had access to and was familiar with many Meisterlieder, hence undoubtedly also with Hans Sachs' "schukknecht"-song. Taylor, too, in his *Lit. Hist. Mg.*, pp. 103-104, thinks that Hans Sachs may have used a jest book for his source, but the first German jest book, Pauli's *Schimpff und Ernst* (a book which Hans Sachs did use of some of his later works) was not published until 1522, six years after the poet had written the Meisterlied under discussion. Taylor states (ibid., p. 104) that Hans Sachs "alludes during the course of the poem to his own love affairs." It would seem, however, that the allusion consists merely in an undertone of gaity.

1, 3 sant stefans dag: the Feast Day of St. Stephen is the oldest one registered in the Martyrologies and Church Calendars, for he was the first Christian martyr of the 1st cent., see Acts 7:58-60; his day is December 26; see also Haltaus, *Jahrzeitbuch*, pp. 163-164.

11 vatter: the innkeeper; Berlepsch (p. 68) quotes from the regulations of Arnstadt: "Soll denen Schumachern eine Herberge erwählt werden und welcher Schuhknecht darin

gewandert, oder sonst kommt, der soll den Hauswirt Vater heißen, seine Frau Mutter, . . ." See also Krebs, p. 82.

18 den werck zeüg: (MHG. *zuig*, stm. n.).
21 erbet: (MHG. *erbeit*, stfn.) *Arbeit*; for the *e* in place of *ei* see W. *BGr.*, § 13.

2, 1 Der rede: gen. with the adj. "fro" (2).
4 mentag: (MHG. *mêntac*, stm.) *Montag*; see also W. *BGr.*, § 47.
8 paczen: according to Schmeller (I, cols. 313-314) a *Batzen* is a coin of fluctuating value which was in circulation in Bavaria and other states. He also quotes (col. 313) an interesting definition (from a manuscript, *s. d.*) for this word with the ending *an* in place of *en*; "Batzan ist leder, daz gemachet ist uz schaffes vellen. Sy (die Schuster) hant den list, daz sy ez machent kordewan glich." Since the vowel *e* is sometimes substituted for an *a* in Hans Sachs' dialect (see 12,2,16), and since sheep's leather would fit into the series of the three other kinds of leather mentioned in the same *Stollen*, this would seem to be the more logical meaning here.
9 bedeüt: *mitteile*.
11 hin heine: (MHG. variant *hein*, stn.) *nach Hause*; dreckt: *trägt*; this is the only time Hans Sachs substitutes *ck* for *g* in this verb, but see W. *BGr.*, § 174.
12 düt . . . schmerczen: a bit of humor.
14 pstost: (MHG. *bestoẓen*, redv. V) *glättet*; for the loss of the *e* in the prefix see W. *BGr.*, § 14.
15 drücknetes: (MHG. *trucken*, wkv.) *trocknet es.*
17 schmere: (MHG. *smër*, stn. m.) *Fett.*
18 maisterein: Weinhold (*BGr.*, § 213) says that the ending *ein* for the fem. *in* continued to be used in the 15th and 16th cents.
19 ers: *er es*; nein: *ein*; for the prefixed *n* see W. *BGr.*, § 165.

3, 2 rüst er sich zw: (MHG. *zuorusten*, wkv.) *kleidet er sich an.*
10 clein al: for an explanation of the technical terms used in the making of shoes see Goedeke, *H. S.* I, pp. 16-17.
12 pech porsten vnd garen: the journeyman made his own shoemaker's thread out of wax, bristles, and yarn.
17 den: (MHG. *den*, adv.) *dann.*

4, 2 stahel: *Werkzeug zum Stechen.*
4 gestempt: (MHG. *gestëmen*, stv. V) *einhält.*
7 fleck: (MHG. *vlec*, stm.) *Lappen.*
8 hantleder: *Lederstück zum Schutz der Hand.*
9 deimling: *Däumling*; according to Grimm, *DW.* 2, col. 851,2 this is "auch jeder überzug zum schutz eines . . . daumens."
11 ne al: *eine Ahle*; gneip: (MHG. *knîp*, stm.) *Messer.*
13 zücket: *ergreift schnell.*
15 aüf züg: *Vorrichtung zum Aufziehen.*
16 füg: (MHG. *vuoc*, stm.) *Kunstfertigkeit.*

5, 11 geschelschafft: i. e. of Meistersinger; for the substitution of *sch* for *s* in the second syllable of this word see W. *BGr.*, § 154.
12 horen: the *n* is by a long mark over the *e*; such an ending for the 1. sg. pres. ind. is common in Middle German according to Weinhold, § 395.
15 han: 3. pl. pres. ind.; for this Middle German form see Weinhold, § 396.
16 gedaüffet: for comment on this custom see Plate, p. 168.

20 den: *denen*; Hans Sachs uses the plural throughout his *Abgesang* to refer to "geschelschafft" (11). Hans sachs: in the spring of 1515 the poet had already signed his name in rhyme in two *Spruchgedichte* (see *H. S.* 2, 222, and 3, 417), but this is the first Meisterlied so signed. He may have been prompted to do this by finding Folz' name woven into the verse in a few of his poems; see, for instance, Berlin 414, foll. 274^r and 477^r (also Ellis, "Solution," p. 455, and Mayer, ed., No. 94, vs. 150, respectively).

No. 22, foll. 33^v-35^r   Orig. 22

Heading: Even though frauenlob's "lang don" is one of the four *gekrönten Töne* (see Taylor, *Lit. Hist. Mg.*, pp. 70-71 and 73), Hans Sachs set only this and one other Meisterlied (No. 30) to it. The reason seems obvious when we read Münzer's caustic comment (*Singebuch*, p. 14, No. 4): "Diese Melodie gehört zu denjenigen, welche die Musik der Meistersinger vor allem diskreditiert haben ..." He then mitigates his statement somewhat by pointing out that we don't know what the original melody may have been. Münzer does not print the music, calls the Puschmann-melody (see Runge, pp. 67-68) *wenig reizvoll*, and Wagenseil's notation (inserted between pp. 554 and 555 as *Das ander Gesetz* of the *Hort*) a *Karikatur*. See also Mey (pp. 167-168) who follows Wagenseil, and von d. Hagen IV, pp. 926-927 and 933. There are twenty-four verses in a strophe, eight in each of the three parts. For the rhyme scheme see Appendix C, and cf. Mey, p. 168, where, however, vs. 20 has six syllables instead of the four found both in Runge (pp. 67-68) and in the two Meisterlieder by Hans Sachs. Frauchiger (pp. 50 and 76, No. XLI) shows a pattern with fewer verses of which some have fifteen syllables. – The significance of the Latin numerals, ^{I} CCCXI, at the top of fol. 33^v to the right, is not apparent.

1, 1   Vss. 1 and 2 are somewhat similar to the first two verses in the *Spruchgedicht, H. S.* 3, p. 406.
    3   dürch einen: the ending of the indef. art. is by abbreviation; in 35,2,17 Hans Sachs uses the dat. with *durch.*
    5   gangen: past part.
    7   alweg: MHG. *allewege*, adv.) *stets;* gedŏn: the vowel is doubtful; it could be either an *o* or a *u*; it is possible that someone other than Hans Sachs modified the *o* by means of the superscribed *e*, for in vss. 15 and 23 below the words "grün" (MHG. *gruo,* adj.) and "kün" (MHG. *kuon,* adj.) were changed by a later hand to *grŏn* and *kŏn*. Since the *ü* in each of these two words is still clearly visible, I am keeping the original spelling.
    9   nahet: (MHG. *nâhet,* adj., adv.)
  12   A virgule after "gesattelt" is a scribal error.
  21   in: note the acc. case.

2, 10   verzoch: *verweigerte sich.*
  13   lüff: *lief*; for the vowel *u* see 19,2,15.
  23   weil: *während.*

3, 3   drack: (MHG. *dracke,* wkm) *Drache.*
  16   ane scherczen: *im Ernst*; see Grimm, *DW.* 8, col, 2595,2c.
  17   anfanck: (MHG. *anvanc,* stm.)
  19   zwanck: *Not.*
  21   an dem rein: a formula to express distance; Hans Sachs' thoughts were probably still in Munich; gedanck: (MHG. *gedanc,* stm.) *Denken.*

4, 1 vrlaüb: *Abschied.*
  3 kürcze: *rasch.*
  4 straücht: *stolperte*; würcze: (MHG. *wurze*, wkstf.) *Wurzel.*
  8 zw füre: (MHG. *zervarn*, stv. VI) *ging auseinander.*
  9 dimerlicher: (MHG. *timmer*, adj.) *heiserer.*
  11 schreitte: *stieg.*
  19 er zalt: (MHG. *erzaln*, wkv.) *berichtete*
  20 palt: the final *t* has been made out of a *d.*

5, 7 rŏslein: the superscript over the *o* may be a later addition; virt: *weiter*; for this meaning see Grimm, *DW.* 4, pt. 1, col. 900.
  8 wilde: here perhaps with the meaning of *seltsam.*
  13 verwilligvng: (MHG. *verwilligunge*, stf.) *Bewilligung.*
  15 vnordenlich: (MHG. *unordenlich*, adj.) *ungehörig*; pegÿrt: *Begierde.*
  19 wist: pl. imp.; since the wise master has addressed the poet with *du* (5), this is a shift to the poet's audience; see also 21, and 7,2 below.
  22 genist: *geheilt wird.*

6, 1 dick: *Tücke.*
  3 clafer: *Schwätzer*; mengerleÿe: (MHG. *menegerleie*, adj.). In a Shrovetide play of 1552 (*H. S.* 14, 198-219) Hans Sachs depicts the havoc a *klaffer* can cause by breaking up a journeyman's marriage.
  4 sie: this refers to "man oder frawen pilde" (5,2 above); beschreÿe: 3. pl. *ins gerede bringen.*
  9 offenlich: (MHG. *offenlich*, adj.) *offenbar*; art: *Ort.*
  12 aneinder: a metathetical error for *einander.*
  13 im: unconsciously, perhaps, Hans Sachs uses the dat. sg. here, where one would expect the pl., because the forced separation from his own beloved still rankles. seczet zw: *plagt*, or *verfolgt.*
  18 münt: synecdoche, a favorite stylistic device for Hans Sachs.
  19 Here and in vss. 20-23 the poet may have been thinking of himself, but then as afterthought added the generalization "mon oder weibe" (24).
  20 in rechtem grünt: *im tiefsten Wesen*; Hans Sachs' love for the girl in Munich was a deep and true love.

7, 1 straüchet: pres. part.; for the loss of the *n* see 19,3,16.
  4 gekrencket: *geschwächt.*
  5 leit: *leidet.*
  10 rach: *Strafe.*
  12 gütte: *Vermögen.*
  18 qüel: (MHG. variant *quêl*, stm.) *Qual.*

No. 23, foll. 12^V-15^V   Orig. 7

Preliminary:

1. See Steinhöwel, *Decameron*, IV, 1, for the Meisterlied and IV, 5, for the tale used in the *Spruchgedicht*, "Der ermört Lorenz" (*H. S.* 2, pp. 216-222).

2. Eyb (*Ehebüchlein*, pp. 52-53) moralizes thus, "Ein hŭbsche histori . . . gibt zuuerstien, das man frawen vnd lunckfrawen zu rechter zeit menner geben soll. Eee das sie durch blŏdigkeit des fleyschs vnd leichtuertigkeit des gemŭtes zu valle vnd schanden kumen mŏgen."

3. See 21,5,20.

4. See Goedeke, *H. S.* I, No. 7: the date 1515 given in Goedeke's note (p. 18) for the *Tragedia* which Hans Sachs made of the same tale is probably a misprint, it should be 1545. In the same note Goedeke says that on November 17, 1549, Hans Sachs wrote another Meisterlied on the same subject, which is to be found in "M 3 174 ohne Namen." Such a song is, however, not recorded in the K-G Index either under the entry for the original Meisterlied of 1516, or under that of the later *Tragedia* of 1545; nor is it to be found among the works written in November of 1549. For the other published copy of this Meisterlied see Goetze-Drescher, *Fab. u. Schw.* 3, No. 4.

Heading: Hans Sachs sets all three of his Meisterlieder which retell tales from the Decameron to the "frawen Eren don" for which see No. 16. 3 xiii: each poem is thirteen strophes long (the usual word "lieder" is omitted); par: (MHG. *bar*, stn.) *meistersängerisches Lied*; for this technical term see also Plate, pp. 180-182; Hans Sachs uses the word again in only three other Meisterlieder, 26, 27, and 28. die 3 neuen historj: (MHG. *histŏrje*, stwkf.) *Erzählungen*, those based on tales 1, 4, and 6 from the Fourth Day of Boccaccio's *Decameron*.

1, 1   nonella: *novella*; not until the third of these songs does Hans Sachs spell this word correctly. The *Decameron* is listed among the books which he had in his library under the entry: "Cento Nouella Johanis Bocacii" (see *H. S.* 26, 152).

    4   memori: Goetze (*Frühneuhochdeutsches Glossar*) lists this as a fem. noun (*Gedächtnis*). Hans Sachs must have had what today is called a "photographic memory," since he so frequently quotes from "memori." He states in one of his summaries (*H. S.* 23, 133, 16-25) that whatever he learned from books "Dis pflanczt ich fleissig in memori."

    5   pocaciüs: although the ending *üs* of this word has been crossed out and a new word *pocaciy* written in by a later hand after the partite sign, I am keeping the original.

    10   der: this word is crossed out in the manuscript and the words *merkt wy* (to rhyme with the new *pocaciy* of vs. 5 above) have been written in by a later hand between the old partite sign and a new one, thereby, however, producing one too many syllables for the verse. As in vs. 5 above, I am keeping the original. concretus: this is *Tancrede* in Steinhöwel's translation; Hans Sachs seems to have had the initial *C* so firmly fixed in his mind that even years later (Nov. 17, 1545), when he wrote a drama on the same subject, he still used it.

    11   was . . . gessessen: *war wohnhaft*; Steinhöwel uses the same verb in the last of these three tales on p. 282, 9-10.

2, 2   vnmasse: *übermäßig*.

    5   Gismonda: Hans Sachs follows Steinhöwel in this name; Eyb calls her Sigismunda.

    7   Capüa: an ancient city in Italy.

    9   eben: *paßlich*.

    14   sie: i. e. Gismonda.

    15   This verse is short one syllable.

    16   Hans Sachs invented the detail in this verse.

3, 3   keim: *keinem.*
7   jüngling: Hans Sachs deletes the fact that the youth was not of noble birth.
10   Güisgardus: Hans Sachs followed Eyb more closely than Steinhöwel with regard to the spelling of this name. A few times he spells the name with an initial *Q* instead of a *G.*
16   prünste: *Glut.*

4, 7   spechte: *spähte.*
8   los: *Zeichen*; for this meaning see Schmeller I, col. 1518, and Grimm, *DW.* 6, col. 1156.
12   wart: pret. *wartete*; seine: MHG. gen. (with an appended *e*) of the pronoun *er.*
14   nossen: (MHG. *niezen,* stv. II, 2) pret. *genossen*; der libe prün: this metaphor may be original with Hans Sachs.

5, 11   denn: def. art.
12   inn: *ihn*; originally this was *im,* but Hans Sachs added another stroke to the *m.*

6, 1   er: the *e* is not capitalized.
5   ein: this is the original word; a dubious letter, possibly *j,* has been made over the *ei*; schloff: (MHG. *sliefen,* stv. II, 1) *schlüpfte.*
8   schir: *schnell.*
9   schaich: a scribal error for the MHG. pret. *schlaich.*
10   pot: *befahl.*
11   zwaien: Hans Sachs uses the dat. with the verb "pot" (10); holen: *die Höhle*; Schmeller (I, col. 1083) cites a fem. noun, *die Holen.*
12   schlüff: (MHG. *slupfen,* wkv.) *schlüpfte*; see W. *BGr.,* § 128 for the substitution of *f* for *ph (pf.).*
15   her aüsser kroch: *heraus erkroch.*

7, 5   plüet: for the spelling see 8,1,23; geschmecht: *geschmäht.*
7   det . . . verkerren: *verwandelte.*
8   wüt: *wütete.*
9   doren: (Middle German variant *torn,* stm.) *Turm.*
10   necht: (MHG. *naehen,* wkv.) *naht.*
11   gangen: p. part.
16   berdrogen: for the insertion of the *r* into the prefix see W. *BGr.,* § 163.

8, 1   Gwisgardo: here and in vs. 12 below Hans Sachs uses the Latin endings.
7   laügen: (MHG. *lougen,* stn.) *Leugnung.*
9   als wol dw: *so wohl wie du.*
16   With the above few verses (8-16) Hans Sachs effectively gives the gist of two and one half pages in his source.

9, 3   schüff: *befahl.*
5   kopff: *Trinkgefäß.*
12   west: pret. *wußte*; see Weinhold, § 419, for the form.

10, 2   pis: Weinhold (§ 363) says this imperative form is common in Alemannic and Middle German.
11   drüeg: probably with the meaning of *brachte.* Even though the attempt was made by a later hand to change the *g* into a *k* or *kt,* I am keeping the original. Steinhöwel uses the verb *nächnet* at this point; the English translation has "carry."

11, 1   jünckfraw: nom. pl.; lüffen: *liefen*; see also 19,2,15.
   2   angsten: *Besorgnissen*; schweiste: (MHG. *sweiẓen*, wkv.) *schwitzte*.
   3   westen: see 9,12 above; bes: *wes*, the MHG. gen. sg. of the interrogative pronoun; des: *das*.
   4   dar: rel. pron. *wo*.
   5   Gwisgardüs dot: Hans Sachs invented the detail in this verse to account for the confusion among Gismonda's ladies-in-waiting.
   8   wart: pres. subj. *warte*; an: *auf*.
  11   Notwithstanding the fact that in the translations by both Steinhöwel and Eyb, Gismonda prepares the poison potion before she receives the heart, Hans Sachs' version seems entirely plausible.
  13   güsse: *goβ*; for the form see Weinhold, § 355.

12, 1   amacht: (MHG. *âmaht*, stf.) *Ohnmacht*.
   4   heisser: *heftiger*.
  11   Congkrette: the Latin voc.; pette: (MHG. *bëte*, stn.) *Bitte*.
  12   bestette: (MHG. *bestaten*, wkv.) imp. *begrabe!* Schmeller (II, col. 796) says there was confusion between the stem *stæt* and *stat*.
  14   vast: gewaltig.

13, 4   ir paider dotter leibe: *die Leiber der beiden Toten*; cf. 19,1,16.
   5   A virgule after "Salerno" is a scribal error.
   7   zw gatte: *zergeht*, i. e. *ein Ende nimmt*.
  11   in: Hans Sachs is here using a dat. pl. pronoun to refer to a noun in the sg. "kint" (10); cf. P-G, § 230; angesiget: (MHG. *anesigen*, wkv.) *besiegt*; this verb is followed by the dat. of person.
  12   abs: *Obst*; Schweitzer ("Sprichwörter u. ... bei Hans Sachs" *Hans Sachs Forschungen*, p. 366) includes this saying among those not found in collections of proverbs.
  16   zeit pringt rossen: the inference is that young people, too, have their time of blossoming.

No. 24, foll. 15ᵛ-18ᵛ   Orig. 8

Preliminary:

1. See Steinhöwel, *Decameron*, IV, 4.

2. Goetze-Drescher, *Fab. u. Schw. 3*, No. 5.

Heading: "in dem vorgmelten don," that is, the "frawen Eren don" (see No. 16); due to an oversight, Hans Sachs omitted the first *e* in the adjective. The *m* is by abbreviation.

1, 1   Mon: the *M* is a rather large ornamental letter; nevella: *novella*.
   3   cecillia: *Sizilien*; Steinhöwel has *Cicilia*.
   4   wilhalmus: Hans Sachs tacks the Latin ending onto Steinhöwel's *Wilhalm*.
  13   degen: (MHG. *dëgen*, stm.) *Krieger*. The details in this and the following three verses have been supplied by Hans Sachs.

2, 3   küng: most probably a scribal error for künig, because the verse needs another syllable.

4   haidenscheffte: the MHG. dat. sg.

5   Tünici: Tunis.

7   Constancia: in the original tale and in Steinhöwel's translation the heroine does not have a name, therefore Hans Sachs transferred the name of Gerbino's sister, whom he does not mention, to her.

14   vorgemelt: *vorher genannt.*

3, 3   the second "ein" in the verse is a scribal error which makes one syllable too many.

10   ein ring: Hans Sachs converts the generalization *kleynet* of his source to a more meaningful token.

13   This verse has a superfluous syllable.

14   Gramata: Granada, formerly a Moorish Kingdom in Spain; for the substitution of *m* for *n* see W. *BGr.,* § 139.

4, 4   wider zeme: (MHG. *widerzëme*, adj.) *widerwärtig.*

6   verschrib: *schriftlich mitteilte*; this is followed by the dat.

7   müsset: this is a strange form. Weinhold (*BGr.,* § 143) does not mention a spurious *t* after an *e.*

15   draüren: (MHG. *drûren*, wkv.) inf. used substantively, *Trauern.*

16   harnisch: *kriegerische Ausrüstung*; were: *Kriegsmacht.*

5, 3   wilhelmo: the Lat. dat.; Hans Sachs deviates from his source by having Constancia's father go to "küng wilhelmo" himself instead of sending an envoy for the request of safe conduct.

5   mocht: pret. subj.

7   die sach: the fact that Gerbino was preparing to take Constancia by force on the sea.

11   der heiden: at the end of the tale Steinhöwel similarly refers to Constancia's father as a heathen.

15   hert: *streng.*

6, 1   reit: the MHG. pret.

3   Missina: the capital of the Sicilian province Messina.

5   galleien: (MHG. *galîe*, stwkf.) gen. pl. *Galeeren.*

8   Sardini: Sardinia, an island in the Mediterranean.

9   vür vare: (MHG. *vürvarn*, stv. VI), inf. *vorfahren.*

10   lenten zw: (MHG. *zuolenten*, wkv.) *landen.*

13   sitiklich: *langsam.*

15   mit schnellen laüf: note the acc. case.

7, 1   in: *ihnen*; although the antecedent is "schiff" (6,16 above), Hans Sachs was probably thinking of the persons within the ship, rather than of the vessel itself. schir: *in kurzer Zeit.*

2   riffe: inf. of the wk. verb.

6   port: *Schiffsrand.*

12   aller seinen sin: gen. pl. with "vergasse"; the final *n* of "seinen" is by a long mark over the *e.*

14   gent: the pl. imp. of the MHG. contracted form of *geben.*

16   zücket: *ergriff schnell.*

8, 1   gral: (MHG. *gral*, stm.) *Schrei.*

3   püchse: *Feuerrohr.*

11   sw: *zu*; Weinhold (*BGr.*, § 150) says that sporadically the initial *z* of the prep. *zu* was pronounced in "Altbaiern" as if it were an *s*.

13   wart . . . ein prechen: *fing an einzubrechen.*

14   wer: *Verteidigung.*

9, 2   Hans Sachs employs understatement.

8   geschwünt: (MHG. *swinden*, III, i) *wurde bewußtlos*, impersonal with the dat.

12   vrgrüeff: *ergriff*; Hans Sachs is here perhaps substituting *ue* for *ie*; see W. *BGr.*, § 110 (Shumway, p. 22, gives two examples of a pret. sg. in rhyme spelled with *ie* from later works). Hans Sachs uses the prefix *vr* for *er* also in 25,10,4, and in 30,3,15.

10, 14   getrieb: without thinking, perhaps, Hans Sachs wrote the NHG. pret. instead of the MHG. one for his rhyme with "leib" (15).

15   lissen irer: a kind of metathetical error for *liss er iren.*

11, 1   heim: i. e. *nach Sizilien.*

3   den heiden: Constancia's father; note the double acc. with "beweist."

8   in wer: *ihnen wäre.*

12   This and the next verse each lack one syllable.

12, 13   gennüge: inf.; note the dat. of thing with this verb.

13, 8   ellich: (MHG. *êlich*, adj.)

11   e': *Ehen.*

12   hant: 2. pl. pres.; Weinhold (§ 396) states that although rare this form does occur in Bavarian; it is more common in Middle German.

13   Hans Sachs shifts to the sg., probably because he wants each individual to consider well that which he is saying.

15   honig: this proverbial saying may be original with Hans Sachs, although Niclas v. Wyle in his *Translationen*, p. 101, ll. 31-33, remarks, "des poeten spruch, der da sagt liebe sin gesencket in wenig hongs vnd vil gallen."

No. 25, foll. 18ᵛ-21ʳ   Orig. 9

Preliminary:

1.   See Steinhöwel, *Decameron*, IV, 6, for this third tale.

2.   Goetze-Drescher, *H. S. Fab. u. Schw.* 3, No. 6.

Heading: the "frawen Eren don" serves Hans Sachs for the third tale.

1, 3   perssia: the name of the place in Hans Sachs' source is Brescia, a town in northern Italy.

4   ritter: this is *edelman* in Hans Sachs' source.

5   misser nigro: Steinhöwel spells this name *Miser Negro.*

13   beste: pret. *weste*; for the form see 23,9,12.

14 pitter lieb: Hans Sachs' use of oxymoron effectively foreshadows the tragic event to come.

2, 4 lobt: pret. with the meaning of *versprach.*

5 ÿ der mon: *jedermann*; the details set down in this *Stollen* are the invention of Hans Sachs.

9 In this and in the following verse Hans Sachs uses poetical language not found in his source.

13 inen: adv. *innen.*

14 irem haüs: this would be Andreola's.

3, 6 im . . . seinem: the dat. of interest in addition to the poss. adj.

8 erschrocklich: *erschrecklich*; for the uncommon substitution of *o* for *ë* see 1,3,10.

16 tas: *daß*; although Hans Sachs frequently substitutes *t* for *d* medially and in final position, there is only one other instance of his doing so initially (26,7,16); see W. *BGr.,* § 140; ir: the maid uses the polite form.

4, 5 vast: *sehr*; heint: (MHG. *hînt*, a variant of *hî-naht,* adv.) *heute zu Nacht oder Abend*; the form is still current in the dialect of Nuremberg according to Gebhart, *Grammatik der Nürnberger Mundart,* §§ 76 and 142.

6 vngemüt: *betrübt.*

10 von erst: *zuerst*; see Schmeller I, col. 122, for this meaning.

11 gesichte: *Traum.*

12 sein: (MHG. *seine,* adv.) *beinahe nicht.*

13 This verse is short one syllable.

15 erst: *vorhin*; this whole verse, omitted from the original, has been written into the right-hand margin, at right angles to the text, by a later hand; the verse is short one syllable.

5, 1 wech: (MHG. *waehe,* adj.) *schön*; the dogs are an invention of Hans Sachs.

3 rech: (MHG. *rêch,* stn.) *Reh.*

7 linden: Hans Sachs supplies this detail of a tree.

8 haimlich: *vertraut.*

10 sein haüpt: the object of "leit" (9).

11 ein graüsamer würme: in the source this is a *kolschwarcz grausam windspil* (greyhound).

12 eines dracken fürme: Schmeller (I, col. 756) cites *der Furm (Form).* Perhaps Hans Sachs thought that a greyhound was not particularly *grausam,* hence changed it into something more formidable.

16 das: *des*; gen. with "er schrack."

6, 6 wider zem: *widerwärtig.*

12 seuffczen: (MHG. *siufze,* wkm.) *Seufzer.*

15 er pidnet: (MHG. *erbidemen,* wkv.) *erbebte*; see also 18,1,24 for *n=m.*

16 saück . . . ein: (MHG. *sûgen,* stv. II, 1) *saugte ein.*

7, 6 sie: the *s* in this first word in the *Stollen* is not capitalized.

9 echczen: (MHG. *ëchzen,* wkv.) *stöhnen.*

11 si: this has been inserted between "haüpt" and "zam" above the line by a later hand; zam: a drastic contraction of MHG. *zesamen*; schlüge: the *u*-hook is a later addition.

8,	1	cleglichen: (MHG. *klegelich,* adj.) Hans Sachs adds an ending to the pred. adj.
	4	hent: *Hand*; Weinhold (*BGr.*, § 12) says that this spurious umlaut in the sg. is sometimes found in the Nuremberg dialect even today; Steinhöwel (*Decameron,* p. 285, line 6) uses the same form for the sg.; stisse: *steckte.*
	5	damit: rel. *womit.*
	15	dissen iüngling: Hans Sachs lets this, the object of "namen," serve also as the object of "wolten . . . dragen" (16) and of "drügen" (9,1).

9,	3	der wachter: Hans Sachs is here using a noun in the sg. for the subject of three verbs in the pl.: "pekamen" (4), "fingen" (5), and "fürten" (6); vngefer: *arglos.*
	4	pekamen: *kamen*; in: dat. pl.
	8	fremden: *seltsamen.*
	9	fregen: (MHG. variant *vrëgen*, wkv.)
	10	sie: i. e., the questions (understood) which the judge is asking.
	11	den iren worte: Hans Sachs uses the dat. pl. of a thing with "glaübet."
	12	im: here the dat. is used with the verb "ermorte."
	16	begriff: *betastete*; an alles zwingen: *ohne Gewalt anzutum.*

10,	3	pastin: (ML. *apostema*) *Geschwür*, probably a *Pulsadergeschwulst* (aneurysm).
	6	aüf der fart: *sogleich.*
	7	freÿ ledig: this may be a formula for acquittal.
	8	pegeren wart: *fing er an zu begehren.*
	12	des richters: gen. with the reflex. verb "erwert sich".
	13	wart . . . kümen aüsse: *wurde bekannt.*

11,	1	lies: *entließ*; this verse is short one syllable.
	2	ritter: Andreola's father.
	11	müt: *dünkt*; there is no ending *et* for the verb, even though there is sufficient space for it, hence the verse is short one syllable; faste: *stark.*
	12	verdrawen: this substantive is masc. for Hans Sachs; see also Grimm (*DW.* 12,1, col. 1955, IV) who cites an example from the year 1505; dw̆: this has been added later above the line, apparently by Hans Sachs.
	13	hestw: here there is complete assimilation of the pret. ending.
	14	gewert: (MHG. *gewërn*, wkv.) *gewährt.*

12,	1	par: *Bahre.*
	3	proces: (MHG. *procëss*, stf.) *Prozession.*
	4	gedŏne: *Getön*; whether Hans Sachs or some one else added the superscript to the *o* in this word and in "schŏne" (9) cannot be determined.
	10	e·: the *e* is capitalized, *Ehe.*
	13	als: *alles*; lide: *litt.*

13,	9	vnwissen: pres. part.; for the loss of the *d* see Weinhold, § 373.
	10	stünst: (MHG. *sunst*, adv.) *sonst*; for the insertion of the spurious *t*, more particularly after an *s*, see W. *BGr.*, § 142.
	12	vmbwatten: (MHG. *umbe-waten*, stv. VI) *herumgehen.*
	16	Saxe: the poet attaches a spurious *e* to his own name.

Preliminary:

1. 1516 is the year which Hans Sachs set down below this Meisterlied in Berlin 414, hence the year 1517 which the K-G Index, No. 46, lists may have been taken from another manuscript into which the Meisterlied had also been copied.

Heading: Similarly to employing the same *Ton* for each of his three tales from the Decameron, Hans Sachs set all three of his songs "von dreÿerleÿ lieb" to just one *Ton*, "der lange marner" (see No. 1). parat: (MHG. *parât*, stf. m.) here perhaps with the broader meaning of *bunter Aufzug*, for that which the poet is presenting in his trilogy is actually a colorful parade of the characteristics of love (but see Plate, p. 181). In 38,2,17 Hans Sachs uses the word in its literal sense of *Fechterkunststück*. güldin: by means of this adjective the poet may have wanted to stress the importance of the subject matter. tablatür: usually spelled *tabulatur* (CL. *tabula*, f., a list) the term the Meistersinger gave to their list of rules, which Hans Sachs, however, in 1540 called "schuelzetel"; here he applies the word to his catalog of characteristics which are both inherent in, and demanded by, the three varieties of love.

1, 1 Space has been left for a large, perhaps ornamental letter, presumably an *O*, which would make the requisite number of syllables for the verse: jerracheÿ: for comment on this see 13,1,2.
  6 süptil: (ML. *subtilis*) *scharfsinnig*.
  8 stat: (MHG. *stat*, stm.) *Stand*.
  12 par: *Lied*.
  13 aigenschaft: here the word seems to have taken on the broader meaning of *Art*, a word which Hans Sachs himself uses in vs. 6 of the second Meisterlied on "dreÿer lieb."
  14 gotlicher lib: possibly a dat. with "penent."
  16 sam: (MHG. *sam*, adv.) *wie*.
  17 Hans Sachs' concept of divine love is, in part, akin to St. Paul's, and with this verse he expresses the substance of the second clause of I Cor. 13:13, ". . . aber die Liebe ist die Größte unter ihnen"; in vs. 21 below he mentions "gelaüb" and "hoffnüng."
  22 köm: the vowel *ö* may be a later correction, for as a rule Hans Sachs employs the vowel *e* in the pret. subj. of this verb (see among others, 23,5,10: 24,3,7; 25,4,14).
  25 heiliger geist: the Meistersinger frequently invoked the Holy Spirit for help in writing a Meisterlied; see, for instance, Berlin 414, foll. 43ʳ, 56ʳ, 59ʳ, 61ʳ, etc.; see also Folz (Mayer, ed.) No. 72 and the third *par* of No. 75.
  26 Aügustinus: St. Augustine, in the last part of his *Inchiridion* on faith, hope, and love, does not spell out the characteristics as Hans Sachs does. Hence the poet may have been reading a commentary on either this work or on I Cor. 13.
  27 hil: (ML. *hyle* from the Greek) *Materie, Urstoff*.

2, 4 hochfart: (MHG. *hôchvart*, stf.) *Hoffart*.
  9 almüs: (MHG. *almuose*, stf.) *Almosen*.
  11 willig armüt: Hans Sachs may here be thinking of those who enter a religious order in which the Three Substantials were Obedience, Chastity, and Poverty, but also of the fact that the vow of Poverty was in decline at this time; see Coulton, Vol. I, chap. XIII, for St. Benedict's Rule, and Vol. III, chap. XXIII, for the decline of the vow.
  13 lie: *Liebe*; for the loss of the *b* see W. *BGr.*, § 126 a.
  25 pit: *bittet*.

3, 3 frassheit: (MHG. *vrâʒheit*, stf.) *Gefräßigkeit.*
5 alle frist: *immer.*
22 Vss. 18-22 may very well be an expression of Hans Sachs' personal faith in God.
23 on wet: (MHG. *anewæten*, wkv.) subj. *ankleide*; a verb in the sg. with three subjects in the following verse.
24 widertigkeit: a scribal error for *widerwertigkeit*; the omitted syllable causes the verse to be short one syllable.

4, 2 reiczvng: (MHG. *reizunge*, stf.) *Anreizung*; ricz: (MHG. *ritzen*, wk.).
3 vnschamheit: (MHG. *unschameheit*, stf.) *Unkeuschheit.*
7 heilliger stet: gen. with "Vil," *Stätte*; heim sücht: *besucht.* Hans Sachs probaly visited some of these himself in one place or another.
8 schiucht: (MHG. *schiuchen*, wkv.) *meidet.*
10 Hans Sachs may have been thinking of Isa. 11:2-3 (Vulgate Bible).
14 in hicziger: (MHG. *inhitzec*, adj.) *sehr heißer.*
15 forcht: (MHG. *vorht*, stm., Middle German *vorcht*) *Furcht*; vndie: *ohne die.*
16 ebigen licht: a metaphor for God.

5, 3 dürch zilt: *durchdrungen*, i. e., with divine love
4 ein plassvng: (MHG. *înblâsunge*, stf.) *Einflüsterung.*
7 Ww: *wo*; the first instance of *w* for *o*; ein gepilt: *eingeprägt.*
11 es: the antecedent is "hercz" (3 above).
18 lerer: Hans Sachs wants his hearers to know that what he says is well documented.
19 der: gen. pl. of the demonstrative pronoun.
25 Cf. vs. 19 above.
27 plos: with the gen., as here, the meaning is *rein von.*

6, 1 sanctus laürencius: St. Laurentius (fl. 253-260), a Spanish martyr who is said to have been roasted to death. Hans Sachs may have included this saint, who lived two centuries after the other four saints cited as examples, because there is a *St. Lorenzkirche* in Nuremberg, and, as a boy, he probably had learned something about the man for whom the church was named. There is also a song to *St. Laurentius* of the 15th or 16th cent. (see *WKL.* II, No. 1237) which may or may not have been current during Hans Sachs' journeyman years. Be that as it may, it is nevertheless interesting to find the words *auff einem glüenden Rost* with which the fourteenth stanza ends, repeated, except for the indefinite article, in vs. 2 below.
4 het genost: (MHG. *genôʒen*, wkv.) *genossen hatte.*
7 Sanctus paülus: during the reign of Nero, Paul was beheaded with the sword.
8 Three of the four hardships quoted in this verse which Paul endured are to be found in his second epistle to the Corinthians, 11:27, but there is no mention of "hicz."
9 benaden: (MHG. *benâden*, wkv.) *begnadigen;* this verse has one syllable too many.
13 Sanctus petrüs: Simon Peter is said to have spent his last years in Rome and there to have been crucified, head down, by order of Nero.
14 ram: *Rom.*
15 sanctüs andreas: St. Andrew, the brother of Simon Peter, was crucified.
17 Sanctüs johannes: St. John lived to an extremely old age; he is said to be the only one of the twelve disciples who died a natural death.
18 ol: (MHG. *ol*, stn.) *Öl;* according to tradition St. John was cast into a vat of hot oil in Rome, but remained unharmed.
21 brifft: *prüft!*
22 was: *was für*; stifft: *stiftet.*

7, 3 selich sag: *gute Belehrung.*
7 Der: this refers to "mensch" (2).
10 auff der erden ring: circumlocution for *auf der Erde.*
18 itlich: (MHG. variant *itlich*, pron. adj.) *jeder.*
21 hor: instead of this Hans Sachs should have written *her*, for this word is the second in a series of five rhymes; there are many examples for both spellings of this imperative.
22 This verse echoes Deut. 6:4-5 and Matt. 22:37-38. The fact that this command is found in both the Old and the New Testament may be the reason for Hans Sachs' calling it "das erst gepot" (19) and "die ewangelisch ler" (20).
23 The commandment in this verse is to be found in Lev. 19:18 and in Matt. 22:39.

No. 27, foll. 3ʳ-5ʳ   Orig. 2

Preliminary:

1.   See Steinhöwel, *Decameron*, X, 8, for the tale of Titus and Gisippus.

Heading: For the *Ton* see No. 1.

1, 1 seraffin: for comment see 2,1,7.
11 pabl: *bald*; the *b* in this word is a scribal error; caim: *Kain*; see Gen. 4:3-8.
12 The statement in this verse is inferred in Gen. 5:3.
13 Prüderlib: the "-lib" may be a scribal error for the suffix *lich*; however, the word is repeated in 7,1 below.
14 figür: here this simply means *Beispiel* and not prefiguration, because it was Abel's sacrifice which was prefigurative; see Watson, *Bibl. and Theol. Dictionary*, pp. 4-6.
17 es: this refers to "mensch" (16) which is both masc. and neut. in MHG.
18 verlon: *überlassen*; note the double accusative; see P-G, § 206.
19 entlichen: *endgültigen.*
25 The point which Hans Sachs makes in this verse was apparently of importance to him, for he repeats it in 6,23 below and prescribes it in 7,22.

2, 1 schlecht: (MHG. *slëht*, adj.) *aufrichtig.*
3 stant: in this verse and in vss. 7 and 8 below Hans Sachs infers his belief that no matter what a person's standing in society, his function in life, or his calling may be, each has been instituted by God (for this same idea see, among others, Huizinga, *Der Herbst d. Mittelalters*, p. 56; see also Münch, *Die sozialen Anschauungen des Hans Sachs*, pp. 31-36 and 114-119). This subject so interested Hans Sachs that years later, under the title of *Die ungleichen kinder Eva*, he used it several times, for a Meisterlied in 1547, a *Fastnachtspiel* and a comedy in 1553, and a *Spruchgedicht* in 1558. specht: (MHG. *spëhen*, wkv.) *schaut.*
4 ir: MHG. refl.
5 geleich: (MHG. *gelîch*, adj.) used substantively.
6 pricht: *erhebt*; see Grimm, *DW.* 2, col. 350, for this meaning.
8 erwelt: Hans Sachs thinks that man does not choose his own place in the world, but that it is chosen for him by God.
11 den dümen ... künsten reich: perhaps this expresses Hans Sachs' charitable attitude toward fellow Meistersinger who lacked talent.
14 on hab: *an Eigentum.*
15 reÿlichen: (MHG. *rîlîche*, adv.) *reichlich*; schenck: (MHG. *schenk*, stf.) *Geschenk.*

284

17 lehen: *geliehenes Gut.*
18 gebert: (MHG. *gewëren*, wkv.) *gebürgt.*
27 drewlich: two marks over the *w* in the manuscript seem meaningless; they were probably added by some later hand, since they slant in the opposite direction from those which Hans Sachs makes over his *u*. vür spricht: *verteidigt.*

3, 4 keines: gen. sg. (with *Mannes* understood) with "begert" (3).
    7 versert: *verwundet.*
    9 schnoder: (MHG. *snœde*, adj.) *rücksichtloser*; wort: for comment on the uninflected gen. in the pl. see Weinhold, § 454; vberhet: the *e* in the stem was made out of an *o*.
   11 hebet . . . aüf: *wirft vor*; for this meaning see Schmeller I, col. 1036.
   14 pillikeit: *Gerechtigkeit.*
   15 vnderscheit: (MHG. *underscheit*, stmnf.) *genaue Auseinandersetzung.*
   22 geschbacht: *gering gemacht.*
   25 wer: pres. subj. *werde*; for the form see W. *BGr.*, § 149.
   26 want: *wohnt*, i. e. *weilt.*

4, 4 küst: *Kunst.*
    6 ginet: *gönnt.*
   10 nit verdolt: (MHG. *verdoln*, wkv.) *läßt es nicht geschehen.*
   15 etwan: *manchmal.*
   16 drogenlich: *trügerisch.*
   17 verdulden: a variant form of *verdoln* (see 10 above), but here with the meaning of *ertragen.*
   25 kart: *kehrt*; a Middle German verb form.

5, 5 geferlich: *auf hinterlistige Weise*; grÿnt: *zürnet.*
    9 dreg: (MHG. *trœge*, adj.)
   11 senfft: *leicht.*
   13 In this *Abgesang* Hans Sachs portrays the social consciousness of brotherly love.
   21 pestet: *bestattet.*
   22 ernert: *rettet.*
   23 parmünge: (MHG. *barmunge*, stf.) *Erbarmung.*
   25 erczeneÿ: (MHG. *erzenîe*, stf.) *Arznei*; leÿt: *verleiht*; note the double acc. with this verb.
   26 neret: *ernährt.*
   27 meret: *vermehrt.*

6, 2 lan: *Lohn.*
    4 gütheit: (MHG. *guotheit*, stf.) *Güte.*
    5 widergelt: (MHG. *widergelt*, stmn.) *Vergeltung.*
    8 zanet nÿmant an: (MHG. *anzannen*, wkv.) *verhöhnt niemand durch spöttische Gebärden.*
   15 widerdries: (MHG. *widerdriez*, stmn.) *Verdruß.*
   16 schimpff: *Kurzweil.*
   18 mit gelimpff: (MHG. *gelimpf*, stwkm.) *mit angemessenem Benehmen.*
   23 Again Hans Sachs refers to the importance of moderation.
   25 schimpffen: *scherzen.*
   26 vür sicht: *trägt Vorsorge.*

7, 1 Prüderlib: cf. 1,13 above.
    2 scham gewant: (MHG. *schamgewant*, stn.) *Kleidungsstück über die Schamteile*; the second object of "dreget" (1).

4 aüf spant: *aufreizt.*
7 gancz: probably with the meaning of *vollständig.*
9 schrancz: (MHG. *schranz*, stm.) *Risse.*
14 perobaldus: *Filippo Berobaldo*, the Elder, an eminent Bolognese Humanist (1453-1505).
15 Dito vnd gisipo: Titus and Gisippus; even though Hans Sachs refers to "perobaldus" he probably read the story of these two friends in Steinhöwel's translation of the *Decameron* where it is the eighth tale of the tenth day.
17 itweder: (MHG. *ietweder*, pron. adj.) *jeder von beiden.*
19 der geschicht: Hans Sachs is using a gen. as object, influenced perhaps by the comparative adv. "mer."
20 von kürczwegen: *zur Unterhaltung.*

No. 28, foll. 5ᵛ-7ᵛ   Orig. 3

Heading: for comment on the *Ton* see No. 1.

1, 2 heraüs der himeldron: *aus dem Thron der Himmel.* In his trilogy Hans Sachs has employed a threefold designation for heaven: "jerarcheÿ" for the Father (26,1,1), "seraffin" for the Son (27,1,1), and "himeldron" for the Holy Spirit.
7 Ovidiüs: Publius Ovidius Naso, 43 B.C. – A.D. 17; for detailed comment see 3,22 below. The *summa summarum* of the evils which follow in the wake of sensual love recorded by Hans Sachs in his *Spruchgedicht* of May 1, 1515 (*H. S.* 3, 415, 1-16) is a kind of embryonic list for the first three strophes of this Meisterlied. The generalizations found there seem to indicate that along with other books he may have been reading Johann Hartlieb's *Das buch Ouidy von lieb zu erwerben, ouch die lieb zu verschmehen*, a translation of Andreas Capellanus' three treatises on love which was published for the first time in 1482 and again twice in 1484; for a discussion of this translation see Wieczorek, *Johann Hartliebs Verdeutschung von des Andreas Capellanus Liber de reprobatione amoris* and the modern translation by Elster entitled *Über die Liebe*; see also Drescher, "Hans Sachs und Boccaccio" (*Zeitschr. f. vergleichende Litteraturgeschichte*, n. F. VII), 405-406, for the suggestion that Hans Sachs may have used the Hartlieb translation (the year 1483 which Drescher gives is probably a scribal error). Hans Sachs did not borrow verbatim from Hartlieb, but there are a few parallels here and there to which I shall call attention using Wieczorek's reprint of the original, but shall refer to it as Hartlieb. Very probably he also found the third chapter of Niclas v. Wyle's *Translationen* fruitful.
11 sie nÿmet . . . krafft: the whole verse may be based on experience, for in *Der buler kercker* (*H. S.* 3, 389, 16-24) Hans Sachs declares that his love for the girl in Munich was so overwhelming that he had no rest, became stupid, deaf, and ill, as if he were bewitched; see also Hartlieb, p. 22, and Niclas v. Wyle, p. 96.
12 vnsinikeit: *Torheit*; gart: (MHG. *gart*, stm.) *Treibstecken.*
13 sczmercz: from out of his own experience Hans Sachs could attest to the fact that love causes this as well as the "herczen leit" (15); Hartlieb too (p. 23) speaks of "smerczen, pin vnd laid."
14 kleiner freit: this echos Hans Sachs' statement of 1515 (*H. S.* 3, 409, 16-17), "Wann lieb ist nichts, dan bitter leyden, / vermischet gar mit kleynen freuden."
17 die . . . mag: even though Hans Sachs does not mention Brant's *Narrenschiff* as a source, he must have read it before writing this Meisterlied, for its influence is apparent in this and in the next several verses (the first edition of the *Narrenschiff* was published in

1494); see chap. 13, "von buolschaft," p. 35, vss. 15-30. He owned a copy of the book (see *H. S.* 26, p. 154).

18 cüpidus nacket stat: in the woodcut on p. 34 of the *Narrenschiff*, Cupid is pictured as a blindfolded, naked boy with a spanned bow, in which there is an arrow, in his hand. Hans Sachs may also have remembered Niclas v. Wyle's statement (*Translationen*, p. 96, ll. 23-24), "ain blindes kinde geflügelt, vnd in seinen henden ainen bogen vnd geschütz habende."

20 proffetten: here used in the larger sense of ML. *propheta*, inclusive of *poeta*; here an indirect reference to Brant.

24 verseren ist: *verwundet.*

25 fraw Venus seil: the woodcut in the *Narrenschiff* (p. 34) also illustrates this.

26 behafft: *umstrickt.*

2, 1 nit zal noch mas: Hartlieb (p. 23) expresses a similar thought, also Brant (p. 37, 23-24), who may have been familiar with Andreas Capellanus' *de reprobatione amoris*; see also *H. S.* 3, 435, 3-15.

8 geper: (MHG. *gebǣre*, stfn.) *Benehmen.*

10 gefer: (MHG. *gevǣre*, stfn.) *Betrug.*

11 wiget: (MHG. *wëgen*, stv. V) *erachtet.*

13 This verse and the following three very probably reflect Hans Sachs' own experience as recounted in *Der buler kercker* (see 1, 11 above); Hartlieb also voices the debilitating effect of sensual love, pp. 22 and 30; Niclas v. Wyle, p. 97, calls it a "siechtum."

16 schlaffen: see also Hartlieb, p. 22.

17 This and the following verse are born out in *Der buler kercker*, *H. S.* 3, 390, from vs. 18 on.

24 lebet . . . finsternis: both Hartlieb (p. 19 and *passim*) and Brant (p. 37, 16-17) declare that sensual love causes withdrawal from God.

26 acht: *achtet*; misseling: (MHG. *misselingen*, stv. III, 1) *missglücke.*

3, 3 dät: this may be a scribal error for *düt* in view of the fact that all of the verbs in this strophe are in the present tense.

4 draurig: see also *Der buler kercker*, *H. S.* 3, 390, 13.

8 vil lügen: see also Hartlieb, p. 24; petracht: *denkt aus.*

10 geschwacht: *geschändet.*

13 This verse repeats that which Hans Sachs had said two years before at the termination of his own love affair (*H. S.* 3, 415, 2), "So ist lieb leydens anefanck."

14 er güt: cf. 22,7,12; schon: (Middle German *schône*, stf.) *Schönheit*. Hartlieb, *passim*, touches on various of the points which Hans Sachs enumerates in vss. 13-20.

15 vnd dügent: *Untugend.*

17 schwervng: *Lästerung.*

18 der dot schlag: (MHG. *tôtslac*, stm.) gen. pl.

19 dettvng: *Tötung.*

20 schwechvng: *Entehrung*; see Grimm, *DW*. 9, col. 2166.

22 Ovidiüm: Hans Sachs' main source was most probably Steinhöwel's translation of Boccaccio's *De claris mulieribus* (the Ulm edition of the translation appeared in 1473, the Augsburg one in 1479, and the Straβburg one, a reprint of the 1473 edition, was published in 1488) rather than Ovid. However, the fact that a quotation from one or another of Ovid's works (*Metamorphoses, Epistolae*, and *Ars amatoria*) precedes the chapters which furnished five of Hans Sachs' pairs of lovers may have led him to refer to the original source as his own, instead of to Steinhöwel or to Boccaccio. The book is listed in Hans Sachs' library as *Johannes Bocacius die 99 durchlewchtig frawen* (see *H. S.*

26, p. 153). There is also the possibility that the poet may have read some of the letters of Ovid's *Heroides*; see 5,6 below.

23 Virgilio: similarly Hans Sachs may be citing Vergil as source, for he found verses from the *Aeneid* superscribed in Steinhöwel's translation for the chapters which bring the unhappy fate of two further pairs of lovers. It is possible however that he had access to Murner's translation of Vergil's *Aeneid* which appeared in Straβburg in 1515. (I have not been able to locate a copy of this.) In all probability he read a German *Volksbuch, Trojas Zerstörung*, which was published in Augsburg in 1474 and 1476 (see Schneider, *Der Trojanische Krieg im späten Mittelalter*, pp. 102-107). I have not been able to find a copy of the *Volksbuch*. See 4, 9 below for almost certain proof that Hans Sachs read this.

26 zeÿch: (MHG. *zeichen*, wkv.) *zeichne*; a virgule after "dail" should be after "zeÿch" in order to provide eight syllables for the verse and a rhyme with "leich:pleich" (5/11).

4, 1 Salamon: see I Kings 11:1-13. Both Hartlieb (p. 25) and Brant (chap. 13, p. 37) cite Solomon as an example of what carnal love does to even the wisest of men; Hans Sachs again referred to this in a *Spruchgedicht* of 1526 (*H. S.* 4, 326, 35-36).

3 Samson: see Judg. 14-16 for the account of Samson and Delilah; Brant mentions Samson also. Hans Sachs had already listed him in his *Spruchgedicht* of 1515 (*H. S.* 3, 410-414) together with eight more of the sixteen pairs of lovers whom he uses as examples in this Meisterlied.

7 Jason: see the sixteenth chapter of Steinhöwel's translation of *De claris mulieribus*.

8 media: Medea, the daughter of the King of Colchis.

9 There is nothing in the Boccaccio tale that warrants the statement in this verse; there is no mention whatsoever of how or when Jason died. Since, however, Hans Sachs had already stated two years before: "Davon hab ich gelesen heindt, / Wie hertzog Jason ward verbrant / Von Medea also genandt" (*H. S.* 3, 410, 34-36), he could only have had another source. This most probably was the *Volksbuch, Trojas Zerstörung* (see 3, 23 above), in which the story of Medea and Jason is incorporated. At the end of the tale, as it is there told, Medea, in revenge for Jason's faithlessness, sends a most beautiful gown into which poison has been woven to Jason and his mistress, Grensa. When the latter puts on the gown the heat of her body causes the poison to burst into flames which are so fierce that they cannot be extinguished. Thus not only Grensa, but Jason and the whole house were burned to "powder."

11 pÿramüs: see *De claris mulieribus*, chap. 12, for the Pyramus-Thysbe tale.

13 Achilles: see ibid., chap. 31, for this story.

19 Paris: the account of Paris and Helen is in ibid., chap. 35.

24 Menelas: the last two letters are a doubtful correction; Menelaus was the King, not "kaisser," of Sparta and the husband of Helen.

26 herfanen: (MHG. *hervane*, wkm.) acc. sg., *Kriegsbanner.*

27 vngemach: *Unglück*; an effective understatement.

5, 3 Demonovm: Demophoon, son of Theseus, ruler of Athens, and his third wife Phaedra.

4 vür pflicht: p. part. *verpflichtet*; see W. *BGr.*, § 31, for the prefix.

6 Phillis: in the second letter in Ovid's *Heroides* Phyllis is writing to Demophoon and reveals her contemplated suicide, because she has not heard from him for some time. She considers four ways in which she might do this: drowning, poison, the sword, hanging, but does not make a choice. (For a modern English translation side by side with the Latin see Showermann, *Heroides and Amores*, pp. 10-31.) It is possible, therefore, that Hans Sachs read the short chapter in Boccaccio's *Genealogie deorum gentilium* (see Romano, ed., chap. XXV) in which it is stated that she ended her life in a noose *(laqueo*

vitam finivit). There were German printings of the original Latin (Cologne, 1472, for instance) which the poet might have seen. (I have not been able to locate a German copy.)

7 leander: I have not been able to find the source which Hans Sachs might have used for Musaios' *Hero und Leander*; the book which he used later for the story, Hyrtzweil's *Etliche historien unnd fabeln*, was not published until 1541 (see Abele, *Die antiken Quellen des Hans Sachs*, p. 107). See the modern German translation of Musaios' *Hero und Leander* by Hans Färber, pp. 6-27; see also v. d. Hagen, *Gesamtabenteuer*, No. 15.

8 gesicht: Hans Sachs may be substituting *s* for *sch* in the 3. sg. pres. *geschicht*; for such a substitution see W. *BGr.*, § 154.

9 ein wasser: the Hellespont.

13 Eneas: chap. 40 of Steinhöwel's translation *De claris mulieribus* concerns itself primarily with Dido. The only mention of Aeneas is that he arrived at the shores of her realm and was well received. Nothing is said of his departure. Perhaps Hans Sachs had indeed read Murner's translation of Vergil's *Aeneid* (see 3, 23 above) and was therefore familiar with Dido's love for Aeneas as told in the fourth book.

15 düren: (MHG. *turn.*, stm.) *Turm.*

16 schwert: the fact that Hans Sachs says Dido plunged a sword into herself would also seem to point to his knowledge of the story related in the *Aeneid*, for Steinhöwel uses the word *messer.*

17 Porkris: Procris; for the metathesis of the *r* in the first syllable see W. *BGr.*, § 163; the tale of Procris and Cephalus is in Boccaccio's *De claris mulieribus*, chap. 26. (For a modern translation see Lindemann, *Ovids Liebeskunst*, . . . , Book III, vss. 685-746, or Rösch, *Metamorphosen*, pp. 267-275.

18 parck: *barg*; koren: *Korn.*

19 Zeffalo: Steinhöwel uses the name *Cephalus.*

21 spir: (MHG. *spür*, stn. f.) *Spur.*

23 ir: this refers to Procris.

24 Herkůle: (the u-hook was probably added later) see Boccaccio's *De claris mulieribus*, chaps. 21-22 for the account of Hercules, Iole ("Jole," vs. 26), and Deianira ("deonira," vs. 25). The two chapters relate separate events in the life of Hercules (one concerns Iole, the other Deianira, his wife) and are very loosely tied together by the brief statement that Deianira knew how much Hercules loved Iole. Hans Sachs confused the names, for it was Deianira, not Iole, who sent the garment to Hercules, not, however, in revenge, but with good intent to regain the favor of her husband. Deianira did not know that the garment was impregnated with Nessus' poisoned blood and thus would kill Hercules (vs. 27).—A virgule after "Herkůle" is a scribal error.

6, 1 Bilhalm von osterreich: *Wilhelm von Österreich* is also the title of the *Volksbuch* which Hans Sachs most probably read, for it was published in 1481 and appeared again in 1491; see *Dt. Lit. in Entwicklungsreihen, Reihe* 12, Vol. 2, pp. 191-284, for this.

3 vür: *fuhr*; des meres deich: this may be the Black Sea because, according to the *Volksbuch*, the *Herzog* went to the kingdom of *Zizia* (Scythia), a name given by the ancient Greeks to the region between the Carpathian and the Caucasus mountains.

5 Agleÿ: the daughter of the King of *Zizia*. At one point in the story Rial, the assumed name of Wilhalm, says to her (*Volksbuch*, p. 204), "die mynn . . . das sy lieb und leid gefügen kan," thereby once more substantiating Hans Sachs' own sentiments.

7 Cainis: the final letter might possibly be an *s*; Caynis is the brother of the other Isolde; the story of the love between Caynis and Gardeloye ("gardoleÿe," vs. 9), the wife of Nampetenis ("nampecenis," vs. 10) is told within the framework of the Tristan-Isolde prose romance, pp. 168-172 and 190-195 (see the note on vs. 13 below).

Notes for page 145

10 nampecenis: not Nampetenis alone, but he together with his knights slew Caynis; schos: that is, with a spear.

13 Dristrant: since the first German edition of the prose romance of *Tristrant und Isalde* appeared in 1484 and four others between then and 1510, Hans Sachs certainly read one or another of these. For the text of the story based on the editions of 1498 (the 1484 edition is no longer extant) and 1557 see *Tristrant und Isalde*, ed. Pfaff.

17 ver huettet: (MHG. *verhüeten*, wkv.) *bewacht*.

18 kissen: (MHG. *kiesen*, stv. II, 2) *wählen*.

20 lessen: here with the meaning of *erzählen*.

21 verkert: *veränderte*.

22 ernert: *errettete*.

26 in dodes farb: euphemistic for *tot*.

7, 2 Quisgardüs: for the story see No. 23.

7 Fillius: Virgilius, known as a great magician throughout the Middle Ages (see, among others, Spargo, *Virgil the Necromancer*). One of the most popular legends connected with him is the episode of the basket to which Hans Sachs refers in this verse. The earliest German account of Virgilius in the basket is to be found in Enikel's *Weltchronik*, an exceedingly long poem of the 13th cent.; see the edition by Massmann, *Kaiserchronik*, pp. 453-458, for the account. Massmann (p. 453) also cites a Meisterlied, *Her Vilius von astronomey ze schule gie*, but gives neither the date for it, nor the location for the manuscript. It is worth noting that, whereas Enikel calls the magician *Virgilius*, the Meisterlied names him *Vilius*. Spargo (ibid., pp. 54-55, 252, and 424, note 1) found "no evidence to indicate that a German Virgilius *Volksbuch* ever existed with the exception of a fragment . . . in verse, *Von Virgilio dem zauberer*, printed about 1520," too late to serve as source for this Hans Sachs Meisterlied of 1517. The fact that the basket incident was depicted during the 14th, 15th, and 16th cents. in stone, tapestries, prints, woodcarvings, and paintings (see Spargo, chap. X, and the *Kaiserchronik*, p. 453) would indicate that it was certainly well known. In addition to the visual evidence there was also casual mention of the incident in literature. Thus Hans Sachs himself probably remembered the brief statement about Virgilius which he had come across in 1515 while reading the first tale in Niclas v. Wyle's *Translationen*, pp. 31-32.

9 Prenberger: Reinmar or Reinmann von Brennenberg was a Minnesinger of the 13th cent. (see v. d. Hagen, *Minnesinger* I, pp. 335-338, and IV, pp. 278-284) to whom the legend of the heart, unknowingly eaten by the beloved, was transferred. According to v. d. Hagen and to Kopp (*Bremberger-Gedichte*) this legend in variant form was widespread in both prose and poetry. (See also Grimm, ed., *Dt. Sagen* II, No. 506, for Bremberger's death.) In Boccaccio's ninth tale of the Fourth Day the story appears with characters from the Provence. Hans Sachs therefore had ample opportunity to become acquainted with the legend. However, the reference to a "ring" seems to have been his own invention.

10 lüs: pret. *ließ*; for the substitution of *u* for *i* (Hans Sachs uses *i* in the pret. in 11,2,5 and 19,5,7) see W. *BGr.*, § 30.

12 Herczogein: the Dutchess of Austria to whom Bremberger paid homage.

13 Darquinus: Hans Sachs has attached the wrong name to the man who dishonored Lucretia, for Tarquinius Superbus was the father. He was the last of the Roman kings and it was he who was expelled together with all of the Tarquins, not just his son Sextus. See Boccaccio's *De claris mulieribus*, chap. 47, for the tale of Lucretia.

14 des keisser sün: Sextus. Hans Sachs follows Steinhöwel in calling the father "keisser."

18 Hans Sachs inadvertently omitted the word *lib*; after "fleischlich"; it is necessary for both the meaning and for the syllable count.

20 am sibenden gepat: it is the sixth, not the seventh commandment which forbids adultery, a fact which either Hans Sachs or some one else realized somewhat later, for the word "sibenden" is underlined and the numeral 6 written beside it.

23 der helle: Hartlieb, too (p. 19), indicates that the result for the person who pursues this carnal love will be "das er ewigklichen in den hellischen flamen gepiniget wirt."

27 Deo gracias: Hans Sachs may have appended these words in order to express his thanks for the completion of his trilogy; but see also the comment at the end of No. 13.

Chapter V / On Meistergesang

Background

1. Martin (*Meistersänger von Strassburg*, p. 13) thinks that a *Singschule* may have existed in Nuremberg as early as 1450. B. Nagel (*Meistersang*, p. 31) cites Martin; Goedeke (*H. S.* I, pp. XXI-XXII) assumes that Folz may have been one of the founders of the *Singschule* when he came to Nuremberg shortly after 1479, but Folz's own words (see note 2 below) deny this assumption; W. Nagel (*Studien zur Geschichte der Meistersänger* [cited W. Nagel], pp. 49-52) and Genée (p. 254) agree with Goedeke's supposition; Weber (p. 26) merely says that after Folz went to Nuremberg it became the most important *Pflegestätte* of Meistergesang; and Plate (p. 162) places the founding of the Nuremberg *Singschule* before that of the one in Straßburg, that is, before 1492.

2. For these verses see Mayer, ed., *Folz*, No. 48, 26-28.

3. See Goedeke, *H. S.* I, pp. 12-14, for this allegorical Meisterlied taken from a Weimar MS. Goedeke affixes the year 1515 to the Meisterlied; the K-G Index, No. 187, places it in the year 1527. 1527 rather than 1515 is undoubtedly the correct year, primarily because the Meisterlied is set to Hans Sachs' *neuen Ton*, a melody which he did not compose until 1526, according to the K-G Index, No. 112. With but one exception all scholars to date have uncritically accepted the year 1515 which Goedeke published. Genée alone, in a note on p. 102, says the year 1515 cannot be correct because Hans Sachs was still *auf der Wanderschaft* and could scarcely be concerned about what was happening in the Nuremberg *Singschule*. – I, too, cited the year 1515 in my "Anal. of Berlin 414," p. 948, note 5, and p. 952, an error which I should here like to correct.

4. See the second strophe and part of the third of the Meisterlied of 1527 for the names and trades of the twelve Nuremberg Masters.

5. See Ellis, "Anal. of Berlin 414," pp. 979-981, for the list of these meisterlieder by Hans Folz, and note also the paragraph on p. 949 on Hans Folz.

6. For the first lines of these see ibid., pp. 981-983, but see also the paragraph on p. 950 dealing with Nunnenbeck's Meisterlieder.

7. These Masters are Kunrat Nachtigall with four, Fritz Ketner with two, and Six Beckmesser, Hans Sachwarz, and Fritz Zorn with one each; see ibid., pp. 985-987.

8. For the *Töne* of the ten Masters see ibid., pp. 973-978.

9. See ibid., p. 978, for the number of Meisterlieder set to each of Zorn's *Töne*.

10. See ibid., pp. 974-975 for Frauenlob, pp. 975-976 for Cünrat Marner, and p. 977 for Regenbogen.

11. This is Ulrich Eislinger for whose *Ton*, his *langer*, only two verses are given on fol. 118^V.

12. Wagenseil (p. 515) lists Veit Pogner, Niclaus Vogel, and Augustin Moser in place of Merten Grim, vom Gostenhof, and Lienhart Nunnenbeck, but calls Fritz Ketner *Kohtner*; W. Nagel (p. 51) substitutes Hans Vogel and August Moser for Grim and von Gostenhof, but retains Nunnenbeck; B. Nagel (*Meistersang*, p. 32) accepts W. Nagel's list of the Twelve Masters as well as the erroneous year 1515 for the meisterlied of 1527; Georg Hager (Bell, ed., *Georg Hager, a Meistersinger of Nürnberg* 1552-1635, Part II, p. 17), in an imaginary conversation with Hans Sachs, makes only one substitution, Vogel for Grim; Lützelberger (*Von den Meistersängern*, p. 219) follows Wagenseil for his names of the Twelve Masters; see also Schnorr v. Carolsfeld, pp. 15-16, for his comments.

13. There is no *Ton* or Meisterlied in Berlin 414 for "Merten Grim, der sechst" nor for "vom Gostenhof, der acht."

14. Mayer, ed. *Folz*, No. 48, 21-24.

15. See 33, 1, 8-12. Folz, too (Mayer, ed.), has references to the lack of talent among Meistersinger in Nos. 89, 90, and 91.

16. See ibid., No. 39, 61-64; this Meisterlied is in the Munich MS. Cgm. 6353, *terminus ad quem* 1496; Folz also warns against envy in No. 52, 9-10, "Das du der hoffart wider strebest / und auch dem neide."

17. Martin (*Die Meistersänger v. Strassburg*, p. 10) thinks that the earlier part of the *Wartburgkrieg* is important for an understanding of the nature of the Meistersinger in that even the greatest medieval poets had to contend with envy.

18. See No. 33.

19. See the Meisterlied of August 19, 1553, "Ein sumari all seiner gedicht," in Goetze's "Monographie über den Meistersänger Adam Pushmann" (*Neues Lausitzisches Magazin*, Vol. LIII), p. 137, vss. 46-49 in which Hans Sachs states: "Vil schuel halff ich verwalten / det auch selber schuel halten / im lant wo ich hin kam / hielt die erst zu franckfurt mit nam;" cf. his last summary of 1567 (*H. S.* 21, 339, 4-7).

20. In view of the fact that Hans Sachs included his name in the last verse in each of the three Meisterlieder which retell stories from the *Decameron* (Nos. 23-25), all three written in 1516, and then for the first time further identified himself as being *von Nürnberg*, it seems more logical to accept the autumn of the year 1516 for his return home, rather than the following year (see also Windolph, *Reiseweg*, pp. 6-7). Thus the poet's statement *Fünff gantze jar ich wandern thet* (*H. S.* 21, 338, 15) would mean the spring of 1512 to the fall of 1516.

21. See Appendix B for a facsimile copy of these two melodies which Hans Sachs recorded in Mg. 2.

No. 29, foll. 31^r-32^r Orig. 20

Preliminary:

1.   The K-G Index, No. 34, assigns the definite date of May 15, "1515 am pfingstag" to this Meisterlied.

2.   Hans Sachs speaks of his father's summons in the *Spruchgedicht* "Kampff-gesprech von der lieb," dated May 1; see *H. S.* 3, 417.

3.   From Hans Sachs' Meisterlied (No. 30) we know that visitors were present at some meetings, for he welcomes them along with the Masters, singers, and *Merker*.

4.   Goedeke, *H. S.* I, No. 4, and Lützelberger-Fromman, *H. S.,* No. 1. From the many changes in wording, (sometimes a whole verse will differ) it is most probable that Goedeke did not use Berlin 414 as a prime source, but one of the three additional manuscripts which he cites in a note; Frommann states in his preface to the second edition, which he edited, that he used the *Nürnberger Handschriften* without, however, defining what he means by these. To judge from the word *schulkunst* in both Goedeke's and Frommann's titles, the Meisterlied must have been so labeled in their sources which, however (except for Berlin 414), were all compiled after 1550 (see Goedeke, *H. S.* I, pp. XLV-XLVI).

5.   Weddingen, *Der dt. Meistergesang*, pp. 67-69.

Heading: Hans Sachs set only this one Meisterlied to Wolfram's "langen don" which consists of twenty-eight verses, eight in each *Stollen* and twelve in the *Abgesang*. For the rhyme scheme see Appendix C, and for the music see Münzer, *Singebuch*, p. 40, No. 49, with the text of the first strophe of a Meisterlied by Hans Sachs of the year 1527; for Münzer's comment see p. 16, No. 49. The third strophe is not numbered. The numbering is mine.

1, 3   plan: *freier Platz*; this word may support the assumption that even this early there were meetings of the Meistersinger which were held elsewhere than in the *Singschule*. For the case see Weinhold, § 333.
  8   verpringen: *vollbringen.*
 16   gewingen: *gewinnen*; the substitution of *ng* for *nn* is still common practice in the Bavarian dialect, according to W. *BGr.,* § 170.
 19   her fire pricht: (MHG. *hervorbrëchen,* stv. V) *empordrängt.*
 20   materÿ: (MHG. *matërje,* stwkf.) *Stoff,* i. e. subject matter.
 22   nit genat: *keine Neigung dazu.*
 25   Hans Sachs advises a singer to keep on practicing until he is competent to sing before the Masters.
 27   wü: *wo*; for the vowel *u* see 4,2,6; dialectically the rhyme with "rw:zw" (25/26) is acceptable, for these are Middle German *rû/rôwe* and *zû/zô* respectively.

2, 4   in: i. e. the Meistersinger.
 12   kar: *Chor*; see 1,2,7 for the meaning.
 16   vnverschlagen: *nicht betrügerisch.*
 22   paissen: (MHG. *beizen,* wkv.) *Vögel mit Falken jagen.*

3, 3 achch: *auch*; MHG. *och* is a variant of *ouch*. The second *ch* in Hans Sachs' word is a scribal error.

6 füg: (MHG. *vuoc*, stm.) *Angemessenheit*.

13 Somewhat later Hans Sachs wrote this entire verse, originally omitted, into the right-hand margin at right angles to the text; two crosses indicate its place in the *Stollen*.

16 gichte: pres. *zugesteht*.

22 solt: Hans Sachs overlooked the fact that this word should be spelled with an *e* instead of an *o*, for it is the second word in a series of four rhymes; for the form with an *e* see 9,3,13.

23 gesang: see 10,3,11 where this word is also neuter; erschelt: (MHG. *erschëllen*, wkv.) pres. *erschallen läßt*.

26 wes: gen. of MHG. *waʒ*.

No. 30, foll. 29ᵛ-30ʳ   Orig. 18

Preliminary:

1. See Windolph, p. 58.

2. See *H. S.* 21, 339,7, for the statement about conducting the *Singschule* in Frankfurt, and the K-G Index, No. 35, for the notation about the day on which the Meisterlied was written.

3. There is no way of knowing whether the rules of Meistergesang prior to those extant, the earliest of which are contained in the *Schuelzetel zw Nürnberg* of 1540 (for this see Hertel, pp. 26-31) were solely transmitted orally, or whether each *Singschule* perhaps had a written set which time and continuous use caused to disintegrate. If such catalogues existed at the time that Hans Sachs visited various *Singschulen* during these journeyman years, he may have had access to them and may have compared them with what he had learned in Nuremberg. Schnorr v. Carolsfeld (p. 17) states that songs which treated the most important rules of Meistergesang antedated the formal *Tabulaturen* and refers to such a song by Hans Sachs written, however, in 1555 (see Hertel, pp. 31-32). Folz takes about a dozen points for granted (mostly with regard to the rhymes) in a satirical Meisterlied written before 1500 (see Mayer, ed., No. 46), and there are a few technical expressions scattered here and there in the Colmar MS. (see, for instance, Bartsch, No. 82). Therefore Hans Sachs' enumeration in this poem of some thirty errors to be avoided in writing a Meisterlied, as well as his explicit definitions of seven of these in the next song, constitutes the very earliest listing which we have.

Heading: This is the second Meisterlied which Hans Sachs set to "des frawenlobs langen don." For comment on it see No. 22. For the sake of convenience I shall refer the reader now and then to Plate, whose definitions, however, are all based on *Schuelzettel* and *Tabulaturen* set down years later than these Hans Sachs' Meisterlieder. A few times I'll call attention to the *Schuelzetel* of 1540.

1, 1 The welcoming words in vss. 1-4 are traditional; in Berlin 414 a number of songs begin somewhat similarly.

5 wer hie hat gesanges günst: these would be the visitors.

7 wel: *wil*; see Weinhold, § 421, for this Middle German form.

16 al straff: penalties for violations of the rules; in 1540, according to the *Schuelzetel* (§ 2), these ranged from one to four syllables; in a few instances, however, where the pattern or melody was altered from that of the traditional *Ton* of a Master, the singer was penalized the sum total of the syllables included in those changes (ibid., § 9). vbersümen: *überrechnen*, i. e., survey.

17 Straffer vnd reiczer: *Spottlieder*; see Plate, p. 190; lonn: *lassen*.

18 loÿca: (ML. *loyca*, MHG. *lôicâ*, f.) *Logik*, but since Hans Sachs tells the Meistersinger not to use this, he may have had a further MHG. meaning of *Schlauheit* in mind. aüiüoca: (ML. *aequivocus*, adj.) used as a noun, *Mehrdeutigkeit*; see Plate, pp. 212-213, for the various kinds of *equivoca*.

19 dencz: *Tänze*; reÿen: (MHG. *reien*, stn.) *Reigentanz*.

20 vberkron: (MHG. *überkrônen*, wkv.) *an Herrlichkeit übertreffen*; this may imply overcomplication of a rhyme scheme, or overelaboration of the coloratura in a melody.

21 vber kürcz vber lange don: in the *Schuelzetel* (§§ 10-11) the limits for short and long were twenty and thirty verses to a strophe, yet at every other meeting much longer *Töne*, could be used.

22 vür geng: (MHG. *vürganc*, stm.) *Erfolg*; the two words have been crossed out in the manuscript and two scribbled, indecipherable words written into the margin. I am keeping the original words.

23 vier haüpton: these two words have also been crossed out and an illegible correction written underneath them. I have kept the original. For the four *Haupttöne* see the Heading of No. 1; every Meistersinger had to know these *Töne*.

24 frümen: (MHG. *vrumen*, wkv.) *förderlich sein*.

2, 2 falsche meinvng: in the *Schuelzetel* (§ 2) this disqualified a singer completely.

3 falsche melodeÿe: divergence from the melody of a Master to which a Meisterlied has been set.

4 gemes: the structure of the strophe; a song had to conform to its original pattern; see Plate, pp. 194-195, for details.

5 falsche latein: (MHG. *latîn*, stf. stn.) Hans Sachs uses the fem. gender, a fact which Hertel (*Schuelzetel*, p. 26, note) failed to take into consideration in his criticism.

6 in congrüa: (ML. *incongruus*, adj.) *nicht übereinstimmend*; this is the technical expression for errors in inflectional forms.

7 zw kurcz zw lanck: a reference to the singing of fewer or more syllables in a verse than the original pattern demanded.

8 merck: *merken*, i. e. *anschreiben als Fehler*; kreiden: (MHG. *krîde*, wkf.) this indicates that chalk was used to note the mistakes.

11 halb: this supposedly belongs to "equiboca" (9 above); schiller: the term for rhymes which have similar, but not identical vowels; see Plate, p. 215; ande: (MHG. *ande*, adj.) *unleidlich*.

12 plos reimen: these are words which have been left unrhymed when they should have been rhymed; pande: the rhyme pattern; see Plate, p. 195.

13 paüs: a singer was not supposed to pause within a verse while singing, only at the end of it; sticz: (MHG. *stütze*, stf.) *Steckenbleiben*.

15 greuf: 3. sg. pres. subj. with the subject *der* understood; see W. *BGr.*, §§ 87,b) and 177,a) for the diphthong, and cf. Folz, Mayer, ed., No. 83, 62. her für noch hinter sich: this expression has reference to three kinds of repetition: 1. if one has forgotten something and goes back to pick it up; 2. if one repeats something to gain time while trying to remember what comes next; and 3. if one inadvertently or carelessly repeats a word or phrase; see Plate, pp. 206-207.

17 ir: confused; see Plate, p. 206.

19 laster: probably mistakes in general; see Plate's comment, pp. 218-219; schbing: imp. *schwinge!* the first three letters are doubtful.

21 vnpequemlich: *unpassend.*

22 differencze: the use of the same word for both the end of one verse and the beginning of the next; but see Plate, pp. 214-215, for additional explanations; cf. Hertel, p. 25.

23 die gespalten: this could belong to the "differencze" of the preceding verse, for *gespaltene Differenz* was the term applied to the situation where two homophonic words were separated by another word, according to Plate, p. 214; or Hans Sachs may here be referring to *gespaltene Reime,* for which see Plate, p. 218.

24 bescheiden: deutlich berichten.

3, 1 Haimlich eqüifoca: see Hans Sachs' definition in 31,2,1-5.

3 reimen die do riren: see 31,2,6-9 for the explanation.

5 cleb silb: this refers to the contraction of a word; see 31, 2,11-18, where Hans Sachs gives greater detail. Hertel (p. 25) comments: "dieser Fehler bei H. Sachs ausserordentlich oft," yet almost every instance in these forty Meisterlieder can be justified by dialectal usage, if we accept the authority of P-G and of Weinhold.

6 verviren: *irre führen.*

7 anhang: see Hans Sachs' definition of this in 31,2,19-22.

8 fünde: p. part. *gefunden.*

9 plinte meinvng . . . plinte wort: obscure or unintelligible meaning or word; see Hans Sachs' definition in 31,3,1-4.

11 halbe wort: pl., *verkürzte Wörter;* see 31,3,6-9 for the definition.

13 ein milb: this term supposedly comes from the MHG. *milwen,* wkv., *zu Mehl oder Staub machen,* hence designates a minute error; Hans Sachs gives details in 31,3,11-18.

14 becleiben: *fest sitzen.*

15 vrlang: *erlange;* see also 24,9,12 for the prefix.

18 dester: (MHG. *dëster,* adv.) *desto.*

19 nit hoch on mas: this may be contained in a part of the fifteenth paragraph in the *Schuelzetel,* "Item wer ein par nider oder höher anfecht den er im anfang angefangen, hat 2 silben versungen."

20 an has: *ohne Hast.*

21 veriren: this is the second time that Hans Sachs refers to becoming confused.

22 die rechte stras: a variant of the more common metaphor *die künste stras.*

No. 31, foll. 30ʳ-31ʳ   Orig. 19

Preliminary:

1. See the first two *Stollen* of the third strophe of No. 30.

Heading: Hans Sachs set only this one Meisterlied to Fritz Zorn's "verhollen don." It is twenty-three verses long with five verses in each *Stollen* and thirteen in the *Abgesang* and seems monotonous in that all save two of the verses in each strophe consist of eight syllables each. For the rhyme scheme see Appendix C, and cf. Mayer, ed., *Folz,* p. 406, where, however, the last word of each *Abgesang* is unrhymed. For comment on Fritz Zorn see the Heading of No. 10.

1, 3 leich: *verleihe!*

4 bewere: *beweise.*

5   scherpff: this was an additional set of rules, over and above the basic criteria, set down to penalize minutiae; sometimes these included common errors, for which, however, the penalty was increased; see Plate, p. 205. gelet: (MHG. *glete*, stf.) *Glätte*, i. e. perfection in all respects.

15   dick: *oft.*

19   vort: (MHG. *vort*, adv.) *weiter.*

21   plint mainvng plinte wort: Hans Sachs treats these together, which accounts for his sum of seven instead of eight items.

23   die stück: these have been set down in exactly the same order in which they occur in the preceding Meisterlied, 30,3,1-14.

2, 1   Haimlich eqüifoca: the following four verses give the definition; verstan: sg. imper.; for the loss of the *t* see 8,1,13.

3   pede: (MHG. *bêde*, num.) *beide*; the infinitive *han* has been omitted at the end of this verse, for not only is the verse short one syllable, but a word is also needed to rhyme with "verstan" (1).

4   ·v·: this stands for the vowel *u* and forms a rhyme with "zw" (2).

5   den: dat. pl.; sein: *sind*; see 5,5,11 for the form.

6   Rürende reimen: Hans Sachs' explanation of these in the next three verses is a very simple one; cf. Plate, pp. 211-212.

10   in die scherpff: note the acc. case.

11   clebsilben: Hans Sachs defines these in vss. 12-18.

17   This is an apt expression for the deletion of a vowel.

18   hinden oder vor an: this may refer to a suffix or prefix, or the "hinden" could be an inflectional ending, in all of which vowels were sometimes omitted.

19   anhang: Hans Sachs' definition of this in vss. 20-22 below differs from that found in Plate, p. 218.

3, 1   Von plinter mainvng: the explanation for this and for "plintem wort" (2) is in verses 3-4.

5   vm: *wegen.*

6   Die halben wort: pl.; Hans Sachs defines these beginning with this verse and on through verse 9; sin: *sind;* see Weinhold, § 364 for this Middle German form and cf. 5,5,11; bw: *wo*; see also 26,5,7.

7   schwancz: a whimsical term for the ending of a word.

11   die milben: Hans Sachs gives concrete examples of these minutiae in vss. 13-18 below.

15   verkürchet: a scribal error for *verkürzet.*

18   ein vocal zweÿ wort reigir: this might refer to such a contraction as "ers" (21,2,19) *er es*, for instance.

20   laüder: *deutlich.*

23   dreit: *trägt.*

No. 32, foll. 32ʳ-33ʳ   Orig. 21

Preliminary:

1.   Since Hans Sachs said that he had learned "Manniches höfliches gedicht" in school (see the Background of Chapter I, Note 17), he may have found a suggestion for his allegory in Kriemhild's *Rosengarten zu Worms*, for he makes a garden the symbol of Meistergesang and is thus the first one to do so. Ellenbeck (*Die Sage vom Ursprung des Deutschen Meistergesangs*, pp. 38-39) does not bring out this point. She gives the

content of Hans Sachs' allegory and his interpretation (with omissions) of it. (Among other items she misreads "veÿel," 1,8, as *viel*.) At the end of her summary she directs attention to a Meisterlied by Holtzmann (see Puschman, *Gründlicher Bericht d. dt. Meistergesangs*, pp. 46-47) and remarks, "In der Deutung des Gartens trägt der Dichter noch zu den von Hans Sachs gegebenen Erklärungen hinzu, daβ das Bäumlein die Melodie und alle meisterlichen Töne bedeutet." This statement does not hold water, for in the first place her *Bäumlein* should be *Brunnlein* (Hans Sachs wrote "prinlein" in 1,10), and in the second place Holtzmann adds nothing to the interpretation. A juxtaposition of the corresponding verses (2,18-19) shows this, for, aside from the spelling and the omission of the ending *e* from the word *all*, which leaves the verse one syllable short, Holtzmann's words are a direct copy of what Hans Sachs wrote.

Hans Sachs	Holtzmann
der prün bedeüt die melodeÿ	Der Brun bedeutt die Melodey
vnd alle meisterliche don süptil	Und all Meisterliche thon Suptill

The entry in the K-G Index (No. 36) also suggests comparison with Holtzmann's *Überarbeitung*. If the latter word is meant to imply revision with the connotation of improvement, it is a misnomer. Out of the sixty-nine verses there are only eight complete verses (1,15 and 20-22; 3,5-8) and six partial ones which show sufficient change of content to be called contributions by Holtzmann. Here and there he also rearranged the words in a verse, attached a prefix or ending, then omitted an article or pronoun, or vice versa, and made a few inconsequential substitutions. He didn't even have to recast the Meisterlied into an entirely different *Ton*, since the only difference between the one he used, Fritz Zorn's *Zugweis*, and the one to which Hans Sachs set his song, Regenbogen's *langer don*, is the one-syllabled verse at the beginning of each *Stollen* in the *Zugweise* and an unrhymed twentieth verse of each *Abgesang* in Regenbogen's *Ton*. Even though Holtzmann rhymed the verses of one syllable, he did not set them off; therefore his strophe, similarly to Hans Sachs', has twenty-three verses instead of the twenty-five of Zorn's *Zugweise*. Moreover the Holtzmann-*Schulkunst* shows thirteen errors in syllable count, seven in rhyme-words, and one whole verse omitted (2,20). It points nicely to one of those men whom Hans Sachs characterized as "hetten gar cleinen verstandt / vnd daüchten sich doch meister sein" (33,1,8-9). – Puschmann apparently didn't know that this Meisterlied had not originated with Holtzmann until he was so informed by Götze (see the Note on p. IX of the *Bericht*). – B. Nagel (*Meistersang*, p. 67) includes the Hans Sachs Meisterlied under his category of *Schulkünste*; Plate (p. 167), on the other hand, does not. Nagel also mentions the above *Schulkunst* by Holtzmann. For a discussion of *Schulkünste* see B. Nagel, *Meistersang*, pp. 63-76. The word does not occur in these early Meisterlieder by Hans Sachs.

2. See *WKL*. II, No. 1405.

Heading: This is the only Meisterlied in Berlin 414 which Hans Sachs set to Regenbogen's "langen don," one of the four *gekrönten Töne*. Although Münzer (*Singebuch*, p. 16, No. 38) lists the *Ton* and comments on it, he does not print the music. For this see Runge, No. 60a, pp. 115-116, for the original and No. 60b, pp. 116-117, for Puschman's version; see also v. d. Hagen IV, p. 935, Wagenseil, pp. 563-565, and Mey with his criticism of Wagenseil, pp. 170-173. Bartsch comments on the *Ton*, pp. 177-178. During the course of time a curious thing happened to it. Apparently the older form had six verses in each of the *Stollen* and eleven in the *Abgesang*, but then the last two verses of each *Stollen* were transferred intact to form the first four of the *Abgesang* with the result that the *Stollen* were reduced to four verses each and the *Abgesang* increased to fifteen, but the total number remained the same, twenty-three. Hans Sachs follows the newer pattern.

For the rhyme scheme he used see Appendix C. – Frauchiger (p. 56, IV) says with regard to the rhyme scheme: "For the scansion cf. GD VI, 379 [i. e., G-D, *Fab. u. Schw. v. Hans Sachs*]; variations occur in rhyme f:f [i. e., vss. 10 and 12] which has 11-11 syllables, while Hans Sachs (in GD) has 10-11." This, however, is true only in the rhyme scheme entered in ibid., p. 379, and is probably a misprint, because the particular Hans Sachs-Meisterlied itself from which the rhyme scheme was taken (No. 813 a, pp. 344-349) has in vs. 10 of each of the seven strophes the requisite number of syllables, namely eleven. Seemingly Frauchiger did not check the Meisterlied in question.

1, 2   het: the object of the preceding prepositional phrase is also the subject of this verb.
    8   veÿel: *Veilchen.*
  10   prinlein: the subject for both the preceding clause and the one in this verse; see 7,2,4 for the construction.
  13   gemein: *vertraut.*
  17   This verse is short one syllable.
  18   die kamen: pl. pro. and verb referring to the abstract noun "feintschafft" (17).

2, 5   zwelff maÿster; for a discussion of the Twelve Masters see Taylor, *Lit. Hist. of Mg.*, pp. 38-42; see also a poem by Folz (Berlin 414, foll. 475^V-477^r, and Mayer, ed. No. 94) in which he ridicules the idea that there should be just twelve by listing more than sixty names from which to choose.
  9   gät: 3. sg. pres. *geht*; since the umlauted *a* is not a correction Hans Sachs may originally have written *gat* (he uses that form more often than *get* for the pres.), whereupon a later hand may have added the two dots with the intent of making the word rhyme with "verstet" (11). For this latter form the poet could just as easily have written *verstat*, since he employs one about as often as the other. Thus, perhaps in copying these verses into Berlin 414, he inadvertently overlooked the discrepancy in his rhyme words "gat" and "verstet." This is the second of the only two *ä*s in these forty Meisterlieder; see 28,3,3 for the first one.
  10   die wein stock: since in 1,5 above Hans Sachs said there were twelve of these, his interpretation that they represent the poems of faith (11) may mean that he had the twelve articles of faith in mind. He had a book in his library which he called "Zwelff artikel des glaubens auf papistisch"; see *H. S.* 26, p. 156; see also Folz (Mayer, ed., No. 52, 97-100) for a reference to twelve articles of faith.
  20   becliben: *gedeihen.*
  23   der edlen fricht: gen. which here serves as the subject.

3, 2   han: 3. pl. pres. ind.; for the form see 21,5,15.
  4   das selbÿg: see 8,3,15-16.
  6   fülereÿ: *Schwelgerei.*
  15   der frücht: gen. pl. with "aüf merckvng han" (14); stan: 3. pl. pres. *stehen*; Weinhold (§ 352) cites an example of this Middle German form in rhyme; in the manuscript an ending *t* or *dt* has been erased to make a rhyme with "han:man:lan" (14/21/23).
  16   fünt: (MHG. *vünt*, stm.) *dichterische Erfindung*; neü fünt: *neue Mode* (one wishes Hans Sachs had been specific about this reference).
  19   The comment in this verse is still pertinent today.
  23   gab: this may be a scribal error for *geb*, the pres. subj.; if not, Hans Sachs may mean that the King has already allocated an eternal award for those who work constantly in the garden.

Notes for page 163

No. 33, foll. 38ᵛ, 40ʳ-40ᵛ   Orig. 27

Preliminary:

1. See Schnorr v. Carolsfeld, pp. 43-46; the phraseology differs *passim* from Berlin 414.

2. Mummenhof, *Hans Sachs,* pp. 19-20; Mummenhof says in a note, p. 5, that he used the "Hans Sachs handschrift Amb. 732, 2° in der Stadtbibliothek" of Nuremberg; some of the wording differs from that of Berlin 414.

Heading: The "vberhohe perck weis" to which this Meisterlied is set is Hans Sachs' third original melody and was composed at Frankfurt in 1516. When he recorded it later in his Mg. 2, foll. 267ᵛ-268ʳ, with the first strophe of this Meisterlied, he apparently did so from memory, for once he changes a word, twice the case of words, and in many instances the spelling. After a long interval the *Ton* was *bewert* on the Sunday after St. Bartholomew's Day (August 24) in the year of our Lord 1548. Its unusual length, fifty-three verses, twelve in each *Stollen* and twenty-nine in the *Abgesang,* is due to the great number of one- and two-syllabled verses, thirteen and eight respectively in each strophe. The rhyme scheme is quite complicated inasmuch as the *Abgesang* is interwoven with each *Stollen* individually. See Appendix C for the pattern. – Primarily, it seems, because of a failure to recognize some of the one-syllabled verses, scholars to date have varied greatly in their presentation of the number of verses which a strophe has. Puschmann, Hertel, Mey, and Genée all had access to the Zwickau-manuscript, Mg. 2, all made use of this very same meisterlied, yet no two of these four arrived at the same result. Puschmann (*Singebuch,* pp. 72-73) with the aid of vertical lines, indicates forty-one verses; Hertel, who mistook the *e* in *berck-* for an *o* and therefore called this *Ton* the *hohe Borckweise* (p. 18), notes forty-five; Mey (pp. 219-221) cites forty-seven, and Genée (pp. 398-400) by using vertical parallel lines shows forty-four, although on p. 108 he states that the strophe has forty-five verses! Mey gives two further versions: the rhyme scheme of a Meisterlied (which is not by Hans Sachs; Mey does not give the author) from the Dresden MS. M 192, 19, with forty-two verses (pp. 129-130), and the music and words of a Meisterlied (again not written by Hans Sachs; no author is mentioned) taken from a Jena-MS, which surprisingly has the correct number of verses, namely fifty-three (pp. 221-223). Sommer, who merely catalogued the Hans Sachs rhyme schemes without words or music, shows forty-one verses (p. 135). He probably took this number from Wackernagel (*WKL.* II, 1406), who published the second of the two Meisterlieder which Hans Sachs set to this *Ton* in Berlin 414 (see No. 4), for Sommer mentions Wackernagel both in connection with the number of verses to a strophe and with regard to the name of the melody. Schnorr von Carolsfeld numbered the verses consecutively throughout the poem, set off those of one-syllable by means of spaces between words, but also added a one-syllable verse, unlike the original of Berlin 414, or of Mg. 2, at the very end of each *Abgesang,* whereby he created an unrhymed verse, contrary to the rhyme scheme. The transcription of the first strophe by both Genée and Mey does not coincide with Mg. 2; both have modernized the forms, and Mey seems also to have resorted to another manuscript. For Münzer's comment on the music and on Puschman's transcription of it see the *Singebuch,* pp. 26 and 72, No. 273. According to Münzer the music is well suited to this first Meisterlied which Hans Sachs set to it.

1, 5 der: Hans Sachs uses the gen. of person with the verb *hören,* influenced possibly by the fact that its antecedent is in the gen.; ane zil: (MHG. *ane zil*) *unaufhörlich.*

7 In contrast to vss. 2, 14, and 53, which have seven syllables and a masculine rhyme-word following a one-syllabled verse, vss. 7 and 19 of each strophe (except vs. 7 of strophe 2) have eight syllables and a masculine rhyme word. Since Hans Sachs makes use of exactly the same pattern in the only other Meisterlied which he set to this *Ton* in Berlin 414 (see No. 4; there, however, 2,7 is not an exception), it indicates that the later rules with regard to such verses were not yet firmly established.

8 Hans Sachs must have been greatly disillusioned when he heard some of the Meistersinger render their songs to speak so bluntly in this verse and on through verse 12.

27 leren: Hans Sachs uses this verb with the meaning of *lernen*; see also Schmeller I, col. 1499.

34 in scherpff: i. e., with the avoidance of the errors set down in the stricter rules; zal: the proper number of syllables in a verse, see Plate, p. 196; masse: see ibid., p. 195, where *mass* is a synonym for *Gemess.*

35 A capital *A* in the right-hand margin after "ich" indicates that the Meisterlied is continued on the folio where the capital *A* is to be found, namely at the top of the left-hand margin of folio 40^r.

37 sprich: pl. *Sprüche.*

43 den: *Töne.*

53 den: this is either the dat. pl. referring to "geschichten" (51), or a scribal error for *dem* which Hans Sachs wrote down in Mg. 2 and which more logically refers to "meister" (45).

2, 2 In this strophe Hans Sachs arranges the personages about whom he would like to know something in a descending order within three similarly descending categories, celestial, ecclesiastical, noble.

7 der parmüng prün: a metaphor for the Virgin Mary.

8 der engel jerarcheÿ: see 13,1,2 for comment.

19 probsten: (MHG. *brobest,* stm.) *Vorgesetzten*; her: *vornehm.*

20 minich: (MHG. *münich,* stm.) *Mönchen.*

22 pehafft: *verpflichtet.*

25 künt: *könnte*; the *k* is not capitalized.

40 springen: this word, as well as "singen" in the next verse, and "erclingen" (42) are substantives in the dat. with the prep. *von* understood for the first two.

42 saiten spil: an uninflected gen. between the prep. and the substantive; erclingen: this was originally omitted, but has been written into the right-hand margin by a later hand, presumably that of Hans Sachs; a cross indicates its place in the verse.

43 zil: this forms a compound with "laufen" (44); vss. 43 and 44 are missing in Berlin 414, but are supplied by the Dresden MS. M 100.

45 von stechen: this phrase, similarly to "erclingen" (42), has been written into the right-hand margin.

51 bezeiten: (MHG. *bezîte,* adv.) *bei Zeiten.*

3, 2 stenden: *Ständen*; vnderzelt: *unerzählt*; cf. 14,3,18 for the spurious *d.*

7 dürck jud heiden: Folz also links Turks, Jews, and heathen in a Meisterlied which Hans Sachs copied into Berlin 414, foll. 130^r-132^r (see also Mayer, ed., No. 75), but whereas Folz shames them, Hans Sachs wants to learn more about them. This may have been because he had heard something about the Turks (Selim I, called "The Terrible," was Sultan from 1512-1520 and was greatly feared by his Christian neighbors to the West); because there were no Jews in Nuremberg (they had been expelled from the city in 1499, and not until 1850 was a Jew again given the privilege of living there); and because in religious instruction in school there had probably been frequent mention of the

heathen. Furthermore there was a 12th-cent. *Heidenturm* in Nuremberg with grotesque figures on it which no doubt aroused the young poet's curiosity. See Merriman, *Suleiman The Magnificant*, Chapter I, for an account of the early history of the Turks, and Priem, *Geschichte der Stadt Nürnberg*, pp. 6 and 696 for the reference to the Jews, and pp. 128 and 592 for the reference to the tower.

16 feür: monosyllabic, because the corresponding verses have eight syllables and a masculine rhyme-word, see 2,1,16 for comment.

18 recht: *genau.*

24 vögel: the vowel *o* has been made out of a *g* and the superscript could be either an *o* or an *e* for there is a line drawn through it.

28 silber: this word with a capital *S* has been written into the left-hand margin, probably by Hans Sachs; a cross indicates its proper place.

31 zalle: (MHG. *zale,* stf.) *Zahl.*

32 dalle: for an occasional pl. form *tal,* see P-G, § 123, Note 2.

33 saüs: (MHG. *sûs,* stm.) *Sausen*; perhaps Hans Sachs had the rushing of fresh waters (34) in mind.

35 Vss. 35-37 may reflect something learned in school.

No. 34, foll. 28ᵛ-29ʳ   Orig. 17

Preliminary:

1.   Schnorr von Carolsfeld, pp. 46-47.

Heading: Hans Sachs set only this one Meisterlied to Mügling's "kürczen don." It is well named in that it consists of just twelve verses equally divided among the three parts of the strophe. For the rhyme scheme see Appendix C and G-D, *H. S. Fab. u. Schw.* 3, p. xx. Since in later years Hans Sachs followed the simple pattern of aaab, cccd, for the two *Stollen,* he no doubt had that in mind for this Meisterlied also. (The Masters were to substitute rhyming words for his unrhymed ones.) However, it is seemingly impossible to find a fitting synonym for the third verse of each *Stollen* which will rhyme with the first two verses. – For the music of the *Ton* see Runge, No. 85, p. 139, and for comment on Puschmann's version thereof see Münzer, *Singebuch,* p. 15. Mayer, ed. (*Folz,* p. 404, No. 13) erroneously labeled the *Ton* the *Grundweise Frauenlobs,* which also has twelve verses to a strophe, divided, however, 3,3,6. plös: the reason for the superscribed *o* is not apparent.

1, 1 güt: the final word of the first verse of each of the three parts of the strophe is the clue to the next rhyme-word.

2 pfleg: Schnorr v. Carolsfeld in a note to this word (p. 61) suggests the synonym *huet,* and for "stras" (vs. 3) the synonym *weg*; thus he did not take into account that the rhyming words for verses 1,2, and 3 were supposed to form a triple rhyme, which "güt," *huet,* and *weg* do not. He too may have had difficulty supplying a third rhyming word, hence thought of the rhyme scheme aabc, ddbc for the two *Stollen.* For such a pattern one can find substitutes, though not always synonyms, for the rhymeless words, as I have done. For "pfleg" the synonym *huot* would be better than *huet,* which v. Carolsfeld suggested, because of the rhyme with "güt." (Schnorr v. C. probably assumed that the *ü* in "güt" was an umlaut, instead of Hans Sachs' way of writing *u.*)

6 plan: the synonym would be *platz* to rhyme with "schacz" (5).

7 hab: with the rhyme scheme implied by Schnorr v. C., aabc, the substitute could be *heg'* to rhyme with *weg*, the synonym for "stras" (3).
8 we: the synonym is *pein* to rhyme with "schrein" (4).
9 singen: the pattern for the *Abgesang* is eeef.
10 beczwicke: the verb *bezwingen* would fit here to rhyme with "singen."
11 verwandlen: *gebringen* could be substituted to make a third rhyme.
12 günst: instead of this word the last word of strophe 3, "gedicht," seems more important as a key word for the final rhyme of each *Abgesang*. With that assumption a substitute for "günst" might be *Licht* with the meaning of *geistige Einsicht*, and for "rank" (2,12) *schicht* (MHG. *schiht*, stf.) meaning *Geschichte*.

2, 2 erclünget: pret. subj. with the meaning *ließet ihr erklingen;* geig: the poet uses metonymy; the substitute would be *harpf* to rhyme with "scharpff" (1).
3 ses: pret. subj. *säße*; the word *wert (werde)* could be substituted.
4 kent: *könnte*; Weinhold (§ 414) says ö (Hans Sachs' *e*) appears in Alemannic as early as the 14th cent. in the pret. subj.
5 wech: *glänzend*.
6 schawt: a synonym to rhyme with "wech" (5) would be *spech* (MHG. *spëhen*, wkv.)
7 verpont: the synonym *versperrt* would rhyme with the new *wert* (3).
8 ort: the substitute would be *ent* to rhyme with "kent" (4).
9 scharpffer künste der sind: both noun and pronoun in the gen. pl. serve as subject, attracted into this case, perhaps, by the original "vile" which Hans Sachs emended to "mengerleÿe," no doubt because he realized that if he retained the original word he would have a rhyme with "mille" (11 below) which would be contrary to his plan for a poem without rhymes. The original verse was better, however, for with the correction, even though "also" was changed to "alss," the verse now has an extra syllable.
10 mite: the substitute *beÿe* would rhyme with "-leÿe" (9 below).
11 mille: (MHG. *müle*, stwkf.) *Mühle*; the substitution might be *dreÿe (Treue)* to rhyme with vss. 9 and 10.
12 melt: (MHG. *malen*, stv. VI) *mählt*; Schmeller (I, col. 1583) cites an example of the same spelling for this verb, "Swelch man in einer mul melt." Hans Sachs is being less than complimentary in this verse. rank: (MHG. *ranc*, stm.) *schnelle drehende Bewegung*, possibly figurative, "turn of a phrase"; see 1,12 above for the suggested substitution for this word.

3, 2 werck: a substitute might be *kram* with the meaning of *Ware* to rhyme with "-sam" of the preceding verse.
3 hol: (MHG. *hol*, stnm.) *Höhle*; a synonym would be *Loch.*
6 das lob: a synonym would be *den preis* to rhyme with "weis" (5).
7 nit schwach: a substitute could be *gar hoch* to rhyme with the suggested *Loch* (3).
8 sin: the substitute would be *Hercz* to rhyme with "ercz" (4).
10 der: pron. gen. sg. with "ein dail"; it refers to "new künst" (8); gemercken: the substitute would be *geleren* to rhyme with "heren" (9).
11 nemen: *keren* might be substituted to rhyme with vss. 9 and 10.
12 in eÿttel gut: (MHG. *îtel*, adj.) *nur in gutem Sinne.*

No. 35, foll. 37ᵛ-38ᵛ   Orig. 26

Preliminary:

1. See Goedeke, *H. S.* I, No. 8; Lützelberger-Fromman, *Hans Sachs*, No. 2; Weddingen, *Der dt. Meistergesang*, pp. 72-73; Mummenhof (*Hans Sachs*, pp. 18-19) quotes the last six verses only.

Heading: This is the second of two Meisterlieder which Hans Sachs set to his "silber weis," for a discussion of which see No. 14. Goedeke does not indicate the verses of one syllable at the beginning of each *Stollen*, hence shows only eighteen verses to a strophe instead of twenty.

1, 3 aüf wülle: inf. used substantively, *Aufwallen*.
    4 hülle: (MHG. *hüel*, stwkf.) *Pfütze*.
    7 besechen: *besorgen*.
   11 grosse hicz: apparently Hans Sachs is using the acc. with "von."
   14 geschmack: *Geruch*.
   18 vnbezwünge: *unbeherrscht*.

2, 2 geleiche: *vergleiche*.
    8 schlechte: *aufrichtig*.
   15 gespor: (MHG. *gespor*, stn.) *Spur*; for the acc. with an intrans. verb of motion see P-G, § 244.
   16 sie: this refers to "gespor" which is fem. for Hans Sachs; see also Schmeller II, col. 683, where he cites *Die, das Gespor*.
   17 dem: Hans Sachs is using the dat. with the prep. "durch."
   19 ane schmerczen: humorously Hans Sachs could say this of himself.

3, 3 gescherpffet: *geläutert*.
    4 geferden: *Hinterlist*.
   12 kron: the first prize; see Plate, pp. 175-176.
   13 krancz: the second prize; see Plate, pp. 176-178.
   15 dotes par: *Bahre des Todes*.
   19 püstaben: i. e. *schriftlich*.

No. 36, foll. 437ᵛ-438ʳ   Orig. 31

Preliminary:

1. The K-G Index, No. 80, lists this Meisterlied under the year 1520 with a question mark and adds that it is "wider ein groben singer."

Heading: Hans Sachs uses Zwinger's "rotten don," which Bartsch considers his best known (p. 183), for this one Meisterlied only. With regard to the melody Münzer (*Singebuch*, p. 18, No. 85) says, "Bei K *(Kol. Hs.)* zwar auch nicht besonders aber interessanter als bei P." He does not publish the music; for this see Runge, No. 18, p. 66, and for the rhyme scheme see Appendix C, and cf. G-D, *H. S. Fab. u. Schw.* 3, p. xxx. Loica: see 30,1,18 for this.

1, 14 wẙrt eüch: i. e., *wird euch zu Teil.*

2, 1 kr$\overset{e}{o}$ne: see 3,2,15 for comment on the superscript.
   2 h$\overset{e}{o}$ne: see 3,2,16.
   5 eich: *eüch*; malvasire: malmsey, a rich, sweet, aromatic wine, originally produced in Malvasia, Greece, from the Malvasira grape.
   6 schaden: probably in a pecuniary sense, since the imported wine would be expensive.
   7 placz: *ein flacher Kuchen*; see Schmeller I, col. 464; pachen: (MHG. *pachen*, stv. VI) *backen.*
   8 prw: *Brühe*; vorhen: *Forellen*; aschen: *Äschen, forellenartige Fische.*
   9 pretlein: *ein kleiner Braten.*
  10 goder: (MHG. *goder*, stm.) *Gurgel.* Instead of a virgule at the end of the verse there is a crossed-out partite sign.
  12 oxen augen: *Spiegelei.*

3, 1 vnholcz: (MHG. *unholz*, stn.) *Abfallholz*; kein note: *nicht nötig.*
   3 ob ir ... penachtet wẙrte (würdet): Hans Sachs probably means, "if dark should overtake you," since he speaks of their staying over night in the next verse.
   6 petstat: (MHG. *bettestat*, stf.) pl. *Schlafstätten*, or *Betten.*
   9 vrten: (MHG. *urte*, wkstf.) *Wirtsrechnungen.*
  12 in dem saüs: *im üppigen Leben.*

No. 37, fol. 438^r-438^v   Orig. 32

Preliminary:

1. See K-G Index, No. 60.

Heading: Hans Sachs set only this one Meisterlied to Frauenlob's "grünt weẙs," concerning which Münzer (*Singebuch*, p. 15, No. 23) says: "Kleine einfache aber nicht ausdruckslose Melodie." For the music see ibid., p. 34, No. 23. The strophe consists of only twelve verses, three in each *Stollen* and six in the *Abgesang*. For the rhyme scheme see Appendix C, and cf. G-D, *H. S. Fab. u. Schw.* 3, p. xv. No. 11. The pattern which Mayer, ed. (*Folz*, p. 404, No. 13), gives for this *Ton* is incorrect; it is actually that of Mügling's *kurzer Ton* which Hans Sachs used in No. 34. In the rhyme scheme which Frauchiger (p. 57, V, 5) has set down for the *Ton* there is a typographical error for vs. 2 of the first *Stollen* in that he shows nine syllables instead of the correct number, seven, which the Meisterlied he transcribed from M 13 (No. VI, pp. 16-17) has.

1, 2 pochen: (MHG. *bochen*, wkv.) *prahlen.*
   3 fechten sein: circumlocution for the simple infinitive *fechten.*
   9 h$\overset{e}{o}$r: höre; the superscribed e may have been added by a later hand because of the fact that Hans Sachs consistently uses either the vowel e or the vowel o in the verb *hören.*
  12 $\overset{e}{o}$r: this word seems strange; possibly the superscribed e, similarly to that of "hor" (9 above), was added later to give the word the meaning of *Ehre*, which Hans Sachs, however, always spells with an e (see, for instance 2,2 and 7 below). Hans Sachs may actually have meant "or" (MHG. *ôr*, wkstn.) acc. pl.; see, for example, Prov. 23:12 where we read: "Gib dein Herz zur Zucht, und deine Ohren zu vernünftiger Rede." Such an assumption would clear up the matter of the rhyme with "hor" (9) and point definitely to the addition of the superscripts by a later hand.

2, 2 gane: MHG. 1. sg. pres. ind. *gönne.*
3 The verse is ironical.
5 frawen lobe: Frauenlob (Heinrich von Meissen, ca. 1250-1318) was considered by the Meistersinger to be their founder; for his status as Meistersinger see Taylor, *Lit. Hist. of Mg.,* pp. 23-25 and 40-41. There is satire in Hans Sachs' comparison.
6 The verse is ironical.
7 haber: *hab' Ehr'.*
12 The verse is satirical. drogenheit: *Verblendung.*

3, 4 Nü: (MHG. *nu,* adv.) *nun;* nichs: a variant MHG. form.
5 zw schar: *zu der Gesellschaft;* meister züngen: Meistersinger; synecdoche, a variant of Hans Sachs' usual "meister münt."
7 nar/en (8): Hans Sachs is less than complimentary.
9 Again irony.
11 one: *ledig.*

No. 38, foll. 462ᵛ-463ᵛ Orig. 36

Preliminary:

1. In the K-G Index, No. 63, this Meisterlied is labeled "Ein maister straff," which is perplexing, for neither Hertel's definition of *Straffer* (*Schuelzetel,* note on pp. 27-28) nor Plate's (p. 109) is applicable to the contents of this particular poem.

2. See Goedeke, *H. S.* I, No. 10; Goedeke's transcription follows Berlin 414 more closely than usual.

Heading: This is the second Meisterlied which Hans Sachs set to his "hohen dag weis," for a discussion of which see No. 7. – The strophes are not numbered. The numbering is mine.

1, 4 man: *Mond.*
6 krage: (MHG. *krage,* wkm.) *Hals.*
15 widhopff: (MHG. *widhopfe,* wkm.) *Wiedehopf, ein Kukucksvogel;* gupffen: (MHG. *gupfe,* stwkm.) *Gipfel,* i. e., *Kamm;* Hans Sachs uses the fem. gender which is that of the Middle German word *kuppe.*
16 stupffen: (MHG. *stupfe,* wkf.) *Stachel;* here no doubt referring to the quill-covered skin of the porcupine.
17 rech: (MHG. *rêch,* stn.) *Reh;* the reason for the superscribed *e* over the *e* in this word and in "spech" (22 below) is not apparent.
21 floch: (MHG. *vlôch,* stm.) pl. *Flöhe.*
22 spech: (MHG. *spæhe,* adj.) *klug.* Since Hans Sachs frequently substitutes *e* for both MHG. *ôe* and *æ* (see, among others, 3,3,28 and 2,1,4 respectively) the series of rhymes *e:ôe:ôe:æ* in vss. 17, 18, 21, and 22, can be justified dialectally.
23 kale: *Bellen;* for this Bavarian meaning see Grimm, *DW.* 5,1, col. 70.
24 vale: (MHG. *falle,* variant of *væle,* stf.) *Mantel;* here the hide.
27 substancze: (MHG. *substanz,* stwkf.) *Wesen.*

2, 3 reuter: *Reiter;* for the diphthong *eu* see 30,2,15.
4 waller: (MHG. *waller,* stm.) *Pilger.*
6 doren: (MHG. *tôre,* wkm.) *Tor, Narr.*

9   gelab: imp. *gelob!* cf. 1,1,5 for the noun "lab."

11 carmen: (CL. *carmen*, n.) *Lied.*

12 retten: *Räten.*

17 parat: *Kunststück.*

21 watt: (MHG. *wât*, stf.) *Kleidung.*

22 mader: (MHG. *mâder*, stm.) *Mäher*; matt: (MHG. *mât*, stnf.) *Mähen.*

23 pfeüfer: *Pfeifer*; see 30,2,15 for the *eü*; fletten: (MHG. floite, *flöute*, wkstf.) *Flöte.*

3, 1 freyden: the *y* has been made out of a *u*.

3 fanthaseÿ: *Einbildung.*

4 achiczen: (MHG. *achzen*, wkv.) *Ach sagen*; Weinhold (*BGr.*, § 20) says that the insertion of an i between consonant combinations is common in the Bavarian dialect.

6 geiden: *Prahlen.*

11 lieb: the *l* is not capitalized.

15 Hans Sachs here expresses a modern viewpoint.

17 rĕtt: (MHG. *rȏete*, stf.) the vowel in this word is a correction in that the e was made out of an *o*, then a tiny e was superscribed.

18 gilb: (MHG. *gilwe*, stf.) *Blässe*; for the hardening of the w into b in a medial or final position in Bavarian see W. *BGr.*, § 125.

22 nett: MHG. dat. sg., *Nöt.*

23 dicken: (MHG. *tücke*, stf.)

25 vernŭnst: (MHG. *vernunst*, stf.) *Vernunft.*

26 stet: *stets*; stŭnd: 3. sg. pret. subj.; for the form see W. *BGr.*, § 271,b). The verse has one syllable too many.

27 ein sach: this may be the lack of rapport between Hans Sachs and the Nuremberg *Singschule* at this time.

Nit on vrsach: Hans Sachs wrote these words underneath the last verse of the Meisterlied. They are part of the mark of the printer Johann Bergmann von Olpe, a mark found at the end of each work which came from his printshop. Hans Sachs no doubt saw them when he was reading Brant's *Narrenschiff*, remembered them, and made use of them here. He changed Bergmann's first word *Nŭt* to "Nit." See both the 1494 and the 1499 editions of the *Narrenschiff*, as well as Weil, *Die dt. Druckerzeichen des XV. Jhr.*, pp. 47 and 50; also Voulliéme, *Die dt. Drucker des XV. Jhr.*, p. 35.

No. 39, foll. 463ᵛ-464ᵛ   Orig. 37

Preliminary:

1.   See the K-G Index, No. 66; Theodor Hampe ("Über Hans Sachsens Traumgedichte," *Zeitschrift für den deutschen Unterricht*, Vol. X, pp. 616-624; the periodical is called *Lyons Zeitschrift* in the K-G Index, No. 66) quotes just a few verses of the Meisterlied. He gives a deeply thoughtful interpretation of the allegory, made, however, from the viewpoint of the late 19th cent., and as he admits, "Bei der Auslegung etwas zu moderne Farben angewandt zu haben." For him Hans Sachs' "societas" is the medieval order of society which, founded on loyalty, could no longer hold its own against the advances made by science, etc., etc. Since Hampe does not think that Hans Sachs could have produced such an allegory, he seems convinced that the poet had a source which, Hampe adds, he has not been able to locate. He believes that Hans Sachs did not understand the true sense of the allegory he found in that source, ". . . sondern ziemlich unverständlich

den Hergang einer Vorlage, die ihn vielleicht durch ihre gelehrt klingenden lateinischen Bezeichnungen angezogen hatte, mit einem ihm aus anderen Gedichten geläufigen kurzen und wirkungsvollen Schlusse versah" (p. 619). True, the interpretation which Hampe offers would be remote from Hans Sachs' thinking, but I doubt that the young poet had a source for this Meisterlied, because as early as 1515 he had already proved his skill in creating an allegorical Meisterlied (No. 22) to portray a certain situation, and in 1516 he was the first to give a detailed, imaginative description of a garden which symbolized Meistergesang (No. 32). Very often Hans Sachs does have a source, but as a rule he indicates what this is. Furthermore, to say that the poet was attracted by the learned Latin designations and that he did not understand what he had read is for me drawing conclusions not based upon facts. Surely a young man who had gone to a Latin school for eight years would not find Latin abstract nouns, which he must have understood, so learned that he would be drawn to some source material because of them. Nor do Hans Sachs' Meisterlieder to date show that he made use of a source, even a Latin one (see Nos. 14, 15, 16, 19, and 28,5,7), which he did not understand. As for the ending, which Hampe thinks is Heineesque and too "frivol" for Hans Sachs, there is really nothing frivolous about it if we look at it in the light of everything else which Hans Sachs has said about the Nuremberg *Singschule* and his fellow Meistersinger. He was longing and wishing very much that matters could be righted between himself and the *Singschule*, even though he knew indubitably that it would take time to bring this about; hence he brought the allegory to its unexpected, effective close by letting his hearers know that he had been dreaming.

Heading: Similarly to the preceding Meisterlied this one is set to Hans Sachs' "hohen dagweis." – Again the strophes are not numbered. The numbering is mine.

1, 1 Ein: the *E* is a very large, black, ornate capital letter.
   4 inmaiginacz: (CL. imaginatio, f.).
   5 zanger: (MHG. *zanger*, adj.) *schwach*; see Grimm, *DW*. 15, col. 227,5.
   6 günt mich riren: *began mich anzutreiben.*
   8 gesicht: *Sinn.*
  16 The figurative language in this and the next verse is pleasingly poetic.
  17 fraw zithera: Cytherea, another name for the goddess Venus which Hans Sachs could have found in Boccaccio's *Genealogia Deorum*; see 28,5,6.
  22 hel: *tönend.*
  24 kinde: (MHG. *künden*, wkv.) *mache kund.*

2, 6 milde: *Freundlichkeit.*
   7 pefilde: (MHG. *beviln*, wkv.) pres. subj. *verdrieβe.*
  12 societas: CL., *Gesellschaft.*
  16 sciencie: gen. of CL. *scientia; Kenntnis.*
  18 der frücht: part. gen.; sŭperbia: CL.; *Übermut.*
  22 in vidia: CL.; *Neid.*

3, 8 simplicitas: CL., *Einfachheit.*
  12 kingin: once before (17,3,22) Hans Sachs used the vowel *i* in the stem of this word.
  16 mich verdribe: the heroine is driven out three times: from the garden (2,27), from the land (3,5), and here from the court of the Queen.
  18 daŭret: (MHG. *dûren*, wkv.) *dauert.*
  22 ÿ: (Middle German *i*, adv.) *zu aller Zeit.*
  23 verstricket: *verbunden.*

No. 40, foll. 468ʳ-469ʳ   Orig. 40

Heading: This is the only Meisterlied which Hans Sachs set to Caspar Singer's "lieben don," which consists of seventeen verses, five in each *Stollen* and seven in the *Abgesang*. Münzer (*Singebuch*, p. 18, No. 82) merely lists the *Ton* with a very brief comment on the music. For the rhyme scheme see Appendix C, and cf. G-D, *H. S. Fab. u. Schw.* 3, p. xxvii, No. 53; see also Mey, p. 146, No. 15. – The strophes are not numbered. The numbering is mine.

1, 1 This and the next verse are a repetition of the two opening verses in Hans Sachs' *Spruchgedicht* of 1515 (*H. S.* 3, p. 406).
  13 wage: (MHG. *wac*, stm.) *bewegtes, wogendes Wasser.*
  14 streichen: *sich schnell bewegen.*

2, 3 sengel: the four fish mentioned in this verse are all small varieties.
  5 praŭssen: (MHG. *brûsen*, wkv.) *laut prahlen.*
  8 das dŭrch: *wodurch.*
  9 hechten: pike; schleÿ; *Schleie*, a European fresh water cyprinoid (of the carp family) fish.
  10 hŭchen: salmon; haŭssen: sturgeon.
  13 los: *leichtfertige.*
  17 ir: gen. pl. with "lachet"; lachet: Hans Sachs overlooked the fact that this word should have formed a triple rhyme with "sachen:machen" (12/14).

3, 2 der dŭmen mercker: gen. pl. with the impersonal "ermant" (1). This and the next verse probably express Hans Sachs' true opinion of the *Merker* at this time. From the fact that he speaks of three fishermen, it is apparent that the *Singschule* in Nuremberg had three *Merker*; some schools had two originally; see Plate, pp. 171-172.
  3 reigister: the list of the items to be penalized.
  4 scharpff . . . gelat: for an explanation of these terms see 31,1,5.
  5 kleb . . . milben: minute mistakes; see 31,2,11-18 and 31,3,12-19 respectively for the definition of these terms.
  7 stŭcz: *Steckenbleiben*; mutirte melodeÿ: *Veränderung der Melodie*; cf. Plate, p. 198. The errors in this and the following verse were gross ones which the *Merker* apparently did not hear.
  8 laster: for the meaning see 30,2,19.
  10 keinen silben: penalties were assessed in syllables.
  13 mer: the rhyme requires the alternate *me.*

PLATES

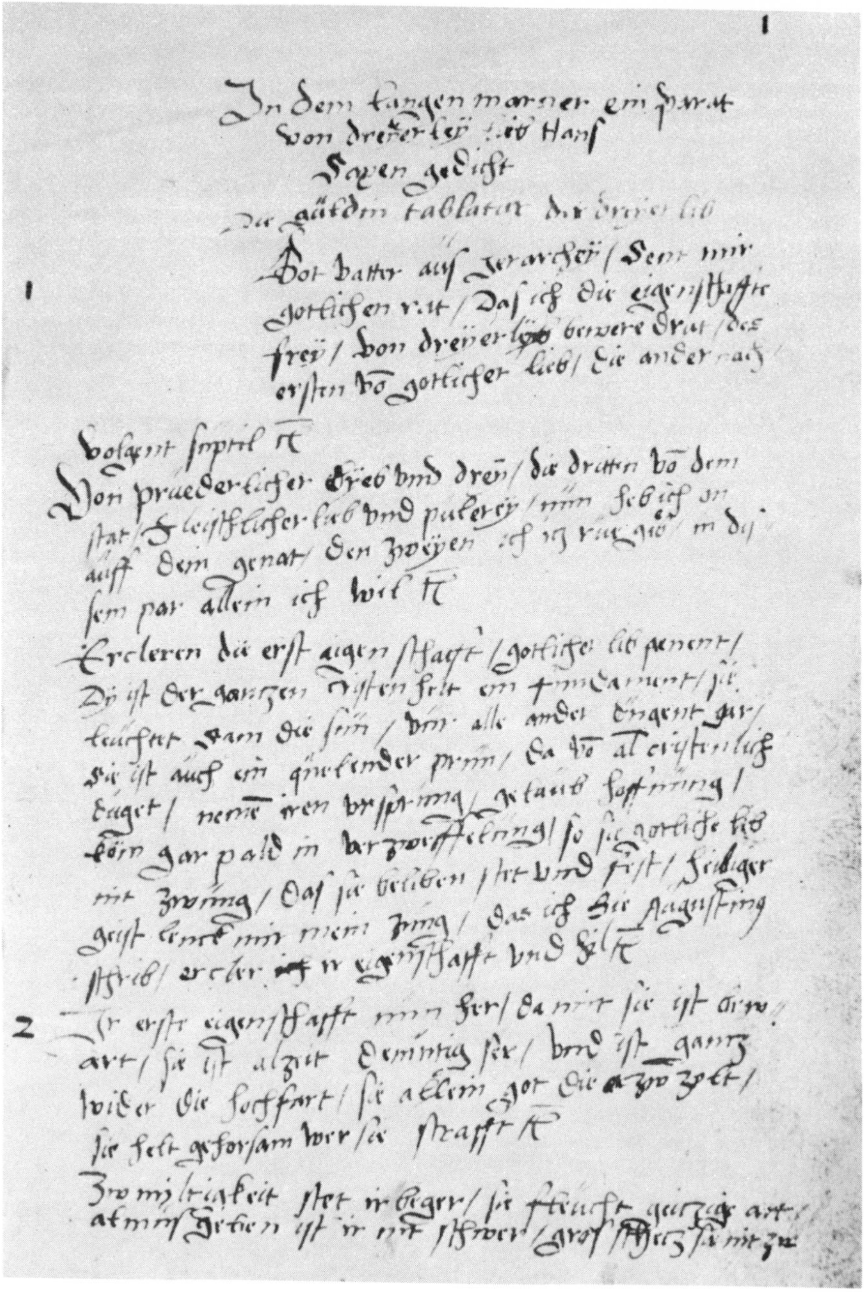

A portion of the first Meisterlied copied into Berlin 414

Vnnßere peÿ hÿnder duſen, wol dem herʒigßken / fur
eÿ auß kant mÿß der vernunfft, des ſter ſtinnd mÿm
herz in freuden ſprinnt / wen mÿr eÿn uß mÿ were ...

Nm on vrjar 1518

In der hohen dagweiß hanß
ſachßen vnd ſein gedicht

Eÿn mal wolt ich ſtudire / da ſ ßg wundler
mÿr mein hirren / dar von wardt mein
gedicht vnd manigmarz gar entwicht /
ſcharpff kunſt die ward mir ʒanßer ...

Mein vernunfft gunt mich nire / ich ſolt
eÿn weil ſpacire / vnd frÿſten mein
erſucht / alſo ich mein ganz hie richt /
auf eÿn grüne anger ...

Vnder em grÿm linde / da ich wardt
ſ ßaten vinde ich leit mich in das gras /
Dar durch ein kleines perßlein flaß von
eÿn kulen prune eÿn ſ ßlaff kam mir
gerune / auß fraw ʒißerg ſol ich er plicket
in ſ ßlaffes qual, em fraw vild mit rone /
ir antliz als die inne durch glemzt
perg vnd dal / ir ſtim hel als der nachtÿ
aul / ir ganz ſ ßmal als der windt / ir
kleid purpur ich vindt / wind ir recht
ßam was ir augen voller ʒißer naß vnd
was von leib groß ſ ßwanger ...

MUSIC

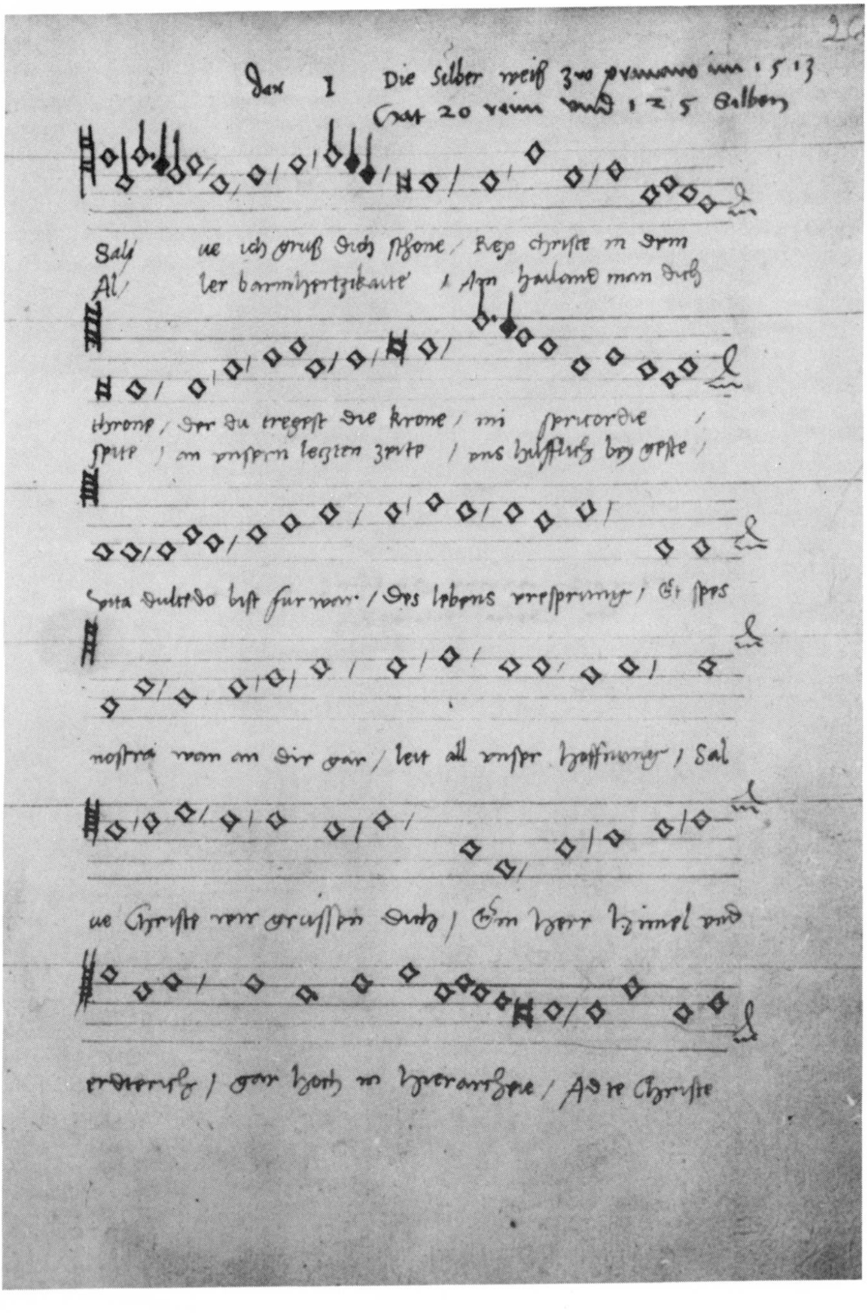

Die Silber weiß 1513

gar frew / Darnomus vor stets schrew / Helff vns

auß allem wee ;

geschort unser ortlich 1 5 3 2
in dem mayen

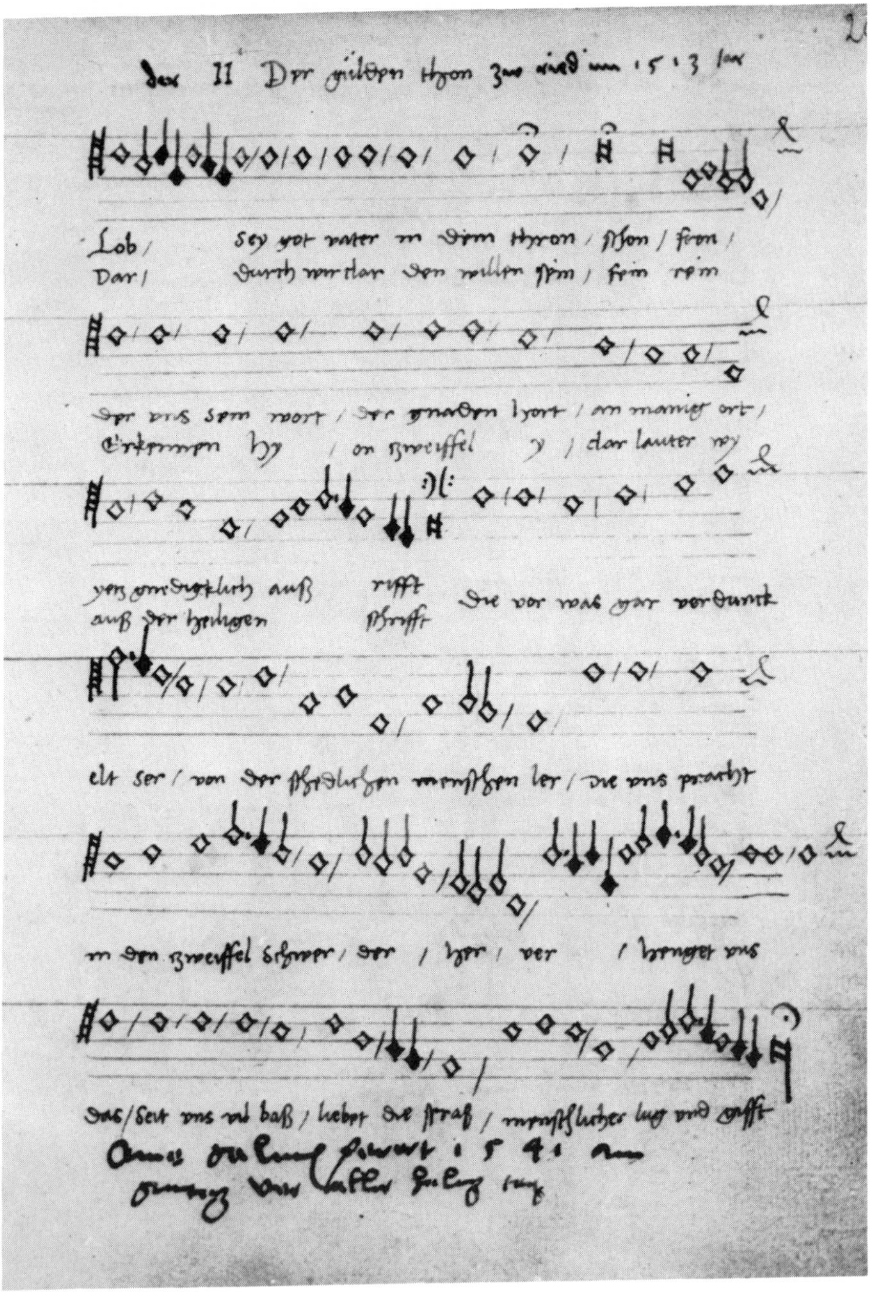

Der gülden thon 1513

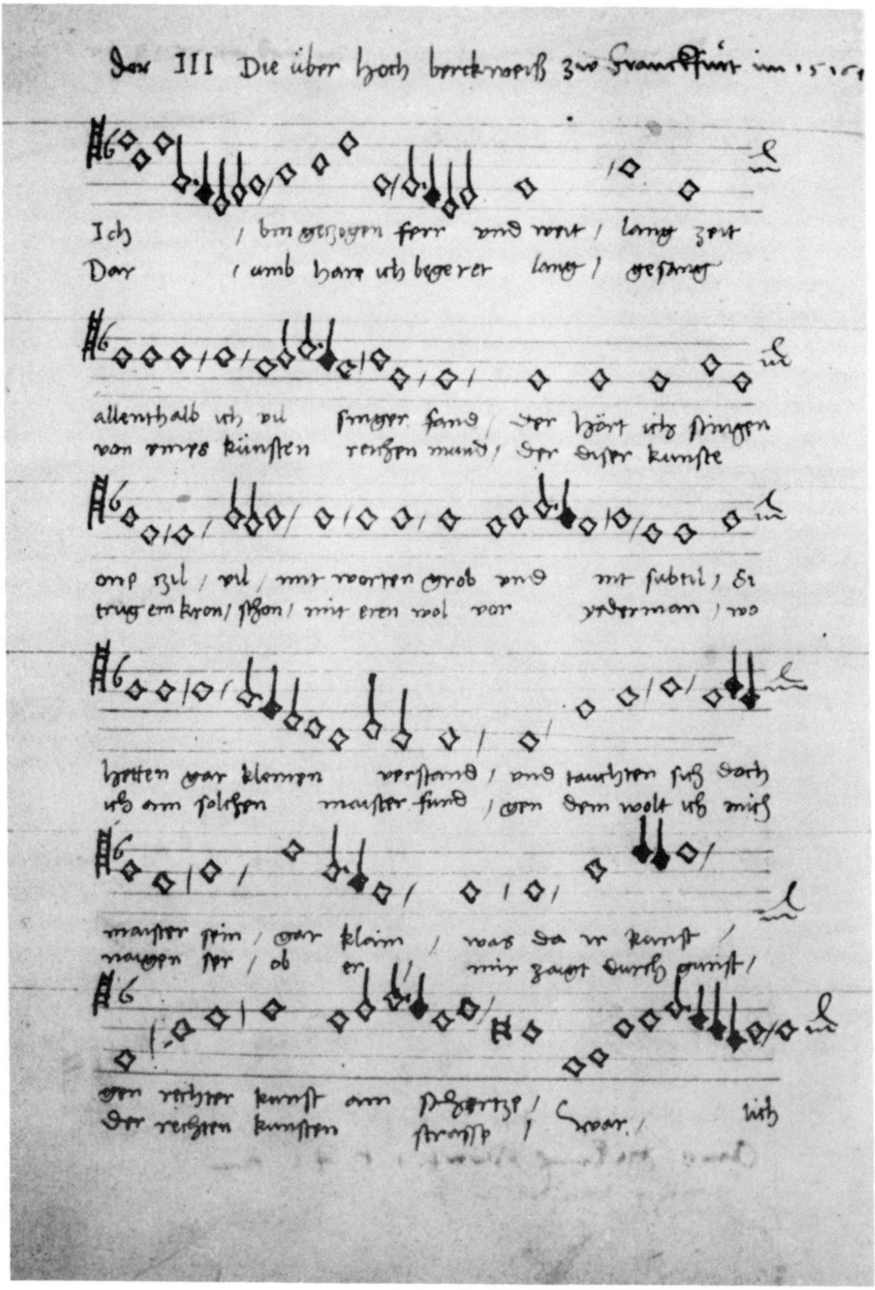

Die über hoch berckweiß 1516

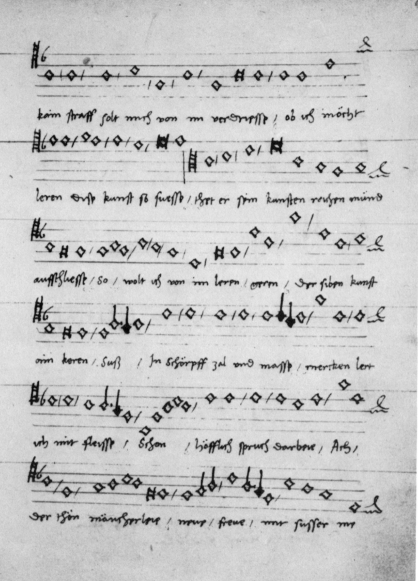

kain straff solt mich von im verdriesse / ob ich möcht

leren dein kunst so suesse / thet er sein kunsten reichen mund

auffschliesse / so / wolt ich von im leren / geren / der siben kunst

ain keren / Suß / In schörpff zal vnd masß / mercken lert

ich mir fleysse / Schon / höfflich sprüch darbeu / Artz /

der thön mancherlen / neu / freue / mit süsser mir

lo dere / den / die frembd selzam spie / dem
maister gab ich breist / gieß / er mir auch mein
hertze / do von das ich lert tichten / schlichten /
von mancherlai ge schichten / nach /
dem offt hat ver langt mich .
1548 am

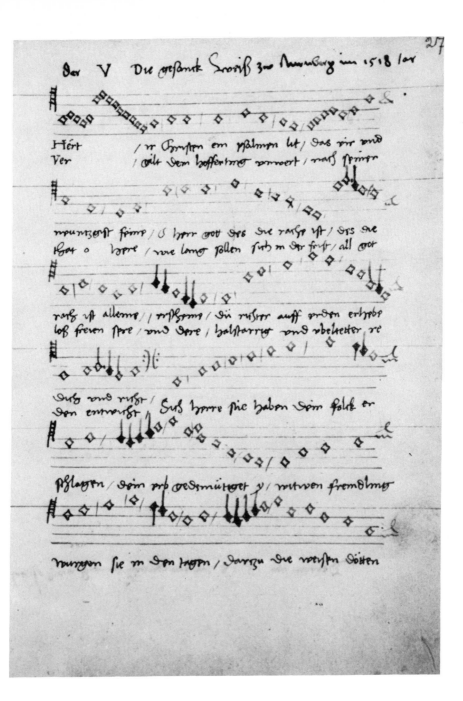

Die gesanck weiß   1518

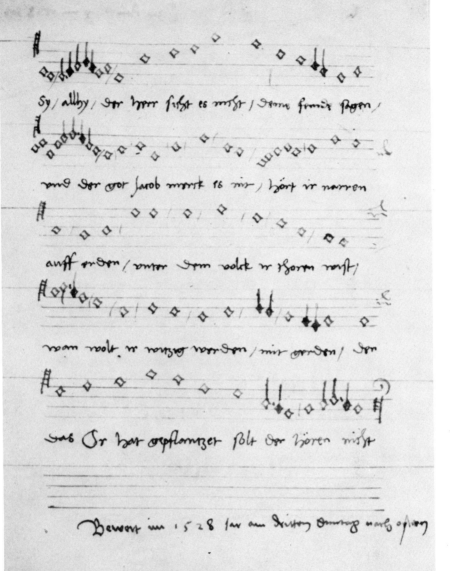

Sy, allhy, der herr sicht es nicht, dem fremd sagen,

vnd der got Jacob marck es mir, hört ir narren

auff erden, vnter dem volck ir thoren rast,

wan wolt ir vernig werden, mir grnden, der

das Er hat gepflantzer solt der hören nicht

Bewert im 1528 Jar am dritten Sontag nach ostern

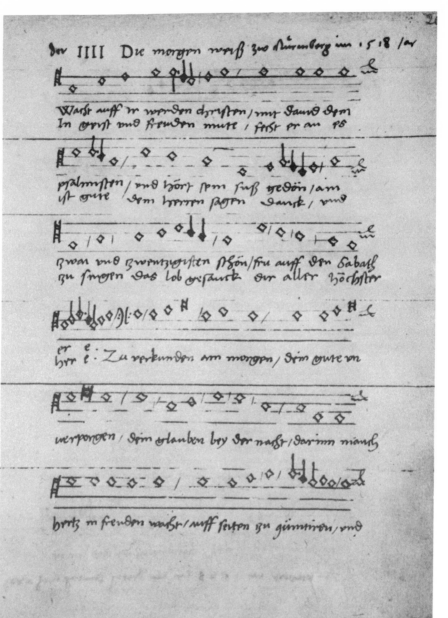

Die morgen weiß   1518

pfalter zu hoffiren / mit gedicht künstlich scharff / herr dir

zu sslahen auff der harff / mit sshonen resonantzen / lieplich

in concordantzen / wan herr du machest mich / ob deinen

werck gar frölich / in freuden ich mich rüm / deiner hand

werck ich plüm / herr wir sind deine werck / So groß vnd

dem gedancken werck / abgrüntloß vy das mer re;

gemacht im 1528 Jar am dritten suntag nach ostern)

The Rhyme Schemes

Hans Sachs set eleven of his forty Meisterlieder in Berlin 414 to the five *Töne* which he had composed by the end of 1518. For the other twenty-nine he used the melodies of fourteen different masters. Of these, ten are represented by one *Ton* only, three by two, and one by three. The *Töne* vary in length from twelve verses to fifty-three: six are from twelve to seventeen; fourteen from twenty to twenty-eight; three from thirty to thirty-eight; and one has fifty-three verses. Four of the *Töne* have verses of twelve syllables: Frauenlob's and Regenbogen's *langer Ton* have one such verse in each *Stollen*; Marner's *langer* has one in each *Abgesang*; and Hans Sachs' *vnser frawen gesanck weis* ends each *Stollen* and each *Abgesang* with a twelve-syllabled verse. Three of the *Töne* have unequal *Stollen*, namely Hans Sachs' *vnser frawen gesanck weis*, Frauenlob's *gülden don*, and *der freÿe don* of Hans Folz.

The number of the Meisterlied set to each *Ton* will be found under the rhyme scheme of that *Ton*. I have quoted Hans Sachs' own words for the *Töne*, but have substituted the nominative ending for the adjective in those instances where he employs the dative.

I. The *Töne* composed by Hans Sachs

1. "Silber weis"   1513 Braunau
1a 6b 7b 7b 6c   5
1a 6d 7d 7d 6c   5 } 20
8e 6f 8e 6f 8g 8g 7h 7h 7h 6c   10
Nos. 14, 35.

2. "güldin don"   1513 Ried
8a 1a 1a 4b 4b 4b 6c   7
8d 1d 1d 4e 4e 4e 6c   7 } 24
8f 8f 8f 1f 1f 1f 4g 4g 4g 6c   10
No. 9.

3. "vberhohe perck weis"   1516 Frankfurt
1a 7b 2b 8c 8d 1d 8d 8c 8e 2e 4f 7g   12
1h 7j 2j 8k 8l 1l 8l 8k 8m 2m 4f 7n   12 } 53
1h 10o 11o 11o 1p 6q 2q 7q 1r 6n 7s 1t 6u 1v 6u 2u 2u
        7u 1t 6u 7s 1r 6g 1p 6w 2w 7w 1v 7a   29
Nos. 4, 33.

4. "hohe dag weis"   1518 Nürnberg
7a 7a 6b 8b 7c   5
7a 7a 6b 8b 7c   5 } 27
7d 7d 6e 8e 7f 7f 6g 8g 7f 7f 6g 8g 7d 7d 6e 8e 7c   17
Nos. 7, 38, 39.

5. "vnser frawen gesanck weis"   1518 Nürnberg
1a 7b 7c 8d 7c 3c 12e   7
     8a 7f 8d 7f 3f 12e   6 } 25
11g 8h 11g 8h 2h 11g 8b 7j 8d 7j 3j 12e   12
Nos. 18, 19, 20.

II. The *Töne* of Other Masters

"Six peckmessers korweis"
1a 7b 4b 7c 7c 6d 2e 8f 2e 8f 8g   11
1a 7h 4h 7j 7j 6d 2k 8l 2k 8l 8g   11 } 38
4m 4m 6n 4n 4n 2o 2o 4n 7p 7p 6q 2r 8s 2r 8s 8q   16
Nos. 3, 6.

"frawen Eren don" (Des Erenbots)
8a 7b 8a 7c 10d   5
8e 7b 8e 7c 10d   5 } 16
11f 11f 11g 8h 8h 11g   6
Nos. 16, 23, 24, 25.

"der freÿe don Meister Hans Volzen"
1a 7b 8c 8b 8c 8d 8d 8e   8
     8f 8g 8f 8g 8h 8h 8e   7 } 30
8j 8k 10l 8j 8k 10l 8m 8n 8o 8n 8o 8p 8p 1a 7m   15
No. 13.

"des frawenlobs gülden don"
1a 6b 1a 6c 1d 1a 5e 1a 6f 1g 5h   11
1g 6j 1k 6l 1k   6m 1n 6o 1p 5q   10 } 37
1q 6e 7l 1p 6b 7o 7j 7m 1n 6c 1d 5h 1r 6f 1r 5q   16
(Strophes 2 and 3)   6f   6c
No. 17.

"grünt weÿs frawenlobs"
11a 7a 10b   3
11c 7c 10b   3 } 12
4d 4d 4e 11f 7f 10e   6
No. 37.

"des frawenlobs lang don"
12a 4a 7b 7b 8c 7b 8d 7e   8
12f 4f 7g 7g 8c 7g 8d 7e   8 } 24
8h 8h 4h 4h 8h 8h 8d 7e   8
Nos. 22, 30.

"Marners langer don"
8a 6b 8a 8b 8c 8d   6
8a 6b 8a 8b 8c 8d   6 } 27
8e 6f 12f 6g 8h 8g 8j 6k 4k 8k 8k 8l 8k 8c 8d   15
Nos. 1, 2, 8, 26, 27, 28.

"der kürcze don Müglings"
6a 8a 8a 8b   4
6c 8c 8c 8b   4 } 12
11d 11d 7d 8e   4
No. 34.

"des Müscaplücz langer don"
4a 4a 4b 4b 7c   5
4d 4d 4e 4e 7c   5 } 22
8f 7g 8f 7g 4h 4h 7j 8k 4k 4l 4l 7j   12
No. 21.

"der lait don nachtigals"
4a 7b 8c 11b 8d 8d 7e   7
4a 7f 8c 11f 8g 8g 7e   7 } 25
7h 11j 7h 11j 8k 11l 8m 8m 7e   11
No. 11.

"der geschiden don Cünracz nachtigals"
7a 8b 8b 7a 7c   5
7d 8e 8e 7d 7c   5 } 17
7f 11g 7f 11g 8h 8h 7f   7
No. 12.

"die schlag weis linhart nünnenpecken"
3a 6b 7c 4d 4d 7e   6
3e 6b 7c 4f 4f 7a   6 } 25
4g 4h 4j 7k 4j 4h 4g 7k 2l 4l 4l 4h 7k   13
No. 5.

"Regenpogens langer don"
9a 12b 8c 11d
9a 12b 8c 11d
8e 11f 8e 11f 8g 6h 10h 8j 10k 8j 10k 8l 10h 8g 10h
No. 32.

$\left.\begin{array}{l}4\\4\\15\end{array}\right\}23$

"der liebe don Caspar singers von eger"
8a 8a 8a 4b 7c
8d 8d 8d 4b 7c
8e 7f 8e 7f 8g 4g 7f
No. 40.

$\left.\begin{array}{l}5\\5\\7\end{array}\right\}17$

"caspars singers schlechter don"
7a 6b 7a 6b 2b 8c
7d 6e 7d 6e 2e 8c
8f 8f 4g 7h 6j 7h 6j 2j 8g
No. 15.

$\left.\begin{array}{l}6\\6\\9\end{array}\right\}21$

"des wolferams langer don"
8a 8a 8a 8a 8b 4b 1b 6c
8d 8d 8d 8d 8e 4e 1e 6c
8f 11g 8f 11g 8h 8h 8h 8h 8j 4j 1j 6c
No. 29.

$\left.\begin{array}{l}8\\8\\12\end{array}\right\}28$

"der verhollen don" (Zorns)
8a 8b 8a 8b 8c
8d 8e 8d 8e 8c
8f 2f 6g 8h 8j 8h 8j 8g 8k 8l 8k 8l 8e
No. 31.

$\left.\begin{array}{l}5\\5\\13\end{array}\right\}23$

"des zorens züg weis"
1a 8b 12c 8d 11e
1a 8b 12c 8d 11e
8f 11g 8f 11g 8h 6j 10j 8k 10l 8h 10j 8h 10j 8h 10j
No. 10.

$\left.\begin{array}{l}5\\5\\15\end{array}\right\}25$

"zwingers rotter don"
11a 11a 11b
11c 11c 11b
8d 11e 8d 11e 7f 6g 4g 7f 8g
No. 36.

$\left.\begin{array}{l}3\\3\\9\end{array}\right\}15$

Bibliography

Abele, Wilhelm. *Die antiken Quellen des Hans Sachs* I and II. Beilage zum Programm der Realanstalt in Cannstadt. Cannstadt: Louis Bosheuyer's Buchdruckerei, Wolfgang Drück, 1897, 1899.

Albrecht, Julius. *Ausgewählte Kapital zu einer Hans Sachs-Grammatik.* [Diss.] Freiburg im Breisgau: Universitätsbuchdruckerei, 1896.

Andreas Capelanus. *Des königlich Fränkischen Kaplans Andreas 3 Bücher über die Liebe aus dem Lateinischen übertragen,* trans. and ed. Hanns Martin Elster. Dresden: Paul Äretz, 1924.

_____ . *The Art of Courtly Love,* trans. and ed. John Jay Parry. Records of Civilization Sources and Studies, No. XXXIII. New York: Columbia University Press, 1941.

Apocryphal Gospels, Acts, and Revelations, trans. Alexander Walker. Ante-Nicene Christian Library; Translations of the Writings of the Fathers down to 325 A.D., Vol XVI. Edinburgh: T. and T. Clark, 1870.

Aretin, Johann Christoph von. "Kritische Beschreibung einer Sammlung alter Meistergesänge in einer Handschrift des XV. Jahrhunderts," *Beyträge zur Geschichte und Literatur,* IX (1807), 1128-1187.

Baader, Joseph. *Nürnberger Polizeiordnungen aus dem XIII. bis XV. Jahrhundert.* Bibliothek des Litterarischen Vereins in Stuttgart, Vol. LXIII. Stuttgart, 1861.

_____ . "Zur Geschichte der Meistersinger in Nürnberg," *Anzeiger der deutschen Vorzeit,* IX (1862), coll. 8-10.

Bächtold-Stäubli. *Handwörterbuch des deutschen Aberglaubens.* 10 vols. Handwörterbuch zur deutschen Volkskunde, Abteilung I, Aberglaube. Berlin und Leipzig: Walter de Gruyter and Co., 1927-1942.

Baesecke, Georg. "Arigo," *Zeitschrift für deutsches Altertum,* XLVII (1914), 191.

_____ . "Zur Geschichte der Meistersinger in Nürnberg," *Euphorion,* XIII (1906), 440 ff.

Barack, Karl August. "Zur Geschichte der Meistersinger in Nürnberg," *Zeitschrift für deutsche Kulturgeschichte,* IV (1859), 376-390.

Bartsch, Karl, ed. *Meisterlieder der Kolmarer Handschrift.* Bibliothek des Litterarischen Vereins in Stuttgart, Vol. LXVIII. Stuttgart, 1862.

Behagel, Otto. *Geschichte der deutschen Sprache.* 5th ed. Grundriss der Germanischen Philologie III. Berlin und Leipzig: Walter de Gruyter and Co., 1928.

Beissel, Stephan. *Geschichte der Verehrung Marias in Deutschland während des Mittelalters.* Freiburg im Breisgau: Herdersche Verlagshandlung, 1909.

Bibliography

Bell, Clair Hayden. *Georg Hager, A Meistersinger of Nürnberg,* 1552-1634. University of California Publications in Modern Philology, Vols. XXIX-XXXII. Berkeley and Los Angeles: University of California Press, 1947.

Benrath, Karl. *Zur Geschichte der Marienverehrung.* Theologische Studien und Kritiken, 59. Jahrgang 1886, 1. und 2. Heft, pp. 7-94; 197-267.

Berlepsch, H. A. *Chronik vom ehrbaren Schuhmacherwerk.* Chronik der Gewerke, Vol. IV. St. Gallen, *s. d.*

Bibel. *Die Bibel oder die ganze Heilige Schrift Alten und Neuen Testaments,* trans. Martin Luther. St. Louis: Concordia Publishing House, 1904.

Biblia pauperŭm. Deŭtsche Aŭsgabe von 1471. Weimar: Gesellschaft der Bibliophilen, 1906.

Biblia Sacra. Vulgatæ Editionis, Sixti V. et Clementis VIII. Londini: Sumptibus Samuelis Bagster et FF, *s. d.*

Bobbe, Heinrich. *Mittelhochdeutsche Katharinen-Legenden in Reimen. Eine Quellenuntersuchung.* Germanische Studien, Heft 19. Berlin: Emil Ebering, 1922.

Boccaccio, Giovanni. *Decameron von Heinrich Steinhöwel,* ed. A. v. Keller. Bibliothek des Litterarischen Vereins in Stuttgart, Vol. LI. Stuttgart, 1860.

————. *De Claris Mulieribus,* trans. Steinhöwel, ed. Karl Drescher. Bibliothek des Litterarischen Vereins in Stuttgart, Vol. CCV. Tübingen, 1895.

————. *Concerning Famous Women,* trans. Guido A. Guarino. New Brunswick, New Jersey: Rutgers University Press, 1963.

————. *Genealogie deorum gentilium,* ed. V. Romano. Bari: G. Laterza, 1951.

Böckmann, Paul. *Formgeschichte der deutschen Dichtung.* Hamburg: Hoffmann und Campe, 1949.

Bonaventura (Saint). *Opera Omnia.* 10 vols. Prope Florentiam, 1882-1902.

Brant, Sebastian. *Das Narrenschiff. Faksimile der Erstausgabe von 1494.* Jahresgaben der Gesellschaft für Elsässische Literatur, Vol. I. Straßburg: Karl J. Trübner, 1913.

Büchner, M. Gottfried. *Hand-Konkordanz.* 29th ed. rev. Heinrich Leonhard Heubner. Leipzig: M. Heinsius Nachfolger Eger und Sievers, 1927.

Catechismus romanus ex decreto concilii Tridentini. Antverpiae, Plantini, 1574.

The Catholic Encyclopedia, eds., Charles G. Herbermann *et al.* 15 vols. New York: Robert Appleton Co., 1907-1912.

Chemnitz, Martin. *De duabus naturis in Christo, Leipzig,* 1578. Trans. and ed. J.S.O. Preus, St. Louis, Mo.: Concordia Publishing House, 1921.

Bibliography

Concordia Triglotta. (The Symbolical Books of the Ev. Lutheran Church) German-Latin-English, eds. F. Bente and W.H.T. Dau. St. Louis, Mo.: Concordia Publishing House, 1921.

Coulton, G. G. *Five Centuries of Religion,* Cambridge Studies in Medieval Life and Thought. 5 vols. Cambridge, England: Cambridge University Press, 1923-1950 (Vol. 1, 2nd ed. 1929).

Curme, George O. *A Grammar of the German Language.* Rev. ed. New York: The MacMillan Co., 1922.

De Boor, Helmut, and Richard Newald. *Geschichte der deutschen Literatur,* Vol. III, 1. München: C. H. Beck'sche Verlagsbuchhandlung, 1962.

Deutsche Philologie im Aufriß II, 2nd ed., ed. W. Stammler. Berlin: Erich Schmidt Verlag, 1960.

Deutsche Sagen II, 2nd ed., eds. the Brothers Grimm. Berlin, 1866.

Delehaye, Hippolyte. *The Legends of the Saints,* trans. of 1st French ed. Donald Attwater. New York: Fordham University Press, 1962.

Diesenberg, Hans. *Studien zur religiösen Gedankenwelt in der Spruchdichtung des 13. Jahrhunderts.* [Diss.] Bonn, 1937.

Dionysius the Areopagite. *Mystical Theology and the Celestial Hierarchies.* Surrey, England: Shrine of Wisdom, 1935.

Drescher, Carl. *Arigo, der Übersetzer des Decamerone . . .* Quellen und Forschungen zur Sprach- und Culturgeschichte der germanischen Völker, 86. Heft. Strassburg: K. J. Trübner, 1900.

———. "Hans Sachs und Boccaccio," *Zeitschrift für vergleichende Litteraturgeschichte,* n. F. VII (1894), 402-416.

———. *Studien zu Hans Sachs* II, n. F. Marburg: N. G. Elwert'sche Verlagsbuchhandlung, 1891, pp. 28-89.

Dreves-Blume. *Ein Jahrtausend Lateinischer Hymnen-Dichtung,* I and II. Leipzig: Reisland Verlag, 1909.

Dreyer, A. "Hans Sachs in München und die gleichzeitigen Münchener Meistersänger," *Analecta germanica Hermann Paul dargebracht.* Amberg, 1906.

Ehrismann, Gustav. *Geschichte der deutschen Literatur bis zum Ausgang des Mittelalters,* II,2,2. München: C. H. Beck'sche Verlagsbuchhandlung, 1935.

Eisenhofer, Ludwig. *Grundriss der Liturgik des römischen Ritus.* Rev. ed. by Joseph Lechner. 5th ed. Freiburg: Herder, 1950.

Bibliography

Ellenbeck, H. *Die Sage vom Ursprung des deutschen Meistergesangs.* [Diss.] Bonn: Heinrich Ludwig, 1911.

Ellis, Frances H. "Analysis of the Berlin MS *Germ. Quart. 414*," *PMLA*, LXI, No. 4 (1946) 947-996.

————. *Hans Sachs Studies I. Das Walt got: A Meisterlied.* Indiana University Publications. Humanities Series No. 4. Bloomington, Indiana, 1941.

————. "The Solution for the Enigmatic Concluding Lines of the Munich Codex *Germanicus 6353*," *PMLA*, LXVII, No. 4 (June, 1952) 446-472.

Eyb, Albrecht. *Das Ehebüchlein*, Vol. I of *Deutsche Schriften des Albrecht von Eyb*, ed. Max Herrmann. Schriften zur Germanischen Philologie. Berlin, 1890.

Folz, Hans. *Die Meisterlieder des Hans Folz aus der Münchener Originalhandschrift und der Weimarer Q. 566,* ed. August L. Mayer. Deutsche Texte des Mittelalters, Vol. XII. Berlin: Weidmannsche Buchhandlung, 1908.

Franz, Adolf. *Die Messe im deutschen Mittelalter.* Darmstadt: Wissenschaftliche Buchgesellschaft, 1963.

Frauchiger, Fritz. *Dresden M 13: A Fifteenth-Century Collection of Religious Meisterlieder.* [Diss.], Chicago: University of Chicago, 1938.

Frauenlob (Heinrich von Meissen). *Frauenlobs Marienleich,* ed. Ludwig Pfannmüller. Quellen und Forschungen zur Sprach und Kulturgeschichte, 120. Heft. Strassburg: Karl J. Trübner, 1913.

Friedman, Clarence William. *Prefigurations in Meistergesang: Types from the Bible and Nature.* [Diss.] Washington, D.C.: The Catholic University of America Press, 1943.

Frommann, Carl, *Versuch einer grammatischen Darstellung der Sprache des Hans Sachs. I Teil: zur Lautlehre.* Nürnberg, 1878.

Gebhardt, August. *Grammatik der Nürnberger Mundart.* Leipzig, 1907.

Geiger, Eugen. *Der Meistergesang des Hans Sachs.* Bern, Switzerland: A. Francke Ag., 1956.

Genée, Rudolph. *Hans Sachs und Seine Zeit.* Leipzig: J. J. Weber, 1902.

Gerhard, J. *Loci Theologici XX,* Tübingen, 1871.

Gesta Romanorum, trans. and ed. Johann Georg Theodor Gräße. 3rd ed. Dresden: Paul Älicke, 1905.

Goedeke, Karl. *Grundriß zur Geschichte der deutschen Dichtung* I, 2nd. ed. *Das Mittelalter* II, 2nd ed., *Das Reformationsalter.* Dresden, 1884 and 1886.

Goetze, Alfred. *Frühneuhochdeutsches Glossar.* 7th ed. Kleine Texte für Vorlesungen und Übungen 101. Berlin: Walter De Gruyter and Co., 1967.

Bibliography

Goetze, Edmund. *Hans Sachs.* Bayerische Bibliotek, Vol. XIX. Bamberg: Buchnersche Verlagsbuchhandlung, 1890.

———. "Monographie über den Meistersanger Adam Puschmann" *Neues Lausitzisches Magazin,* Vol. LIII (1877), 59-157.

Grabmann, Martin. *Die Gesch. d. Katholischen Theologie seit dem Ausgang der Väterzeit.* Freiburg im Breisgau: Herder and Co. G. m. B. H. Verlagsbuchhandlung, 1933.

Grimm, Jacob. *Ueber den altdeutschen Meistergesang.* Göttingen: Heinrich Dieterich, 1811.

Grimm, Wilhelm. "Marienlieder," *Zeitschrift für Deutsches Altertum,* X (1856), 1-42.

Grimm, Jakob und Wilhelm. *Deutsches Wörterbuch.* 16 vols. in 33. Leipzig: S. Hirzel, 1854-1960.

Hagen, Karl. *Deutschlands literarische und religiöse Verhältnisse im Reformationszeitalter,* Vol. II. Frankfurt a/M: Völker, 1868.

von der Hagen, Friedrich Heinrich. *Minnesinger,* Vols. I-V. Leipzig: J.A. Barth, 1838-1861.

———. *Sammlung zur altdeutschen Literatur und Kunst* I, 1. Breslau, 1812.

———. *Gesammtabenteuer.* Stuttgart und Tübingen: J.G. Cottascher Verlag, 1850.

Hahn, Karl August. *Das alte Passional.* Frankfurt a/M, 1845.

Haltaus, Christian Gottlob. *Jahrzeitbuch der Deutschen des Mittelalters.* Erlangen, 1797.

Hampe, Theodor. "Über Hans Sachsens Traumgedichte," *Zeitschrift für den deutschen Unterricht,* X (1896), 616-624.

Handschin, Charles Hart. *Das Sprichwort bei Hans Sachs.* Bulletin of the University of Wisconsin, No. 103. Philology and Literature Series, Vol. III, No. 1. Madison, Wisconsin, 1904.

Heerwagen, Heinrich Wilhelm. *Zur Geschichte der Nürnberger Gelehrtenschulen* (1485-1526). Nürnberg, 1860.

Der Heiligen Leben und Leiden, ed. Severin Rüttgers. Leipzig: Insel-Verlag, 1922.

Henze, Helene. *Die Allegorie bei Hans Sachs.* Halle: Max Niemeyer, 1912.

Herolt, Johann. *Promptuarium Discipuli de Miraculis Beate Marie Virginis, ca.* 1435-40. Nuremberg, 1486.

Hertel, F. G. W. "Nürnberger Schulzettel vom Jahre 1540," *Jahresbericht des Gymnasiums zu Zwickau* (1853-54), 1-36. *(Der Schuelzetel zw Nürnberg* is on pp. 26-31; Hertel capitalized Hans Sachs' small *s* in *schuelzetel.)*

Bibliography

Hintner, Florian. "Hans Sachs in Wels," *II. Jahresbericht des Städtischen Gymnasiums in Wels* (1903), 1-19.

Hoffmann, J. L. *Hans Sachs.* Nürnberg, 1847.

Holter, Kurt and Gilbert Trathnigg. *Wels von der Urzeit bis zur Gegenwart.* Wels: Verlag Eugen Friedhuber, *s. d.*

Holzschuher, Hanns. *Hanns Sachs in seiner Bedeutung für unsere Zeit.* Die Literatur, Sammlung illustrierter Einzeldarstellungen, ed. Georg Brandes, Vol. 31. Berlin: Bard Marquardt et Co., *s. d.*

Hopper, Vincent Foster. *Medieval Number Symbolism.* Columbia University Press, 1938.

Huizinga, J. *Herbst des Mittelalters.* 6th ed. Stuttgart: Alfred Kröner, 1952.

Hulme, F. Edward. *Symbolism in Christian Art.* New York: The MacMillan Co., 1909.

Hymni Latini medii sevi . . . , ed. F. J. Mone. 3 vols. Freiburg im Breisgau: Herder, 1853-1855.

Jacobsthal, G. "Über die musikalische Bildung der Meistersinger," *Zeitschrift für deutsches Altertum und deutsche Literatur,* Vol. XX, n. F. VIII (1876), 69-91.

Jacobus de Voragine. *The Golden Legend or Lives of the Saints,* trans. William Caxton. Vols. I-VII. London W. C., 1931-1939.

James, Arthur W. *Die starken Praeterita in den Werken von Hans Sachs.* [Diss.], München, 1894.

Jungmann, Joseph A. *The Mass of the Roman Rite,* trans. the Rev. Francis R. Brunner, rev. the Rev. Charles K. Riepe. New York: Benzinger Brothers, Inc., 1961.

Kaiserchronik, Gedicht des zwölften Jahrhunderts. Dritter Theil, ed. Hans Ferd. Massmann. Bibliothek der gesammten deutschen National-Literatur, Vol. IV, 3. Quedlinburg und Leipzig, 1854.

Kienast, Richard. "Die deutschsprachige Lyrik des Mittelalters," *Deutsche Philologie im Aufriß,* Vol. II, coll. 2-131. Berlin: Erich Schmidt, 1960.

Kluge, Friedrich. *Etymologisches Wörterbuch der deutschen Sprache.* 19th ed. rev. by Walther Mitzka. Berlin: Walther de Gruyter, 1963.

Kober, A. "Geschichte der deutschen Mariendichtung," *Zeitschrift für deutschen Unterricht (Zeitschrift für Deutschkunde)* XXVIII (1914), 595-619; 697-700.

Koch, Max. *Festschrift zur Hans Sachs Feier.* Weimar: Emil Weber, 1894.

Kochs, Theodor. *Das deutsche geistliche Tagelied.* Forschungen und Funde, Heft 22. Münster in Westfalen: Verlag der Aschendorffschen Verlagsbuchhandlung, 1928.

Bibliography

Konrad von Würzburgs Goldene Schmiede, ed Edward Schröder. Göttingen: Vandenhoeck und Ruprecht, 1926.

Köpke, Friedrich Karl. *Das Passional. Eine Legenden-Sammlung aus dem dreizehnten Jahrhundert.* Quedlinburg und Leipzig, 1852.

Kopp, Arthus. *Bremberger Gedichte, Ein Beitrag zur Brembergersage.* Quellen und Forschungen zur deutschen Volkskunde, Vol. II. Wien: Rud. Ludwig, 1908.

Krebs, Werner. *Alte Handwerksbräuche.* Basel, 1933.

Krieg, Franz. *Katholische Kirchenmusik.* St. Gallen: Niggli und Willy Verkauf, 1954.

Kusch, Eugen. *Nürnberg / Lebensbild einer Stadt.* Nürnberg: Nürnberger Presse GMBH, 1951.

Lexer, Matthias. *Mittelhochdeutsches Handwörterbuch*, Vols. I-III. Leipzig: S. Hirzel, 1872, 1876, 1878.

_____. *Mittelhochdeutsches Taschenwörterbuch.* 32nd ed. Stuttgart, 1966.

von Liliencron, Rochus. *Über den Inhalt der allgemeinen Bildung in der Zeit der Scholastik.* (Festrede) München, 1876.

Linker, Robert White. *Music of the Minnesinger and Early Meistersinger.* Chapel Hill: The University of North Carolina Press, 1962.

Lütcke, Heinrich. *Studien zur Philosophie der Meistersänger.* Palaestra CVII. Berlin: Mayer und Müller, 1911.

Lützelberger, Ernst Karl Julius. "Einiges von den Meistersängern," *Album des Literarischen Vereins in Nürnberg für 1864,* pp. 210-234. Nürnberg: Bauer und Raspe, 1864.

_____. *Hans Sachs. Sein Leben und seine Dichtung.* 2nd ed., rev. Carl Fromman. Nürnberg: Hermann Ballhorn, 1891.

Manual of Catholic Theology. See Wilhelm-Scannell.

Das Märterbuch, ed. Erich Gierach. *Deutsche Texte des Mittelalters,* Vol. XXXII. Berlin, 1928.

Marienlegenden, ed. Franz Pfeiffer. Wien, 1863.

Marienlegenden aus dem Alten Passional, ed. Hans-Georg Richert. Deutsche Textbibliothek, No. 64. Tübingen: Max Niemeyer, 1965.

Martin, Ernst. *Die Meistersänger von Strassburg.* Strassburg: R. Schultz und Comp., 1882.

_____. "Wolfhart Spangenberg, Geschichte des Meistergesangs," *Jahrbuch für Geschichte, Sprache und Literatur Elsass-Lothringens,* XXVI (1910), 231-233.

Mechthild von Magdeburg. *Das fliessende Licht der Gottheit.* Einsideln, Zürich / Köln: Benziger Verlag, 1956.

Bibliography

Meier, P. Gabriel. *Die sieben freien Künste im Mittelalter.* Jahresbericht über die Lehr- und Erziehungs-Anstalt des Benekiktiner-Stiftes Maria-Einsiedeln im Studienjahre 1885/1886. Part I, pp. 3-30; Part II, Studienjahr 1886/1887, pp. 4-36. Einsiedeln, New York, 1886 and 1887.

Merriman, Roger B. *Suleiman the Magnificent.* Cambridge, Massachusetts: Harvard University Press, 1944.

Messenger, Ruth Ellis. *The Medieval Latin Hymn.* Washington, D.C.: The Capitol Press, 1953.

Mey, Curt. *Der Meistergesang in Geschichte und Kunst.* Leipzig: Hermann Seemann Nachfolger, 1901.

Michels, Victor. A review of Karl Drescher's *Studien zu Hans Sachs* in Anzeiger für deutsches Alterthum und deutsche Literatur, Vol. 18 (1892), pp. 353-359.

Miracles of the Blessed Virgin Mary, trans. C. C. Swinton Bland. London: George Routledge and Sons, Ltd., 1926.

Mittellateinisches Glossar, ed. E. Habel. Paderborn: Ferdinand Schöningh, 1931.

Morris, Ramona and Desmond. *Men and Snakes.* New York and San Francisco: McGraw-Hill Book Company, 1965.

Moser, Virgil. *Frühneuhochdeutsche Grammatik,* Vol. I, *Lautlehre,* 1. Hälfte: and 3. Teil, 2. Hälfte (Schluβ). Germanische Bibliothek, 1. Reihe. Heidelberg: Carl Winter-Universitätsverlag, 1929, 1951.

Mummenhof, Ernst. *Der Handwerker in der deutschen Vergangenheit.* Monographien zur deutschen Kulturgeschichte, Vol. VIII. Leipzig: E. Diederich Verlag, 1901.

————. *Hans Sachs.* Zum 400 jährigen Geburtsjubiläum des Dichters. Im Auftrag der Stadt Nürnberg. Nürnberg: Kommissionsverlag der Friedrich Kornschen Buchhandlung, 1894.

Münch, Jette. *Die sozialen Anschuungen des Hans Sachs.* [Diss.], Erlangen-Bruck: M. Krahl, 1936.

Münzer, G. *Das Singebuch des Adam Puschman nebst den Originalmelodien des M. Behaim und Hans Sachs.* Leipzig: Breitkopf und Härtel, 1906.

Muscatblut. *Lieder Muscatbluts,* ed. E. v. Groote. Cöln: Du-Mont-Schauberg, 1852.

Mussafia, A. *Studien zu den mittelalterlichen Marienlegenden,* I-IV, Sitzungsberichte der Kaiserlichen Akademie der Wissenschaften, Philosophisch-Historische Klasse, Vols. 113 (1886), 917-994; 115 (1888), 5-91; 119 (1889), 1-66; 123 (1891), 1-85.

Musaios. *Hero und Leander,* trans. (from Greek) Hans Färber. München: Ernst Heimeran, 1961.

Nagel, Bert. *Der Deutsche Meistersang.* Heidelberg: F.H. Kerle, 1952

Bibliography

————. "Der frühe Meistersang und das Christentum," *Germanisch-Romanische Monatsschrift*, XXIII (1935), pp. 348-360.

————. *Meistersang*. Sammlung Metzler, Realienbücher für Germanisten. Abt.: Literaturgeschichte. Stuttgart: J.B. Metzlersche Verlagsbuchhandlung, 1962.

Nagel, Wilibald. *Studien zur Geschichte der Meistersänger*. Muzikalisches Magazin. Heft. 27. Langensalza, 1909.

Nicolaus (Niclas) von Wyle. *Translationen von Niclas von Wyle*, ed. Adelbert von Keller. Bibliothek des Litterarischen Vereins in Stuttgart, Vol. LVII. Stuttgart, 1861.

Nürnberger Polizeiordnungen aus dem XIII. bis XV. Jahrhundert. Bibliothek des Litterarischen Vereins in Stuttgart, Vol. LXIII. Stuttgart, 1861.

Ovid (Publius Ovidius Naso). *Heroides and Amores*, trans. Grant Showerman. The Loeb Classical Library. Cambridge, Massachusetts: Harvard University Press, 1947.

————. *Ovids Liebeskunst, Heilmittel der Liebe und Schönheitsmittel*, trans. Heinrich Lindemann. Leipzig, 1861.

————. *Metamorphosen*, trans. Erich Rösch. München: Ernst Heimeran Verlag, 1952.

Paul, Hermann. *Mittelhochdeutsche Grammatik*. 13th ed. rev. E. Gierach. Halle/Salle: Max Niemeyer, 1939.

Pauli, Johannes. *Schimpf und Ernst*, ed. H. Osterley. Bibliothek des Litterarischen Vereins in Stuttgart, Vol. LXXXV. Stuttgart, 1866.

Physiologus, ed. Th. G. v. Karajan. Deutsche Sprach- und Denkmale des 12ten Jahr., Vol. IV. Wien, 1846.

Der Physiologus, trans. and ed. Otto Seel. Lebendige Antike. Zürich und Stuttgart: Artemis Verlag–AG, 1960.

Plate, O. "Die Kunstausdrücke der Meistersinger," *Strassburger Studien* III (1888), 147-237.

Priem, Joh. Paul. *Geschichte der Stadt Nürnberg*. Nürnberg: Jacob Zeiser, 1875.

Puschmann, Adam. *Gründlicher Bericht des deutschen Meistergesangs*, ed. Richard Jonas. Neudrucke deutscher Literaturwerke des XVI. und XVII Jahrhunderts, No. 73. Halle a. S.: Max Niemeyer, 1888.

Ranisch, Salomon. *Historischkritische Lebensbeschreibung Hanns Sachsens*. Altenburg: Richterische Buchhandlung, 1765.

Reese, Gustave. *Music in the Middle Ages*. New York: W.W. Norton and Co., 1940.

Roth, F. W. E. "Zur Geschichte der Meistersänger zu Mainz und Nürnberg," *Zeitschrift für Kulturgeschichte* III, n. F. 4 (1896), 261-290.

Bibliography

Runge, Paul, ed. *Die Sangesweisen der Colmarer Handschrift und die Liederhandschrift Donaueschingen.* Leipzig: Breitkopf und Härtel, 1896.

Hans Sachs-Forschungen. Festschrift zur Vierhundersten Geburtsfeier des Dichters Hans Sachs, ed. A. L. Stiefel. Nürnberg: Joh. Phil. Raw'schen Buchhandlung, 1894.

Hans Sachs. Werke. *Dichtungen von Hans Sachs* I, ed. Karl Goedeke. Deutsche Dichter des 16. Jahrhunderts IV. Leipzig: F. A. Brockhaus, 1870.

———. *Hans Sachs,* eds. Adelbert v. Keller and Edmund Goetze. 26 vols. Bibliothek des Litterarischen Vereins in Stuttgart. Tübingen: H. Lauf, 1870-1908.

———.*Sämtliche Fabeln und Schwänke von Hans Sachs.* 6 vols., eds. Edmund Goetze and Carl Drescher. Neudrucke deutscher Litteraturwerke des 16. und 17. Jahrhunderts, Halle a/S.: Max Niemeyer, 1893-1913.

———. *Sämmtliche Fastnachtspiele von Hans Sachs.* 7 vols., ed. Edmund Goetze. Neudrucke deutscher Litteraturwerke des 16. und 17. Jahrhunderts, Halle a. S.: Max Niemeyer, 1880-1887.

———.*Dichtungen von Hans Sachs* III. *Dramatische Gedichte,* ed. Julius Tittmann. Deutsche Dichter des sechzehnten Jahrhunderts. Vol. VI. Leipzig: F. A. Brockhaus, 1871.

———. *Hans Sachs Werke* I, ed. Bernard Arnold. Deutsche National Literatur, Vol. XX. Berlin und Stuttgart, *s. d.* [1884-1885].

Saint Augustine. *Saint Augustine's Enchiridion,* trans. Ernest Evans. London S. P. C. K., 1953.

Saint Katherine. *Die Legende der Heiligen Katharina von Alexandrien,* ed. Siegfried Sudhof. Texte des späten Mittelalters, Heft 10. Berlin: Erich Schmidt, 1959.

Salzer, Anselm. *Die Sinnbilder und Beiworte Mariens in der deutschen Literature und lateinischen Hymnenpoesie des Mittelalters.* Programm des k. k. Ober Gymnasiums der Benedictiner zu Seitenstetten XX-XXVIII. Linz, 1886-1894.

Scheeben, Matthias Joseph. *Handbuch der katholischen Dogmatik,* I and II. Freiburg im Breisgau, 1873 and 1878.

———. *Fünftes Buch, Erlösungslehre.* Erster Halbband und Zweiter Halbband. 2nd ed., ed. Carl Feckes. Freiburg: Verlag Herder, 1954.

———. *Mariology,* trans. T. L. M. J. Geukers. St. Louis, Mo. and London: B. Herder Book Co., 1946 and 1947.

Schirokauer, A. "Studien zur Mittelhochdeutschen Reimgrammatik," *Beiträge zur Geschichte der deutschen Sprache und Literatur* XLVII (1923), 1-126.

Schmeller, J. Andreas. *Bayerisches Wörterbuch,* Vols. I, II. 2nd ed. rev. G. Karl Frommann. München, 1872, 1877.

Bibliography

Schneider, Karin. *Der Trojanische Krieg im späten Mittelalter.* Philologische Studien und Quellen, Heft 40. Berlin: Erich Schmidt Verlag, 1968.

Schnorr von Carolsfeld, Franz. *Zur Geschichte des dt. Meistergesangs.* Berlin, 1872.

Schroeder, Sister Mary Juliana S. S. N. D. *Mary-Verse in Meistergesang.* The Catholic University of America Studies in German, Vol. XVI. Washington, D.C.: The Catholic University of America Press, 1942.

_____. "Topical Outline of Subject Matter in the Berlin MS *Germ. Quart. 414,*" *PMLA*, LXI, No. 4 (December 1946), 997-1017.

Schweitzer, Charles. *Hans Sachs.* [Diss.] Nancy: Berger-Levroualt et Cie, 1887.

_____. "Sprichwörter und sprichwörtliche Redensarten bei Hans Sachs," *Hans Sachs Forschungen*, ed. A. L. Stiefel. Nürnberg, 1894.

Schwiebert, E. G. *Luther and His Times.* St. Louis, Mo.: Concordia Publishing House, 1950.

Shumway, Daniel Bussier. *Das ablautende Verbum bei Hans Sachs.* [Diss.] Einbeck, 1894.

Sibyllinische Weissagungen. Urtext und Übersetzung, ed. Alfons Kurfess. München: Heimeran, 1951.

Siebenkees, Johann Christian. *Materialien zur Nürnbergischen Geschichte* I. Nürnberg, 1892.

Sommer, W. *Die Metrik des Hans Sachs.* Halle: Max Niemeyer, 1882.

Spangenberg, Cyriacus. *Von der Musica und den Meistersängern.* Bibliothek des Litterarischen Vereins in Stuttgart, Vol. LXII. Stuttgart, 1861.

Spargo, John Webster. *Virgil the Necromancer.* Harvard Studies in Comparative Literature, Vol. X. Cambridge: Harvard University Press, 1934.

Specht, Franz Anton. *Geschichte des Unterrichtwesens in Deutschland.* Stuttgart, 1885.

Stammler, Wolfgang. "Zur Sprachgeschichte des 15. und 16. Jahrhunderts." *Vom Werden d. dt. Geistes:* Festgabe G. Ehrismann, pp. 171-189. Berlin, W. De Gruyter and Co., 1925.

Strauss, Gerald. *Nuremberg in the Sixteenth Century.* New York: John Wiley and Sons, Inc., 1966.

Strecker, Karl. *Einführung in das Mittellatein.* 2nd ed. Berlin: Weidmannsche Buchhandlung, 1929.

Taylor, Archer. *The Literary History of Meistergesang.* New York: Modern Language Association of America. London: Oxford University Press, 1937.

Taylor, Archer, and Frances H. Ellis. *A Bibliography of Meistergesang.* Indiana University Studies, Study No. 113, Vol. XXIII. Bloomington, Indiana, 1936.

Bibliography

Taylor, Henry Osborn. *Thought and Expression in the 16th Century* I. 2nd ed. rev. New York: Frederick Ungar, 1930. Republished 1959.

Tucher, Endres. *Endres Tuchers Baumeisterbuch der Stadt Nürnberg: 1464-1475,* ed. Matthias Lexer. Bibliothek des Litterarischen Vereins in Stuttgart, Vol. LXIV. Stuttgart, 1862.

Tristrant und Isalde, Prosaroman des fünfzehnten Jahrhunderts, ed. Fridrich Pfaff. Bibliothek des Litterarischen Vereins in Stuttgart, Vol. CLII. Tübingen, 1881.

Volksbücher vom sterbenden Rittertum, ed Heinz Kindermann. Deutsche Literatur . . . in Entwicklungsreihen; Reihe Volks- und Schwankbücher, Vol. 1. Leipzig: Philipp Reclam jun., 1942.

Volksbücher von Weltweite und Abenteuerlust, ed. Franz Podleiszek. Deutsche Literatur . . . in Entwicklungsreihen; Reihe 12, Band 2. Leipzig: Philip Reclam jun., 1936.

Voulliéme, Ernst. *Die deutschen Drucker des fünfzehnten Jahrhunderts.* 2nd ed. Berlin: Reichsdruckerei, 1922.

Wackernagel, Philipp. *Das deutsche Kirchenlied,* Vol. II. Leipzig: B. G. Teubner, 1867.

Wagenseil, Johann Christof. *De Sacri Rom. Imperii Libera Civitate Noribergensi* (pp. 433-576 contain *Buch von der Meistersinger Holdseligen Kunst*). Altdorf / Noricorvm: Typis Impensisqve Jodoci Wilhelmi Kohlesii, 1697.

Walther von der Vogelweide, ed. W. Wilmans. Halle a. S., 1883.

Wander, Karl Freidrich Wilhelm. *Deutsches Sprichwörter-Lexikon,* 5 vols. Leipzig: F. A. Brockhaus, 1867-1880.

Watson, Richard. *A Biblical and Theological Dictionary.* New York: B. Waugh and T. Masco, 1833.

Weber, Rolf. *Zur geschichtlichen Entwicklung und Bedeutung des deutschen Meistergesangs im 15. u. 16. Jahrhundert.* [Diss.], Berlin, 1921.

Weddingen, Otto. *Der deutsche Meistergesang.* Berlin, 1894.

Wehrhan, Karl, ed. *Die deutschen Sagen des Mittelalters,* zweite Hälfte; *Deutsches Sagenbuch,* dritter Teil. München: C. H. Beck, 1920.

Weil, Ernst. *Die deutschen Druckerzeichen des XV. Jahrhunderts.* München: Münchner Drucke, 1924.

Weinhold, Karl. *Mittelhochdeutsche Grammatik.* 2nd ed. Paderborn: Ferdinand Schöningh, 1883.

———. *Bairische Grammatik.* Berlin: Ferd. Dümmlers Verlagsbuchhandlung, 1867.

Weller, Emil. *Der Volksdichter Hans Sachs und seine Dichtungen.* Eine Bibliographie. Nürnberg: Jacob Sichling, 1868.

Bibliography

Wickram, Georg, *Georg Wickrams Werke, dritter Band: Das Rollwagenbüchlein,* ed. Johannes Bolte. Bibliothek des Litterarischen Vereins in Stuttgart, Vol. CCXXIX. Tübingen, 1903.

Wieczorek, Hans Georg. *Johann Hartliebs Verdeutschung von des Andreas Capellanus Liber de reprobatione amoris.* [Diss.], Breslau, 1929.

Wilhelm, Joseph, and Thomas B. Scannell. *A Manual of Catholic Theology Based on Scheeben's "Dogmatik,"* Vols. I and II. 4th ed. rev. London: Kegan Paul, Trench, Trubner and Co. Ltd.; New York, Cincinnati, Chicago: Benziger Bros., 1935.

Windolph, Friedrich. *Der Reiseweg Hans Sachsens in seiner Handwerksburschenzeit nach seinen eigenen Dichtungen.* [Diss.] Greifswald: Hans Adler, 1911.